Rethinking the 1898 Reform Peric

Political and Cultural Change
in Late Qing China

Harvard East Asian Monographs 214

Contributors

Richard Belsky

Tze-ki Hon

Hu Ying

Joan Judge

Rebecca E. Karl

Xiaobing Tang

Timothy B. Weston

Seungjoo Yoon

Peter Zarrow

Rethinking the 1898 Reform Period

Political and Cultural Change
in Late Qing China

Edited by

Rebecca E. Karl & Peter Zarrow

Published by the Harvard University Asia Center
and distributed by Harvard University Press
Cambridge (Massachusetts) and London 2002

Printed in the United States of America

The Harvard University Asia Center publishes a monograph series and, in coordination with the Fairbank Center for East Asian Research, the Korea Institute, the Reischauer Institute of Japanese Studies, and other faculties and institutes, administers research projects designed to further scholarly understanding of China, Japan, Vietnam, Korea, and other Asian countries. The Center also sponsors projects addressing multidisciplinary and regional issues in Asia.

Library of Congress Cataloging-in-Publication Data
Rethinking the 1898 reform period : political and cultural change in late Qing China / edited by Rebecca E. Karl & Peter Zarrow
    p. cm. -- (Harvard East Asian monographs ; 214)
    Includes bibliographical references and index.
    ISBN 0-674-00854-5 (alk. paper)
    1. China--History--Reform movement, 1898. I. Karl, Rebecca E. II. Zarrow, Peter Gue. III. Series
    DS768.R48 2002
    951'.035--dc21
                                                 2001051782

Index by the contributors and editors

❦   Printed on acid-free paper

Last figure below indicates year of this printing

12 11 10 09 08 07 06 05 04 03 02

Acknowledgments

The editors would like to acknowledge the hard work of the contributors to this volume. In addition, we would like to thank the two anonymous readers selected by the Harvard University Asia Center for their detailed and helpful suggestions for revisions; and our editor at the Press, John Ziemer, for his editorial assistance, cooperation, and speedy processing of the manuscript.

R.E.K. and P.Z.

Contents

Contributors   ix

Introduction   1
Rebecca E. Karl and Peter Zarrow

1 The Reform Movement, the Monarchy, and
Political Modernity   17
Peter Zarrow

2 Literati-Journalists of the *Chinese Progress* (*Shiwu bao*)
in Discord, 1896–1898   48
Seungjoo Yoon

3 Zhang Zhidong's Proposal for Reform: A New Reading
of the *Quanxue pian*   77
Tze-ki Hon

4 The Founding of the Imperial University and the
Emergence of Chinese Modernity   99
Timothy B. Weston

5 Placing the Hundred Days: Native-Place Ties and
Urban Space   124
Richard Belsky

6 Reforming the Feminine: Female Literacy and the
   Legacy of 1898   158
   Joan Judge

7 Naming the First "New Woman"   180
   Hu Ying

8 "Slavery," Citizenship, and Gender in Late Qing China's
   Global Context   212
   Rebecca E. Karl

9 "Poetic Revolution," Colonization, and Form at the Beginning
   of Modern Chinese Literature   245
   Xiaobing Tang

   Index   269

Contributors

RICHARD BELSKY 白思奇 is Associate Professor of History at Hunter College, City University of New York. He is currently working on a book about the operation of native-place ties among scholar-officials in Beijing during the late imperial and early Republican periods.

TZE-KI HON 韓子奇 teaches history at State University of New York at Geneseo. He has published articles and book chapters on premodern and modern China. He is completing two book manuscripts, one on the self-identity of literati in eleventh-century China, and the other on modern Chinese historiography from 1890 to 1949.

HU YING 胡纓 is Associate Professor in the Department of East Asian Languages and Literatures at the University of California at Irvine. She is the author of *Tales of Translation: Composing the New Woman in China, 1899–1918* (Stanford University Press, 2000). She has published numerous papers on late Qing literature and culture.

JOAN JUDGE 季家珍 is Associate Professor of History at the University of California, Santa Barbara. She is the author of *Print and Politics: 'Shibao' and the Culture of Reform in Late Qing China* (Stanford University Press, 1996). Her current project is tentatively entitled "China's 'Women's Question': Female Literacy, Cultural Transformation and Modern Nationalism in the Late 19th and Early 20th Centuries."

REBECCA E. KARL is Assistant Professor of East Asian Studies and History at New York University. Her book, *Staging the World: Chinese Nationalism at the Turn of the Twentieth Century*, is forthcoming from Duke University Press. She is also the co-editor (with Saree Makdisi and Cesare Casarino) of *Marxism Beyond Marxism* (Routledge, 1996).

XIAOBING TANG 唐小兵 teaches modern Chinese literature and culture in the Department of East Asian Languages and Civilizations, University of Chicago. His most recent publication is *Chinese Modern: The Heroic and the Quotidian* (Duke University Press, 2000). His current research project is a study of the theory and practice of the woodcut movement in twentieth-century China.

TIMOTHY B. WESTON 魏定熙 is Assistant Professor of History at the University of Colorado at Boulder. He is co-editor with Lionel M. Jensen of *China Beyond the Headlines* (Rowman & Littlefield, 2000) and is currently finishing a book-length work on the early history of Beijing University and Chinese political culture.

SEUNGJOO YOON 尹聖柱 is Assistant Professor of History at Carleton College. He is the author of "Hsieh Ts'an-T'ai's Abortive Uprising of 1903: A Case for the Rise of Non-Gentry Social Elite in Late Ch'ing Coastal China," *Papers on Chinese History*, vol. 1, Harvard University (1992); and "The Green Gang Nexus in Shanghai General Labor Union, 1924–1927," *Papers on Chinese History*, vol. 2 (1993). He is working on a manuscript entitled "The Formation, Reformation, and Transformation of Zhang Zhidong's Document Commissioners, 1885–1909."

PETER ZARROW 沙培德 is an Associate Research Fellow of the Institute of Modern History, Academia Sinica, Taipei. He specializes in the intellectual history of China in the late nineteenth and early twentieth centuries and is currently engaged in research on changing attitudes toward the kingship through the 1911 revolution. He is also completing a manuscript entitled "Twentieth-Century China: An Interpretive History."

Rethinking the 1898 Reform Period

Political and Cultural Change
in Late Qing China

Introduction

Rebecca E. Karl and Peter Zarrow

The nine chapters in this volume re-examine the reform period in late Qing China that began, unsuccessfully, in 1898 with the "hundred days" (also known as the *wuxu* reforms, *wuxu bianfa* 戊戌變法 or *wuxu weixin* 戊戌維新)[1] and continued until the end of the dynasty in 1911. They focus in particular on the extended historical significance of this important period. The editors and contributors are united in wishing to invest the 1898 era with fresh meaning, even as each retains his or her respective disciplinary, methodological, and perspectival differences. Although none of us claims that our work has superseded the excellent scholarship of our predecessors, our intention is to refocus historiographical inquiry away from the event-based political narrative of a failed reform effort that has been the dominant mode of treating this period. In this fashion, we hope to create for "1898" the kind of historical space that has long been associated with the later New Culture / May Fourth period (1915–27).[2] At the same time, we are far from wishing to reify "1898" or to (re)establish it as a marker of an absolute break from its immediate past; we also do not find it productive to locate in the reform period "backward residues" of that past. As such, the chapters in this volume look at the 1898 period as an extended moment during which a series

---

1. The "hundred days" refers to the fact that the actual reform movement captured the imperial court's attention for around one hundred days (103, to be exact), before being cut short by a palace coup d'état that was powerfully opposed to the movement. "Wuxu" is the designation for 1898 in the Chinese sixty-year cycle for counting years.

2. We thank one of the anonymous readers of our manuscript for this felicitous phrasing of the problem.

of historical questions that have since powerfully informed China's modernity were first posed in a systematic and systemic fashion.

Most of the contributors to this volume first came together as part of a double panel organized by Peter Zarrow at the 1998 Association for Asian Studies meeting. The chapters in this anthology are thus the products not so much of a symposium as of individuals whose work loosely revolves around a particular set of historical, scholarly, and theoretical issues. For the purposes of this introduction and the organization of the contributors' work in this book, we, the editors, have attempted to impose some order on the essays. Although such impositions are always partial, on our reading, the included essays are united thematically by a commitment to asking new questions about 1898. There is, at least in part, a common focus among all the authors on exploring how new bodies of knowledge, or new knowledge-formations, contributed to the creation of new concepts of the political and the social in China at the turn of the twentieth century. The organization of the chapters in the book reflects this unifying theme. This introduction, then, is intended to give a brief account of the historiographical and historical problematics and contexts for our separate reconsiderations and to introduce the various authors' approaches to those problematics.

The Problem

Our reconsideration of the 1898 period comes at a particular time in historiographies of modern China and in historiographies of 1898. Over the past two decades in the People's Republic of China, the 1898 reform period has re-emerged as a historical moment not only worthy of, but in fact demanding, rethinking.[3] Indeed, with the relatively complete repudiation of the

---

3. For trends in PRC scholarship on the 1898 reforms and modern China, see, e.g., the special issue of *Jindaishi yanjiu* (Researches in modern Chinese history), 1998, no. 5, published on the hundredth anniversary of the event; Yang Nianqun 楊念群, *Ruxue diyuhua de jindai xingtai: san da zhishi qunti hudong de bijiao yanjiu* 儒學地域化的近代形態：三大知識群體互動的比較研究 (The modern models of regional Confucianism—Comparative research into the interaction of three intellectual groups) (Beijing: Sanlian and Harvard Yenching Institute, 1997); and Liu Zhen'gang 劉振崗, *Wuxu weixin yundong zhuanti yanjiu* 戊戌維新運動專題研究 (Specialized topics in the study of the *wuxu* reform movement) (Beijing: Shoudu shifan daxue chubanshe, 1999); among many others.

In August 1998, the Chinese Historical Association and Beijing University sponsored a conference in Beijing at which papers on the reform movement were delivered by over 160 scholars from around the world. Sixty-three of these papers were then published in Wang

Maoist revolutionary premises of socialist modernization and thus within the larger context of the current Chinese debate over reformist (rather than revolutionary) paths to modernization, the "bourgeois" reformers of the turn of the last century—the political activists, intellectuals, and other social elements who participated most vigorously in the 1898 reforms—are being rediscovered and mobilized to speak, as if directly, to contemporary reformers at the turn of the twenty-first century. One indication of this trend was a remark by the editors of *Researches in Modern Chinese History* in their introduction to a special anniversary issue marking the centennial of the 1898 reforms: "the dream of a strong nation of the [1898] reformers remains an ideal for which the Chinese people still work today."[4] More specifically, an emblematic figure in this historical recuperation of 1898, Wang Xiaoqiu, senior historian at Beijing University, wrote in the introduction to a recently published anthology that he co-edited: "Currently, the sons and daughters of China are increasing the pace of reform and opening so as to face the twenty-first century. Socialist modernization with special Chinese characteristics is entering a critical historical phase. At this time, to reflect on and deepen research on the century-old history of late Qing reform not only is valuable academically but also has contemporary significance."[5]

The contemporary significance of 1898, Wang continued, lies primarily in the fact that reform must be reconceived as a legitimate historical path, for, as he pointed out, historiography in the PRC has predominantly understood reform as the antonym of revolution, so much so that "the value of violent revolution tended to get rigidly upheld, and the value of reformist tendencies

---

Xiaoqiu 王曉秋, ed., *Wuxu weixin yu jindai Zhongguo de gaige: wuxu weixin yibai zhounian guoji xueshu taolunhui lunwenji* 戊戌維新與近代中國的改革: 戊戌維新一百週年國際學術討論會論文集 (The 1898 reform movement and reform in modern China: collected papers from the international scholarly conference on the hundredth anniversary of the 1898 reform movement) (Beijing: Shehui kexue wenxian chubanshe, 2000).

4. *Jindaishi yanjiu bianjibu* 近代史研究編輯部, "Wuxu weixin yundong yanjiu de huigu yu qianzhan xueshu zuotanhui zongshu" 戊戌維新運動研究的回顧與前瞻學術座談會綜述 (A summary of the academic conference on the past and future of research on the 1898 reform movement), *Jindaishi yanjiu* 1998, no. 5: 1.

5. Wang Xiaoqiu 王曉秋, "Zonglun: wan Qing gaigeshi yanjiu lungang" 總論: 晚清改革史研究論綱 (Introduction: outline to research on late Qing reform history), in *Wuxu weixin yu Qingmo xinzheng: wan Qing gaigeshi yanjiu* 戊戌維新與清末新政: 晚清改革史研究 (The 1898 reforms and the late Qing new policies: studies on late Qing reform history), ed. Wang Xiaoqiu and Shang Xiaoming 尚小明, p. 1 (Beijing: Beijing daxue chubanshe, 1998).

was relatively ignored." In view of the fact, Wang concluded, that the contemporary period of socialist modernization is one of reform and not of revolution, the rigid valorization of revolution must be rethought, and the value of reform must be restored to historical research.[6] The 1898 reform period must hence be rescued, as it were, from its previous entanglement in an official narrative of Chinese history dominated by a revolutionary paradigm in which the 1898 reforms could only be seen as a failed moment (no matter how temporarily progressive in its own right). By contrast, the 1898 reform period is now often raised as the originary moment of (an aborted effort at) nonsocialist modernization, to which China now has (finally) returned. This view of the historical place of the 1898 reform movement, by implication, delegitimates the 1949 revolution, although this implication is seldom explicitly spelled out.[7]

---

6. Ibid., pp. 6, 1. As the editors of the summary article in *Jindaishi yanjiu* (see esp. pp. 2–6) make clear, before the onset of the Cultural Revolution in 1966, Chinese assessments of 1898—particularly influenced by Feng Ziyou's early narrative—participated in a different, albeit perhaps no less rigid historiographical tradition; that is, one dictated by the "inevitability" of the 1911 revolution, which presented the 1898 reforms as a "progressive" albeit abortive episode in a narrative paradigm that established a teleological revolutionary unfolding of the modern Chinese nation.

7. Although, as Liu Zhen'gang (*Wuxu weixin yundong zhuanti yanjiu*, pp. 11–12) notes, "Approximately from the end of the 1980s forward and originating from 'conservative' trends in cultural critique . . . all modern events and people that sought fundamental change [in modern Chinese history] have been labeled 'radical' and [thereby] condemned. . . . They [contemporary conservative critics] believe that it is precisely 'radicalism' that interrupted China's normal development and laid obstacles in the way of China's progress towards modernization." In light of these critiques, in the 1990s, a large-scale debate emerged over whether the 1898 reformers were "too radical" (*guo jijin* 過激進); this is a trend, Liu points out, that praises the self-strengthening period of the 1860s–1890s for its modernizationism, while condemning the 1898 reforms, the 1911 revolution, the May Fourth period, etc., for their radicalism.

For the most concentrated examples of the "radicalism" debate, see various issues of the journal *Ershiyi shiji* 二十一世紀 (*Twenty-first Century*), from the beginning of the 1990s on. It appears that this debate was touched off by the circulation in 1988 of Ying-shih Yu's lecture at Hong Kong University entitled "Radicalism and Conservatism in Modern Chinese History." In a recent analysis, Wang Hui ("The 1989 Social Movement and the Origins of Chinese 'Neo-liberalism': A Reconsideration of Intellectual Trends on the Chinese Mainland and the Question of Modernity," trans. Rebecca Karl, *positions*, forthcoming) attributes the persuasiveness of this debate in the PRC in the 1990s to the rethinking of the 1989 student movement, whose "radicalism" was partially blamed for its failure.

Of course, one could simply cynically dismiss this scholarly interest in 1898—and Wang Xiaoqiu's seemingly paradigmatic sentiments along with it—as yet one more effort, in a long series of such efforts, to "use the past to serve the present." And, on one level, the current rush—in Japan and the United States, no less than in the PRC—to study late Qing chambers of commerce and industrial developments; the possible formation of a "public sphere" and a civil society in the press and journalistic practices and in philanthropic organizations (whether Chinese entrepreneurial or missionary-inspired) and other nonstate or semi-state associations; streamlined bureaucracies and so on does lend a certain support to the suspicion that, once more, a long-disregarded, or at least long-misunderstood, lesson from the "past" is indeed being mobilized to serve the "present."[8] However, as scholars and historians, it is perhaps more fruitful for us to move beyond such utilitarian and functionalist notions of the relationship between past and present and, rather, to note the larger historical context in which the 1898 period is being discovered in the PRC and elsewhere to have contemporary relevance.

In this regard, one can think in terms not of "making the past serve the present" but, as Wang implies, of seeking a nexus of problems or a conjunction of historical problematics confronting Chinese intellectuals and society, then and now.[9] Those problems—in their general similarity—can be encapsulated as problems *of* and *in* modernity, understood as simultaneously a local and a global crisis.[10] That is to say, at the most general level, these

---

8. For this type of utilitarian interpretation of "using the past to serve the present," see the various essays in Jonathan Unger, ed., *Using the Past to Serve the Present: Historiography and Politics in Contemporary China* (Armonk, N.Y.: M. E. Sharpe, 1993).

9. One of the most incisive of such rethinkings in China was one of the earliest to discard explicit judgmentalism—"failure/success," "approve/condemn" (*kending* 肯定 / *fouding* 否定); see Wu Tingjia 吳廷嘉, *Wuxu sichao zongheng lun* 戊戌思潮縱橫論 (A comprehensive discourse on intellectual trends in the *wuxu* period) (Beijing: Renmin daxue chubanshe, 1988). Wu names the *wuxu* period as such (*wuxu shiqi* 戊戌時期) and avoids both an event-based account and a value-laden teleological narrative of Chinese history and nation-building. Unfortunately, Wu died before finishing her historiographical project, which was to move general Chinese historiographical discussion away from narrow concerns with judgments (*pingjia* 評價).

10. Whether today's problems are *also* problems of and in *postmodernity* is currently a hotly contested issue. For a summary discussion of these debates, see Xudong Zhang, "Postmodernism and Post-Socialist Society: Cultural Politics in China After the 'New Era,'" *New Left Review*, no. 237 (Sept./Oct. 1999): 77–105; see also Arif Dirlik and Xudong Zhang, eds., *Postmodernism and China* (Durham: Duke University Press, 2000).

are historical problems that arise when a seemingly stable set of historical politico-cultural meanings and socioeconomic arrangements (no matter how contested in their particulars) confronts a competing claim to universalism that, then and now, apparently emanates and intrudes from elsewhere (for example, global capitalism and the host of questions and issues—cultural, economic, political, intellectual—that this intrusion helps [re]shape). In the current period, the historical confrontation could be figured as a move from revolutionary socialism, with all its cultural, intellectual, economic, social, and political formations and claims, to the current "socialism with Chinese characteristics," which seeks to link China to the global capitalist world, with all the disjunctures, unevenness, and sociopolitical, economic, and cultural forms, both emergent and residual, that this linking has spawned and made visible.[11] In short, today's historical confrontation can be seen as marking a move from the "particularism" of Chinese socialism (however much that was historically linked to a global socialist moment, which has now, in any case, been forgotten) to the "universalism" of nonsocialist, globalized capitalist modernization and development.

By contrast and yet similarly, a century ago, the historical confrontation could be figured as a move from a disintegrating particularistic dynastic order toward a globalized national future that was deeply constrained by the imperialist context of capitalist expansionism.[12] At that time, despite these constraints, or perhaps because of the urgency the constraints imposed on that historical moment, within the move from the particular to the national-universal also resided the hope for China's entry into the global universality of modernization.[13] This urgent hope and task—as Wang Xiaoqiu, Liu Zhen'gang, and many other PRC historians remind us—remains an important issue in China today. In our view, then, it is the similar context of

---

11. Co-existing "emergent" and "residual" forms draws from Raymond Williams's insights into eighteenth- and nineteenth-century England; see his *The Country and the City* (London: Oxford University Press, 1973).

12. Joseph Levenson in part framed the problem in this way in his *Confucianism and Its Modern Fate: A Trilogy* (Berkeley: University of California Press, 1968).

13. We emphasize here that we are not claiming that everything needs to or should be encapsulated in a "narrative" of nation. We are speaking here at the most general level of nationalism as a historical problematic. We also emphasize that we do not claim or believe that China was inert prior to the 1898 period, but merely that the *historical problematic* of modernity—as a Chinese and global problem—was only systemically and systematically raised in the 1898 period.

China's encounter with the two global capitalisms—that of the late nineteenth and that of the late twentieth century—that renders "1898" so full of meaning today. It is this, rather than the functionalist exhumation of 1898, that endows the re-emergence of scholarship on the 1898 reforms with contemporary historical significance, for Chinese scholars as for anyone interested in the local effects of globalizing trajectories.

The chapters in this volume, although not speaking in one voice about this or any other issue, reconsider the nature of the historical confrontation at the turn of the last century when a weakened and nominally sovereign China was compelled to acknowledge, articulate, and grapple with the multifaceted crises produced by its forced incorporation into the uneven global system of states, capital, and knowledge. In contrast to the PRC reconsiderations sketched above, however, the connections between the past and the present made by the authors in this volume are implicit rather than explicit. They are not directly concerned with contemporary policy issues or with the specific problems of the present. They do nevertheless draw many of their historical questions precisely from the intersection between the past and the present and, more specifically, from the century-long history of modernity in China that, as the various chapters in this volume imply, began with the 1898 reform period. As such, along with Wang Xiaoqiu and many other Chinese scholars—from Taiwan and the PRC alike—the contributors to this volume have found it not only intellectually productive but historically necessary to rethink 1898 not as an event *per se* but, more important, as a vital conjunctural historical moment, as an extended moment during and through which Chinese intellectuals and society *consciously* confronted and began to reformulate the Chinese historical problematic.

In this light, another historiographical context for this volume is China studies in the West, particularly in the United States. For, even as 1898 is being rediscovered in the PRC, the turn of the twentieth century has, relatively speaking, fallen out of favor in American scholarship on China; indeed, it continues to be treated in an isolated fashion and is seldom drawn into the main currents of "Chinese modernity," which are seen as more properly placed in the later May Fourth period.[14] This recent neglect in the

---

14. We could note here some exceptions, such as the new subfield of Shanghai studies, which, however, generally fails to connect Shanghai to the rest of China, and studies of literature such as David Der-wei Wang's *Fin-de-siècle Splendor: Repressed Modernities of Late Qing Fiction, 1849–1911* (Stanford: Stanford University Press, 1997). Wang, however, figures the late

United States seems to be due to at least two related developments in China studies. First, the Republican period and the Nanjing decade (1920s and 1930s) are now receiving a full-scale reappraisal. This reappraisal stems in part from the growing disrepute of communism and revolution and the previous overly political-factional focus of historiography on the period, as well as from the availability of new sources on the period in the PRC itself. Beyond that, the reappraisal of the 1920s and 1930s also encompasses and emerges from a wide-scale reconsideration of the New Culture / May Fourth period, whose liberal (rather than radical revolutionary) potentials are being re-emphasized. The brief pre-revolutionary decades during which quasi-capitalist-style modernization spawned a new set of social, cultural, economic, and intellectual configurations have thus drawn much recent historiographical and historical attention.

Second, the late imperial period (pre-1800) is also being completely remapped. Scholars of this period have successfully questioned many of the historical paradigms established and informed by May Fourth scholarship on Chinese history. Indeed, these scholars, especially those working on gender and economic issues, have irrefutably demonstrated how May Fourth perspectives have, since the 1920s, consistently construed Chinese history along narrowly focused lines. In essence, by defining China's past as a stagnant traditionalism, May Fourth scholarship and its heirs—in Taiwan, the PRC, and most China studies around the world—established a set of binary lenses for the study of Chinese history: tradition/modern (or feudal / capitalist-socialist [modern]), China / West (Japan), failure/success, stagnation/modernization, continuity/discontinuity, and so on. In liberating late imperial history from the grip of May Fourth paradigms and by demonstrating the vitality and complexity of pre-1800 China, late imperial historians have contributed powerfully to allowing others, such as late Qing scholars, to liberate their fields in similar fashion. The contributors to this volume have drawn, implicitly or explicitly, from these developments in historiography.

In the past, and to a large extent still in current textbook accounts, which are dominated by May Fourth paradigms, there has been a widespread focus on a teleological, outcome-based narrative of the events of the summer of

---

Qing period in terms of a "belated modernity," a formulation that only succeeds in reinscribing a unitary notion of "modernity" that is Western-defined and Western-centered, temporally teleological, and spatially neutral.

1898—of the 103 days during which specific proposals for political, economic, and educational restructuring were submitted to the dynastic authorities by reform-minded men with the support of the Guangxu 光緒 emperor, a brief and frenetic period that ended with the coup d'état by the Empress Dowager Cixi 慈禧 and the "martyrdom" of six prominent reformers and the long exile abroad of many others. This focus has often limited 1898 to being defined narrowly as an *event* and as a political agenda—a failed event and political agenda at that. Moreover, since the 1911 revolution was "successful," in the minimal sense of bringing down the dynastic order, the "failure" of 1898 as a political event can be seen as having been historically superseded—even inevitably so—by the success of the revolution as an event. To be sure, the mutuality of reformist and revolutionary thought in the pre-1911 period has long been recognized by historians—Joseph Levenson, Benjamin Schwartz, Hao Chang, Mary Rankin, and many others, past and present—and any historical interpretation of the period based on a rigid separation of the camps has long been discarded. Nevertheless, given the firm focus on the political institutional premises of modernization, the 1898 reforms and the resulting coup can only be—and have generally been—construed as an example of China's failure to modernize. Implicit and explicit comparisons to Japan's Meiji Restoration period only make this "failure" more abject, an abjectness not mitigated by any appeal to the ostensible "success" of the dynastic-sponsored new policy reforms of 1901–11.

Hence, in this volume, the contributors approach the problem of 1898 with new historical questions. The essays range across considerations of political thought and structural change, educational institutions and knowledge-formations, gender, and urban history, as well as broad socio-cultural-historical questions. We do not provide a narrative of the events *per se*, nor do we enter into the thousands of documentary debates over who did what when and to whom. Nor do we pass judgment on the period as a whole; even less do we propose to make an inventory of "the modern," usually understood as a list of institutional characteristics (derived from European and American, or Japanese history) against which China can but fall short. Moreover, with our new questions, we believe not only that the very judgment-laden binary structure of reform versus revolution indicated by Wang Xiaoqiu is now clearly impossible to maintain, but also that we must discard the narrow "eventness" of 1898, not to mention the other dichotomies customarily used to encapsulate either the period or its primary actors and ethos, such as "conservative" versus "reformer," "traditional" versus "modern," "essence" versus "function," "Chinese" versus "Western" (or "Japanese"), and so on. This turn away from a narrower focus on institutional modernization and state-based politics allows us to concentrate on exploring the period in the context of a larger framework: as part of a multifaceted process of transforming the relationships of society, knowledge, and politics. This transformation intertwined the local and the global, a process that surely remains to this day one of the most dynamic and traumatic processes of and in modernity for any society, polity, or people.

In sum, then, "modernity" in this volume is taken to be a fluid set of institutional, cultural, political, and economic practices. In this, we wish to distinguish "modernity" from "modernization," which describes and prescribes particular state- and economic-forms derived from Western or Japanese history. Rather, "modernity" is understood as a loose and yet overdetermined conceptual framework deriving from and simultaneously informing a particular Chinese experience of a diverse global historical process, an experience through which new problems were raised and old problems were rethought in creative, inventive, and contradictory ways. In the Chinese case (as, we suspect, in many other such historical cases), these problems initially centered around the relationship among politics, knowledge, and social change; or, more abstractly, on how to recognize and understand the world (including China) and how to reorganize China (and sometimes, the world) by mobilizing such new recognitions. Thus, by neither taking a teleological modernizationist approach nor focusing on the "failures" of the reform movement, the contributors to this volume treat the 1898 period as a symbolic and material historical conjuncture, during which issues of continuing relevance to China were first systematically raised and received comprehensive airings in the Chinese context. It is these airings, in all their variety and contradictoriness, that we see as one of the most important aspects of the moment and that we seek to explore.

The Essays

The chapters in this volume discuss—each in its own way—Chinese experiences of modernity, as these experiences were reflected in and through the crises of the late Qing. Directly or indirectly, they explore the ways in which the status of the dynastic state and indeed the state in general was thrown open to question. What becomes most apparent here is that, as the boundaries of "the state," not least the dynastic grip on the state, were being questioned, new spaces of political activity were opened up through new social and cultural practices and the elaboration of new institutions and bodies of knowledge. Perhaps most noteworthy in this regard is what could be called the widespread destatification of political discourse in the wake of, and despite, the apparent "failure" of the reform initiatives as a coherent movement. This destatification was not, in other words, merely part of an accumulating process of the weakening and fall of the Qing dynasty in particular or of the dynastic state as representative of the historical Chinese polity per se—although it was both of those, to be sure. This destatification was more importantly part of a process of the redefinition of "politics" *and* of "Chineseness."

Indeed, as Peter Zarrow argues, not only did the reform effort permanently open the way for the lower-level gentry to participate in policy making but the very notion of "popular power" (民權 *minquan*) that arose during the period worked to delegitimate the entire imperial order as a form of politics. Focusing on the reformers' imaginary of the monarchy, Zarrow shows that, paradoxically, the use of the powers of the monarchy to promote the reform agenda was in fact seriously undercut by the simultaneous radical critique of that institution by reform movement activists. This contradiction led to the diffusion of a concept and practice of "politics" as separate from the dynastic state and its civil servants and an epochal, albeit incomplete, shift of the basis of Chinese identity away from the dynastic house to new concepts of citizenship and ethnicity. By the same token, as Seungjoo Yoon argues in his chapter, through the notion of the "interstitial bureaucracy," the very practice of politics in this period was also significantly complicated from within the state proper. A group of bureaucrats were able to promote change by using quasi-official powers that had developed by the late Qing between the statutory and nonstatutory regimes. In his examination of the fraught relationship between Zhang Zhidong 張之洞, one of the key officials of the period, and the intern-commissioners who edited the "reformist" *The China Progress* (*Shiwu bao* 時務報), Yoon opens up the historical question of how a new space of "politics" was created in one critical instance in late Qing China. More broadly, one of the most interesting aspects of this relationship—indeed, the aspect that Yoon's investigation explores—was the role newspapers and their editors were coming to assume in late Qing political processes.

If the status of the existing state and the growth of print media are crucial aspects of most modern transitions, as Benedict Anderson has famously argued[15] and as many in China understood quite clearly by 1898, then the definition of what constitutes proper knowledge—for government officials and an informed citizenry alike—was also quickly apprehended as a critical problem and brought to the fore of discussion. As Tze-ki Hon indicates, this was precisely the issue at stake in Zhang Zhidong's famous essay, *An Exhortation to Learning* (*Quanxue pian* 勸學篇). As Hon argues, Zhang's essay must be understood as part of a larger transformation in political discourse and the social practice of politics in the late Qing and not simply as a "conservative" rebuttal to Kang Youwei's "radicalism." Thus, contrary to standard interpretations suggesting that Zhang used the *ti-yong* 體用 (essence/use) formula to privilege Chinese learning as essence (*ti* 體) and Western learning as function (*yong* 用), Hon demonstrates that Zhang proposed reforms in the examination system, made knowledge of the world a qualification for the civil service, and emphasized Western learning at every level of the educational system. Hon concludes that Zhang and the reformist scholars during the 1898 period shared a determination to change Chinese institutions (*fa* 法) and to alter the very bases of knowledge for the bureaucracy and education in China.

The emphasis on the combination of new knowledge and new institutions is also reflected in Timothy Weston's discussion of the process of curriculum formation during the first years of Beijing University (or, until the 1911 revolution, the Imperial University), which was a direct product of the 1898 reforms. As Weston notes, the Imperial University received support from many factions within the Qing state; this surprising situation can be explained in part, according to Weston, by reconsidering the *ti-yong* dichotomy. Rather than a rigid separation between "Western" and "Chinese," the dichotomy is, Weston argues, an imaginative and forthright approach to the inherent syncretism of modern knowledge itself. In this light, Weston examines how new attitudes toward "knowledge" were mobilized in late Qing politics through the organization of the university from 1898 to 1904.

These four chapters deal largely with the changing realm of the state and the political; the remaining chapters diffuse this reconsideration of the political into various aspects of the social and cultural realms. Indeed, by not taking "the social" as a pre-existing reality, the authors of the next five chap-

---

15. Benedict Anderson, *Imagined Communities* (London: Verso, 1991).

ters demonstrate in different ways how a simultaneously unified and fractured notion of "society" was being formed through this period. If the will to rethink and reconstruct "China" as a unified national society and polity was one clear aspiration of both critics and even officials of the dynasty—as it would be articulated shortly after the 1898 reform movement—then it is equally clear that the actual results of social change and modern transformations thwarted and sometimes openly contested this aspiration at every turn. Richard Belsky's consideration of the 1898 reforms as urban history figures this double movement precisely. Belsky's essay not only locates us firmly in a place—Beijing—but argues that an urban-historical approach to the reform movement—as opposed to the more customary "national" approach—reveals much about the nature of the movement while helping explain how Beijing as an urban space evolved in its aftermath. As he demonstrates, the influence of locally based institutions, such as native-place lodges, on the national reform movement were profound; yet, as he also notes, in the wake of 1898 the Qing government moved to assert greater control over these local organizations, just as they were assuming more and more public functions, such as organizing education. If the Imperial University, as Weston discusses, was a national-level approach to integrating new attitudes toward knowledge and education, there were also, as Belsky shows, more locally based approaches to some of the same problems.

The complex rearticulation of social space throughout the extended 1898 period that Belsky points to in Beijing can be noted more abstractly by examining the arguments over both new and old concepts that erupted in the post-1898 period. Indeed, as Joan Judge, Hu Ying, and Rebecca Karl discuss in different ways, the inclusion of women in the discursive and practical notion of the "social" and the "political" became one of the most vexed legacies of 1898; it also represents one of the most vexed questions of and in modernity, in China as elsewhere. All three of these "gender" essays—albeit carried out in different fashions and pointing to surprisingly different conclusions—demonstrate how discourses on the "female," the "nation," and the "modern" were fraught with contradiction from the very beginning in China.

Joan Judge takes up the problem by analyzing two competing sets of discourses that focused on the relationship between female literacy and national empowerment. Judge uses the debates over female literacy—whether female literacy was "good" merely because it had a political function—to demonstrate that the assumed transparent connection between literacy, political agency, and the national project is hardly as uncomplicated as it has subsequently been depicted. Indeed, she argues, as women were exhorted to become educated, educated women's political roles became increasingly circumscribed to family productive and reproductive roles. This circumscription not only limited women as political actors but, in a more long-term sense, limited the development of a specifically female subjectivity to channels prescribed by male nationalists.

While Judge focuses on female literacy, Hu Ying's essay illumines in a contrasting fashion the resituating of the category of *cainü* 才女 (talented women) in the 1898 period. In her analysis of the discursive fate of *cainü*, Hu examines the extraordinary career of Kang Aide 康愛德 (AKA Ida Kahn), one of the first Western-trained Chinese women doctors, by looking at Kang through three different versions of her life: that of her contemporaneous Chinese biographer, Liang Qichao 梁啓超, who defeminized her; then, through the eyes of the Western missionaries who trained her but who rendered her into a pure servant of God; and third, through a semi-biographical pamphlet Kang herself produced in English, entitled "An Amazon in Cathay," which restored her femininity and politics, albeit by combining them in surprising fashion.

Rebecca Karl, taking a different approach and indeed reaching different conclusions from Judge, considers the explosive emergence of the term "slavery," which was widely used to depict and describe the nature of female oppression in late Qing China. She ties this particular locution to the simultaneous appearance of new phrases and concepts used to describe and define the global context in which China was situated. Karl argues, through a multivalent discussion of "slavery" discourses, that at the very moment when gender issues entered the debates on citizenship and nationalism—as modes and figurations of social and political participation—there developed an immediate disjuncture in attitude toward both the general problems of the Chinese nation and the specific problems of female politicization, particularly in regard to the relationship between the family and the nation. By problematizing the question of "family" through her consideration of "slavery" discourses, Karl seeks to contest the notion of male-imposed limitations on "female subjectivity" by linking local, national, and global levels of analysis so as to open new historical questions on the relationship between gender and modernity.

All the preceding essays implicitly or explicitly argue that modernity must be seen as both a local Chinese and a global category. Xiaobing Tang's essay takes up this question quite directly; it focuses attention on a revolutionized form of poetry through an examination of the relationship between Liang Qichao's poetic imagination and modern colonization. In a specific sense, most literary considerations of Liang at the turn of the century focus on his advocacy of political novels and the subsequent rise of the novel and short-story forms; by contrast, Tang argues that the content of poetry, too, was profoundly affected by the global recognitions of the period. Tang illuminates Liang's attitude toward the global by noting his advocacy of the dual movement of "colonization," that is, of China by the West and of the West by Chinese literary practice. On the other hand, as Tang analyzes Liang Qichao's position, it is only from within this new-content / old-style paradigm that the long Chinese poetic tradition could be reinvigorated. Located at the beginning of modern Chinese literature, the revolutionizing of poetry, Tang argues, was a first attempt to bend native form to new content, surely one of the most basic and intractable contradictions of and in modernity worldwide.

In sum, then, these essays cannot be called "revisionist" in the sense that they directly attack received wisdom about the role and significance of 1898; nor does this collection pretend to cover every possible aspect of the questions asked. Nonetheless, the contributions attempt to examine the broader significance of this extended historical moment in terms of the new historical problematic of modernity that was posed to and in early twentieth-century China. In so doing, the authors examine what is arguably an originary moment of modern Chinese concepts of the political and the social. They pose their questions and seek their answers from perspectives that are both distinct in certain ways from those of Chinese historians working in China today and also, in other ways, overlap with those of their PRC colleagues.

In the wake of the centenary year of 1998, which witnessed the gathering of scholars from around the globe in several international symposia, and since the historical problematics that animated the beginning of the twentieth century are widely seen as relevant to the contemporary historical moment, it is clear that the study of 1898 is just beginning. We intend this anthology as a modest contribution to that new beginning.

CHAPTER ONE

The Reform Movement, the Monarchy, and Political Modernity

Peter Zarrow

Historians have generally seen the failure of the reform movement of 1898 as a tragic lost opportunity, as a sign of the dangers of court politics, or as proof of the weakness of reformist ideas or the reform-minded bourgeoisie.[1] For

---

For numerous useful suggestions on earlier versions of this chapter, I thank the audience and participants at the "1898" panels at the Association of Asian Studies annual meeting in Washington, D.C., in 1998, including those represented in this volume; the members of the University of Sydney China Seminar, especially David D. S. Goodman and Helen Dunstan; and Young-tsu Wong; as well as the two anonymous readers for the Harvard University Asia Center; needless to say, I have obdurately refused to accept some suggestions and forced others into my own interpretive scheme, but I remain grateful for all criticisms.

1. Useful (and representative) works dealing with the reform movement include Hao Chang (Zhang Hao 張灝), *Liang Ch'i-ch'ao and Intellectual Transition in China* (Cambridge, Mass.: Harvard University Press, 1971); idem, "Intellectual Change and the Reform Movement, 1890-8," in *Cambridge History of China*, vol. 11, *Late Qing, 1800–1911*, ed. John K. Fairbank and Kwang-ching Liu, pp. 274-338 (Cambridge, Eng.: Cambridge University Press, 1980); idem, *Chinese Intellectuals in Crisis: Search for Order and Meaning, 1890–1911* (Berkeley: University of California Press, 1987); idem, *Lieshi jingshen yu pipan yishi: Tan Sitong sixiang de fenxi* 烈士精神與批判意識 — 譚嗣同思想分析 (The spirit of martyrdom and critical consciousness: an analysis of the thought of Tan Sitong) (Taibei: Lianjing, 1988); Li Zehou 李澤厚, *Kang Youwei Tan Sitong sixiang yanjiu* 康有爲譚嗣同思想研究 (Studies on the thought of Kang Youwei and Tan Sitong) (Shanghai: Renmin chubanshe, 1958); Tang Zhijun 湯志鈞, *Wuxu bianfa shiluncong* 戊戌變法史論叢 (Collected essays on the history of the 1898 reform movement) (Wuhan: Hubei renmin chubanshe, 1957); Wang Rongzu (Young-tsu Wong) 汪榮祖, *Wan Qing bianfa sixiang luncong* 晚清變法思想論叢 (Collected essays on reform thought in the late Qing) (Taibei: Lianjing, 1990); Wu Tingjia 吳廷嘉, *Wuxu sichao zonghenglun* 戊戌思潮縱橫論 (Views on the intellectual tide of the 1898 reform movement) (Beijing: Renmin

good or ill, the failure of reform led to the success of revolution, since the Qing's "new policies," whose implementation began in 1902, came too late. The failure of the reform movement, which climaxed in the "hundred days" of imperial edicts in the summer of 1898, has seldom been questioned; after all, it resulted in the "coup d'état" of the Empress Dowager Cixi 慈禧 (1835–1908) and the execution or exile of the movement's leaders. Nonetheless, this negative view of the reform movement overlooks the fact that it was also a turning point in the shaping of China's modern political culture. Before 1898, participation in the affairs of government by non-office-holding literati was limited to informal and largely illegitimate networks under the loose protection of high officials.[2] Even the system of private secretaries and aides (*muyou* 幕友) of officials that flourished in the wake of the Taiping Rebellion was just that: private and non-official.[3]

Between, say, 1895 and 1898 an explosion of open and openly politicized literati clubs and journals and academies—sometimes with only the most nebulous of links to officialdom—challenged the court's right to limit social forces and determine policy behind closed doors. After 1898, it was the Manchu court that lacked legitimacy. After 1898, new forms of political engagement and new standards of state-society relations came to be accepted as just by China's townspeople, young literati, and even rural gentry. This chapter

---

daxue chubanshe, 1988); Paul A. Cohen and John E. Schrecker, eds., *Reform in Nineteenth-Century China* (Cambridge, Mass.: Harvard University, East Asian Research Center, 1976); Kung-chuan Hsiao, *A Modern China and a New World: K'ang Yu-wei, Reformer and Utopian, 1858–1927* (Seattle: University of Washington Press, 1975); Kong Xiangji 孔祥吉, *Kang Youwei bianfa zouyi yanjiu* 康有爲變法奏議研究 (Studies of the Reform memorials of Kang Youwei) (Shenyang: Liaoning Jiaoyu chubanshe, 1988); idem, *Wuxu weixin yundong xintan* 戊戌維新運動新探 (New inquiries into the 1898 reform movement) (Changsha: Hunansheng xinhua shudian, 1988); and Luke S. K. Kwong, *A Mosaic of the Hundred Days: Personalities, Politics, and Ideas of 1898* (Cambridge, Mass.: Harvard University Press, 1984).

2. James M. Polachek, *The Inner Opium War* (Cambridge, Mass.: Harvard University, Council on East Asian Studies, 1992).

3. My intention here is not to deny that a public sphere (*gong*) and possibly a kind of civil society were evolving in the late Qing—as outlined in Mary Backus Rankin, "The Origins of the Chinese Public Sphere: Local Elites and Community Affairs in the Late Imperial Period," *Etudes chinoises* 9, no. 2 (1990): 13–60; idem, "Some Observations on a Chinese Public Sphere," *Modern China* 19, no. 2 (Apr. 1993): 158–92; and William T. Rowe, "The Problem of 'Civil Society' in Late Imperial China," *Modern China* 19, no. 2 (Apr. 1993): 139–57; however, this trend was not recognized as fully legitimate by the court or, perhaps, even by public opinion, such as it was, until the reform movement was well under way.

shows how a new conception of the monarchy encapsulated a self-consciously "modern" sense of political justice.

The reformers lost their heads, or at least the freedom to reside safely in China, but won the argument. For since 1898, it has proved exceedingly difficult for small leadership circles to lay claim to a legitimate right to rule without popular sanction, although of course the twentieth century has been marked by repeated and occasionally long-lived attempts to do so. By 1898, as the reformers looked to the West and Japan, they saw that political modernity lay in popular power (*minquan* 民權) and a strong state. Popular power did not imply enfranchising the ignorant masses, but in the years following the Sino-Japanese War of 1895 it legitimated literati calls for reconstituting the Qing state.[4] Furthermore, the very ambiguity of "popular power" proved to be a persuasive factor in reconceptualizing the legitimate state, as sovereignty (*zhuquan* 主權) shifted from the monarchy to the populace in the eyes of radical literati. In other words, the center of the polity moved from the dynastic house to the nation; 1898 marked a pivotal moment in the creation of a distinctively *Chinese* national identity defined in political terms through a mass citizenship that implied—at least potentially—full-fledged political rights and participation and immediate membership in a community of ethnic, historical, and cultural ties.

The monarchy became particularly destabilized during the course of 1898 for at least three reasons. First, the rise of Cixi had already created two foci of power, the empress dowager and the young emperor, neither of which was fully legitimate by itself.[5] Second, 1898 climaxed in a clash between the factions of the empress dowager and the emperor that left the emperor permanently wounded and destroyed the balance between the two that had provided at least a precarious political and ritual stability earlier in the decade.[6] And third, the very reforms advocated in 1898 created a contradiction at the root of the institution of the monarchy. The first two points are widely accepted; the third inspires this chapter. For the reformers, on the one hand, the emperor was to be all-powerful and all-wise, pushing reforms

---

4. Xiong Yuezhi 熊月之, *Zhongguo jindai minzhu sixiangshi* 中國近代民主思想史 (The history of democratic thought in China) (Shanghai: Renmin chubanshe, 1987), pp. 216–27.

5. Marianne Bastid, "Official Conceptions of Imperial Authority at the End of the Qing Dynasty," in *Foundations and Limits of State Power in China*, ed. S. R. Schram, pp. 147–85 (London: School of Oriental and African Studies, 1987).

6. Kwong, *Mosaic of the Hundred Days*.

to completion against obscurantist opposition; on the other hand, he was to be literally self-effacing, creating new power structures that would replace the court with a government dominated by reformist literati, and was eventually to acknowledge that sovereignty lay in the people.

China's early transition to a post-feudal order ("early modern" in European historiography)—strong imperial rule, a rationalizing bureaucracy, the center's suppression of local power structures, and the dissemination of a kind of civil religion—was under way as early as the eighth century.[7] But educated Chinese at the end of the nineteenth century, no matter how great their pride in their culture's general accomplishments, saw China as a loser, not a pacesetter, in the historical race. They were willing to forgo many long-accepted ideas about political order to build a modern nation-state, taking as models various examples of success: Britain, Germany, France, the United States, Russia, and Japan. No one wished to copy any of these models in its entirety, but they were seen as sources of knowledge about China's possible future—as roadmaps to its survival and prosperity in the modern world. The reform movement engaged in a creative appropriation, based on limited knowledge of the West, of several notions that were seen as compatible with Chinese culture: the nation-state, mass citizenship, a constitutional monarchy and representative government (local self-government and national parliaments), and commercial development. In other words, for the reformers, "political modernity" did include the institution of the monarchy.

At the same time, the reform movement attempted to use the monarchy for modernizing purposes. For both practical and theoretical reasons, the reformers sought no changes in the lineage basis of China's rulership. Practically, they hoped for the court's support to reshape the bureaucracy and were in no position to challenge its authority. Theoretically, they favored using all the autocratic powers of a modernizing emperor along the lines of Peter the Great and the Meiji emperor; they could imagine but not yet build any alternative sources of power and legitimacy.

The reformers were to some extent advocates of democratic thought and constitutionalism, but paradoxically these self-proclaimed modernizers at least ostensibly supported an especially autocratic monarchy. At the same time, they sometimes used a transcendental language derived from New

---

7. Alexander Woodside, "Territorial Order and Collective Identity: Tensions in Confucian Asia: China, Vietnam, Korea," *Daedalus* 172, no. 3 (Summer 1998): 216–17.

Text Confucianism that posited progressive forces rooted in the cosmos.[8] This was a critical step in expanding the scope of the "public" (*gong* 公), for Confucius was no longer the private property of the emperor, whose own claims to authority were now seen as derivative. The category of the "public" was deeply embedded in reform discourse long before 1898, and by the 1890s it was providing a critical step for creating a modern politics of open, legitimate contestation.[9] The reformers' claims to a voice were based squarely on their moral scholarship, and they implicitly acknowledged that no single person in the political realm could claim final interpretive authority. Nothing, perhaps, was new here, but the political crises of the late Qing forced what had once been but a factional tactic into the open. As Liang Qichao 梁啓超 (1873–1929), Kang Youwei 康有爲 (1858–1927), and other reformers began rethinking the nature of monarchical power (*junquan* 君權), claims to authority that were in effect based on mere birth—the sanctity of the impe-

---

8. For New Text Confucianism, see Benjamin A. Elman, *Classicism, Politics, and Kinship: The Ch'ang-chou School of New Text Confucianism in Late Imperial China* (Berkeley: University of California Press, 1990); and Anne Cheng, "Nationalism, Citizenship, and the Old Text / New Text Controversy in Late Nineteenth-Century China," in *Imagining the People: Chinese Intellectuals and the Concept of Citizenship, 1890–1920*, ed. Joshua A. Fogel and Peter Zarrow, pp. 3–38 (Armonk, N.Y.: M. E. Sharpe, 1997).

9. See Mizoguchi Yūzō 溝口雄三, "Chūgoku no 'kō' 'shi'" 中國の「公。私」 ("Public" and "private" in China), 2 pts., *Bungaku* 56, no. 9 (1988): 88–102, no. 10 (1988): 73–84; and William T. Rowe, "The Public Sphere in Modern China," *Modern China* 16, no. 3 (July 1990): 309–29. Huang Kewu (黃克武, "Cong zhuiqiu zhengdao dao rentong guozu—Qingmo Zhongguo gong si guannian de chongzheng" 從追求正道到認同國族—清末中國公私觀念的重整 [From the pursuit of rights to national identity: renovating the Chinese conception of public and private in the late Qing], paper delivered at the conference "The Public and the Private: The Restructuring of Collective and Individual Bodies in Modern China [1600–Present]," Academia Sinica, Taibei, May 21–25, 1999), has recently stressed the link between such seventeenth-century critics of the monarchy as Huang Zongxi and Gu Yanwu on the one hand and the late Qing reformers on the other in terms of the equation of dynastic succession with "selfishness" (*si*)—the opposite of "public" (*gong*). Nor were such views unusual in the seventeenth century (see Xiong Bingzhen 熊秉眞, "Shiqi shiji Zhongguo zhengzhi sixiangzhong feichuantong chengfen de fenxi" 十七世紀中國政治思想中非傳統成份的分析 [An analysis of nontraditional elements in seventeenth-century China's political thought], *Zhongyang yanjiuyuan jindaishi yanjiusuo jikan*, no. 15A [June 1986]: 1–31). In the hands of the reformers, "public" was associated with democracy, a widespread view by the 1890s (Huang Kewu, "Cong zhuiqiu zhengdao," p. 14). The point here, however, is that even if democracy remained a utopian projection, "public" functioned as an immediate challenge to traditional imperial prerogatives.

rial line—could not survive. This gives rise to several questions. Did Kang Youwei and the other reformers seek (merely) to use the existing monarchical institution to press for reforms that would eventually lead to democracy? Did they wish, on the other hand, for reforms that would strengthen the state but fall short of what we now consider democracy? Did they seek to fashion a new basis of authority and power that would replace the monarchy? Did they seek to replace the entire system of authority resting on the examination system, the gentry class, the system of sacred-classical learning, the bureaucracy, and the monarchy? What future did they envision for the Qing court? How radical were they?

In fact, the reformers' views were shifting, ambiguous, and uncertain. This was not mere political weakness or the odd result of particular circumstances but a central intellectual dilemma in the reformers' political philosophy as they attempted to redefine kingship without abandoning it. One can trace something of a division among the reformers, with Liang Qichao and Wang Kangnian 汪康年 (1860–1911) more or less on the "people's" side and Kang Youwei and Mai Menghua 麥孟華 on the "ruler's" side; more to the point, however, each individual reformer was divided internally and dealt with the ambiguity of power in different ways. It can, on the other hand, be argued that the contradictions were more apparent than real.[10] In this view, when Kang praised "popular power" and even envisioned a post-Qing polity, he was expressing his long-term goals. For the immediate future, however, the reformers sought only reform: fundamental institutional changes within the existing framework of the monarchy and the bureaucracy. In this view, when the reformers praised autocratic methods and glorified the emperor, they were only recognizing the political realities and challenges facing reform in the late Qing and attempting to harness the emperor to pull the cart of reform in the direction of democracy or, at any rate, constitutional monarchy. The "paradox" of the reformers' willingness to rely on imperial power is explained by lack of alternatives: young literati-intellectuals could scarcely lead bottom-up reforms capable of changing the entire system, nor could they imagine a popular revolution at this point. It is also true that in the

---

10. The case for the fundamental consistency of the reformers, and Kang Youwei in particular, is well expressed by Wang Rongzu (汪榮祖, *Kang Youwei* 康有為 [Taibei: Dongda tushu, 1998], pp. 18–32, 63–81), who explains apparent contradictions as tactical shifts in terms of the overriding goal of institutional change (*bianfa* 變法).

Guangxu 光緒 emperor (r. 1875–1908) they found a willing, if ultimately ineffective, supporter.

Nonetheless, to explain a paradox is not to diminish its paradoxical nature. If the reformers' views of the monarchy were consistent at a discursive level—autocratic reform now, constitutional monarchy later, perhaps full-fledged democracy someday—they nonetheless spoke of the institution, powers, and charisma of the monarchy in contradictory ways. At a rhetorical level and, I think, in terms of the ideas and imaginations of the reformers, the monarchy retained much of its potency and mystical awe. After the failure of the 1898 reforms, although Kang remained loyal to the Guangxu emperor, Liang moved in a more secularizing direction. Nonetheless, in 1896 Liang began his noted analysis "China's Weaknesses Are Due to Avoiding Problems" ("Lun Zhongguo jiruo youyu fangbi" 論中國積弱由於防弊) by emphasizing the "public mindedness" of the former kings.[11] In other words, he simply took for granted the origins of the monarchical institution in the ancient myth of civilizing sage-kings. Liang's goal was to contrast their impartiality with the selfishness (si 私) of the later emperors. In this, he did not go beyond the earlier views of Huang Zongxi 黃宗羲 (1610–95), whose views, indeed, Liang was vigorously promoting.[12]

The cosmological foundations of the Chinese monarchy thus were beginning to be questioned by the 1890s, but by no means had faith in them disappeared even among the most "advanced" of China's educated classes. This is not to imply that the Chinese monarchy's legitimating techniques were stationary; the eighteenth century in particular had seen large discursive shifts,[13] but it is to emphasize that we should hardly be surprised at finding individuals expressing differing views of the monarchy. The consistency of the reformers' views is discussed below, but it is ultimately less central to this chapter than the twists and turns in their efforts to reconceptualize the monarchy. The problem of the monarchy was but one part of a larger complex of questions about institutional reform, but it was intimately

---

11. Liang Qichao 梁啓超, *Yinbingshi heji: wenji* 飲冰室合集：文集 (Collected essays from the Ice-drinker's Studio) (Zhonghua shuju, Beijing, 1996), 1: 96.

12. Wm. Theodore de Bary, trans. and ed., Huang Zongxi, *Waiting for the Dawn: A Plan for the Prince* (New York: Columbia University Press, 1993), pp. 78–80.

13. Pamela Kyle Crossley, *A Translucent Mirror: History and Identity in Qing Imperial Ideology* (Berkeley: University of California Press., 1999); Angela Zito, *Of Body & Brush: Grand Sacrifice as Text/Performance in Eighteenth-Century China* (Chicago: University of Chicago Press, 1997).

connected with the deepest layers of cultural and national identity and even existential orientation. To put it crudely, if the sage-kings' creation of civilization (that is, China) did not survive the debacle of 1898, then what became of national identity? It was one thing to criticize historical emperors for selfishness; it was quite another to overturn the foundations not just of the central political institution but of the very culture itself. And if the monarchy was fundamentally corrupt from the beginning, what did that imply about Tian 天 (Heaven) and humanity's place in the cosmos? This chapter cannot investigate these larger questions systematically, but, even as mere questions, they illustrate that more than politics was at stake in the late 1890s. I begin with a discussion of Kang Youwei's early writings on the monarchy, which established the case for autocratic reform; then show how Liang Qichao and other reformers adapted these views to the needs of the reform movement after 1895; and finally suggest how New Text Confucianism fostered a reconceptualization of rulership that was profoundly destabilizing for the existing monarchy but offered a path toward a new cultural identity.

Kang Youwei's Early Views on the Monarchy

By the mid-1880s, Kang Youwei had produced a systematic synthesis of his political and philosophical position.[14] In *A Complete Book of Substantial Truths and Universal Principles* (*Shili gongfa quanshu* 實理公法全書), a kind of outline of his views, Kang sought to delineate absolute moral truths based on a scientific or mathematical approach that supported his universalism.[15] Using the Confucian value of benevolence (*ren* 仁), he proclaimed the equality of humanity as well as a notion of individual autonomy (*ge you zizhu zhi quan* 各有自主之權). This in turn led him to a condemnation of despotism.

---

14. San-pao Li (Li Sanbao), "K'ang Yu-wei's *Shihli kung-fa chüan-shu* (A complete book of substantial truths and universal principles)," *Zhongyang yanjiuyuan jindaishi yanjiusuo jikan* no. 7 (June 1978): 683–725.

15. Kang Youwei 康有爲, *Kang Youwei quanji* 康有爲全集 (The complete works of Kang Youwei), ed. Yuan Shiping 遠世平 (Shanghai: Shanghai guji chubanshe, 1987), 1: 245–306; Wang Rongzu (Young-tsu Wong) 汪榮祖, "'Wuxue sasui yicheng': Kang Youwei zaonian sixiang xilun" 「吾學卅歲已成」: 康有爲早年思想析論 ("My Learning Was Complete at Thirty": an interpretation of the early thought of Kang Youwei), *Hanxue yanjiu* 12, no. 2 (Dec. 1994): 53–54.

Kang was a Guangdong native, a precocious student, and a man who assigned himself the mission of saving China. He was perhaps the most influential politico-philosophical writer of the 1890s in China and one of the key
figures in the project of creating modern Chinese thought. Although Kang
had not yet formulated the principles of his utopian vision by the 1880s,
many of his radical notions were already developed. Marriages should be
freely contracted and subject to change; children should be raised in public
nurseries with no filial obligations (nor would parents have obligations toward their children); and sages and teachers would have no special authority.[16] Kang's vision of the king was that of a mediator (*zhongbao* 中保), chosen by the people for their own protection as two individuals chose a
mediator in a dispute.[17] Kang's general approval of democracy is clear. He
favored republican forms such as parliaments but criticized direct democracy
as inferior. Unlimited monarchical powers (*junzhu weiquan wuxian* 君主威
權無限), however, contravened scientific truth. In other words, despotism
not only was an artificial institution but also lacked any basis in justice. Kang
supported a system of indirect democracy in which officials would be elected
to carry out administrative functions.[18] Such officials would themselves be
regarded as kings, a nomenclature implying that potentially anyone could be
king (*junzhu* 君主). Indeed, the notion that "power belongs to all" (*quan
guiyu zhong* 權歸於眾) suggests that human institutions should be built on
the basis of equality (*pingdeng* 平等).

However, at the same time, in his *Esoteric and Exoteric Essays of Master
Kang* (*Kangzi neiwai pian* 康子內外篇), Kang presented a vision of an absolute and highly active monarchy.[19] He defined the sage as one who pos-
sesses transformative powers. Sagely rulers can manipulate and control the
people. At the same time, they must understand the circumstances and
trends (*shi* 勢) around them in order to lead and correct. China is uniquely
suited for this task:

---

16. Kang Youwei, *Kang Youwei quanji*, 1: 245–306; San-pao Li, "K'ang Yu-wei's *Shihli kung-
fa chüan-shu*," pp. 696–708.

17. Kang Youwei, *Kang Youwei quanji*, 1: 288; San-pao Li, "K'ang Yu-wei's *Shihli kung-fa
chüan-shu*," p. 708. Kang's idea here may be an echo of the "social contract." Rousseau's *Social
Contract* had been translated into classical Chinese in Japan in the late 1870s. The notion of
mediation seems to have little to do with traditional notions of kingship but resonates with
the informal authority of local gentry.

18. Kang Youwei, *Kang Youwei quanji*, 1: 288, 298.

19. Ibid., 1: 165–200.

not because of China's huge territory or its large population or its abundant natural resources, but because of its unique respect for imperial power (*junquan duzun* 君權獨尊). This respect was indeed not stolen from circumstances, nor was it teased out of profit; rather, it was achieved through the accumulation of the benevolence (*ren*) of the founding emperors, the righteousness (*yi* 義) of the Han, Tang, Song, and Ming dynasties, and the promotion of honorable rewards by millions of sages and worthies over millions of years.[20]

Kang was not here exalting the supreme power of the emperor for its own sake, but he noted that it could be used to supplement deficiencies in the bureaucracy, the populace, and the military. Yet it is also clear that the emperor can have only the best interests of his people in mind; he cannot act for his own benefit. Following the ancient "Legalist" thinkers Guanzi 管子 and Shang Yang 商鞅, Kang wrote that the "way of the sages is to take care of the people and correct their virtue" and create prosperity.[21] This is not merely what a king does; it is what a king *is*: "The distinction between the hegemon and the true king lies solely in the mind-and-heart. When the mind is sincerely devoted to the people, leading them to wealth and power, this is the kingly way. When the mind is obsessively devoted to oneself and leads the self to wealth and power, this is the method of the hegemon." At the same time, the root of kingly behavior is not mysterious; it is simply the "mind that cannot bear to see suffering." Suffering requires action to cure it. Rotten old customs are deeply rooted. Kings must therefore use power. By no means did Kang think the people would naturally follow the ruler willy-nilly; rather, kings must use "the method of rewards and punishments" (*kaisai zhi shu* 開塞之術) to threaten and coerce.[22] This, too, defines the sage, and at this point in his argument Kang referred to the Confucian dictum: "Restrain the people with rites, pacify the people with music," making them good and joyful without their even knowing how this comes to pass. "Thus it is said, 'The people can be made to follow [the Way] but not to understand [it].'"[23] Governance follows from punishing evil and rewarding

---

20. Ibid., 1: 165–66.

21. Ibid., 1: 166.

22. This is the primary theme of "Hebi" 闔闢, the first chapter. The term *hebi* is virtually untranslatable, referring on different levels to closing and opening (the most literal level), strategies, magical powers, and these very techniques to reward virtue and punish evil. It is derived from the *Classic of Changes* (*Yijing* 易經, *xici shang*), which defined "change" (*bian* 變) in its terms: *yihe yibi wei zhi bian* 一闔 ·闢謂之變.

23. Kang Youwei, *Kang Youwei quanji*, 1: 166; *Lunyu* 8.9.

good; the loyalty of the masses comes from benefiting them. Kang cited numerous historical cases of kings not only gaining and retaining power in this
way, but also converting entire populations—to Buddhism in the case of the
Liang, to Western customs in the case of the Meiji emperor, and even to
various changes of fashion. Kang was thus talking about a good deal more
than what we normally mean by political power.

Rulers need to possess an understanding of history and the models of the
past, techniques of administration, a sense of priorities, and the ability to assess the present situation. Kang here promoted an activist style of ruling.
Although the "mind that cannot bear suffering" lies at the root of government, rulers cannot be merciful to evildoers. Citing Ming Taizu's (r. 1368–
99) harsh treatment of malfeasance, Kang praised the Ming founder's love of
the people in this regard. First, the system must be reformed, and only then
can one "nourish the people with magnanimity."[24] Then will ordinary people
obey the laws, the talented rush forward to prove their merit, and culture
flourish. The powers of the ruler will be virtually unlimited. He can encourage and nourish talent; build schools; spread knowledge; develop infrastructure, industry, commerce, and farming; train armies; and clarify the
rites and music (or government). When the nation thereupon becomes
wealthy and strong, domestically customs will be uplifted and externally foreigners will be subjugated. This will be the time to "avenge the anger and
shame of our ancestors, recover China's culture (*shengjiao* 聖教), preserve the
sacred relations (*shenglun* 聖倫) from imminent destruction, and save the
kingship (*wangjiao* 王教) from gradual disintegration."[25]

Passages such as these can be understood in terms of the Confucian
statecraft tradition, as Hao Chang suggests,[26] or of Legalist influences, as
San-pao Li suggests.[27] Both are present, and Kang's faith in what we may
call behaviorism is obvious. The point here, however, is that Kang exalted
not so much the monarchy as power—or, more precisely, transformative
power—itself. It is true that he associated this power with the traditional

---

24. Kang Youwei, *Kang Youwei quanji*, 1: 169.

25. Ibid., 1: 170.

26. Chang, *Chinese Intellectuals*, pp. 26–27.

27. Li Sanbao (San-pao Li) 李三寶, ed. and trans., "*Kangzi Neiwaipian* chubu fenxi—
Kang Nanhai xiancun zuizao zuopin" 康子內外篇初步分析－康南海現存最早作品
(An analysis of the *Esoteric and Exoteric Essays of Master Kang*—the earliest extant writings of
Kang Youwei), *Qinghua xuebao* 11, no. 12 (Dec. 1975): 217.

kingship represented by both the Yao-Shun ideal and the historical dynasts. This led Kang to assert the supremacy of the monarch, and his prose is redolent, in the final analysis, of the Confucian ideal of the "kingly way," which was associated with the glorification of imperial institutions. Nonetheless, as in mainstream Confucianism, his final concern is the welfare of the people and the morality of rule. The kingship is instrumental in that sense; it is historically determined, and there is little indication in these passages that Kang treated it as rooted in the nature of the cosmos. He has preserved the omnipotent, almost magical, kingship but separated it from its old moorings. A later essay in the volume perhaps clarifies this point. Kang borrowed the second-century B.C. thinker Dong Zhongshu's 董仲舒 distinction between benevolence (ren), associated with others, and righteousness (yi), associated with the self.[28] But unlike Dong, Kang emphasized the contradictory aspects of the two virtues—benevolence representing regard for others, unselfishness, and egalitarianism; and righteousness, self-regard and hierarchy. The traditional Chinese reverence for the ruler over the subject, the male over the female, and the good over the base all represented "righteousness"; more to the point, they should be replaced with more egalitarian attitudes. Kang thus clearly preferred benevolence and even the Mohist "universal love" (jian'ai 兼愛) and Buddhist egalitarianism to the traditional Confucian regard for righteousness. In regard to the monarchy, he concluded that a king should behave with universal love even though the people could be self-regarding.[29] The moral responsibilities of the ruler thus demanded his administrative perfection; equally, rulership was infused with moral meaning.

Kang was concerned with the history of governing insofar as it offered models of imperial decisiveness; he showed no such interest in institutions. The monarch must be devoted to the welfare of the nation and that in turn required fundamental, sweeping change. Change, in turn, was dictated by and must be in accord with circumstances and trends, even while it was the test of leadership. Kang simultaneously suggested that in some ultimate sense the monarch and the people were equal but that for the time being the king stood far above the nation. Kang's activist emperor possessed charisma in the sense of having almost-but-not-quite magical powers. Kang did not

---

28. Kang Youwei, Kang Youwei quanji, 1: 187–88.
29. Ibid., 1: 189.

discuss Yao, Shun, or later dynasts as anything but human, but because these particular men "could understand the trends and penetrate into people's minds" and because they knew the "methods of power," they could accomplish anything.[30] This was ultimately a moral and even spiritual vision of leadership, however, because Kang firmly planted the monarchy in the soil of benevolence and selflessness. If there seems to be a contradiction between what in the end boils down to a fairly traditional conception of the monarchy and a strong egalitarianism, this was resolved for Kang in the stringent moral demands he placed on the monarchy as a personal institution.

Yet any sense of an actual emperor's personality disappears under the weight of the responsibility Kang assigned to him. If imperial charisma for Kang, as noted above, derived from skills of an incredible order, another part came from the mind-and-heart rooted in benevolence. Kang wrote as a would-be advisor or prime minister to the king, and there is much in his approach, in terms of both style and substance, that had a long Confucian pedigree. His rhetoric is heightened so that the ruler is discussed in an exalted language. Kang's ruler was, in his capacities, greater than an ordinary individual who happened to hold a certain post, but he was also less than an ordinary human, stripped of desires and required to deny himself ordinary pleasures and self-regard. Yet the ruler nonetheless remained an individual: in no sense was the power of the collectivity immanent in him. What Kang made him was the sole, personal focus of sovereignty.

In these early essays, Kang did not separate the state from the person of the ruler nor, for all Kang's egalitarianism, did he treat the people with any great respect. If anything, it was their duty to be passively transformed; after that, they conceivably might form a nation. Kang's thought moved in two separate directions. He desired fundamental reform, including reform of the monarchy, even as he would strengthen the institution, not least by recalling its cultural resources to it. Kang maintained a "more or less conciliatory attitude toward the existing political order,"[31] and he justified this with a synthesis of Confucian statecraft and Legalist ideas. Kang's thinking was divided not so much between conservative and radical tendencies, for Kang felt no conflicts between different goals and his radical vision was moored safely

---

30. Ibid., 1: 165.
31. Hsiao, *A Modern China*, pp. 80–81.

to the future, as between means and ends.[32] For all practical (immediate) purposes, he could not envision a Chinese state except as the creature of the emperor. Yet, as Young-tsu Wong has pointed out, Kang's main concern in these texts was not to exalt the ruler but to press for reform. In other words, Kang's stress on the powers of the emperor was a recognition of the historical reality that reforms could be legislated only from the top.[33]

However, there is no direct contradiction between the view that Kang exalted the emperor and the view that he remained firmly committed to fundamental reform; in other words, Kang was neither a hypocrite cynically using an emperor he reduced to a tool nor was he a mental slave of the traditional imperial ideology. It is true that a careful, literal reading of the *Esoteric and Exoteric Essays of Master Kang* shows Kang to be describing, not praising; yet, on the other hand, what Kang describes—in lyrical prose—is an essentially charismatic kingship. Indeed, Kang's vision of an activist emperor was at odds with the mainstream of imperial Confucianism, which, generally speaking, promoted a more passive sage-ruler. Nonetheless, Kang was within the mainstream in portraying the emperor's moral and cosmic authority even while he clearly condemned autocratic power as outside the bounds of the Confucian value of benevolence or the Mohist-Western value of universal love. Whatever Kang "really" thought of the origins and institution of the monarchy, he portrayed it in terms that ranged from "artificial" to "sacred" and from dysfunctional to both moral and powerful. We should also remember that he was to invest the efforts of a lifetime in Guangxu and the Chinese monarchy.

For Kang, there was nothing incongruous about combining the "traditional" monarchy with reform—any more than building progress on the past ever need seem strange. In retrospect, we may isolate tensions in Kang's

---

32. In this sense, I cannot agree with Hao Chang's (*Chinese Intellectuals*, pp. 29–34) emphasis on the dichotomy between radicalism and conservatism in Kang, but the distinction he notes between the political and moral layers of Kang's thought is extremely useful.

33. See Wang Rongzu, "'Wuxue sasui yicheng,'" p. 58; idem, *Kang Youwei*, pp. 63–90. Wang thus criticized Hao Chang's and Richard Howard's emphasis on Kang's "conservatism" in this regard. Howard ("K'ang You-wei [1858–1927]: His Intellectual Background and Early Thought," in *Confucian Personalities*, ed. Arthur Wright and Denis Twitchett, pp. 294–316 [Stanford: Stanford University Press, 1962]) stated that Kang saw the monarchy as valid and the emperor as magical. See also Chang (*Chinese Intellectuals*, p. 29): Kang "spoke expansively not only of the cultural glories of the Chinese tradition, but also of the irresistible, absolute moral authority of the Chinese emperor."

thought, but the direction he gave the reform movement of 1898 directly contributed to what we may call political modernity. First, his stress on activism and wholesale, transformative change was a profound challenge to the status quo. The modernist project of rebuilding society was, for Kang, to be accomplished through the cosmological kingship. Whether, for Kang, its powers stemmed from Heaven or the imagination of the people need not detain us here; rhetorically, at least, traditional kingship was alive and well. Yet, second, a possibly unintended but necessary consequence of Kang's conception of the Chinese emperor was to show that rulership itself could be consciously reformulated. The search for the roots of monarchism led not merely to its exaltation but also to its moral purpose. The implication that an immoral—or simply passive—monarchy was not legitimate did not have to be made explicit, but it could not be ignored. It remains true, however, that if Kang could reconcile such disparate views—Confucianism, statecraft thinking, Legalism, even Mohism—within an ideal kingship, he had less to say about the institutions that might support reform. Rulership for Kang lay in meeting challenges, creating (undefined) institutions, and overcoming danger.

During the 1890s, Kang did, of course, have much to say about specific institutional reform, and he cannot be accused of ignoring the issue for long.[34] Indeed, the association between the New Text school and statecraft interests from the early nineteenth century virtually guaranteed that Kang, who emerged from this tradition, would pay a great deal of attention to institutions. His radical claims for Confucius "as a reformer," for the "three ages" as an evolutionary scheme, and for a re-reading of the entire Confucian tradition shocked a generation but established the intellectual basis for sweeping political and social reforms. He explicitly linked the Age of Disorder with the absolute monarchy, the Age of Approaching Peace with constitutional monarchy, and the Age of Universal Peace with republicanism. At best, monarchism might be associated with the Age of Approaching Peace. As a long-civilized nation, though one still far short of perfection, China needed a constitutional monarchy that recognized the people's rights.

Kang's views of the monarchy in the mid- and late 1890s contrasted in significant ways with his earlier views. Like other reformist thinkers, he treated a parliament as a means for promoting national unity and connecting

---

34. Hsiao, *A Modern China*; Kong Xiangji, *Kang Youwei bianfa zouyi yanjiu*; Wang Rongzu, *Kang Youwei*.

ruler and people, but Kang also offered a picture of the emperor outside politics and administration yet no longer above the nation. At the beginning of the hundred days, Kang memorialized the emperor to establish a parliament, so that "the ruler and the citizens discuss the nation's politics and laws together."[35] He advocated the separation of powers: the parliament makes the laws, legal officials adjudicate them, and the government administers them. What, then, does an emperor do? "The ruler remains in general charge" (*renzhu zongzhi* 人主總之). Not only did Kang thus preach the doctrine of Western-style constitutional monarchy, but he also clearly implied that the emperor, although establishing the constitution, is also subject to it. Under such a system, the government "represents" the emperor, who is sacred but without responsibility and (thus?) forms "one body" with all the citizens.

Rulership here is attenuated and edging toward the symbolic rather than practical. Nonetheless, Kang claimed that this was a recipe for strengthening China, just as autocracy had proved to weaken the country. In his famous but undelivered "second memorial" to the throne of May 1895 opposing the proposed peace terms with Japan, Kang had complained of the growing gaps between ruler and officials and the officials and people.[36] This charge had long been fundamental to the reformist position, but later Kang elaborated in another memorial: a unified country was strong and orderly, whereas autocracy led to a system in which the people paid their taxes but did not participate in government, fought with one another, and thought only of their own benefit.[37] The lesson Kang drew was that unity and assimilation under the great umbrella of benevolence would prevent ethnic strife, at least on the political level. Kang thus implied that the institution of a parliament (or constitutionalism generally) would unite not only ruler and people but also the people themselves.

He cited the usual mythical sage-kings (Huangdi, Yao, Shun) to show that in ancient times China had been governed with a democratic spirit

---

35. Kang Youwei 康有爲, "Qing ding lixian kaiguohui zhe" 請定立憲開國會摺 (Memorial requesting the establishment of a constitution and parliament), in Jian Bocan 翦伯贊, *Wuxu bianfa* 戊戌變法 (The reform movement of 1898) (Shanghai: Shenzhou guoguangshe, 1953), 2: 236–37.

36. Kang Youwei 康有爲, "Shang Qing di di er shu" 上清帝第二書 (Second memorial to the Qing emperor), in Jian Bocan, *Wuxu bianfa*, 2: 152.

37. Kang Youwei 康有爲, "Qing jun min hezhi Man Han bufen zhe" 請君民合治滿漢不分摺 (Memorial requesting the joint rule of ruler and people and the joining of the Manchu and Han peoples), in Jian Bocan, *Wuxu bianfa*, 2: 238.

but—tellingly—noted that the ancient kings had lacked the institution of a parliament to assure cooperation between ruler and people. Kang praised the emperor for being willing to give up power if it would benefit China,[38] while at the same time he repeatedly promised the Guangxu emperor that his sacred rule (*shengzhi* 聖治) would surpass that of the earlier rulers and even spread beyond China itself. Given his views of Chinese history and culture, as well as the political needs of the reform movement at its height in the summer of 1898, Kang had no choice but to emphasize monarchical power (*junquan*). In a June memorial, for example, Kang used language reminiscent of the "Hebi pian" 闔闢篇, reminding the emperor of his "inexhaustible powers," his duty to take action, and his ability to change customs and arouse the people.[39] The Guangxu emperor's powers in fact were quickly exhausted. No notion of imperial charisma could survive 1898. Reformers—and revolutionaries—thus turned increasingly to various sorts of secular, popular organization to build a more open and contestatory politics in the wake of the hundred days and, in the process, relocated the myth of sovereignty to "the people."

Liang Qichao and Reforming the Monarchy

In the mid- and late 1890s, Liang Qichao used Kang's evolutionary notion of the Three Ages to explain the historical role of the monarchy. Kang's most important disciple, Liang would begin to break away from Kang after they were forced into exile in the autumn of 1898, but at this time he was still a close follower. Already a prominent spokesman for reform in his own right, Liang had also begun his wide reading in Western history and politics.[40] In an essay written on the eve of the hundred days entitled "Reasons for the Replacement of the Monarchy by Democracy" ("Lun junzheng minzheng xiangshan zhi li" 論君政民政相嬗之理), Liang equated the monarchy not with the Age of Disorder (as had Kang at times) but with the following Age of Lesser Peace; democracy in his scheme marks the Age of Universal Peace.[41] Liang thus moved China further up the ladder of political evolution

---

38. Kang Youwei, "Qing ding lixian kaiguohui zhe," 2: 237.

39. Kang Youwei 康有爲, *Kang Youwei zhenglunji* 康有爲政論集 (Collected political writings of Kang Youwei), ed. Tang Zhijun 湯志鈞 (Zhonghua shuju, Beijing, 1981), 1: 277; cf. Hsiao, *A Modern China*, pp. 208.

40. Chang, *Liang Ch'i-ch'ao*, pp. 59–72.

41. Liang Qichao, *Yinbingshi heji: wenji*, 2: 7–11.

than had Kang, and constitutional monarchy disappeared as an independent stage. In Liang's imaginary of origins, the Age of Disorder was marked by "multiple lords," by which he meant both tribal and feudal-aristocratic systems. Monarchism thus represented a higher stage of civilization than feudalism.[42] Liang completely junked the sage-king founders of Chinese civilization here and replaced them with warring tribal chieftains, cruel lords, harsh punishments, high taxes, a caste system, and even slavery. Confucius, however, emerged to lead China to the next stage of civilization by criticizing the hereditary lords, promoting independent farmers, and even envisioning the final Universal Peace. Thus was China rescued by the "uncrowned king" (*suwang* 素王) from the worst excesses of aristocratic misgovernment and made strong by the recruitment of the talented into a national bureaucracy. Liang felt that disunity led to weakness since rulers pursue their selfish interests (*jun zhi siyu* 君之私有) by encouraging their peoples to fight one another. That is why unitary kingship represented at least a "lesser peace" that saw relatively little warfare and other disturbances.

Liang thus followed Kang's New Text–derived adulation of Confucius. This provided the basic operating framework of his reformism, although Liang already showed signs of a more pragmatic, even hard-headed approach. He also believed (like Kang) in a kind of historical determinism: there was no use in pushing history faster than it could move, but when the time was right, trying to stop progress was futile. Yet Liang was already publicly postulating a new kind of relationship between ruler and people. Democracy was essentially a higher stage of unity for Liang, related both to communal property (*gongchan* 公產) and popular unity (*hezhong* 合眾); indeed, his essay "Grouping" ("Shuo qun xu" 說群序) began by emphasizing that the ruler should be "a member of the same group as the people."[43] Still, the point here is that once a particular stage is reached, no country can revert to a simpler, less advanced political form. What, then, of contemporary

---

42. With a considerable degree of historical justification, Liang classified ancient Athens as an aristocratic slave state, not a democracy, thus saving his evolutionary scheme and allowing him to claim equivalence between China and the West in terms of ancient historical development. Liang argued that both the ancient Mediterranean world and the ancient Chinese states of Xia and Shang contained some of the seeds of democracy, but neither developed them. However, in a letter to Yan Fu, Liang explicitly condemned attempts to find equivalence between China and the West ("Yu Yan Youling xiansheng shu" 與嚴幼陵先生書, in Liang Qichao, *Yinbingshi heji: wenji*, 1: 108).

43. Ibid., 2: 2–3; see Chang, *Liang Ch'i-ch'ao*, pp. 95–107.

political forms? In what stage was China and the world today? The vision of a world beyond China was important, for Liang emphasized that the laws of history were universal. Broadly speaking, it made no sense that some parts of the world would be significantly advanced over others. Thus Liang argued that even republics like the United States and France were not in fact approaching the Age of Universal Peace, since major powers like Britain, Russia, and, for that matter, China were still monarchies and significant portions of the globe remained mired in tribal forms. The world as a whole, marked by selfish struggles among nations, was thus a world of chaos. The stage of Universal Peace might be far, far in the future.[44] If Westerners had realized the virtues of public-mindedness, they still had not eliminated the selfish struggles among nations, families, and individuals. Liang concluded: China needed the West's knowledge of legal matters but only (China's) "laws of the sages" could finally civilize the whole world ("China Should Seek Legal Knowledge" ["Lun Zhongguo yi jiangqiu falü zhi xue" 論中國宜講求法律之學]).[45]

In the meantime, however, what of China's monarchy? When was democracy to replace it? Liang was not to answer these questions directly in the years leading up to 1898. In fact, he vacillated between sharp criticism of the monarchy and a call for popular participation in government on the one hand and an appreciation of the special powers of the monarch and skepticism about the abilities of the Chinese people on the other. Like Kang, Liang judged rulership itself on the basis of ultimate or moral standards, but he emphasized public-mindedness (*gong*), which was conceptually related to the practical question of grouping, rather than benevolence (*ren*), which remained open to a more spiritual interpretation. Liang maintained his loyalty

---

44. Liang's new awareness of the international context and "global consciousness" undoubtedly led to a sense of local difference, but his sense of temporal progress remained universal; that is, if the West was "ahead" of China, this was not because it had a unique historical trajectory. China would catch up quickly since world historical trends mandated change (or else—without reform, extinction). He cited Kang Youwei's notion that the West was 80–90 percent civilized whereas China was 10–20 percent; neither had completed the evolutionary trajectory ("Yu Yan Youling xiansheng shu," in Liang Qichao, *Yinbingshi heji: wenji*, 1: 109; cf. Xiaobing Tang, *Global Space and the Nationalist Discourse of Modernity: The Historical Thinking of Liang Qichao* [Stanford: Stanford University Press, 1996]; and Rebecca E. Karl, "Creating Asia: China in the World at the Beginning of the Twentieth Century," *American Historical Review* 103, no. 4 [Oct. 1998]: 1096–118).

45. Liang Qichao, *Yinbingshi heji: wenji*, 1: 93–94.

to the monarchy as an institution, the Qing dynasty specifically, and to Confucianism (*baojiao* 保 教), but his political critique grew increasingly sharp and even bitter.

Liang's case *for* the monarchy was made most convincingly in his first major essay, "A General Discussion of Reform" ("Bianfa tongyi" 變法通議), published serially in 1896–97.[46] Basically, this work assumed the existence of the monarchy rather than arguing for it; nonetheless, this assumption led Liang to assign an essential role to the emperor. He argued for the necessity and desirability of change, opposing the conservative prejudice against changing the "inviolable" ways of former kings. "Those who cannot create laws are not sages, and those who cannot act according to the times are not sages." Indeed, this applies not only to the founders of new dynasties but to all rulers. Without change, inertia will lead to weakness, but if leaders consider their faults and change, "this is renewal of the kingship" (*si wei xinwang yi* 斯爲新王矣).[47] In this sense, Liang was following Kang's early insistence on an activist kingship and emphasizing the historical innovations—*in response to the trends of the day*—of dynasts from the earliest times through the Qing itself. Liang considered this responsiveness to be the essence of sagehood, and if Kang claimed Confucius as a reformer and the founder of Ming as a sage, Liang added the Kangxi (r. 1662–1722) and Yongzheng (r. 1723–35) emperors to the list. Replying, in effect, to the conservative charge that the reformers were slavish imitators of the West, Liang proclaimed that a characteristic of sages was that they felt no shame in learning from others. Nonetheless, Liang's ultimate goals remained conservative in their own way. He demanded "improvements" in order to preserve the nation, the race, and Confucianism. He challenged neither the institution of the monarchy nor the Qing's right to rule.

Another Kang disciple and a fellow student with Liang Qichao, Mai Menghua, wrote even more explicitly in favor of a disciplinary state. In his essay "Should China Follow Monarchical Power or Democracy?" ("Lun Zhongguo yi zun junquan yi minquan" 論中國宜尊君權抑民權), Mai praised the monarchy as the best way to achieve reform.[48] Mai, who was one

---

46. Ibid., 1: 1–92.

47. Ibid., 1: 4, 1.

48. Mai Menghua 麥孟華, "Lun Zhongguo yi zun junquan yi minquan" 論中國宜尊君權抑民權 (Should China follow monarchical power or democracy?), in Jian Bocan, *Wuxu bianfa*, 3: 111–13.

of the most active proponents of reform, argued that the essence of sovereignty (*daquan* 大權) lay in the "ability to create a political system, to establish new precedents, and to kill people or let them live." For Mai, power was indivisible. The key point was not that the Chinese people were backward, although this was a consideration, but that (legitimate) power stemmed from the top and attended to the needs of the people. Mai's analogies were to the way individuals ran their own lives—unless they lost control—or the way family heads ran their families—unless they allowed the servants to take over. When kings command the empire, the people depend on them; if rulers lose power, however, then corrupt officials will emerge, and the nation will lack the (sovereign) power it needs to survive. "Democracy," according to Mai, describes a situation in which rebels emerge and all seize power for themselves. This disaster occurs when the king neglects his duties and loses or gives up his power.

Mai did not rule out the possibility that democracy might be workable, but he thought this course would be practical only after the entire population was properly equipped to manage its own affairs. Meanwhile, at least, China needed discipline like that found in the Western nations with their population registers, efficient tax systems, compulsory education, health and safety regulations, meritocratic civil services, and stable currencies. Mai looked to the West and saw not freedom but efficiency, order, and unity. He looked at China and saw laxity, corruption, and favoritism. The Confucian family model of government remained the core of Mai's political thinking, but this was a paternalism more severe than kindly. As in the contemporary West, "The Former Kings ruled by taking the people as their children and themselves as parents and taking the people as their students and themselves as teachers." They made all the decisions for the people. In effect, Mai urged that this model be applied to contemporary China, which was suffering from a lack of monarchical power.

It might be argued that Mai's "monarchical power" is close to a notion of state sovereignty rather than specifically tied to personalized power. Aside from the single reference to the Former Kings, Mai did not celebrate the monarchical institution in anything like the terms Kang used in some of his early essays. Mai presumably understood that the actual rulers of the Western nations were not themselves kings, however much power they had. Perhaps Mai in some sense foresaw a split between duties and power on the one hand, which he celebrated, and a potentially symbolic kingship on the other.

If so, however, this represented a step Mai himself did not take. Mai offered no defense of even bad rule, but he was like Hobbes in his desire to locate sovereignty at a clear and specific point. It is hard to imagine a more specific point than a single ruler. The activist ruler is theorized in Mai's writings not through charisma but through administrative power.

Liang's concerns were broader. The theme of unity emerged more clearly in Liang than that of discipline or administration. Liang demanded cooperation and an end to discrimination between the Manchu and Han peoples. The corollary to this was to end divisions between ruler and people. Both propositions rested on the assumption of the "great principle of making the empire public" (gong tianxia zhi dayi 公天下之大義).[49] In trying to prove that the Manchus had nothing to fear and much to gain from reform, Liang did not treat the Qing emperor as a Manchu king. Rather, the emperor was a kind of embodiment or symbol of the group. The meaning of "group" (qun 群), for Liang, was based more on history and culture than on "race." The group, in turn, was a nation defined by the state rather than ethnicity. The historical role of the monarchy in uniting state and nation was critical. Liang praised the putatively reformist tendencies of the present emperor ("sagacious, benevolent, indomitable, and open-minded") and cited the historical contrast between the English and French revolutions in regard to the monarchy. The English kings—in Liang's view—compromised with popular demands, and so the imperial system survived and England had peace, prosperity, and an empire. In France, however, monarchical and aristocratic obduracy had led to disaster. In other words, China's national unity depended on reform rather than revolution, moderation and compromise rather than extremism, and monarchism rather than republicanism.

These remarks serve to confirm the general view of Liang's politics at this time. He was cautious, reformist, antirevolutionary, and committed to gradual change within the existing system. But the worldview that underlay his political position was increasingly radical. Aside from his growing sympathies with racial analysis, there can be no doubt that for Liang the monarchy had already become somewhat attenuated. For all his rhetorical flourishes, and for that matter for all his skepticism about the capabilities of the Chinese people as such, he nonetheless looked outside the monarchy for the main motive force for reform. Specifically, Liang seemed to place most of his hopes in the gentry-activists (zhishi 志士), and a great deal of "A General

---

49. Liang Qichao, Yinbingshi heji: wenji, 1: 80.

Discussion of Reform" focused on institutional reforms in the areas of education, the civil service, and the role of the gentry. There is a sense of both top-down, court-derived reforms and bottom-up, popular changes. Nonetheless, Liang retained a real fascination with the charisma of the monarchy. Given China's great population, abundant minerals, fertile soils, and intelligent people, "when monarchical power is uniform (*junquan tongyi* 君權統一), the emperor need fear no obstacles to whatever he wishes to establish."[50]

Liang also had to support the monarchy for lack of other options. Democracy or republicanism he considered premature, given the backwardness of the Chinese people, whom he called "ignorant" and "weak" although certainly educable.[51] Orderly, top-down reforms were necessary to avoid the kind of disorder that revolutionary plots threatened. Thus, in his short essay "An Examination of Ancient Parliaments" ("Gu yiyuan kao" 古議院考), Liang presented the institution in terms long familiar to the reform movement: not as an institution that allowed policy to be made by the people but as a technique of "uniting" the ruler and the people in order to concentrate their powers.[52] Although Liang praised parliaments for allowing the efficient separation of legislative from administrative functions, his tone remained paternalistic, and he praised kings who ruled by discovering what the people wanted.

Nonetheless, Liang indulged in some sharp attacks on the institution of kingship itself, most frankly in a letter to Yan Fu 嚴復 (1853–1921). Although he denied that China's history was fundamentally inferior to that of

---

50. Ibid., 1: 4.

51. Ibid., 1: 80, 110. It is sometimes suggested that "democracy" and "popular power" in writings from this period actually refer to what might be called "gentry democracy"; however, although it is true that the publicists of the 1898 generation advocated nothing like universal suffrage and could not imagine giving the vote to porters and maids (any more than could their Victorian counterparts in Britain), nonetheless "popular power" was certainly not restricted to *gentry* (*shenshi* 紳士) in the legal sense of the term but to educated men (*shi* 士) broadly defined. The operative dichotomy was not between elite and populace but between those who were officials and those who were not, although of course the late Qing's educated stratum wished to educate the masses before allowing them political participation (Li Xiaoti 李孝悌, *Qingmo minchu de xiacengshehui qimeng yundong, 1901–1911* 清末民初下層社會啟蒙運動 [The enlightenment movement for lower-class society in the late Qing, 1901–11] [Taibei: Zhongyang yanjiuyuan, Jindaishi yanjiusuo, 1992]). In turn, their advocacy of popular education, although scarcely new in the Confucian tradition, also demonstrated their ultimate commitment to democracy.

52. Liang Qichao, *Yinbingshi heji: wenji*, 1: 95–96.

the West, Liang accepted Yan's judgment that the reasons for the decline of the "yellow race" boiled down to rulership (*junzhu*).[53] Furthermore: "The strength of a country stems ultimately from democracy. This is the nature of democracy. Monarchism is simply selfishness (*si*), whereas democracy is simply public-mindedness (*gong*). 'Public-mindedness' is the ultimate standard of governance, whereas 'selfishness' is rooted in humanity."[54] In equating the monarchy with selfishness, Liang was not, however, issuing a blanket condemnation. He urged that a balance be struck between *gong* and *si*. Excessive self-suppression (*keji* 克己) could lead to self-destruction, and selfishness was, after all, natural. Liang started with the proposition that the Chinese people were still ignorant and aimless. To unify them, they needed to be given a goal that was already popular. Such a goal could be gradually broadened until the people learned to trust the reformers (and finally themselves?). The question was whether under the immediate circumstances it was or was not the role of "monarchical power" to transform them.

The ancient dichotomy between *gong* and *si* was central to Liang's views of the monarchy.[55] It was also related to another reformist assumption. The reformers tended at times to dismiss China's entire post-Qin history as a kind of wrong turn, a 2,000-year detour. One point was to use the ancient past to attack the recent past, but more was involved as well. To denigrate the Han and the Tang along with the traditionally despised Qin was to attack, above all, a particular form of dynastic rule. If the relationship between Confucianism and monarchism, as between the gentry and the court, had never been entirely easy, still the reformers were attacking imperial Confucianism as it had developed over centuries. This is, of course, one reason why conservatives and even less radical reformers were so shocked by Kang and Liang. The only form of kingship that generations had known was at stake. Referring to the pre-Qin past, Liang proclaimed: "The Former Kings treated the empire with public-mindedness, and thus did they manage affairs. Later ages treated the empire with selfishness, and thus they avoided problems."[56]

What Liang meant, as he explained in "China's Weaknesses Are Due to Avoiding Problems," was that the duty of rulers was to take care of the people actively, not simply to try to maintain the status quo and ignore real

53. Ibid., 1: 108.
54. Ibid., 1: 109; cf. Chang, *Liang Ch'i-ch'ao*, pp. 104–5.
55. Huang Kewu, "Cong zhuiqiu zhengdao."
56. Liang Qichao, *Yinbingshi heji: wenji*, 1: 96.

problems. The attitude of "avoiding problems" arose from selfishness.[57] As rulers became isolated and ignorant, chasms developed, and the ruler treated his officials like animals, and officials regarded the ruler as a common man. For 2,000 years, laws became stricter as politics and education declined, and "monarchical power became ever more exalted" (*junquan ze rizun* 君權則日尊) as national prestige decreased. People were left helpless; oppressors (*minzei* 民賊) intensified their exploitation.[58] The entire system, in Liang's reading, became more and more elaborate, with the emperor isolated from the people and the bureaucrats tripping over one another. This he naturally contrasted with ancient times when the rulers of the various kingdoms (*guo* 國), large and small, were all close to the people and unified under the emperor (*ge qin qi min er shang tong yu tianzi* 各親其民而上統於天子).

If much of Liang's critique derived from long-standing Confucian criticisms of the monarchy, his reading of Chinese history also led him to praise emperors who appointed commoners to advise them and went on tours to make contact with the people. That emperors should seek and heed advice was scarcely a new idea. That their failure to do so would lead not merely to mistakes but to the depletion of the popular spirit (*minqi* 民氣) and ultimately the weakening of the state rested on a sense of the utility of popular activism—the converse of imperial "selfishness." Again, the issue that lay behind Liang's immediate concerns was the problem of grouping (*qun*). In this vein, he also critically noted the tendency of the ancient emperors to call themselves "I, the one man," to separate themselves from the people.[59]

In contrast to the weak nations of selfish monarchs, strong nations of citizens are formed when the people exercise their rights or powers (*quan* 權).[60] Such powers cannot be exercised by one person, since no one is strong

---

57. Ibid., 1: 99.

58. Ibid., 1: 96.

59. Ibid., 2: 3–4.

60. Ibid., 1: 99. There is a good deal of ambiguity in this use of *quan*, which was coming to mean "rights" but still retained strong overtones of "power." For different perspectives, see Roger Ames, "Rites as Rights: The Confucian Alternative," in *Human Rights and the World's Religions*, ed. Leroy S. Rouner, pp. 119–216 (Notre Dame, Ind.: University of Notre Dame Press, 1988); Wm. Theodore de Bary, "Neo-Confucianism and Human Rights," in *Human Rights and the World's Religions*, ed. Leroy S. Rouner, pp. 183–98; and Stephen C. Angle, "Did Someone Say 'Rights'? Liu Shipei's Concept of *Quanli*," *Philosophy East and West* 48, no. 4 (Oct. 1998): 623–51. Liang here seems to mean something like legitimately held powers, that is,

or wise enough for such responsibilities. The "Former Kings" thus understood that equality was essential. Yet, again, Liang does not condemn selfishness totally. He seems to derive rights from the Western doctrine of
autonomy (*zizhu zhi quan* 自主之權) and acknowledges that autonomy,
with its emphasis on duties and rewards, represents a kind of selfishness.
Without this selfishness, citizens would have no basis on which to exercise
their rights. As long as no one seizes the rights of others, these rights accu-
mulate to form a strong nation.[61] Such rights should not be subject to struggle, which harms others, nor can they be neglected, which harms oneself. If
neither the emperor nor the people are willing to assume responsibility, the
result is disaster. Yet if one party pushes the struggle for power to the utmost selfishness, this situation, too, results in powerlessness.

An even sharper defense of popular power, "Reform of the Various Nations Stems from the People" ("Lun dadi geguo bianfa jie you min qi" 論大
地各國變法皆由民起),[62] was penned by Ou Qujia 歐榘甲 (1858–1912),
another of Kang's disciples. Like Wang Kangnian, Liang Qichao, and even
Kang Youwei, Ou cited the advantages of communication and unity between high and low. However, this did not mean that Ou believed China
was ready for democracy; indeed, he, too, followed the hoary family model of
government and emphasized the ruler's dual roles in taking care of the people and maintaining order. Ou defined the ruler in terms of his ability to
unite the people (*neng qunmin wei zhi jun* 能群民謂之王). The ruler formed
"one body" with the people, representing the collectivity (*min zhi ji* 民之積),
and was himself constituted by combining all the people (*he zhongmin er
chengjun* 合眾民而成君), just as in physics bodies are composed by combining particles or as nations are formed by combining ethnic groups. At the
same time, Ou drew a distinction between ruler and the "king." The king
does not actively unite the people but seems to draw them to himself: "those

---

not civil or negative rights (e.g., the right not to be tortured) but the positive rights of citizens
to speak out and to participate in political events. Such rights are, after all, powers of a sort.

61. We may thus conclude that even the radical reformers of 1898 were still operating consciously and unconsciously within a Confucian framework; however, Tan Sitong 譚嗣同
(1865–98) did directly attack the three bonds (*san'gang*); for the political import of this, see
Chang, *Chinese Intellectuals*, pp. 93–103.

62. Ou Qujia 歐榘甲, "Lun dadi geguo bianfa jie you min qi" 論大地各國變法皆
由民起 (Reform of the various nations stems from the people), in Jian Bocan, *Wuxu bianfa*,
3: 152–56.

to whom the people come are called king" (*min suo guiwang wei zhi wang* 民所
歸往謂之王).[63]

Ou's approach to the monarchy, emphasizing national integration even
more than the "wealth and power" of the state, comes close to Liang
Qichao's position at the time but without Liang's counterbalancing criticisms of the monarchical institution. Where Ou went beyond the other reformers, however, was in the lessons he drew from China's immediate dire
circumstances. If the king had lost power, like a father who could no longer
feed or educate his children, the solution lay not in some attempt to revive
long-lost institutions but in creating new ones. With proper education and
ethics, the people themselves could be energized to renew the nation. Reform in China was the responsibility of the people, not the leaders. Logically
enough, Ou concluded that the people were therefore to blame for the failure to reform. Similarly, the political successes of the West were attributable
to the people, not the rulers. But Ou was caught in a trap, unable to suggest
how to get from here to there. He had no faith in China's historic institutions, although he found much of the traditional sage-king model attractive.
He had no faith in the people as presently constituted, although he could
imagine no other source of fundamental change. He took some hope in the
historical fact that the peoples of the West were once equally backward, but
he noted that Chinese culture could hardly revive while China was being enslaved by those very same Western Powers.

Sages and Kings

The reformist ideology—and its views of kingship—derived from the New
Text tradition as reshaped by Kang Youwei, who turned Confucius into a
leader and prophet. Liang not only used Kang's evolutionary understanding
of the Three Ages to make sense of the impending transition to democracy,
but in his "An Interpretation of the *Spring and Autumn Annals*" ("Du Qunqiu
jieshuo" 讀 〈 春秋 〉 界說), he also exalted Confucius as the "uncrowned
king" (*suwang*).[64] The point here is that Liang separated sagehood from the

---

63. The *locus classicus* for this remark is the *Guliang* commentary on the *Spring and Autumn
Annals* (*Guliang zhuan*, Zhuang Gong, third year): *wangzhe min zhi suo guiwang ye* 王者民之所
歸往也.

64. Liang Qichao 梁啓超, "Du Chunqiu jieshuo" 讀 〈 春秋 〉界說 (Interpreting the
Spring and Autumn Annals), in *Jieshuo Liang Qichao zhexue sixiang lunwenxuan* 界說梁啓超哲學

monarchy and clearly valued the former more highly; at the same time, the
purpose of the sage was to help the king. Specifically, Liang explained the
Spring and Autumn Annals as Confucius' attempt to "carry out the matters of
the emperor" at a time of general decline, that is, to reform the age. Now,
how could Confucius, a mere commoner, speak of such matters as rituals
and regulations? Because being a sage, he understood the need to save the
world from chaos and to clarify universal principles (*gongli* 公理).[65] Confucius' means was to influence and "use" the king. Charges that Confucius
sought to usurp power were mistaken—although Confucius surely could
have gained power if he had wanted to. Although Liang would seem to be
implying that both sages and kings were necessary, his main point was that
Confucius possessed the "great virtue and magnificent achievements of a
founder of a teaching."

Liang also noted that Confucius was a lawgiver. His greatness resided in
his use of laws to establish order in the Age of Disorder, as well as in looking
ahead to the laws for the ages of Approaching Peace and Universal Peace.[66]
Today, Liang urged, China needed to pursue the study of the law because it
was through laws that the group was linked together to form a political
community. Intelligent emperors in the past had recognized this truth, but it
was a wisdom that had been forgotten after the Qin; even as the population
increased, laws were simplified, and no attempt was made to keep them up
to date. Turning to the *Spring and Autumn Annals*, Liang claimed its emphasis on rites (*li* 禮) was the equivalent of universal principles or truths (*gongli*),
which in the West were used to circumscribe power.

Thus for Liang what distinguished Chinese civilization was not the institution of the monarchy but the perfection of sagehood. The sage possessed many of the attributes of the king. He was a lawgiver and retained
great charismatic powers, influencing events as he recognized and responded
to contemporary trends. Nonetheless, the sage worked only through indi-
rection, and Liang never imagined that sages were so plentiful that they
could replace real kings. Liang's criticisms of the monarchy as an institution
and his respect for democracy stand out more clearly than Kang's at this
time, although the two men agreed that the emperor had to lead the neces-

思想論文集 (Selected writings defining Liang Qichao's philosophical thought), ed. Ge Mao-
chun 葛懋春 and Jiang Jun 蔣俊, pp. 19–28 (Beijing: Beijing daxue chubanshe, 1984).

　65. Ibid., p. 27.

　66. Liang Qichao, *Yinbingshi heji: wenji*, 1: 93.

sary reforms to create a more democratic order. But much more clearly than Kang, Liang linked the Chinese emperor with the nation or "group." The dichotomies shifted as well. If Kang's emperor was to be *benevolent* rather than *righteous* and Liang's emperor was to be *public-minded* rather than *selfish*, what change has occurred? The key factor was probably Kang's universalism. Although Kang certainly stressed the need for reforms to make China strong, he still spoke largely in terms of the universal, cosmic kingship. Liang, on the other hand, although still devoted to an ultimately universal vision, pictured an emperor more clearly defined as Chinese. Liang could not, however, quite decide if the emperor still served as a necessary symbol of unity, the core around which the Chinese nation was to be formed, or if this role was largely obsolete.

The reform movement generally and the Kang-Liang radicals are often subsumed under the theme of building up the "wealth and power" of the Chinese state; almost equally prominent has been the theme of a struggle between pro-democracy forces and defenders of despotism.[67] Yet the reformers were capable of advocating strong imperial rule. My intention is not to deny that the reformers on balance contributed to the development of an opposition to despotism, but to note that their attitudes toward the monarchy were in fact complex and shifting. It seems more useful to conceptualize what was going on as a partly unconscious effort to rethink the Chinese notion of kingship. This was not, of course, the main goal of the reformers, but one consequence of their intellectual and political work was to enlarge the space of politics. The traditional form of the Chinese state—revolving around court, bureaucracy, and dynasty (the imperial family through time)—would not long survive such changes in political consciousness. Perhaps most important, the shift of China's historical center from kings to sages created a new space for a Chinese identity to emerge that was independent of the dynasty. Of course, "new knowledge" from the West played a major role in this process, but the essential framework remained Confucian. In the 1890s, the Next Text tradition in the hands of the radical reformers encouraged a massive reorientation of Chinese politics.

At the same time, for all the reformers, the Chinese notion of kingship represented a lever for change. In China's institutional and legal framework, the ancient pedigree and traditional charisma of the monarchy were seen as

---

67. See, inter alia, Chang, "Intellectual Change"; and Xiong Yuezhi, "Minzu juexing de yikuai lichengbei," esp. pp. 217–26. But the approach is general in the literature.

advantages. Reformers seized on the long-standing links between the sage-king ideal and the Mencian notion of popular legitimacy (minben 民本). On the other hand, the historical monarchy was also a symbol of the decadence and dissipation of an entire civilization. All the evils of the post-Qin system were captured by the notion of the ruler who failed to take care of the people, to create a system of order, or even to extend his raw, coercive powers. Instead, broad chasms had developed between the emperor and his subjects, between the officials and the people, and even between the emperor and his officials—gaps that marked the sheer impotence of the Chinese state and the gross ignorance of the people. There had been little sense in imperial Confucianism of the king as a leader of a *people*, and the reformist ploy of legitimating a certain kind of monarch served also to legitimate the people itself.

Nonetheless, this was an unstable formulation: the monarchy as a symbol of national unity turned out to be a hollow hope. The emperor was firmly delinked from the cosmos and even Tianxia 天下, and perhaps even from the nation. What the reformers did not want to do, of course, was to allow ethnic antagonisms to come to the fore. They therefore had to treat the actual monarchy as a "Chinese" kingship with no reference to unique Manchu-Qing elements: they had to develop a conception of the nation that explicitly denied the importance of ethnicity. If the Guangxu emperor was in fact ready to play the role of a national king, others in the court were not about to let this happen. Yet the deeper problem the radical reformers faced was to determine whether the emperor was an asset or a liability to the nation. By historicizing the kingship, the reformers separated it from one of its traditional charismatic bases, sagehood. This break from Kang's early essays revived a Legalist-influenced notion of (imperial) sagehood. Although it had long been recognized that the emperor, being mortal and prone to mistakes and ethical lapses, should take the advice of the wise men about him, nonetheless the Chinese idea of kingship had become rooted in the concept of sagehood. The moral authority of an emperor's critics never extended to challenging the institution itself; nor did it even match the charismatic authority of the emperor, which was rooted both in ancient cosmological notions and in the Three Bonds (san'gang 三綱) of the Confucian social tradition.

By the 1890s, however, ultimate authority was being removed from the emperor, slowly and unevenly but inevitably. The reformers, like their predecessors, focused some of their harshest criticism on the isolation of the emperor. Unlike their predecessors, they turned instead to the "people" and discovered that popular power was exceedingly difficult to comprehend in terms of the traditional cosmology. Yet if the emperor were to become a committee chairman of a desacralized state, what would become of the basis of its legitimacy? It was the promise of "popular power" both to replace the emperor institutionally (eventually) and to be self-legitimating. Yet when the reformers looked at the Chinese people, they seemed sadly wanting. The monarchy was thus simultaneously necessary and utterly decadent.

CHAPTER TWO

Literati-Journalists of the Chinese Progress (Shiwu bao) in Discord, 1896–1898

Seungjoo Yoon

The role of the Shanghai-based *Chinese Progress* (*Shiwu bao* 時務報) in the reform movement of 1898 is well known. Most historians agree that the newspaper was the harbinger of the literati-led modern press in late Qing China. It is also generally agreed that the paper played an important role in introducing new political ideas from Europe, most notably "popular power" (*minquan* 民權), an idea profoundly radical in the context of the late Qing constitutional order.[1] Moreover, as many scholars have pointed out, its impact on the late Qing polity was not limited to just a few reformist literati but extended to the broader reading public. It circulated far beyond Shanghai and reached the imperial city of Beijing and other major cities, both along the coast and in the interior. In short, the *Chinese Progress* and the editors and writers associated with it stood at the center of the reform effort from the journal's appearance in 1896 to its demise in the summer of 1898.[2]

A draft version of this paper was presented at the annual conference of the Association of Asian Studies in April 1998 in Washington, D.C. I am grateful to Philip Kuhn, Peter Zarrow, and the two anonymous reviewers for the Harvard University Asia Center for their valuable comments on earlier versions of this paper.

1. I am indebted to Peter Zarrow and Stephen Angle for the translation of the term *minquan* as "popular power" instead of now-dated "popular rights." The Qing state did not employ the concept of rights in the sense found in the Roman legal tradition.

2. For this standard view, see Fang Hanqi 方漢奇, *Zhongguo xinwen shiye tongshi* 中國新聞事業通史 (General history of the newspaper business in China) (Beijing: Zhongguo renmin daxue chubanshe, 1992), pp. 553–75; and Tang Zhijun 湯志鈞, *Wuxu shiqi de xuehui*

It is not well known, however, that the paper was an extension of the private bureaucracy of Zhang Zhidong 張之洞 (1837–1909), one of the most influential reform-minded scholar-officials in the lower Yangzi region in the late Qing. The paper's employees were drawn mostly from the pool of Zhang's private secretaries, who were known as document commissioners (*wen'an weiyuan* 文案委員). Document commissioners were a special category of private secretaries, and their main duties involved the processing of important papers from various "Western affairs" (*yangwu* 洋務) enterprises. In terms of social standing, they were among the lower echelons of the literati trained in the Confucian classics in preparation for the civil service examinations. In terms of expertise, however, they had some command of foreign languages and Western affairs and to some extent were privy to official discussions and policy proposals. The document commissioners compiled, translated, and edited diplomatic, commercial, and journalistic reports as reference materials for their superiors. The emergence of document commissioners was thus intimately related to trade and diplomacy as it developed after the mid-nineteenth century.[3] Historians have paid less attention to the problems faced by writers of the *Chinese Progress*, both ideological and institutional, as they tried to advance new political ideas in the paper. These were not independent "journalists"; the document commissioners were constrained in terms of their thought and behavior, however innovative and radical they might have been and however liberal their political orientations. They did not aspire to form "a fourth estate" independent of political patronage. In other words, as members of Zhang Zhidong's extended advisory board, the paper's literati-journalists strove to place themselves within the orthodox order of Confucian statecraft.

In this chapter, I hope to show how the institutional configuration of the *Chinese Progress* shaped ideological conflicts among the writers associated with it. I will argue that the political debates and forums the paper created were directed more toward the reinvigoration of the "statecraft" (*jingshi* 經世) ideal within Confucian tradition than toward the establishment of a "public sphere," at least in the sense used by the German social philosopher

---

he baokan 戊戌時期的學會和報刊 (Study societies and newspapers during the reform period of 1898) (Taibei: Taiwan Shangwu yinshuguan, 1993), pp. 143–211.

3. For a further discussion of document commissioners, see Seungjoo Yoon, "The Formation, Reformation, and Transformation of Zhang Zhidong's Document Commissioners, 1885–1909" (Ph.D. diss., Harvard University 1999), esp. chap. 2.

Jürgen Habermas.[4] I begin by discussing the changing milieu of late Qing elite culture and its accommodation of a literati-led press as a legitimate political forum. I then examine the ideological schism that developed between Zhang Zhidong and the literati-journalists of the *Chinese Progress* as they introduced radical political ideas for administrative renovation. Finally, I conclude by looking at the unsuccessful attempt of the more radical associates of the paper to found a government gazette by finding another patron.

Zhang Zhidong and the Formation of the Chinese Progress

At first glance, the story of the *Chinese Progress* seems to support an interpretation of the newspaper more as "servant of the state" than as an independent force in politics.[5] As noted above, it was managed and written by Zhang Zhidong's private bureaucracy, not by a civic organization. Various factors contributed to Zhang's decision to establish a newspaper. Himself an avid reader of foreign newspapers, from which he liked to quote in his official government reports, Zhang envisioned a newspaper company as an effective means of gathering and disseminating information from foreign journals useful for the management of foreign affairs.[6] More broadly, the changing intellectual environment among Chinese literati and officials alike after the mid-nineteenth century favored the launching of such an enterprise. Most important, after the 1860s it became customary for the Zongli yamen 總理衙門, the highest body in the Beijing bureaucracy to handle

---

4. For a discussion of the late Qing press in the light of the expansion of "public sphere," see Joan Judge, *Print and Politics, 'Shibao' and the Culture of Reform in Late Qing China* (Stanford: Stanford University Press, 1996). Previous scholarship has also touched on the issue in passing. These include the case of *Han bao* in William Rowe, *Hankow: Conflict and Community in a Chinese City, 1796–1895* (Stanford: Stanford University Press, 1989), pp. 24, 29; the *Shen bao* in Mary Rankin, *Elite Activism and Political Transformation in China: Zhejiang Province, 1865–1911* (Stanford: Stanford University Press, 1986), pp. 129, 133, 141–47 *et passim*; Leo Ou-fan Lee and Andrew J. Nathan, "The Beginnings of Mass Culture: Journalism and Fiction in the Late Ch'ing and Beyond," in *Popular Culture in Late Imperial China*, ed. David Johnson, Andrew J. Nathan, and Evelyn S. Rawski, pp. 360–95 (Berkeley: University of California Press, 1985).

5. For a discussion of different approaches to the interpretation of the role of the media in Japan, see Susan Pharr and Ellis Krauss, eds., *Media and Politics in Japan* (Honolulu: University of Hawaii Press, 1996).

6. Zhang Zhidong 張之洞, *Zhang wenxiang gong quanji* 張文襄公全集 (Complete works of Zhang Zhidong; hereafter cited as ZZD) (Beijing, 1928; facsimile reproduction—Taibei: Wenhai chubanshe, 1963), 134: 23a–b, May 15, 1890 (GX 16/03/27) *et passim*.

foreign affairs, to have customs officials in the treaty ports collect foreign newspapers; the yamen then circulated information gleaned from these papers to interested boards in the central government. It is not unusual to find clippings or excerpts of foreign newspapers in diplomatic documents from the period.[7]

By the early 1890s, two intellectual developments made the idea of newspapers published by the literati attractive to Chinese intellectuals. First, a broader spectrum of literati were coming to regard journalism as a legitimate endeavor for themselves rather than clerical work reserved for minor functionaries.[8] Second, both central and local governments began to recognize the positive functions of newspapers and to rely heavily on journalistic reports in policy deliberations. Members of the Chinese elite, both inside and outside the government, were increasingly turning to foreign newspapers to obtain swifter and more reliable information, especially about foreign relations. The Qing officialdom's quest for foreign news began with an interest in trade, diplomacy, technology, and science and eventually expanded to include news about the laws and administration of foreign countries.[9] Underlying this desire for information was a sense of China's humiliation at the hands of foreign powers, most recently in the Chinese defeat in the Sino-Japanese War of 1894–95. By 1895, more than 200 newspapers published by foreigners were being read in China. The literati judged the government's military briefings as inadequate, untimely, and even unreliable. In contrast, they found the accounts in foreign news media that relied on telegraphed reports more effective. Hanlin scholars, the cream of the scholar-officials, for instance, preferred quoting from foreign newspapers rather than from official briefings in their memorials about the war.

---

7. Such references are found in *Zouban yiwu shimo*, reprinted in Zhongyang dang'anguan 中央檔案館, Ming Qing dang'anbu bianjishi 明清檔案部編輯室, ed., *Zhongguo jindaishi yanjiu congkan: Yangwu yundong* 中國近代史研究叢刊洋務運動 (Studies of modern Chinese history: the Self-Strengthening movement) (Shanghai: Shanghai renmin chubanshe, 1961), 1: 5–9 *et passim*.

8. See Judge, *Print and Politics*, pp. 17–31; Fang Hanqi, *Zhongguo xinwen shiye tongshi*, pp. 243–374; and Ma Guangren 馬光仁, *Shanghai xinwen shi* 上海新聞史 (A history of journalism in Shanghai) (Shanghai: Fudan daxue chubanshe, 1996), pp. 11–103.

9. A few examples can be found in memorials submitted by Junliang, Wen Tingshi, Wenhai, Shen Enjia, Yude, and Shouchang; see Number One Historical Archives of China, *Lufu zouzhe, neizheng lei* 錄副奏折內政類 (Grand Council memorial file copies relating to internal affairs; hereafter *LFZZ*) (Microfilm), 1895.

Zhang Zhidong was responsive to this emerging literati-official culture. During the Sino-Japanese War, Zhang, then the governor-general of the Jiangsu-Jiangxi-Anhui region, used his document commissioners as virtual war correspondents whose main function was to bring military telegrams and foreign press clippings to Zhang's attention.[10] In late 1895, when he was appointed governor-general of Hunan-Hubei, Zhang inaugurated the Hubei Translation Bureau (Hubei yishu ju 湖北譯書局) at the provincial capital of Wuchang. Dispatched to various coastal cities, the bureau's document commissioners, mostly foreign-language experts, some with experience in Western countries, collected documents, both commercial and diplomatic, and translated them into Chinese.[11] The bureau also compiled an encyclopedia of foreign information, *A Compendium of Western Affairs* (*Yangwu congshu* 洋務叢書), and circulated it among reform-minded officials in Hunan and Hubei.[12]

At the same time, Zhang Zhidong decided to establish his own newspaper company with funds he had appropriated from the mining businesses in Hunan under his supervision. The Hubei Translation Bureau would supervise personnel and financial management of his new private bureaucratic institution. Named the *Chinese Progress*, this new enterprise was to perform multiple roles as a book-purchasing agency, a publishing house, and, most important, a translation office.[13] Even though Zhang was interested in the institutional and technological innovations of modern Europe and Japan for his reform initiatives, he certainly did not desire a wholesale Westernization of the Qing polity. He also did not intend his new enterprise to be vulnerable to accusations of "heterodoxy." Zhang envisioned the *Chinese Progress* as consisting solely of translators to the exclusion of editorial writers or reporters. The Hubei Translation Bureau itself provided the *Chinese Progress* with most of its translators; graduates of foreign-language schools in China, Chinese students abroad, and translators in Chinese legations in foreign capitals

---

10. Ye Han 葉瀚, "Kuaiyusheng ziji" 塊餘生自記 (Ye Han's autobiography), manuscript at the Shanghai Municipal Library; ed. Gu Tinglong and reprinted in *Zhongguo wenhua yanjiu jikan* 1987, no. 5: 480–81.

11. Wu Dexiao to Wang Kangnian, undated, late 1895, *Wang Kangnian shiyou shouzha* 汪康年師友手札 (Correspondence between Wang Kangnian and his masters and friends; hereafter WKN); reprinted with punctuation and editing by Wang Genlin (Shanghai: Shanghai guji chubanshe, 1986), p. 383.

12. Ye Han to Wang Kangnian, WKN, pp. 2566, 2568, *et passim*.

13. Ye Han to Wang Kangnian, WKN, pp. 2532, Mar. 17, 1896 (GX 22/02/24) *et passim*.

were also hired. Zhang made sure that the Hubei Translation Bureau, not the main office of the *Chinese Progress*, supervised the worldwide network of translators so that no sensitive foreign materials would flow directly to the *Chinese Progress*. It was the Translation Bureau that would feed the newspaper with publishable documents. This arrangement was meant to ensure the dissemination of correct "public opinion," in the words of a *Chinese Progress* supervisor—the firm stance that a leader should adopt irrespective of his underlings' opinions.[14] This understanding of the "public" was important for Zhang and his protégés since the readership of his newspaper consisted mainly of officials or literati with semi-official positions. To emphasize his vision of the *Chinese Progress's* editorial stance, he chose Confucius' dictum: "Transmit, but do not innovate."[15] In short, Zhang defined the newspaper as an extension of his document commission—the Hubei Translation Bureau. The *Chinese Progress* was a far cry from a free press for the general public.

Editorial Writing, Political Participation, and Schism

The employees of the *Chinese Progress* were not content with their role as Zhang's passive publishers, however. None of the literati-journalists wanted to identify himself as a "politico-cultural broker" or what his Japanese counterparts would call a "masterless samurai" (*rōnin* 浪人), fatefully pinned between the state and society or, more immediately, between bureaucratic institutions and mass media.[16] Just like journalists working for the reform newspapers in Japan, the people associated with the *Chinese Progress* found in the newspaper a new avenue of political expression as they tried to reach out to the public.

Nevertheless, it would be misleading to assume that their "public" was the general populace. Like other late Qing reformist intellectuals, they resorted to the idea of "*qun*" 群 (lit. "groupings") popularized by the famous publicist Yan Fu 嚴復 (1854–1921), who appropriated the term from the ancient Chinese text of *Xunzi* 荀子 to translate the Western concept of "soci-

---

14. Ye Han to Wang Kangnian, WKN, p. 2539, June 10, 1896 (GX 22/04/29).

15. *Lunyu* 7.1. Wu Dexiao to Wang Kangnian, WKN, p. 389, Mar. 18, 1896 (GX 22/02/05).

16. For the "political and cultural broker," see Judge, *Print and Politics*. James Huffman (*Creating a Public: People and Press in Meiji Japan* [Honolulu: University of Hawaii Press, 1997]) argues that the early Meiji journalists "created a new public" on a mass base in defiance of state censorship.

ety."[17] The journalists of the *Chinese Progress*, however, employed the term to refer not so much to society as opposed to the state as to a new political community—a legitimate clique or social network consisting of like-minded educated men. This was in fact a literati association (*wenshe* 文社) writ large in a modern context. It could be a literary club, a religious discussion group, a study society (*xuehui* 學會), or a newspaper company (*baoguan* 報館). Like traditional literati associations, however, the proper *qun* entity, a cultured association of superior persons (*junzi* 君子), was to be distinguished from a "private" association, that is, a club of inferior persons or a secret society of bandits.[18] Only certain educated elite could legitimately form this privileged society of knowledge. In their worldview, Heaven had endowed the literati with the distinctive trait of "grouping through the cultured exchange of knowledge." Theoretically speaking, the *qun* could admit other strata of Chinese society only if they shared the idiosyncratic nature of literati. It was, however, a role of the cultured elite to disseminate "popular enlightenment" (*minzhi* 民智) to the general populace in a piecemeal fashion.[19]

The journalist-activists of the *Chinese Progress* mobilized all available *qun* components to increase their autonomy from the paper's patron, Zhang Zhidong, and to assert their voice in the realms of editorial policy and personnel management. Wang Kangnian 汪康年 (1860–1911), the director-general of the *Chinese Progress*, is the best illustration of the *qun* ideal even though he was Zhang's choice to lead the newspaper. A native of Zhejiang and a graduate of the metropolitan examinations, Zhang became one of Zhang's private secretaries when he served as a tutor for his grandsons. Since the Sino-Japanese War he had been interested in managing a newspaper as his lifetime vocation and had planned to publish his own newspapers before Zhang's invitation.[20]

---

17. For a discussion of the concept of *qun*, see Hao Chang, *Chinese Intellectuals in Crisis: Search for Order and Meaning (1890–1911)* (Berkeley: University of California Press, 1987), pp. 109–16; and Chen Shude 陳樹德, "'Qunxue' yiming kaoxi" 群學譯名考析 (An analysis of the Chinese rendering of "sociology"), *Shehuixue yanjiu*, no. 6 (June 1988): 74–78.

18. Wang Yinian 汪詒年, *Wang Rangqing xiansheng zhuanji* 汪穰卿先生傳記 (A biography of Wang Kangnian), in *Jindai paihai* 近代牌海, ed. Rong Mengyuan and Zhang Bofeng, 12: 167–344 (Chengdu: Sichuan renmin chubanshe, 1988), pp. 198–202.

19. Zhang Binglin, "We Should Protect Study Societies Since They Render Great Benefits to the Yellow Race," *Chinese Progress* (*Shiwu bao* 時務報; hereafter CP), 19, 3b–6b, Mar. 3, 1897 (GX 23/02/01).

20. Wang Yinian, *Wang Rangqing xiansheng zhuanji*, pp. 29–30, 198–99.

In the interstices of Zhang's private bureaucracy, Wang Kangnian and the writers for the *Chinese Progress* gingerly expanded all the ties available to them, both associational and ascriptive: native place, common educational and examination backgrounds, master-disciple relations, and membership in literati associations. They shared critical information with one another through such informal channels as club gatherings, poetry contests, philosophical discussions, the circulation of personal letters and diary entries, and wine parties. The *Chinese Progress*, however, represented an important departure from the existing literati associations. The new networks of communication blurred the line between the official and the private realms, and the paper came to form a qualitatively new *qun* entity.

Zhang's admonitions to the contrary, editorial writers and essayists participated in free-ranging discussions of reform on the pages of the *Chinese Progress*, and over time, the paper's editorials and articles dealt increasingly with sensitive constitutional issues. References to popular power and parliaments occupied significant portions of the pages of the paper. This did not mean, however, that writers for the *Chinese Progress* called for immediate constitutional change. For the present, they thought a wholesale transformation of political system, such as the French Revolution, was out of the question since Chinese officials, unlike the French ministers under the *ancien régime*, would not support the idea of popular power and equality.[21] In their minds, constitutionalism and monarchism were perfectly compatible, and the *Chinese Progress* advocated gradual evolution toward a constitutional monarchy like those found in Meiji Japan or Britain. "Popular power" and "parliament" referred not so much to direct representation as to the broadening of literati participation in politics. In short, they envisioned a more accommodative political community, that is, a countrywide *qun*.

How could they realize such a political vision? One answer was to incorporate semi-official deliberative organs, most notably private advisory boards, into the regular officialdom. In an early contribution to the *Chinese Progress*, Sun Tongkang 孫同康, like Wang Kangnian a graduate of the metropolitan examinations of 1892, for example, proposed that the private secretariat be replaced by a "chamber of talents," or a British-style parliament.[22] Zhang Zhidong did not like the "bandit Sun's" article and

---

21. Ye Han to Wang Kangnian, WKN, p. 2553, Oct. 7, 1896 (GX 22/09/12).

22. Sun Tongkang, "On the Establishment of the Chamber of Talents," CP 4, 10a–12b, Sept. 9, 1896 (GX 22/08/01).

demanded that Wang exercise editorial prudence.[23] Zhang's discontent notwithstanding, demands for broader political participation increasingly assumed ethno-nationalistic overtones. Liang Qichao 梁啓超 (1873–1929), the paper's editor-in-chief and a pioneer in the intellectual revolution in modern China, condemned the foreign advisors in Zhang's private bureaucratic institutions. In Liang's judgment, they denied salaries to Chinese officials and served "that ethnic group" (bizu 彼族), the Manchus![24] Zhang's reaction was to consider terminating his patronage of the Chinese Progress.[25]

Despite Zhang's disapproval, Liang tried to give philosophical explanations for his proposals linking anti-reform attitudes with opposition to the New Text scholarship that he and his mentor Kang Youwei 康有爲 (1858–1927) advocated. In the ideological charges against his adversaries, it did not matter whether these thinkers followed Song Learning or the Old Text School of Han Learning, since both neglected the utopian dimension of Confucianism. Liang blamed Old Text scholarship for conservative opposition to the introduction of European political thought, especially the notion of popular power. He singled out the famous mid-Qing scholar Ji Yun 紀昀 (1724–1805) as a "ringleader" of Han Learning who had laid the theoretical grounds for prohibiting the literati from forming study societies. Nor was the Song Learning immune from Liang's attack. Woren 倭仁 (1804–71), the author of one of the most famous reactionary statements of the late Qing, "harmed" people and country, in Liang's judgment, since he was opposed to the introduction of Western learning.[26] Liang's attacks on these cultural conservatives, however, greatly embarrassed one of Zhang's chief document commissioners, Ji Juwei 紀鉅維 (1848–1920), who happened to be Ji Yun's grandson. The incident was even more embarrassing since Ji supported Liang's basic editorial stance. Efforts to mediate between Liang Qichao and Ji Juwei went nowhere, and a few supervisors at the Hubei Translation Bureau planned to write defenses of Ji Yun and Woren.[27] Zhang Zhidong rep-

---

23. Liang Qichao to Wang Kangnian, undated, WKN, p. 1900.

24. Liang Qichao, "On Schools: Introduction," CP 5, 1a–3b, Sept. 17, 1896 (GX 22/08/11).

25. Wu Qiao to Wang Kangnian, WKN, pp. 518–19, Dec. 17, 1896 (GX 22/11/13).

26. Liang Qichao, "On the Civil Service Examination System," CP 8, 1a–3b, Oct. 17, 1896 (GX 22/09/11); idem, "On Schools," CP 10, 1a–3a, Nov. 5, 1896 (GX 22/10/01).

27. Liang Qichao to Wang Kangnian, undated, late 1896, WKN, p. 1900.

rimanded Wang Kangnian once again for not censoring "harmful articles" before publication.[28]

In addition, Liang demanded effective discipline of quasi-officials, especially those who worked in government-sponsored enterprises. His continued criticism of the incompetence of certain private secretaries testified that ethnic nationalism was not his real point. In an essay written in mid-1897, Liang warned that the "experts" in Western affairs could turn out to be mere reincarnations of the old-style "evil gentry" without proper training. Liang expressed his concern that many of them had "supervised armies without having acquired military skills, intervened in monetary affairs without having learned accounting, and interfered in legal disputes without having practiced law." The worst of them, he continued, became "experts after having merely served Western businessmen as interpreters or as tutors for compradormerchants." His article might have been regarded as mild if not for his criticisms of Empress Dowager Cixi 慈禧, the behind-the-scenes leader of the Qing dynasty from the 1860s until her death in 1908. Liang insinuated that Cixi was following in the footsteps of "evil female rulers" of ancient dynasties.[29] In response, Zhang Zhidong banned Liang's "extremely erroneous and disloyal" article lest it should bring a "great disaster" to his jurisdiction.[30] At the same time, he ordered Wang Kangnian to warn Liang against spreading "heterodox teachings" in the *Chinese Progress*.[31]

It was Wang Kangnian, however, who came up with an even more ambitious proposal. In his vision, newspapers like the *Chinese Progress* were to constitute a legitimate branch of the government, and the literati-journalists were to enjoy the same rights to criticize as the censors and the Hanlin scholars.[32] Alarmed, Zhang demanded that Wang cease writing editorials, which he deemed as too "naïve" and even "stinking rubbish." The paper's legitimate function, Zhang insisted, was the translation of foreign journals and books. Editorials and articles in the *Chinese Progress*, if written at all, had

---

28. Gu Yinwu to Wang Kangnian, undated, late 1896, WKN, p. 3284.

29. Liang Qichao, "The Preface to Know-Shame Study Society," CP 40, 3a–4a, Sept. 26, 1897 (GX 23/09/01).

30. ZZD, telegrams, p. 29.

31. Wang Yinian, *Wang Rangqing xiansheng zhuanji*, 2: 17.

32. Wang Kangnian, "Proposals for Self-Strengthening in China," 3 pts., CP 4, 1a–4a; Sept. 7, 1896 (GX 22/08/01).

to be limited to the introduction of foreign institutional models, not bold policy proposals.[33]

Wang's response was to publish an editorial calling for broader literati participation in politics based on the theory of popular power.[34] Moreover, he published more translations of foreign articles that discussed political parties, political philosophies, and the exercise of constitutional prerogatives in Western countries. Few of these translations were of the most recent and fundamental Western writings. Nor were they remarkably insightful. Nevertheless, the thought of such articles being disseminated to the newspaper's subscribers was enough to frighten the cautious. A *Chinese Progress* translation of "Postscript to a Biography of George Washington" in late 1897, for example, made officials in Beijing uneasy.[35] Zhang Zhidong's confidants in his private bureaucracy also expressed concern that such articles would destabilize the emperor-centered polity of China.[36] The supervisors in the Translation Bureau ordered Wang to abandon writing and concentrate on management.[37] Zhang himself intervened in the *Chinese Progress*'s editorial process in order to reassert his vertical patronage ties within the company. Even as he shielded the paper against the central government's reaction, he incessantly reminded the editorial board not to address certain "taboo subjects," that is, constitutional issues. Also, he warned that he could not tolerate attacks on central government policies or criticisms of Zhang or his private bureaucracy, the very foundation of the newspaper.

Warnings against political heterodoxy notwithstanding, the literati-journalists continued to use the paper as a forum for debate. In the spring of 1897 the *Chinese Progress* published perhaps its most provocative article to date. In "Refuting Han Yu," Yan Fu, the famous essayist for another reformist journal, *China Herald* (*Guowen bao* 國 聞 報), in Tianjin, wrestled squarely with the issue of the monarchy. Yan juxtaposed Han Yu 韓 愈, a ninth-century forerunner of the Neo-Confucian movement and one of the most polemical political thinkers in Chinese intellectual history, with the proponents of democratic theories and Social Darwinism in modern

---

33. Ye Han to Wang Kangnian, WKN, p. 2547, Sept. 19, 1896 (GX 22/08/13).
34. Wang Kangnian, "On Popular Power," CP 9, 3a–5a, Oct. 27, 1896 (GX 22/09/21).
35. Zhang Yuanji to Wang Kangnian, undated, late 1897, WKN, pp. 1713–14.
36. Gu Hongming 辜 鴻 銘, *Gu Hongming wenji* 辜 鴻 銘 文 集 (Haikou, Hainan: Hainan chubanshe, 1996), pp. 220–21.
37. Liang Qichao to Wang Kangnian, undated, WKN, p. 1897.

Europe. Han did not come off well. Yan criticized Han for being unable to transcend the existing monarchical system of government even as he made a radical philosophical departure from the past. In Yan's opinion, all the monarchs since the Qin dynasty were, in actuality, "giant housebreakers" who had stolen the idealized community of China's ancient civilization from the Chinese people. Yan did not call for the establishment of a democratic system of government. Nor did he explicitly call the Empress Dowager Cixi or the Guangxu emperor housebreakers. Nevertheless, his message could be interpreted as antimonarchical. First, his choice of Han Yu was polemical. Han was revered as an icon of the Neo-Confucian orthodoxy among Yan's contemporaries, including Zhang Zhidong. Second, in his juxtaposition of Han Yu with modern European political thinkers, Yan did not emphasize that China's historical trajectory was distinct from that of Europe. He concluded, without reservation, that the principles of Social Darwinism dictated that the political logic of popular power would prevail in China as well.[38]

What the cultural conservatives found most distasteful in Yan's essay was his reinterpretation of Han Yu from the amoral worldview of Social Darwinism. Ironically enough, it was Han Yu, not Yan Fu (whose identity was protected), who became the "forerunner" of Social Darwinian discourse in China, even though this theory developed more than a millennium after Han's time. The anachronism, however, was willfully adopted in the conservative commentators' ideological attacks on Social Darwinism. According to one essayist, Han Yu was a radical visionary who advocated "self-rule" by the people in the late Tang dynasty when its subjects were far from enlightened (*minzhi weikai* 民智未開), even by the most liberal standards. Due to Han's rash political program, the essayist argued, the entire populace of China fell under the sway of "parties of disorder," a Social Darwinian world of the jungle.[39]

In response, another commentator tried to defend Yan Fu's argument by disassociating him from Social Darwinism. The conventional understanding of Confucian sagehood, he pointed out, overemphasized the heroic elements

---

38. CP 23, 5a–6b, Apr. 12, 1897 (GX 23/03/11). For another discussion of Yan's article, see Benjamin Schwartz, *In Search of Wealth and Power: Yen Fu and the West* (Cambridge, Mass.: Harvard University Press, 1964), pp. 64–66.

39. Sun Baoxuan 孫寶瑄, *Wang shanlu riji* 忘山廬日記 (Diary of Sun Baoxuan; hereafter SBX); reprinted with punctuation and editing by Ren Zong (Shanghai: Shanghai guji chubanshe, 1983), May 3, 1897 (GX 23/04/02), p. 95.

of the sage as both the giver of primal law and order and the personification
of moral idealism. This narrow definition included just a few cultural heroes
like the Yellow Emperor (Huang Di) or the Divine Farmer (Shen Nong) in
China's legendary past. A more liberal interpretation of sagehood, however,
was more inclusive. To justify his position, the commentator blended the
fourth-century B.C.E. Confucian philosopher Xunzi and Buddhism. In this
interpretation, Xunzi opened the way for calling "anyone who could establish a primal institution" in a disorderly age a sage. In addition, Buddhist
views of the present as an age of degeneration provided opportunities for
new cultural heroes. If this world was not improving, numerous sages would
appear. The implicit message was that even in the context of the late Qing
crisis one could expect a sage.[40]

A lifelong admirer of Han Yu, Zhang Zhidong could not tolerate the
grouping of Han with the Social Darwinists, either positively or negatively.
Zhang determined that the article was a symptom of the contemporary intellectual malaise. What he detested most was the enthusiasm for such unorthodox ideas as popular power, Social Darwinism, and historical progress.
In Zhang's judgment, any theory of political evolution was tantamount to
the advocacy of "parochialism, disintegration, and eventually chaos."[41] He
feared an attack by the censors on the newspaper, perhaps even demands for
its closure.[42] Zhang ordered Wang Kangnian to admit his "blunder" and to
give a satisfactory explanation to readers[43] and had his longtime document
commissioners write a critique of Yan Fu's essay to the effect that it had
"completely reversed the proper relationship between the monarch and his
subjects, the backbone of the three cardinal bonds, out of ignorance." In addition, apologies were made to the readers of the *Chinese Progress* for having
published such a "reckless" article.[44] Furthermore, Zhang had a public announcement posted on the front gates of the new schools that subscribed to

---

40. Gao Fengqian to Wang Kangnian, WKN, p. 1628, July 12, 1897 (GX 23/06/13).

41. For Zhang's aversion to *minquan*, see Daniel Bays, *China Enters the Twentieth Century:
Chang Chih-tung and the Issues of a New Age, 1895–1909* (Ann Arbor: University of Michigan
Press, 1978), pp. 29–32.

42. Zhang Zhidong to Chen Baozhen and Huang Zunxian, Sept. 11, 1897 (GX 23/09/16),
ZZD, telegrams, 153: 32.

43. Ye Han to Wang Kangnian, WKN, p. 2596, received June 6, 1897 (GX 23/05/07).

44. Tu Renshou, "Critique of 'Refuting Han Yu,'" CP 30, 20a–22a, June 20, 1897 (GX
23/05/21).

the newspaper. Zhang's message: the students of the schools should take care to discriminate good articles from bad.[45]

A group of young essayists on the editorial board of the *Chinese Progress*, however, did not budge and instead tried to expand Yan's theory of political evolution further. If progress is universal in human history, they reasoned, a representative system of government based on the principles of mass participation and popular sovereignty will surely appear in China. In an editorial, for instance, Liang Qichao predicted that every political system would eventually evolve toward its highest form, that is, democracy. What mattered was not its inevitability, but the proper guidance of its pace and form according to the needs of each country. The Chinese monarch should not be alarmed at this prospect, he continued, since the monarchy was compatible with a "democratic" system. The Qing government could, moreover, leapfrog the intervening steps and reach the final phase of a democratic polity—"self-rule without a presidency." Liang did not explain how the Chinese version of "democracy" could be achieved. He merely introduced the Chan Buddhist theory of "sudden enlightenment" to supplement Yan's theory of political evolutionism. China could bypass all tedious, unnecessary steps through the intense concentration of political and intellectual energies of enlightened elite.[46]

In support of Liang, other editorial writers saw the theory of popular power more as an expedient means of political renovation than as an end in itself. Liang's assistant editor opined that the theory of popular power could be used to eradicate "deep-seated evils" in the Chinese system of government by broadening the base of political awareness and participation.[47] Another editor identified these evils: corruption, ineptitude, inertia, the obsolete civil service examinations and official recruitment system, and the lack of smooth coordination between the monarch and local officials in the field. His solution was what Max Weber would call "rationalization"—clear job descrip-

---

45. Zhang Zhidong, "Public Announcement," cited in Wang Yinian, *Wang Rangqing xiansheng zhuanji*, p. 216; Zhang Yuanji to Wang Kangnian, WKN, p. 1706, Sept. 5, 1897 (GX 23/08/09).

46. Liang Qichao, "The Law of Evolution from Monarchy Toward Democracy," CP 41, 1a–4a, Oct. 6, 1897 (GX 23/09/11).

47. Xu Qin, "How to Eradicate the Evils of China," 4 pts., CP 42, Oct. 16, 1897 (GX 23/09/21); 44, Nov. 5, 1897 (GX 23/10/11); 46, Nov. 24, 1897 (GX 23/11/01); 48, Dec. 14, 1897 (GX 23/11/21).

tions, specialization, and abolition of the law of avoidance.[48] In short, these essayists tried to stress the usefulness of new political theories, including democracy, for the Qing monarchy.

Despite these young editorialists' circumspect rhetoric, the notion of democracy was too provocative to be raised legitimately. Any serious discussion of the idea unavoidably entailed a negative portrayal of existing political institutions. At the same time, novel political ideas, however carefully worded, would certainly make cultural conservatives suspicious. In this light, it was quite prudent for a distribution manager of the paper in Beijing, for example, to withhold the issue that carried Liang's essays and to advise his counterparts in other cities not to circulate it.[49] Likewise, the Translation Bureau supervisors of the newspaper found the essays "improper" and considered ways to gain more effective control over the *Chinese Progress* editorial board. If unchecked, they understandably worried, such essays would damage the reputation of Zhang Zhidong. Therefore, it became critical to reshuffle the paper's editorial board and to espouse an orthodox political philosophy.[50]

Statecraft, Regionalism, and the Search for New Orthodoxy

In mid-1897, Zhang Zhidong decided to reshuffle the leadership of the *Chinese Progress* after concluding that indirect intervention in the paper's editorial board through his confidants in the Hubei Translation Bureau was not sufficient. In Zhang's original plan, most of the paper's staff, including Wang Kangnian and Liang Qichao, were to be replaced by members of his pool of document commissioners.[51] Zhang and his confidants tried not to

---

48. Mai Menghua, "China Should Embark on Reform from the Reorganization of Government Structure," 2 pts., CP 22, 1a–4a, Apr. 2, 1897 (GX 23/03/01); 24, 1a–5a, Apr. 22, 1897 (GX 23/03/21).

49. Zhang Yuanji to Wang Kangnian, undated, late 1897, WKN, pp. 1713–14.

50. Liang Qichao to Wang Kangnian, WKN, p. 1901, received Dec. 20, 1897 (GX 23/11/14); ibid., 1901, Dec. 20, 1897 (GX 23/11/27).

51. The CP reorganization drew much attention; see Song Shu to Hu Daonan and Dong Xueqi, Oct. 12, 1897 (GX 23/09/17), Song Shu 宋恕, *Song Shu ji* 宋恕集 (Collection of Song Shu's writings; hereafter SS); reprinted with punctuation and editing by Hu Zhusheng (Beijing: Zhonghua shuju, 1993), p. 585; Chen Qingnian 陳慶年, "Wuxu jihai jianwen lu" 戊戌 己亥見聞錄 (Reminiscences of the years between 1898 and 1899; hereafter CQN), *Jindaishi ziliao* 81 (1990): 107.

make the reorganization process seem punitive. The reshuffling of the editorial staff went relatively smoothly. Zhang arranged a furlough for the old members at West Lake in Hangzhou and teaching positions in the newly established Current Affairs School (Shiwu xuetang 時務學堂) in Changsha, Hunan.[52] Nevertheless, the reorganization of the paper's managerial board did not go entirely as planned due to considerable factional infighting among Zhang's document commissioners. In the winter months of 1897–98, Wang Kangnian and new candidates engaged in importunate lobbying of their patrons and negotiations with one another over the paper's director-generalship. Most notably, Huang Zunxian 黃遵憲 (1848–1905), the author of *A History of Japan* (*Riben guozhi* 日本國志), a major inspiration for reformist thought in the late Qing, strove to gain direct control of the paper by planting many of his men on its board of overseers, a move supported by Zhang and the Hubei Translation Bureau.[53]

Meanwhile, in the late summer and early fall of 1897, Zhang Zhidong helped set up additional newspapers to counter the editorial position of the *Chinese Progress* and thus effectively ended the *Chinese Progress*'s monopoly under his patronage.[54] These were the *Statecraft Journal* (*Jingshi bao* 經世報), the *Journal of Substantial Study* (*Shixue bao* 實學報), and the *Seek-the-Truth Journal* (*Qiushi bao* 求實報).[55] As if to demonstrate his preferential patronage, Zhang placed the *Statecraft Journal* under the direct supervision of the Hubei Translation Bureau and arranged an office near the governor-general's yamen in Wuchang for the paper's headquarters until he moved them to Shanghai.[56] Most of the staff of these new journals, drawn from Zhang's document commissioners, happened to be thinkers from the state-

---

52. Zou Daijun to Wang Kangnian, WKN, p. 2743, Sept. 8, 1897 (GX 23/08/12), *et passim.*

53. Huang Zunxian to Wang Kangnian, WKN, pp. 2343–44, Aug. 17, 1896 (GX 22/07/09) *er passim*; Zheng Xiaoxu 鄭孝胥, *Zheng Xiaoxu riji* 鄭孝胥日記 (Diary of Zheng Xiaoxu; hereafter ZXX); reprinted with punctuation and editing by Lao Zude (Beijing: Zhonghua shuju, 1993), p. 610, July 30, 1897, *et passim.*

54. Song Shu to Zhang Binglin, July 14, 1897 (GX 23/06/15), SS, p. 572.

55. SS, July 15, 1897 (GX 23/06/16), pp. 574–55; Wang Renjun, CP 44, Aug. 18, 1897 (GX 23/07/21); CQN, Dec. 9, 1897 (GX 23/11/16); CP 39, front cover, Sept. 17, 1897 (GX 23/08/21).

56. Wang Renjun to Wang Kangnian, WKN, p. 3526, received Feb. 10, 1898 (GX 24/01/20).

craft school and natives of the eastern coastal area of Zhejiang province.[57] Identifying themselves as bearers of the orthodox statecraft tradition, these Zhejiang literati strove to place the discussion of administrative renovation within the confines of Confucian moral world order. In the face of the formidable challenges posed by European political thought, these statecraft writers raised the fundamental question: Who is civilizing whom? In particular, they detested a search for wealth and power at the expense of Confucian moral self-cultivation. Judged by such a standard, the *Chinese Progress* was off the track. Therefore, the new journals' motto was to be "to straighten the minds of the people and develop public morale."[58]

With the establishment of these newspapers, Zhang Zhidong was to implement a more far-reaching philosophical critique of the philosophical foundations of the radical essayists. Most of the former members of the *Chinese Progress* editorial board were followers of Kang Youwei, who inspired the utopian currents of the late Qing reform movement. Kang was deeply influenced by the so-called Guangdong Learning (*Yue xue* 粵 學), which stressed the exegetical scholarship of Han Learning. Out of the eclectic tradition of Han Learning, Kang had chosen the New Text position for his philosophical exposition of institutional reforms based on what Confucius himself would have supposedly wished. In opposition to Kang, Zhang had his chief document commissioners examine Kang's first treatise, *An Inquiry into the Classics Forged During the Xin Period* (*Xinxue weijing kao* 新 學 僞 經 考), and prepare for a thoroughgoing refutation of Kang's unorthodox views.[59] He also had the statecraft essayists writing for the new journals belittle Kang's intellectual credentials and criticize his free-ranging writing style and philosophical orientations. Kang's famous draft for the "Joint Petition of 1895," a virtual reform charter, for example, was disparaged as "vulgar" by the standards of the statecraft writing tradition. In addition, Kang was accused of "vulgarizing" his disciple Liang Qichao's writing style in the *Chinese Prog-*

---

57. This special group of statecraft scholars is yet to be studied. See Hao Chang, "On the Ching-shih Idea in Neo-Confucianism," *Ch'ing-shih wen-t'i* 3, no. 1 (Nov. 1974): 36–61; and Philip Kuhn, "Ideas Behind China's Modern State," *Harvard Journal of Asiatic Studies* 55, no. 2 (Dec. 1996): 295–337.

58. CQN, Dec. 9, 1897 (GX 23/11/16).

59. CQN, p. 111, May 17, 1898 (GX 24/leap month 03/27). This critique would eventually become the *Exhortation to Study* (*Quanxue pian*). For further discussion of this, see the chapter by Tze-ki Hon in this volume.

ress. Kang was also suspected of having dictated the editorials that appeared under Liang's name.[60]

The statecraft literati-journalists' next move was to refute Kang's messianic view of Confucius and his "manipulation" of the Confucian classics for institutional reform. The *Journal of Substantial Study* compared Kang to Wang Mang 王莽, the infamous usurper and institutional innovator of the first century C.E. In a critique of Kang's famous treatise *Confucius as a Reformer* (*Kongzi gaizhi kao* 孔子改革考), an article in the journal criticized Kang for intentionally misinterpreting the Chinese classics for "ulterior political motives" in the manner of Wang Mang.[61] The comparison was, indeed, not without merit: both men instituted a religious ceremony for Confucius and based their calls for radical institutional renovation on an eccentric exegesis of the Confucian canon. Moreover, both exalted the *Rites of Zhou* (*Zhou li* 周禮), the classic attributed to the Duke of Zhou. But the critique missed the point that Kang's *Inquiry into the Classics Forged During the Xin Period* specifically criticized Wang's support of the pioneers of the Ancient Text scholarship. Wang Mang's patronage of false scholarship, in Kang's view, had caused all the intellectual malaise of the preceding two millennia. Moreover, the essay did not distinguish Kang's futuristic utopianism from Wang's idealistic restorationism.[62] Nevertheless, it did reflect the concern of cultural conservatives that Kang was manipulating the Confucian classics for an ideology that would support his own ambitions.

Intended or not, the Zhejiang statecraft essayists' criticism of Kang Youwei echoed the concerns of moderates within the *Chinese Progress* and assumed factional overtones along regional lines. Earlier, before Zhang Zhidong's reorganization of the *Chinese Progress,* a number of more middle-of-the-road journalists had tried to reduce Kang's influence on the arguments of his disciples or followers (*Kangmen* 康門 or *Kangtu* 康徒) within the paper, most notably Liang Qichao. The moderates thought that they had restrained certain "radical" or "unorthodox" New Text views.[63] One Zhejiang literati-journalist on the *Chinese Progress* was one of the most vocal critics of

---

60. Song Shu to Hu Daonan and Dong Xueqi, SS, p. 578, July 26, 1897 (GX 23/06/27).

61. *Journal of Substantial Study* (*Shixue bao* 實學報; hereafter *JSS*) 14, Jan. 3, 1898 (GX 23/12/11).

62. On Kang's futuristic utopianism, see Chang, *Chinese Intellectuals*, pp. 56–65.

63. Wu Qiao to Wang Kangnian, undated, early 1896, WKN, p. 467 *et passim*; Zhang Yuanji to Wang Kangnian, WKN, pp. 1703–4, Aug. 24, 1897 (GX 23/07/27) *et passim.*

what he termed the "Cantonese faction" (*Yuedang* 粤黨). Zhang Binglin 章
炳麟 (1869–1935), soon to emerge as a major proponent of ethnic nationalism and an inspiration of the 1911 revolution, had long disliked the New Text
scholars on the editorial board. Zhang believed that their philosophical orientations tended to suppress universal human desires—an old topic of debate within Neo-Confucianism—and also that they were increasingly exalting Kang.[64] The journalists from Guangdong, on the other hand, found
Zhang difficult to work with and finally managed to expel him from the
editorial board on the grounds that his antiquated writing style was unsuit-
able for journalism.[65] The Guangdong-Zhejiang factional conflict within the
Chinese Progress was so emotionally charged that Zhang Binglin got into a
fistfight at a drinking party with Kang Youwei, who was visiting the paper's
office in Shanghai. Zhang joined the editorial boards of the *Journal of Substantial Study* and the *Statecraft Journal* and continued to attack his former
colleagues.[66]

The Cantonese literati-journalists, now mostly in Changsha, allied with
Hunan reformist literati of a New Text bent to accuse Wang Kangnian,
who was from Zhejiang, of mismanagement, embezzlement, immoral behavior, and even separatist maneuvers. According to their ill-grounded rumors, Wang was either "hatching a secret scheme in Japan to launch a rebellion" or teaming up with the "renegade" Sun Yat-sen 孫逸仙 (1866–1925).[67]
The second accusation could have been fatal to Wang because Sun and his
followers had organized the "Political Reform Society" (Bianzheng hui 變政
會, *sic*, the Revive-China Society) in Honolulu, and were spreading anti-
Manchu revolutionary propaganda.[68] In response, the Zhejiang literati-
journalists claimed that Kang was a follower of the Progressive Party (Shin-
pōtō 進步黨), an opposition party influential during the popular rights

---

64. Zhang Binglin to Tan Xian, cited in Tang Zhijun, *Wuxu shiqi de xuehui he baokan*, p.
728n134; SBX, p. 89, Apr. 15, 1897 (GX 23/03/14).

65. Huang Zunxian to Wang Kangnian, undated, early 1897, WKN, p. 235; Wu Dexiao
to Wang Kangnian, WKN, p. 422, undated, late 1896; Tan Sitong conversation with Zheng
Xiaoxu, ZXX, p. 598, May 3, 1897.

66. SBX, p. 260, Sept. 28, 1898 (GX 24/08/13) *et passim*.

67. Liang Qichao telegram to Huang & Xu to Han Shuyuan, quoted in Zou Daijun to
Wang Kangnian, WKN, p. 2756, May 31, 1898 (GX 24/04/12); CQN, p. 111, May 20, 1898
(GX 24/04/01).

68. Wu Qiao to Wang Kangnian, WKN, p. 484, Apr. 25, 1896 (GX 22/03/13); ZXX, p.
658, Jun. 2, 1898.

movement period in Japan, with Arao Sei, a member of the party and a Japanese spy, as his liaison.[69]

With the escalation of this regional animosity, the statecraft essayists shifted their attacks from Kang Youwei's New Text scholarship to the radical political thought of modern Europe. Their initial target, however, was not an antidynastic revolutionary like Sun Yat-sen, but Mo Di 墨翟, an ancient Chinese philosopher of the fourth century B.C.E. According to their interpretation, Mo Di's ideal of universal love had inspired political theories of democracy (*minzhu* 民主) in modern Europe. If this was the case, they argued, Mo Di had contaminated not only the Chinese people but also Westerners. In "A Critique of Democracy" in the pages of the *Journal of Substantial Study,* for example, the statecraft thinkers criticized the naïveté of the new Chinese followers of democratic theories, who did not realize the "calamities" that democracy had brought to Europe, such as electoral corruption and mob politics. If Mo Di was the progenitor of democratic theory, they concluded, rehashing his theory in its currently vulgarized version was a matter of an even greater shame for the Chinese literati. Such a vulgar theory could captivate the minds of the "traitor" Sun Yat-sen, they contended, but not the literati-journalists of the *Chinese Progress.*[70] In the words of the *Statecraft Journal,* advocates of popular power were "blind followers" of European models and ignorant of "our cherished Chinese political tradition."[71] Even Wang Kangnian was not saved from this strident attack on the theory of democracy. In the words of the paper, Wang had virtually called for "anarchy" by ignoring the "administrative authority" (*liquan* 吏權) essential for the Qing government.[72] In short, the statecraft essayists wanted to make sure that administrative renovation followed the Confucian statecraft tradition with due stress on its moral strain.

In order to keep his post on the *Chinese Progress,* Wang Kangnian had to draw a line between himself and those "blind followers" of European radical political thought, most notably, Kang Youwei and Sun Yat-sen.[73] Wang decided to regain Zhang's favor by changing the tone of his writings to

---

69. Ye Han to Wang Kangnian, WKN, pp. 2600–601, July 29, 1898 (GX 24/06/11).

70. Wang Renjun, "A Critique of Democracy," *JSS* 3–15.

71. Chen Qiu, "Preface to the *Statecraft Journal,*" *Statecraft Journal* (*Jingshi bao* 經世報), 1, Aug. 2, 1897 (GX 23/07/05).

72. Ma Yongxi, "A Critique of 'Popular Power,'" SS 10, Oct. 30, 1897 (GX 23/10/05).

73. Qian Xun to Wang Kangnian, July 14, 1898 (GX 24/05/26), WKN, p. 3004.

Zhang's taste. In subsequent essays, Wang used Social Darwinian rhetoric to make a case for state nationalism for the Qing.[74] He warned of the colonialist nature of Western encroachment on the Qing. Wang capitalized on the German occupation of Jiaozhou in the Shandong peninsula, which occurred at the time of his writing and triggered a series of territorial acquisitions by the European powers, the infamous "scramble for concessions." In this time of national humiliation, things Western, Wang warned, must be monitored with vigilance for the sake of the Chinese state.[75] Not surprisingly, Zhang Zhidong and the Translation Bureau supervisors welcomed Wang's new posture.[76] Encouraged, Wang criticized "naïve followers" of Western methods in a subsequent editorial. He pointed out the seamy side of colonialism and charged that the colonized subjects did not enjoy the universal legal protection that the colonizers were propagating. In the end, Wang predicted, the colonizers would deprive the colonized of their native religion and language. If the Chinese blindly followed the advice of the Westerners, he concluded, the Qing state would become a colony as had Poland and India.[77]

Zhang Zhidong and the Translation Bureau were greatly pleased with Wang's editorial and praised it as "the best since the newspaper was established." Zhang's document commissioners at the Translation Bureau encouraged Wang to write follow-up essays to elucidate his state nationalism in defense of the current political regime. Chinese nationalism, they argued, should be based on the principle of the preservation of the Qing state. In response to imperialist maneuvers in China, the most crucial element for state nationalism was unity between Manchus and the Han Chinese. If these two groups had insisted on their ancestral territories, they argued, the current situation in Central Asia suggested that the Russians would have swallowed the Manchus. Likewise, Britain, Germany, and France would have carved up China proper had it not been for the Manchus' military might and determination. In other words, Wang's nationalism opposed ethnic nationalism that

---

74. Hao Chang (*Chinese Intellectuals*, p. 2) distinguishes two strains in late Qing nationalism, conservative "state nationalism" or "reactive nationalism" and more radical "ethnic nationalism."

75. Wang Kangnian, "On the German Occupation of Jiaozhou Bay," CP 52, 1a–3a, Feb. 21, 1898 (GX 24/02/01).

76. Qian Xun to Wang Kangnian, WKN, p. 3001, Mar. 16, 1898 (GX 24/02/24).

77. Wang Kangnian, "Inevitable Courses for China in the Near Future," CP 65, 1a–3b, Jun. 29, 1898 (GX 24/05/11).

contained anti-Manchu sentiments, which only would help the Westerners colonize the entire "Chinese race."[78] Even though Wang provided no further philosophical answers as to how state nationalism would synthesize the inner moral dimensions of self-cultivation and the outer concern for statecraft, his espousal of these views surely saved Wang's job. Wang proved himself to be an orthodox statecraft thinker to his Zhejiang compatriots and a loyal document commissioner to his patron, Zhang Zhidong.[79]

Network Building, Censorship, Ghostwriting, and the Government Gazette Campaign in Beijing

The dominance of the Zhejiang statecraft persuasion over the Cantonese New Text persuasion within the *Chinese Progress* did not end the complicated interplay between knowledge and power in the context of the late Qing reforms. When Liang Qichao and his associates moved to Hunan, they were successful for a moment in enlisting young converts and supporters. In the spring and summer of 1898, however, increasing hostility toward Kang Youwei and his teachings culminated in conservative campaigns throughout the province and elsewhere.[80] A shakeup in the leadership of the Current Affairs School prompted Liang Qichao and his colleagues to leave for Beijing, where they hoped to build alternative patronage networks.[81] The Kang-Liang group had been enjoying protection from important sections of the Beijing bureaucracy, most notably Zhang Yinhuan 張蔭桓 (1837–1900), minister of the Zongli yamen, and Weng Tonghe 翁同龢 (1830–1905), the Guangxu emperor's former tutor and an influential grand councilor.[82] In addition, this group of *Chinese Progress* journalists had earlier tried to involve as many influential officials as they could into the paper's donation and subscription network. These included Li Hongzhang 李鴻章 (1823–1901), a grand councilor

---

78. Qian Xun to Wang Kangnian, WKN, p. 3004, Jul. 14, 1898 (GX 24/05/26).

79. CQN, pp. 110, 116; Zou Daijun to Wang Kangnian, WKN, pp. 2757–59, July 13, 1898 (GX 24/05/30).

80. For the interplay between reformers and conservatives in Hunan, see Hao Chang, "Intellectual Change and the Reform Movement, 1890–8," in *The Cambridge History of China*, vol. 11, pt. II, *The Late Qing, 1800–1911*, ed. Denis Twitchett and John K. Fairbank, pp. 300–318 (Cambridge, Eng.: Cambridge University Press, 1980).

81. Zou Daijun to Wang Kangnian, WKN, pp. 2757–59, July 13, 1898 (GX 24/05/30).

82. Luke Kwong, *A Mosaic of the Hundred Days: Personalities, Politics, and Ideas of 1898* (Cambridge, Mass.: Harvard University, Council on East Asian Studies, 1984), pp. 135–39.

and the linchpin of late Qing diplomacy, and Ronglu 榮祿 (1836–1903), a nephew of the Empress Dowager Cixi.[83] Not all these patrons, however, remained sympathetic. Li Hongzhang, a strong rival to Zhang Zhidong in court politics, opined that the paper's articles were "of no use in the actual administration of state affairs, no matter how well phrased and full of enthusiasm." None of the statecraft proposals made by the "nit and locust" literati-journalists, in his view, would catch the emperor' attention.[84]

The Cantonese faction was also aware that Beijing officials, especially those with censorial rights, remained unfavorable to the paper's tenor. Even before the publication of its first issue, there was a rumor that it would carry a series of sensational articles, including draft memorials criticizing the Empress Dowager Cixi. Moreover, censors and Hanlin academicians did not like the literati-journalists' use of the newspaper to discuss administrative reform, a privilege reserved for senior officials. For example, a censor prepared 10,000 copies of a critique immediately after Liang Qichao began publishing a series of articles calling for the abolition of the civil service examination system in favor of a national school system.[85] In their eyes, the journalists of the *Chinese Progress* were merely "profit-seekers" after liquor fees or mindless followers of unorthodox teachings.[86] As early as 1897, Beijing officials' uneasiness with the paper became more vocal at banquets and wine parties. In their judgment, the paper, out of its enthusiasm for administrative reform, was insulting historical monarchs.[87] The anti–*Chinese Progress* mood among Beijing officials reached an apex in January of that year when a Hanlin scholar prepared a draft memorial to request the closing of the newspaper—just as Zhang Zhidong had feared. In the Hanlin scholar's opinion, the paper had "propagated groundless rumors defaming the imperial court and high officials." Furthermore, the paper, if unchecked, would turn literati minds from Neo-Confucian orthodoxy toward "heterodox" teachings. Attached to the memorial were Liang Qichao's

---

83. Liu Tizhi 劉體智, *Yicilu* 異辭錄 (Anecdotal memories) (Beijing: Zhonghua shuju, 1988), p. 162; Wu Baochu to Wang Kangnian, undated, WKN, p. 338 *et passim*.

84. *Zhilin bao*, cited in Dou Zongyi 竇宗彝, *Li Hongzhang nian(ri)pu* 李鴻章 年(日)譜 (Taibei: Wenhai chubanshe, 1980), Feb. 14, 1896 (GX 22/01/02), p. 5091; SBX, p. 123, Aug. 2, 1897 (GX 23/07/05).

85. Liang Dingfen to Wang Kangnian, WKN, p. 1900, Dec. 1896.

86. Huang Zunxian to Wang Kangnian, WKN, p. 2335, July 4, 1896 (GX 22/05/24); Wang Daxie to Wang Kangnian, WKN, p. 747, Sept. 1, 1896 (GX 22/07/24).

87. Wang Daxie to Wang Kangnian, WKN, p. 756, Jan. 12, 1897 (GX 22/12/10).

essays.[88] Zhang Zhidong had to intervene to protect the paper by winning the cooperation of Li Hongzao 李鴻藻 (1820–97), a grand councilor and president of the Board of Civil Appointments, to block the memorial from being delivered to the throne on the grounds that it contained "inappropriate" expressions in it. However, Linshu 麟書, an imperial clansman and a grand secretary, and Xu Tong 徐桐 (1819–1900), a Bannerman and a grand secretary in charge of the Board of Civil Appointments, cosigned the memorial and submitted it to the throne.[89]

Censorial criticism of the *Chinese Progress* never diminished. In early 1898, a censor proposed placing all newspapers in China under the central supervision of the Book Depot (Guan shuju 官書局), a branch of the Zongli yamen. This measure was crucial, he contended, since Westerners were feeding sensitive information about Chinese court politics to the literati-journalists in order to intervene in the internal affairs of China and spread "theories of democracy." Even though the censor did not name the *Chinese Progress* specifically, it was widely considered one of the most radical among the handful of native newspapers.[90]

In order to counteract the anti–*Chinese Progress* mood, the Kang-Liang group sought censorial protection by rendering aggressive ghostwriting services for Beijing officials with censorial rights. They volunteered to compose draft memorials for censors and Hanlin scholars and even bribed them on a regular basis in order to serve as ghostwriters, which in actuality meant borrowing of the names of persons authorized to write memorials.[91] To get

---

88. Gu Yuan, "To Eradicate Heretical Doctrines," *LFZZ*, Jan. 7, 1897 (GX 22/12/05).

89. Wang Daxie to Wang Kangnian, WKN, p. 756, Jan. 12, 1897 (GX 22/12/10); Liang Dingfen to Wang, WKN, p. 1902, Jan. 15, 1897 (GX 22/12/13); Wen Tingshi 文廷式, *Wen Tingshi ji* 文廷式集 (A collection of Wen Tingshi's literary works); reprinted with punctuation and editing by Wang Shuzi (Beijing: Zhonghua shuju, 1993), 2: 727.

90. Huang Kuijun, "A Proposal Calling for the Control of the Press," *LFZZ*, May 22, 1898 (GX 24/04/03).

91. The bribes given two censors, for example, reached 100 taels a month (Liu Tizhi, *Yicilu*, pp. 161–62, 163). We do not know the source of this money, but most historians point out that Kang and his associates conducted active ghostwriting activities during their sojourn in Beijing; see Kwong, *A Mosaic of the Hundred Days*, pp. 139–42; Kong Xiangji 孔祥吉, *Kang Youwei bianfa zouyi yanjiu* 康有爲變法奏議研究 (Studies of Kang Youwei's reform memorials) (Shenyang: Liaoning jiaoyu chubanshe, 1988), pp. 127–50 *et passim*; and Kuang Zhaojiang 鄺兆江, "Wuxu zhengbian qianhou de Kang Youwei" 戊戌政變前後的康有爲 (Kang Youwei before and after the 1898 reform movement), *Lishi yanjiu* 1996, no. 5: 9–10.

their voices heard by higher officials and hopefully the throne, Kang and his followers skillfully combined ghostwriting with journalism. Unused draft memorials would find their way into the paper. Conversely, drafts of journal essays could be used as writing samples to demonstrate their policy expertise. Thanks to their patronage-building efforts, Kang and his disciples obtained considerable sympathy from a number of censors and eventually the protection of the throne.

Under this new patronage, one of the next moves of the Kang-Liang group was to monopolize the distribution networks of all dozen or so reformist journals, including the *Chinese Progress*, in the imperial city. Capitalizing on disputes among managers of distribution routes, Kang and his associates were able to set up the General Distribution Depot (Paibao zongju 派報總局) at Liulichang, the hub of literati activities.[92] Meanwhile, they discredited Wang Kangnian among Beijing officials. Pointing to the financial losses of the *Chinese Progress* under Wang, they demanded that either Kang or Liang manage the newspaper. Consequently, Wang lost his reputation among Beijing officials, a few of whom even came to believe the widely circulated rumor that Wang was funding Sun Yat-sen from the paper's purse.[93]

With this success, the Cantonese group moved to obtain the court's endorsement of their takeover of the paper. They launched a campaign to make the *Chinese Progress* a central government organ under the direct supervision of the Zongli yamen, not of Zhang Zhidong's Hubei Translation Bureau. Kang Youwei recommended that Liang Qichao lead the government newspaper. They also submitted to the yamen all the published issues of the *Chinese Progress* in which Liang's essays loomed comparatively large in the hope of impressing yamen officials. Finally, in spite of Wang Kangnian's resistance, Kang won the support of Sun Jia'nai 孫家鼐 (1827–1909), a former imperial tutor and a minister in the Zongli yamen, to submit a memorial, with all the issues of the paper attached, to the throne.[94] The Guangxu emperor approved Sun's proposal and issued edicts endorsing the Zongli

---

92. Zhang Yuanji to Wang Kangnian, WKN, pp. 1729–30, Mar. 7, 1898 (GX 24/02/15); pp. 1731–32, Apr. 13, 1898 (GX 24/03/23).

93. Wang Daxie to Wang Kangnian, WKN, pp. 781–82, June 2, 1898 (GX 24/04/14); p. 778, May 28, 1898 (GX 24/04/09); Zhou Xuexi to Wang Kangnian, WKN, p. 1210, July 27, 1898 (GX 24/06/09).

94. Zhang Yuanji to Wang Kangnian, WKN, p. 1737, July 27, 1898 (GX 24/06/09); Huang Zhuanji to Wang Kangnian, undated, WKN, p. 2314; Wang Daxie to Wang Kangnian, WKN, pp. 790–91, July 31, 1898 (GX 24/06/13) *et passim*.

yamen's supervision of the *Chinese Progress* and conferring a new name on it, the *Chinese Progress Government Gazette* (*Shiwu guanbao* 時務官報). The emperor ordered Kang to take charge of the new government organ using funds from the Board of Revenue and the Imperial Household.[95] Kang submitted a memorial of thanks to the throne with a request that its employees be put on the government payroll, thus nullifying the need for subscription fees. As if to show his financial expertise, he proposed that the central government depository could be augmented from the provincial coffers of the Board of Supreme Reorganization and the Western Affairs Bureau for the estimated thousand taels needed for the paper's monthly expenditures. In addition, he also pointed out that the use of reporters was not necessarily unprecedented since their functions were similar to those of folksong-collecting officials (*caishi guan* 採詩官) in the *Book of Odes* (*Shijing* 詩經).[96] At the same time, Kang consulted with Sun Jia'nai over the promulgation of a press law. In an appendix attached to his memorial, Kang stressed the need for firm supervision of existing newspapers, both native and foreign. In the selection of editorial writers, for example, he placed special emphasis on loyalty and patriotism, principles to be implemented universally by all the managers of newspapers in foreign concession areas.[97] Kang's proposals unmistakably indicated that he and his followers, the radical wing of the *Chinese Progress*, were not intent on establishing a fourth estate. On the contrary, they made the paper utterly dependent on state power even at the sacrifice of whatever remained of the semi-autonomous *qun* elements of the paper. This is not to say, however, that they compromised their political vision or ideological persuasion. Rather, the Kang-Liang group envisioned a paradoxical, and thus unachievable, political goal: to advance "independent" political ideas from within the imperial court by making full use of government gazettes and official funds.

---

95. Number One Historical Archives of China, *Shangyu dang* 上諭檔 (Grand Council record book of imperial edicts; hereafter *SYD*) (Microfilm), July 26, 1898 (GX 24/06/08); Aug. 16, 1898 (GX 24/06/29); Sept. 12, 1898 (GX 24/07/27); Sept. 17, 1898 (GX 24/08/02).

96. The *locus classicus* for such an official remains unclear. However, Kang quotes Feng Guifen's *Essays of Protest* (*Jiaobinlu kangyi*); see Kang Youwei, memorial, July 31, 1898 (GX 24/06/13), in idem, *Jieshi shangshu huilu* 杰士上書匯錄; draft copy of the Imperial Household Department at the Imperial Palace Museum, originally copied in 1898; reprinted in *Kang Youwei zaoqi yigao shuping* 康有為早期遺稿述評, ed. Huang Mingtong and Wu Xizhao, pp. 306–7 (Guangzhou: Zhongshan daxue chubanshe, 1988).

97. Kang Youwei, appendix slip, *Jieshi shangshu huilu*, pp. 307–8.

Kang and his associates, with the strong patronage of the Zongli yamen and the emperor, placed their government gazette campaign on a safe track. Sun Jia'nai appointed Liang Qichao to a position at the government-sponsored Translation Depot (Yishu ju 譯 書 局), the Zongli yamen's branch office, where he drew up new regulations on the translation of foreign books and journals.[98] At the same time, Sun arranged for the Zongli yamen to send an official telegram to Liu Kunyi 劉 坤 一 (1830–1902), the governor-general of Jiangsu-Jiangxi-Anhui, to help Huang Zunxian, now the leader of the *Chinese Progress* transfer team on Kang's behalf, to take over the newspaper in Shanghai. Kang was in such a triumphant mood that he sent a telegram to Wang Kangnian asking for a cooperative transfer.[99] In the summer of 1898, the *Chinese Progress's* metamorphosis almost became a fait accompli as the news caught the attention of the nation when Sun Jia'nai's memorial appeared consecutively in the *Beijing Gazette* (*Jing bao* 京 報) in Beijing, the *Shen bao* 申 報 in Shanghai, and the *Asahi shimbun* in Osaka.[100] The transfer, however, stalled when the Wang Kangnian group, relying on Zhang Zhidong's protection, refused to hand over the paper's assets. In their judgment, the imperial court did not fully understand the paper's internal affairs and was thus caught up in the Cantonese faction's maneuver. They expected that they would be able to obtain the imperial court's support if the true ideological face of the Cantonese could be exposed.[101]

At this juncture, Zhang Zhidong had his document commissioners present the *Exhortation to Study* (*Quanxue pian*) to the throne. A program of neo-orthodoxy in the statecraft tradition of the Song Learning persuasion, the treatise was the culmination of his ongoing ideological battle against unorthodox political discussion of popular power and equality. His work won enormous moral support not only from his colleagues in the five provinces of south China but also from the emperor.[102] In expectation of imminent

---

98. *SYD*, Aug. 16, 1898 (GX 24/06/29); Aug. 26, 1898 (GX 24/07/10).

99. Kang Youwei to Wang Kangnian, quoted in Wang Daxie to Wang Kangnian, WKN, pp. 788–89, July 29, 1898 (GX 24/06/11).

100. Wang Liyuan to Wang Kangnian, WKN, p. 1030, Aug. 4, 1898 (GX 24/06/17); Sun Gan to Wang, WKN, p. 1447, Aug. 5, 1898 (GX 24/06/18); Yao Xiguang to Wang Kangnian, WKN, p. 1266, Aug. 10, 1898 (GX 24/06/23).

101. *CQN*, p. 118, Aug. 9, 1898 (GX 24/06/22); Wang Liyuan to Wang Kangnian, WKN, p. 1030, Aug. 4, 1898 (GX 24/06/17); Wang Youling to Wang Kangnian, p. 1085, Aug. 26, 1898 (GX 24/07/01).

102. *ZXX*, p. 668, July 27, 1898 (GX 24/06/09).

changes in the ideological milieu in the imperial city, the Zhejiang faction resorted to a waiting game: the Wang group attacked the Kang-Liang group in
the influential journals in Tianjin, Shanghai, and Macao.[103] At the same
time, Wang changed the name of the *Chinese Progress* to the *Verax* (*Changyan
bao* 昌言報) and continued publication. The influential governor-general
Liu Kunyi supported the move, and Zhang Zhidong demanded that Sun
Jia'nai at the Zongli yamen ignore the unauthorized moves of the Cantonese
faction.[104] The final fate of the *Chinese Progress* was in suspense until late
September when Ronglu staged a palace coup in support of Cixi. Shortly
thereafter, the imperial court closed all newspapers, including the abortive
Chinese Progress Government Gazette.[105]

Conclusion

The rise and fall of the *Chinese Progress* illustrates the intricate interplay between political power and knowledge. The episode also shows how the paper's peculiar configurations, both institutional and interpersonal, helped its
journalists occupy a special place in the unfolding of late Qing reform politics. Zhang Zhidong, the major patron of the *Chinese Progress*, and its literati-
journalists had different visions of the role of the newspaper in their efforts
at administrative renovation. Zhang regarded the newspaper as an extension
of his private bureaucratic organization or as a depot for reference materials
on the management of foreign affairs. Many of the ambitious men associated
with the paper regarded it as an innovative *qun* entity, a fresh mediating
ground between the state and the elite stratum of society. The literati-
journalists envisioned the paper as a half-official, half-civic literati association
and an alternative avenue for broadening political participation. It is tempting
to conclude that the literati were endeavoring to expand the "organizational
capacity" of society vis-à-vis the state and hence to see the emergence of "civic
consciousness" through the medium of the political press.

---

103. For a discussion of the debate among them, see Tang Zhijun, *Wuxu shiqi de xuehui he
baokan*, pp. 143–54.

104. *Changyan bao* 昌言報, 1898; reprinted in *Jindai Zhongguo shiliao congkan* 近代中國
史料叢刊, no. 329 (Taibei: Wenhai chubanshe, 1987), Oct. 1, 1898 (GX 24/08/16); Zhongguo jindaishi yanjiusuo 中國近代史研究所, ed., *Zhongguo jindai ziliao congkan: Wuxu bianfa* 中國近代資料叢刊戊戌變法 (Shanghai: Shenzhou guoguang chubanshe, 1953),
2: 612.

105. SYD, Sept. 26, 1898 (GX 24/08/11); Oct. 9, 1898 (GX 24/08/24).

However, a careful analysis of the unfolding of the *qun* elements and the statecraft ideals in the intellectual interchanges of the *Chinese Progress* demonstrates that the paper remained more a "servant of the state" than an independent voice. One cannot deny that to a certain degree the flexibility of the paper's semi-official configuration accommodated unorthodox, and even dissident, modes of political thought. Nevertheless, the literati-journalists, however radically oriented, had to define their roles within the parameters of the existing power relations. In their attempt to expand the scope of political participation, they had to identify themselves as the faithful successors of legitimate statecraft thinkers, be they from the Song Learning or the Han Learning tradition. Furthermore, the journalists' persistent efforts to reach out to officialdom, not to the general public, for readership and protection unmistakably indicated that the paper functioned in the service of the state. Even the paper's most radical wing, the Cantonese faction, sought to use the paper as a means for alternative patronage building within existing power configurations—as demonstrated in their campaign for reorganizing the *Chinese Progress* as a government gazette.

Intellectually, however, the tensions between patron and clients over the newspaper's stance stemmed from their different ideological positions over the meaning of the new statecraft orthodoxy in the context of reform politics. In the absence of a definite philosophical justification for reform programs until mid-1898, Zhang initially adopted a negative editorial policy, even when he was pursuing active administrative policies. When he found such a passive posture had its limitations, he played the more culturally conservative statecraft essayists of eastern Zhejiang off the New Text editorialists from Canton. The regional conflict reflected a deeper chasm dividing reformist literati. The paper's literati-journalists, both radical and moderate, strove to produce a culturally acceptable program for administrative renovation in the late Qing. Although they might have found a Western-style parliament or constitutional monarchy a viable political vision, it still remained difficult for them and their contemporaries to reach a consensus concerning the means to implement such a vision and the pace of such a reform. The literati search for a new political order, as seen in the ideological and institutional battles around the fate of the *Chinese Progress*, continued to be shaped by power configurations and factional alignments, as well as the emergence of new social formations and ideas.

CHAPTER THREE

Zhang Zhidong's Proposal for Reform: A New Reading of the Quanxue pian

Tze-ki Hon

Zhang Zhidong 張之洞 (1837–1909) plays a pivotal role in recent scholarship on the "hundred days" of reform in 1898 as an open-minded official who set the stage by advocating a broader scope for reform in China. Particularly, he is credited with implementing a series of substantial changes in the economy, transportation, and education in Hubei and Hunan as governorgeneral from 1890 to 1907.[1] However, he is also considered a member of the

---

I thank Mary Mazur, Peter Zarrow, Henry Y. S. Chan, Lee Chiu-chun, and the two anonymous reviewers of this volume for the Harvard University Asia Center for their critical comments on earlier versions of this essay. Their constructive criticisms have deepened my understanding of the complexity of late Qing reform. Of course, I bear full responsibility for all the mistakes in this essay.

1. See, e.g., William Ayers, *Chang Chih-tung and Educational Reform in China* (Cambridge, Mass.: Harvard University Press, 1971), pp. 137–95; Daniel H. Bays, *China Enters the Twentieth Century: Chang Chih-tung and the Issues of a New Age, 1895–1909* (Ann Arbor: University of Michigan Press, 1978), pp. 33–53; Wang Ermin 王爾敏, *Wan Qing zhengzhi sixiangshi lun* 晚清政治思想史論 (A study of late Qing political thought) (Taibei: Xuesheng chubanshe, 1969), pp. 72–100; Wang Rongzu 汪榮祖 (Young-tsu Wong), *Wan Qing bianfa sixiang luncong* 晚清變法思想論叢 (A collection of essays on late Qing reform thinking) (Taibei: Lianjin chuban, 1984), pp. 1–134; Xiao Gongquan 蕭公權 (Kung-chuan Hsiao), *Zhongguo zhengzhi sixiang shi* 中國政治思想史 (A history of political thought in China) (Taibei: Lianjin chuban, 1996 [1977]), pp. 833–90; Xue Huayuan 薛化元, *Wan Qing zhongti xiyong sixiang lun* 晚清「中體西用」思想論, *1861–1900* (A study of the theory of Chinese essence and Western function in the late Qing, 1861–1900) (Taibei: Daoxiang chubanshe, 1991), pp. 163–206; and Zhou Hanguang 周漢光, *Zhang Zhidong yu Guangya shuyuan* 張之洞與廣雅書院 (Zhang Zhidong and the Guangya Academy) (Taibei: Zhongguo wenhua daxue, Chubanbu, 1983), pp. 1–122.

conservative camp—headed by the Empress Dowager Cixi 慈禧 (1835–1908)—who put an abrupt end to the reforms. He is perceived as an opportunist who at first helped the reformers but then participated in their suppression as the political winds shifted.[2] This controversial figure deserves our special attention today as we ponder the complex origins of Chinese modernity. If indeed, as David Der-wei Wang points out, the incipient modernity of the late Qing has been "repressed" due to our preoccupation with the revolutionary ethos and May Fourth radicalism,[3] we need to re-examine Zhang's reformism as part of our efforts to evaluate late Qing modernity.

One often-cited example of Zhang's "conservatism" is the *Quanxue pian* 勸學篇 (An exhortation to learning).[4] Many scholars consider the work a political ploy, written to counter such radical reformers as Kang Youwei 康有爲 (1858–1927) and Liang Qichao 梁啓超 (1873–1929).[5] Written in 1898, this work is understood as an argument for limited reform, delineating what could and could not be changed. With the statement "Chinese learning for the fundamental principles and Western learning for the practical applica-

---

2. See, e.g., Cai Zhensheng 蔡振生, *Zhang Zhidong jiaoyu sixiang yanjiu* 張之洞教育思想研究 (A study of Zhang Zhidong's educational thought) (Shenyang: Liaoning jiaoyu chubanshe, 1994), pp. 125–27; Chen Jun 陳鈞, *Rujia xintai yu jindai zhuiqiu—Zhang Zhidong jingji sixiang lunxi* 儒家心態與近代追求－張之洞經濟思想論析 (The Confucian mentality and contemporary pursuits—a study of Zhang Zhidong's economic thought) (Huanggang: Hupei renmin chubanshe, 1990), pp. 163–91; Feng Tianyu 馮天瑜, *Zhang Zhidong pingzhuan* 張之洞評傳 (A critical biography of Zhang Zhidong) (Zhengzhou: Henan jiaoyu chubanshe, 1985), pp. 201–33; Tang Zhijun 湯志鈞, *Jindai jingxue yu zhengzhi* 近代經學與政治 (Classical studies and politics in modern China) (Beijing: Zhonghua shuju, 1989), pp. 216–29; Zhang Bingduo 張秉鐸, *Zhang Zhidong pingzhuan* 張之洞評傳 (A critical biography of Zhang Zhidong) (Taibei: Zhonghua shuju, 1972), pp. 19–46.

3. On the repressed modernity of the late Qing, see David Der-wei Wang, *Fin-de-Siècle Splendor: Repressed Modernities of Late Qing Fiction, 1849–1911* (Stanford: Stanford University Press, 1997), pp. 13–52.

4. This study of the *Quanxue pian* is based on the version in Zhang Zhidong, *Zhang Wenxiang gong quanji* 張文襄公全集 (The complete works of the Honorable Zhang Wenxiang [Zhang Zhidong]) (Taipei: Wenhai chubanshe, 1963); hereafter cited as "*QJ*" followed by *juan* and page numbers.

5. Cai, *Zhang Zhidong jiaoyu*, pp. 125–27; Feng, *Zhang Zhidong pingzhuan*, pp. 201–33; Tang Zhijun 湯志鈞, *Wuxu bianfa shi* 戊戌變法史 (The history of the 1898 reforms) (Beijing: Renmin chubanshe, 1984), pp. 325–33; Zhang Bingduo, *Zhang Zhidong pingzhuan*, pp. 19–46; Zhou, *Zhang Zhidong yu Guangya shuyuan*, pp. 117–22.

tions" (*Zhongxue wei ti, xixue wei yong* 中學爲體，西學爲用), the *Quanxue pian* is remembered as yet another example of resistance to modernization.[6]

Although there is much to be learned from this reading, nonetheless it ignores the context in which the work was produced. The original intent of the *Quanxue pian* was to offer, in a time of crisis for China, a proposal for comprehensive reform. Rather than a summation of late Qing reformism or a rebuttal of Kang and Liang, it was part of the ongoing debate on how to change the country based on critical re-examination of its institutions and substantial borrowings from the West. This chapter offers a new reading of the *Quanxue pian* as Zhang Zhidong's attempt to reconcile two extreme views that appeared around 1898—the radical reformers' plan for drastic sociopolitical changes with little regard to their practicality, and the conservative reformers' preoccupation with preserving Chinese tradition at all costs. The work was intended for a wide audience with different opinions on reform. A detailed analysis of the reform proposals in the *Quanxue pian* will show, I think, Zhang's contribution to expanding the scope of reform from superficial technological transfers to thoroughgoing social and educational changes. Despite the Empress Dowager Cixi's suppression of the reforms, many of Zhang's proposed social and educational changes were eventually implemented. Some of them even outlasted the Qing and continued in effect after the 1911 revolution.

Quanxue pian *and* Ti-yong

The *Quanxue pian* is often read as Zhang Zhidong's proposal for limited reform in China. One often-cited example of Zhang's conservatism is his bifurcation of Chinese learning and Western learning. By privileging Chinese learning as primary and essential (*ti* 體), and downplaying Western learning as secondary and supportive (*yong* 用), Zhang is said to have found a justification for limited reform. He camouflaged his conservatism, some scholars suggest, by sponsoring reform in areas designated *yong* and rejecting reform in areas labeled *ti*.[7]

---

6. Chen, *Rujia xintai*, pp. 163–91; Li Zehou 李澤厚, *Zhongguo xiandai sixiangshi lun* 中國現代思想史論 (A study of the intellectual history of modern China) (Beijing: Dongfang chubanshe, 1987), pp. 311–43; Joseph Levenson, *Confucian China and Its Modern Fate: A Trilogy* (Berkeley: University of California Press, 1958), pp. 59–78; Tang Zhijun, *Wuxu bianfa shi*, pp. 571–84.

7. Li, *Zhongguo xiandai*, pp. 311–43; Levenson, *Confucian China*, pp. 59–78.

Among the early critics who saw the *Quanxue pian* in this light was Liang Qichao. In his *Intellectual Trends in the Qing Period* (1921), Liang distinguished Zhang's reformism from that of Kang Youwei, Tan Sitong 譚嗣同 (1865–98), and himself. He saw Zhang as a conservative reformer, who wanted to restrict China's imports of Western learning to technical skills such as weaponry, mapping, navigation, and military training. By privileging Chinese learning and downplaying Western learning, Zhang denied the younger generation of reformers a chance to found a new school of learning that would be "neither Chinese nor Western but in fact both Chinese and Western."[8] In a subtle way, Liang attributed the failure of the reforms to the rigid mind-set of Zhang, who failed to realize that Chinese learning and Western learning could be freely mixed.[9]

In depicting Zhang negatively, Liang's intention might have been to make him a scapegoat for the failure of the reforms,[10] but in the process he drew scholars' attention to the alleged difference between Zhang's reformism and that of Kang and himself. The *ti-yong* 體用 formula has subsequently been seen as the main point separating the two groups of reformers. Some contemporary scholars even see this division as illustrating the different social origins of the late Qing reformers. In this view, Zhang is a "feudal bureaucratic reformist," whose scholar-gentry background led him to employ *ti-yong* to reject change in the Confucian sociopolitical order. In contrast, Kang and

---

8. Liang Qichao, *Yinbing shi heji* 飲冰室合集 (Collected writings from the Ice-Drinker's Studio) (Beijing: Zhonghua shuju, 1989 [1939]), "zhuanji" 34: 71. Cf. Immanuel C. Y. Hsu, trans., *Intellectual Trends in the Ch'ing Period* by Liang Qichao (Cambridge, Mass.: Harvard University Press, 1959), p. 113.

9. Besides Liang Qichao, Yan Fu 嚴復 (1854–1921) was another early critic of Zhang's usage of *ti-yong*. In an open letter to the editor of *Waijiao bao* 外交報 (Foreign affairs magazine) in 1902, he compared Zhang's bifurcation of Chinese learning and Western learning to mixing "the *ti* of an oxen with the *yong* of a horse" (*Yan Fu ji* 嚴復集 [Collected works of Yan Fu], ed. Wang Shi [Beijing: Zhonghua shuju, 1986], pp. 557–65). But, as Wang Ermin (*Wan Qing zhengzhi*, pp. 51–55) points out, Yan Fu's criticism attracted less attention from later scholars than Liang's because he did not explicitly direct his criticism toward Zhang.

10. Wang Rongzu 汪榮祖 (*Wan Qing bianfa*, p. 122), for one, has found Liang Qichao's picture of Zhang Zhidong's reformism suspicious. Wang's suspicion is not unwarranted if we keep in mind that, from 1895 to early 1898, Liang had worked for Zhang in various capacities, including editing the *Shiwu bao* 時務報 in Shanghai and teaching in the Current Affairs Academy (Shiwu xuetang 時務學堂) in Hunan. Since after the failure of the hundred days of reform, Zhang remained in power and Liang was forced to flee the country, Liang had reason to clarify his relationship with Zhang during the eventful months of 1898.

Liang are "capitalistic reformers" suspicious of *ti-yong* because of their desire for more radical change.[11]

Certainly, to gain a complete picture of the 1898 reforms, we need to compare Zhang's reformism with that of Kang and Liang. But the comparison is too narrow in scope when it is based exclusively on *ti-yong*. We need to remember that *ti-yong* consists of two key concepts—*ti* (substance or fundamental principle) and *yong* (function or practical application). Together they denote an organic relationship between two subjects or two kinds of learning, but their specific meanings vary according to usage and context. Because of its creative ambiguity, *ti-yong* was widely used in late nineteenth-century China to characterize the reformers' attempts to balance the need for reform with the need to preserve the status quo. The term did not, however, prescribe the specific contents of reform or strategies of implementation.[12] More important, since the 1860s, many reformers had used the notion to justify a critical evaluation of the Chinese tradition and substantial imports of Western learning. Zhang was neither the first, nor the only one, to use the pair of concepts. Although it is acceptable to say that Zhang's *Quanxue pian* captured the spirit of the times, it is a distortion to say that Zhang perpetuated conservatism in the late Qing by inventing *ti-yong*.[13]

Furthermore, the *Quanxue pian* makes few references to *ti-yong*. And Zhang seldom used the two terms to make broad sweeping generalizations about the nature of Chinese learning and Western learning. In those few instances in which he referred to Chinese learning as *ti* and Western learning as *yong*, he was less rigid than some critics have suggested. For instance, in discussing the curriculum for the proposed nationwide school system,

---

11. Tang Zhijun 湯志鈞, *Wuxu bianfa renwu zhuan'gao* 戊戌變法人物傳稿 (Draft biographies of historical figures in the 1898 reforms) (Beijing: Zhonghua shuju, 1982), pp. 571–84; idem, *Jindai jingxue*, pp. 216–29.

12. To draw attention to this creative ambiguity of *ti-yong*, I avoid giving *ti* and *yong* a definite translation in this chapter. Instead, I explain what *ti* and *yong* mean in different situations. For a discussion of the changing meanings of *ti-yong* in late nineteenth-century China, see Tze-ki Hon, "Ti-yong Theory," in *Modern China: An Encyclopedia of History, Culture, and Nationalism*, ed. Wang Ke-wen, pp. 354–55 (New York: Garland, 1998). For a discussion of the manifold intellectual possibilities that *ti-yong* generated during the late Qing period, see Timothy Weston's chapter in this volume.

13. On the widespread use of *ti-yong* during the late Qing period, see Wang Ermin, *Wan Qing zhengzhi*, pp. 55–81; and Xue, *Wan Qing zhongti xiyong*, pp. 39–159.

Zhang said, "[Students should] be studying both the new learning and the old learning. The old learning includes the Four Books and the Five Classics, Chinese historical facts, political treatises, and geographical studies. The new learning includes Western politics, technology, and history. The old learning is the *ti* and the new learning is the *yong*. Both should be given equal attention."[14] In Zhang's mind, Western or the new learning included a broad range of humanistic studies such as history and politics. It was not limited to technological skills, as Liang Qichao suggested. Furthermore, Zhang regarded both Chinese and Western learning as equally important subjects for students to master. His statement "the old learning is the *ti* and the new learning is the *yong*" was not intended to privilege Chinese learning over Western learning, but to indicate that students should master Chinese learning before beginning to study Western learning. Here *ti-yong* represents not so much a judgment of cultural value as a temporal sequence. Zhang wanted students to "give equal attention" to both types of learning in order to come to terms with the drastic changes facing China.

As Luke Kwong has pointed out, the *ti-yong* formula in the *Quanxue pian* should be placed in the wider context of the late Qing search for talent.[15] For Zhang as well as for other reformers, the pair of concepts expressed the desire for a new "late Qing personality ideal" to deal with the country's domestic and foreign problems. The new talents, well versed in both Chinese and Western learning, were to shoulder the responsibility for rejuvenating China based on an understanding of Confucian statecraft and a command of global knowledge. Despite their unconventional interpretations of Confucianism, Kang and Liang were exemplars of this late Qing ideal. Both of them had received a traditional Chinese schooling and had passed the civil-service examinations. They also possessed, by the standards of the times, a good grasp of foreign knowledge (based on translations). Their "biculturalism," one may argue, was one reason why Zhang initially endorsed their quest for broadening the reforms. For instance, he gave Liang a chance to spread his views by employing him as an editor of newspapers such as *Shiwu bao* 時務報 (Current affairs news) and allowing him to teach in the academies he had recently opened.

---

14. *QJ* 203.9b.

15. Luke S. K. Kwong, "The T'i-yung Dichotomy and the Search for Talent in Late-Ch'ing China," *Modern Asian Studies* 27 (1993): 253–79.

Hence, rather than separating Zhang from Kang and Liang, *ti-yong* was probably what brought them together from 1895 to early 1898.[16]

Quanxue pian *and Popular Power*

The *Quanxue pian* is also seen as Zhang's attempt to stop Kang and Liang from launching constitutional reform based on popular power (*minquan* 民 權).[17] As Ding Weizhi has argued, the *Quanxue pian* shows the fundamental difference between Zhang as a Qing official interested in "foreign affairs" (*yangwu pai* 洋務派) and Kang and Liang as "constitutional reformers" (*weixin pai* 維新派).[18]

There is both internal and external support for this reading. A few contemporary accounts, including a memoir by Zhang's secretary Gu Hongming 辜鴻銘 (1857–1928), suggest that Zhang's intention in writing the work was to "refute Kang and Liang."[19] Furthermore, the biography of Zhang in the *Qingshi gao* 清史稿 (Draft of Qing history) even identifies the publication of *Quanxue pian* as the sole reason for Zhang's not being disciplined after the 1898 coup.[20] Of course, the most important evidence of Zhang's opposition to popular power can be found in the *Quanxue pian* itself. Zhang devoted all of Chapter 6 of Part I to refuting the ability of the people

---

16. As Timothy Weston points out in his chapter in this volume, in 1898 Liang Qichao used the *ti-yong* formula in his proposal for the establishment of the Imperial University in Beijing. William Ayers (*Chang Chih-tung and Educational Reform*, pp. 138–44) also acknowledges the intellectual link between Zhang on the one hand and Kang and Liang on the other.

17. On rendering *minquan* as "popular power," see Peter G. Zarrow, "Introduction," in *Imagining the People: Chinese Intellectuals and the Concept of Citizenship, 1890–1920*, ed. Joshua A. Fogel and Peter G. Zarrow, pp. 3–38 (Armonk, N.Y.: M. E. Sharpe, 1997); and Joan Judge, *Print and Politics: "Shibao" and the Culture of Reform in Late Qing China* (Stanford: Stanford University Press, 1996), pp. 146–60. On the *Quanxue pian* as Zhang's attempt to stop Kang and Liang from launching constitutional reform, see Bays, *China Enters the Twentieth Century*, pp. 32, 43–53; and Feng, *Zhang Zhidong pingzhuan*, pp. 201–33.

18. Ding Weizhi 丁偉志, "Zhongti xiyong lun zai wuxu weixin shiqi de shanbian" 中體 西用論在戊戌維新時期的嬗變 (The development of the debate on Chinese substance and Western practicality during the 1898 reform period), *Lishi yanjiu* 1994, no. 1: 137–54.

19. Gu Hongming 辜鴻銘, "Zhang Wenxiang mufu jiwen" 張文襄幕府紀文 (Remembrances of the governor's office of Zhang Wenxiang [Zhang Zhidong]), in *Gu Hongmin wenji* 辜鴻銘文集 (Collected writings of Gu Hongming), pt. I, ed. Wang Xingtao, p. 416 (Haikou: Hainan chubanshe, 1996 [1902]). Cf. *QJ* 228.18a.

20. Zhang's biography in the *Qingshi gao*, reprinted in *QJ* 1a.27a.

to govern themselves. For him, advocates of the sovereign power of the people misunderstood what the concept meant in the West. Instead of the people having the power to govern themselves, popular power meant the government should listen to the people. The Western advocacy of popular power was meant to encourage a controlled dialogue between the ruler and the ruled through such institutions as parliament and provincial assemblies. This dialogue was not meant to disrupt the existing social and political hierarchy.[21]

Although Zhang's knowledge of Western concepts of popular power was rudimentary, he had a point in separating the parliamentary system from popular power. Zhang affirmed the value of the parliamentary system as a political institution for public discussion of governmental affairs (*gongyi* 公議), although he thought that China had no immediate need to adopt it.[22] For him, based on a reading of *Mencius*, the people had the right to air their grievances to the government, and the government had the responsibility to take care of the people. He did not doubt that the introduction of a Western-style parliamentary system would help improve communications between the rulers and the ruled. What he objected to, however, was the hasty attempt to introduce the system without sufficient preparation. Since many Chinese were still ill-informed about their own country and the world, he foresaw a danger in allowing the masses to engage in "unfocused talk and useless speech" (*youtan yiyu* 游談囈語) in a parliament.[23] One danger was the waste of time and resources in electing representatives who had little to offer in governing the country. Another was the disruption of social order that would result when idlers took advantage of the parliamentary debates to advance their own interests.[24] For Zhang, who vividly remembered the widespread destruction and the many deaths that had resulted from the Taiping Rebellion (1851–64), the second danger could have particularly serious consequences. He wrote:

Although today's China is not powerful, its people are contented with their work due to the law and order provided by the [Qing] government. If the advocacy of popular power continues to spread, then fools will be happy to adopt it and rebels

21. *QJ* 202.24b–25a.
22. Ibid., 26a–b.
23. Ibid., 23a.
24. Ibid., 23a–24a.

will be ready to take action. Subsequently law and order will be difficult to maintain, and rebellions will arise in all corners of the country.[25]

In categorically rejecting the people's power to govern themselves (but endorsing their power to air grievances), Zhang was in disagreement with the Kang-Liang group. On several occasions, he intervened to stop the discussion of popular power in *Shiwu bao* and *Xiang xue bao* 湘學報.[26] However, it is doubtful that he wrote the *Quanxue pian* (particularly Chapter 6 of Part I) solely to refute Kang and Liang. The late Qing discussion of popular power involved a large number of people. Certainly Yan Fu 嚴復 (1854–1921) was one of the first to criticize the imperial system for not letting the people govern themselves,[27] and in some sectors he was considered the spokesman for the idea.[28] There were as well many advocates of popular power in the Chinese littoral, which Zhang referred to as "the foreign sphere on the coast" (*haibin yangjie* 海濱洋界).[29] For example, Hu Liyuan 胡禮垣 (1874–1916) and He Qi 何啓 (1858–1914), known to some as the "comprador ideologists," wrote extensively in Hong Kong promoting parliamentary government in China.[30] Some Westerners residing in the treaty ports (such

---

25. Ibid., 24a. For the impact of the Taiping Rebellion on Zhang, see Hu Jun 胡鈞, *Qing Zhang Wenxiang gong Zhidong nianpu* 清張文襄公之洞年譜 (An annotated biography of Zhang Zhidong of the Qing dynasty) (Taiwan: Shangwu yinshuguan, 1978), pp. 11–15.

26. For an account of Zhang's intervention in the discussion of popular power in *Shiwu bao*, see Seungjoo Yoon's chapter in this volume. For Zhang's suppression of discussion of popular power in *Xiang xue pao*, see Su Yu 蘇輿, ed., *Yijiao congbian* 翼教叢編 (A general collection to protect the faith) (Taibei: Tailianfang chubanshe, 1970 [1898]), 6.1a; and Ayers, *Chang Chih-tung and Educational Reform*, pp. 144–52.

27. Yan, *Yan Fu ji*, pp. 32–36; Benjamin Schwartz, *In Search of Wealth and Power: Yen Fu and the West* (Cambridge, Mass.: Harvard University Press, 1964), pp. 130–48.

28. Su Yu, *Yijiao congbian*, 3.26a–29b.

29. *QJ* 202.14b–15a.

30. He Qi and Hu Liyuan are called the "comprador ideologists" because they were based in Hong Kong and spent most of their lives working with the British. See Jung-fang Tsai, "The Predicament of the Comprador Ideologists He Qi and Hu Liyuan," *Modern China* 7, no. 2 (1981): 191–225. In the 1890s, He and Hu published a series of essays promoting parliamentary government in China. These essays were later grouped together in *Xinzheng zhenquan* 新政眞詮 (A true interpretation of the New Policies; reprinted—Shenyang: Liaoning renmin chubanshe, 1994) in 1902. In the book, they criticized Kang for forcing Western political institutions to fit his own interpretation of Confucianism and condemned Zhang for refusing to adopt parliamentary government in his reform proposal. Based on Social Darwinism, they believed that the evolution of human society had rendered the Chinese political system obso-

as Timothy Richard, 1845–1919) freely offered advice on how to reform Chinese political institutions. By not specifying the target of his refutation in the *Quanxue pian*, Zhang was apparently addressing the broad discussion of popular power rather than Kang and Liang in particular.

Zhang's opposition to the discussion of popular power can be contextualized in other ways as well. As Joseph Esherick has suggested, although the notion of "the people" (*min* 民) was frequently invoked in the debate on popular power before 1898, there was little interest in discussing individual liberty.[31] The focus of the debate was not the equality of all members of the polity but the right of the lower-level gentry and scholars to participate in policy discussions and decision making so that peripheral members (for example, Liang Qichao, Tan Sitong) would be included in the political process. It is anachronistic to inject ideas such as republicanism and democracy into the popular power debate. In suppressing the discussion of popular power, Zhang's intention was to stop what he considered to be the unregulated increase of power among the lower echelons of the scholar-gentry.

Balancing Two Extreme Views

If the *Quanxue pian* was not intended just to refute Kang and Liang, then why was it written? One way to answer the question is to examine Zhang's introduction (*xu* 序) to the work and his explanation of his purpose in writing the piece. He began with a reminder to his readers that China was experiencing a "drastic transformation" (*shibian* 世 變).[32] His use of the phrase "drastic transformation" is noteworthy. It is significant because he employed exactly the same wording that the reformer Yan Fu had used three years earlier in the wake of China's defeat in the Sino-Japanese War

---

lete, and hence China needed a more advanced political system such as parliamentary government (*Xinzheng zhenquan*, pp. 247–75, 335–427).

31. Joseph Esherick, *Reform and Revolution in China: The 1911 Revolution in Hunan and Hubei* (Berkeley: University of California Press, 1979), pp. 16–18. See also Luke S. K. Kwong, *T'an Ssu-T'ung, 1865–1898: Life and Thought of a Reformer* (Leiden: E. J. Brill, 1996), pp. 171–94; and Ingo Shafer, "The People, People's Rights, and Rebellion: The Development of Tan Sitong's Political Thought," in *Imagining the People: Chinese Intellectuals and the Concept of Citizenship, 1890–1920*, ed. Joshua A. Fogel and Peter G. Zarrow, pp. 82–112 (Armonk, N.Y.: M. E. Sharpe, 1997).

32. *QJ* 202.xu 1a. For Yan Fu's discussion of the "drastic transformation," see Yan, *Ji*, pp. 1–5.

(1894–95) to describe China's immense problems in entering the modern age. More important, he stressed (once again following Yan Fu) the uniqueness of the problems by characterizing them as unprecedented in the history of China. Unique problems called for drastic measures to change the country. Hence, by stressing China's urgent need to reform itself, he expressed his strong support for reforming Chinese society and political institutions.

As a response to this drastic transformation, Zhang found the intense debate on reform healthy because it was bringing the best minds in the country together to solve its internal and external problems. However, he was deeply troubled by the division of the literati into opposing camps. He was particularly saddened by the intense debate between the advocates of the new learning, who favored substantial borrowing from the West, and the advocates of the old learning, who wanted to preserve the Chinese tradition.[33] Blinded by their extreme positions, both groups, he charged, failed to realize their own shortcomings. The advocates of the new learning were "horses without reins" (*qiduo er yangwang* 歧多而羊亡), because they knew only about borrowing extensively from abroad but failed to relate the borrowing to Chinese needs. The advocates of the old learning were people who "stopped eating altogether because of a hiccup" (*yinyi er shifei* 因噎而食廢), because they ignored the problems confronting China once the authority of traditional learning was challenged.[34]

The tragedy of the debate, according to Zhang, was that both sides were partially right and yet they held on to their side of the solution at the expense of the other. The advocates of the old learning were right in wanting to preserve Chinese cultural identity and historical continuity. Yet, by opposing any change in the Chinese traditional institutions, they offered nothing to solve the country's current problems (*bu zhi tong* 不知通). In the same vein, the advocates of the new learning were right in trying to update

---

33. *QJ* 202.xu 1a. In the late Qing writings, "Chinese learning versus Western learning" and "the old learning versus the new learning" were often used interchangeably to denote the literati's anxiety about mastering domestic and foreign knowledge. Xiaobing Tang (*Global Space and the Nationalist Discourse of Modernity: The Historical Thinking of Liang Qichao* [Stanford: Stanford University Press, 1996], pp. 16–18) points out that around 1895 the emphasis shifted to "the old learning versus the new learning." Zhang Zhidong's introduction to *Quanxue pian* appears to exemplify this trend.

34. *QJ* 202.xu 1b.

Chinese institutions by borrowing from the West. But, by making too many changes, they were turning China into a foreign country (*bu zhi ben* 不 知 本).[35] Worse yet, with both sides refusing to listen to each other, the debate had turned into a nationwide polemic that divided the country and delayed the effort to strengthen it. For this reason, Zhang considered the source of China's problems no longer to be from without but from within. It was the debate over reform, rather than the threat coming from the West, that was causing the country's downfall.[36]

Zhang was not exaggerating when he described the reform debate as the source of China's downfall. The intensity of the debate is apparent in the polemical writings collected in *Yijiao congbian* 翼 教 叢 編 (A general collection to protect the faith) and *Xiangbao leizuan* 湘 報 類 纂 (*Hunan Journal*, topically arranged). Representing the views of conservatives in Hunan, the writings in *Yijiao congbian* condemn the Kang-Liang group for forsaking the Way of the Sage. In contrast, the essays in *Xiangbao leizuan* blame the conservatives for living in the past. This polemic shows the extent to which the reform debate had split the literati in Hunan. To some degree, the split was generational, particularly between the established scholars (like Zhu Yixin 朱 一 新 [1846–94]) and young and rising scholars (like Liang Qichao). But the split was also between open-minded officials like Governor Chen Baozhen 陳 寶 箴 (1831–1900) and Educational Commissioner Xu Renzhu 徐 仁 鑄 (1860–1900) and conservative scholars, such as Wang Xianqian 王 先 謙 (1842–1917) and Ye Dehui 葉 德 輝 (1864–1927). The split among the literati was so widespread that it had the potential for paralyzing the provincial government of Hunan.

To redirect the attention of the literati away from the reform polemics and toward concrete efforts at reforming the country, Zhang wrote *Quanxue pian*. His goal was to remind the two sides in the debate that China needed everyone to cooperate in order to survive in the global competition for power and wealth. To come to terms with the unprecedented drastic transformation facing the country, Zhang argued, China required a critical evaluation of its traditional institutions as well as a global vision. Because of this, both the advocates of the old learning and the advocates of the new learning had a role to play in rejuvenating the country. True to its title—an exhortation to

---

35. Ibid.
36. Ibid.

learning—Zhang intended *Quanxue pian* to be an invitation to both groups to learn to appreciate one another.[37]

Following the Right Sequence of Learning

Given Zhang's purpose in writing the *Quanxue pian*, the division of the work into Inner Chapters (*nei pian* 內篇) and Outer Chapters (*wai pian* 外篇) makes sense. The two parts, each directed to a specific audience, were attempts to locate the common ground between the two opposing camps in the debate over reform.

In the Inner Chapters, Zhang aimed his remarks at the advocates of the new learning and addressed their indiscriminate borrowing from the West by stressing the importance of "being concerned with the basis" (*wu ben* 務本).[38] In the nine chapters in this section, he discussed, among other issues, the way the Qing government had improved the livelihood of the people, the Three Bonds (emperor-official, father-son, husband-wife) as the cornerstone of Chinese tradition, the embodiment of the truth in the Confucian classics, and why the idea of popular power did not fit China's needs. Seemingly didactic and uncreative from today's perspective, Zhang vigorously defined the boundaries of reform. For him, any reform was welcome so long as it strengthened the country and did not challenge the legitimacy of the Qing rule, the primacy of the Three Bonds, and the authority of the Confucian classics.

Why did Zhang want to set limits on reform when China seemed to require more widespread borrowing from the West? Was Zhang not conservative in laying down preconditions for reform? In the "Following the Sequence" ("Xun xu" 循序) chapter, he explained the reasons a proper sequence in learning was needed.

Nowadays if we want to strengthen China and preserve Chinese learning, we must study Western learning. Yet, if someone [studies Western learning] without first firmly being rooted in Chinese learning to cultivate his character, he may become a rebel leader if he has a strong body and a slave if he is weak. He will cause more harm [to society] than a person who knows nothing about Western learning.[39]

---

37. Ibid., 3b–4a; *QJ* 228.14a. Daniel Bays (*China Enters the Twentieth Century*, pp. 43–45) aptly calls Zhang's attitude the "distinct middle-of-the-road position."

38. *QJ* 202.xu 2a.

39. *QJ* 202.27a.

In emphasizing the importance of a proper sequence of learning, Zhang was responding to the rapid increase in the demand for Western learning after China's defeat in the Sino-Japanese War. The defeat further exposed China's military weaknesses and demonstrated the inadequacy of the technological reforms pursued by the Self-Strengthening Movement. The defeat made many Chinese aware of how far their country lagged in the global competition. Many of them were convinced that more drastic reform—especially in education, social practices, and political institutions—was necessary to modernize China. On the one hand, Zhang was delighted to see this increase in the demand for Western learning because it helped to widen the scope of reform in China from superficial technological transfers to basic changes in social and educational structures. On the other hand, he was worried that the desire to learn from the West might have gone too far. To his knowledge, some Chinese in treaty ports and coastal cities had already demonstrated their sense of cultural inferiority by adopting foreign names, foreign clothing, the seven-day Christian calendar, and foreign citizenship. Some of them even publicly advocated the abolition of the Three Bonds.[40]

It was in response to this rise in a sense of cultural inferiority in the coastal treaty ports that Zhang suggested the three preconditions for reform. His intent was to address the problem of excessive Westernization of some coastal Chinese, rather than to counter the radical reformism of Kang and Liang. For Zhang, Chinese learning had to come first in training the new talent, because it provided the literati with a cultural identity and a historical consciousness. It helped them clarify the purpose and the scope of reform in China.[41]

Were Zhang's political, social, and cultural preconditions for reform restrictive? At first glance, Zhang's "conservatism" is apparent in his reaffirmation of the Qing's legitimacy, the patrilineal hierarchy, and Confucian dogma. He appeared to set a limit to the reforms by excluding change in those three areas. Arguably, Zhang's success in reforming Hunan and Hubei provinces may have led him to think that he had found an ideal model for a government-led, top-down reform in China.[42] Nonetheless, we should

---

40. Ibid., 14b–17b.

41. Ibid., 17b–18a.

42. Three years before the hundred days of reform, Zhang helped to lead a massive social and economic reform in the backward and parochial provinces of Hunan and Hubei. With the help of the local gentry and the able governor Chen Baozhen, he brought mining, tele-

not forget that in his time Zhang's three preconditions were equivalent to a least common denominator for defining "China." In the late 1890s, although there were some rumblings in the background questioning Qing rule and Confucian orthodoxy, there was no overt opposition to the existing social and political system, let alone plans to replace it. Furthermore, looked at from a slightly different angle, Zhang's alleged conservatism can be seen as the basis for aggressive reform. Having set minimum requirements for what should remain unchanged, he earned the freedom (particularly from the constraints that the narrow-minded conservatives would impose) to initiate reform in almost all areas outside the three preconditions. The preconditions, one might say, were the façade for drastic reform.

This radical aspect of Zhang's thought was made apparent in his discussion of the Way (*dao* 道) and the institutions (*fa* 法). For him, the Way never changed. Speaking like a dogmatist, he identified the unchanging Way as the social hierarchy and the moral codes defined by Confucian teachings. In a nutshell, the Way was the Three Bonds and the Four Basic Virtues (ritual behavior, justice, integrity, and honor).[43] But although he was rigid about the Way, he was extremely flexible about changing traditional institutions. Not unlike Kang Youwei,[44] Zhang told his readers that all institutions were malleable, for they were meant to change in accordance with the needs of the times. He cited numerous examples from history—including the eleventh-century reformer Wang Anshi 王安石 (1021–86)—to prove that institutional change had been common in Chinese history.[45] To the stubborn opponents of reform, he proclaimed: "What remains constant

---

graph, electricity, and a new road system to the two provinces. He also experimented with testing candidates on Western knowledge in the provincial examination and revitalizing the old academies as an alternative means of spreading Western learning. Many of these reforms, especially the educational reform, found their way into the *Quanxue pian*. For a study of Zhang's educational reform in Hunan and Hubei, see Ayers, *Chang Chih-tung and Educational Reform*, pp. 137–95; and Bays, *China Enters the Twentieth Century*, pp. 37–43.

43. *QJ* 203.19b–22b.

44. In *Kongzi gaizhi kao* 孔子改制考 (A study of Confucius as a reformer; 1897), Kang Youwei reinterpreted Confucianism as a philosophy of institutional reform; see Kung-chuan Hsiao, *A Modern China and a New World: K'ang Yu-wei, Reformer and Utopian, 1858–1927* (Seattle: University of Washington Press, 1975), pp. 97–136. Although Zhang did not express his aspiration for institutional reform in bold terms or espouse a grand reinterpretation of Confucianism as Kang did, he underscored that none of the tradition-honored institutions remained unchanged throughout history.

45. *QJ* 203.20a–22b.

is the human bonds, not the tradition-honored institutions; the Way of the Sage, not the machinery; the moral codes, not the technical skills."[46] By specifying what had to be preserved, he marked out a huge area in which change was welcome. With a nuanced argument, he turned what at first appeared to be an attempt to set limits to reform into a plea for drastic change.

Social and Economic Reform

Whereas Zhang targeted the Inner Chapters at the advocates of the new learning, he aimed the Outer Chapters at the advocates of the old learning. The goal of the Outer Chapters, as he put it, was to remind his readers "to be concerned with current affairs" (wu tong 務通).[47] In the fifteen chapters in this section, he repeatedly admonished his readers that they were not allowing reform to take its own course. He called them narrow-minded for wanting to preserve the status quo and living in the past. To show his own vision of reform, he laid out a blueprint for drastic social and economic reform.

To change China socially, Zhang planned to reform the civil-service examination system. He wanted to change the contents of the examinations— the ladder of success for all educated males—so that a new type of scholarship would emerge throughout the country and a new kind of talent would enter the government. Although he did not recommend the abolition of the eight-legged essay as Yan Fu and Liang Qichao had proposed,[48] he was equally committed to testing candidates' practical knowledge and global vision. The centerpiece of his examination reform was the establishment of three separate examinations—testing knowledge of Chinese statecraft at the district level, testing world knowledge at the provincial level, and testing mastery of the Confucian classics at the national level.[49] By removing poetry and the eight-legged essays altogether from the examinations and by delaying the examination of the candidates' command of the Confucian classics until the very end, Zhang stressed the importance of mastering practical knowledge in government and managing the economy in the new examination system. In Zhang's vision, the source of practical knowledge, as shown

---

46. Ibid., 19b.
47. QJ 202.xu 2a.
48. Yan Fu, Ji, 5–15; Liang, Yinbing shi heji, "wenji," 1: 21–30.
49. QJ 203.24b–25a.

in the first two levels of the examinations, was both China and the rest of the world. This arrangement was a tacit acceptance of China's membership in the global community of nations. And by capping the examinations with testing the examinee's knowledge of the Confucian classics, Zhang silenced his conservative critics and addressed the problem of the excessive Westernization of coastal Chinese.

Supporting this new examination system was a nationwide school system. This new school system would have a standard curriculum to train examination candidates.[50] Paralleling closely the three levels of the civil-service examination system—district, provincial, and national—the school system would likewise be divided into three levels: primary schools at the district level, secondary schools at the provincial level, and a university at the national level.[51] At each level, students were to be taught a mixture of Chinese and Western learning that emphasized mathematics, geography, and politics. Increased efforts to translate foreign books and to publish newspapers would give both students and readers at large better access to global knowledge. By combining training in school and the knowledge gained through outside reading, students in the new educational system would have a global vision.[52] Certainly, Zhang's proposals for reforming the civil-service examinations and the school system were not entirely his own creation; there had been a discussion of reform in these two areas since the 1880s.[53] Nonetheless, he deserves credit for proposing a coherent plan for founding a system for training new talent.

In economics, Zhang focused on ensuring the self-sufficiency of the Chinese economy. He suggested the introduction of better mining technology (particularly in coal mining) to reduce China's reliance on foreign imports.[54] He recommended building an efficient railroad system to improve transportation and bring the whole country together with a strong sense of na-

---

50. Ibid., 12a–13b.

51. Ibid., 8a–b.

52. Ibid., 9a–11b, 14a–18b.

53. For an account of different proposals for changing the civil-service examination and the school systems, see Wang Dezhao 王德昭, *Cong gaige dao geming* 從改革到革命 (From reform to revolution) (Beijing: Zhonghua shuju, 1987), pp. 93–170; and Benjamin A. Elman, *A Cultural History of Civil Examinations in Late Imperial China* (Berkeley: University of California Press, 2000), pp. 569–94.

54. *QJ* 203.40b–41a.

tional identity.[55] To improve China's competitiveness in the global market, he proposed the establishment of specialized vocational schools to train skilled labor in agriculture, manufacturing, and commerce.[56]

More a social than an economic reformer, Zhang believed that the success of economic reform ultimately depended on the success of social reform. Without first eliminating social values that were hindering economic growth, genuine economic reform would not be possible. For instance, the traditional Confucian system of four classes (scholars, peasants, artisans, and merchants) not only perpetuated a long-standing prejudice against agriculture, craftsmanship, and commerce, it also gave the educated elite an excuse not to exercise leadership in any of the other three areas. To rectify this situation, Zhang asked the scholar-gentry and the officials to stop looking down on peasants, artisans, and merchants.

In general, agriculture, craftsmanship, and commerce are interpenetrative and interdependent. If agriculture performs poorly, then artisans suffer. If the standard of craftsmanship declines, then merchants suffer. If both craftsmanship and commerce have lost their vitality, then peasants suffer. If all of the three sectors are in decline, then the whole country is in trouble. . . . Hence, [to make sure that the three sectors are not in decline,] the scholar-gentry and the officials have to participate in reforming their practices.[57]

Although delivered in a measured tone, Zhang's suggestion was radical by the standards of his times. What he advocated was a reduction in the long-standing social barriers separating the four classes so that they would work together as an organic whole.

Partly because of Zhang's plan for reducing social barriers, Min Tu-ki reminds us, some of his contemporaries thought the *Quanxue pian* was written to support the radical reforms of Kang and Liang.[58] One of these perceptive readers was Zhang Binglin 章炳麟 (1868–1936). As a young scholar, he read a draft of *Quanxue pian* in early 1898 when he visited Zhang Zhidong in Wuchang. He did not like the Inner Chapters because of their advocacy

---

55. Ibid., 43b.

56. Ibid., 30a–34b.

57. Ibid., 34a.

58. Tu-ki Min, *National Polity and Local Power: The Transformation of Late Imperial China*, ed. Philip Kuhn and Timothy Brook (Cambridge, Mass.: Harvard University, Council on East Asian Studies, 1989), pp. 74–75.

of loyalty to the Qing court. But he approved of the Outer Chapters, which, he said, "offer an accurate picture" of China's problems.[59]

It is also interesting to note that none of the Outer Chapters was included in the *Yijiao congbian*. To prove that Zhang Zhidong was on their side, the Hunan conservatives included chapters of the *Quanxue pian* in the *Yijiao congbian*. But they selected only four of the Inner Chapters—"On Being Faithful to Confucian Teachings," "On the Three Bonds," "On Knowing One's Race," and "On Popular Power." Those who read only the excerpts in the *Yijiao congbian* but not the entire text of *Quanxue pian* would certainly have the impression that Zhang was an opponent of reform. In their selective inclusion of *Quanxue pian*, the Hunan conservatives appeared to realize that Zhang's reform proposal was a double-edged sword. They embraced the Zhang of the Inner Chapters but kept their distance from the Zhang of the Outer Chapters.

Political Implications of Social and Economic Reform

As noted above, Zhang is identified in current scholarship as a conservative because he rejected the notion of popular power and questioned the desirability of introducing a parliamentary system to China. Zhang seems to be a Janus-like figure, who was aggressive in pursuing social and economic reform but hesitant in initiating political change. For some scholars, this "double nature" reveals Zhang's cunning as an experienced bureaucrat who knew how to bend to the political winds.[60] For others, Zhang's "lack of thoroughness" in reform demonstrates his tragic role in the transition from tradition to modernity, from empire to nation.[61] Despite the apparent absence of political reform in *Quanxue pian*, can we say that it offers no plan for political change? To assess *Quanxue pian* as a proposal for comprehensive reform, we need to examine the political implications of Zhang's proposals.

By reforming the civil-service examinations and establishing a nationwide

---

59. Zhang Binglin 章炳麟, *Taiyan xiansheng ziding nianpu* 太炎先生自訂年譜 (Master Taiyan's annotated year-by-year chronicle of his life) (Taibei: Wenhai chubanshe, 1966), p. 16.

60. Cai, *Zhang Zhidong jiaoyu*, p. 127; Tang Zhijun, *Wuxu bianfa renwu zhuan'gao*, pp. 571–84.

61. Li, *Zhongguo xiandai*, pp. 311–343; Levenson, *Confucian China*, pp. 59–78; Ding, "Zhongti xiyong lun," pp. 150–51.

school system, Zhang wanted to produce people with both practical expertise and global vision. By combining Chinese and Western learning, he intended to cultivate a social milieu in which the two kinds of learning were
seen as an organic whole rather than mutually exclusive. But in initiating
these reforms, one may argue, he also wanted to create a new educated elite
who would enter government service through an improved civil-service examination system. As an official who had spent more than half of his life
working in the Qing bureaucracy, he realized that the conservatives had
many reasons to object to reform, especially political reform. Some were an-
tiquarians; others were by nature skeptical of change. But a large number
were "corrupt bureaucrats" (*suli* 俗吏) who had a vested interest in preserving the political status quo.[62] In other words, the conservatives were not as
ignorant of China's problems as many people assumed; nonetheless, they
would do what they could to protect their interests.

For this reason, Zhang considered social and educational reforms to be
the prerequisite for fundamental change in China. He believed that the conservatives would remain in power unless a new corps of cosmopolitan leaders
emerged to replace them. He also believed that there would always be people
receptive to conservative views until a new set of social values arose. Thus,
genuine change in Chinese political institutions had to begin from the bottom—first in the classroom and then in the examination hall. To under-
score the long-term nature of social and educational reform, Zhang wrote:
"To respond to the pressing problems of the time, we have to reform the
tradition-honored institutions; to reform the tradition-honored institutions,
we have to begin with reform of the civil-service examination system."[63] The
key word in this statement is "to begin" (*shi* 始). For Zhang, the reform of
the civil-service examinations was more than a refinement of the process of
official selection; it was the first step in creating a new society and a new government. It might take years or perhaps decades to take effect, but once the
new society took root, fundamental change in political institutions was possible. It is noteworthy that as late as the beginning of 1898 Liang Qichao appeared to adopt the same approach to political reform as Zhang. In an essay
suggesting changes in Hunan, Liang told Governor Chen Baozhen that
proper training of the masses (by which Liang meant the scholar-gentry and

---

62. *QJ* 203.20b–21a.
63. Ibid., 24a.

the scholar-officials) was fundamental to spreading popular power in China.[64]

In this regard, what separated Zhang from the Kang-Liang group during the reform period was not such abstract notions as the *ti-yong*, and popular power or the commitment to profound change in China. Their main difference lay in the practical steps to be taken to rejuvenate China, including the outmoded political system. The Kang-Liang group, perhaps fueled by youthful euphoria, believed that a few imperial edicts would be sufficient to change the political institutions.[65] For his part, Zhang believed that permanent reform of political institutions entailed changing the bureaucracy and the enormous human network that supplemented it. The Kang-Liang group was optimistic that political reform could be achieved overnight; Zhang thought of reform as a long-term process.

Conclusion

At the end of his introduction to *Quanxue pian*, Zhang stressed that the Inner Chapters and Outer Chapters combined were to explicate the "five kinds of understanding" (*wu zhi* 五 知) needed by the Chinese in the 1890s: (1) the understanding that China was not as good as countries like Japan and Turkey; (2) the understanding that China could be colonized as India and Vietnam had been; (3) the understanding that in order to survive, China had to undertake drastic changes not only in technology but also in institutions and social practices; (4) the understanding that the essence of Chinese learning lay in its application to practical matters and the essence of Western learning lay in its institutions; and (5) the understanding that the Chinese should remain Chinese wherever they were.[66]

In these five kinds of understanding, Zhang cleverly mixed the views of the advocates of the new learning (the first four) with those of the advocates of the old learning (the last). In this regard, *Quanxue pian* achieved what its title claimed—it was an exhortation to learning. It urged the advocates of

---

64. Liang, *Yinbing shi heji*, "wenji" 3: 40–47; *Xiangbao leizuan* 湘 報 類 纂 (*Hunan Journal*, topically arranged) (reprinted—Taipei: Dadong shuju, 1968 [1902]), pp. 222–35.

65. For an insightful discussion of the youthful euphoria of Kang and Liang, see Kong Xiangji 孔 祥 吉, *Wuxu weixin yundong xintan* 戊 戌 維 新 運 動 新 探 (New studies of the 1898 reform movement) (Changsha: Hunan renmin chubanshe, 1988), pp. 358–84.

66. *QJ* 202.xu 3a.

the new learning to treasure their tradition and to reflect on their cultural identity. It encouraged the advocates of the old learning to accept change and to open their eyes to global knowledge. Ultimately, the *Quanxue pian* exhorted both groups to learn from each other, for each of them offered something that China needed at that time—a critical examination of its traditional institutions on the one hand and a global vision on the other.

However, as it turned out, *Quanxue pian* did not alleviate the polemics. Nor did it prevent the bloodshed of the September palace coup d'état and the subsequent crackdown on the reformers. The work remained more Zhang's personal dream for balancing the competing claims of the reformers and the conservatives than an effective measure to calm the country. Some of the proposals in *Quanxue pian*, including the restructuring of the civil-service examinations and the building of a nationwide school system, were implemented in the early 1900s. Yet the opportunity for peaceful and orderly reform based on a critical re-evaluation of Chinese traditional institutions and substantial borrowings from the West seems to have been lost after 1898. In hindsight, the hundred days of reform were tragic not only because they were cut short by the palace coup d'état, but also because after the summer of 1898 the moderate approach to reform that bridged East and West was less and less a viable option. For many decades to come, the attempt to modernize China without sacrificing its cultural uniqueness and history was deemed "conservative," "reactionary," or "fence-sitting." Even onetime radical reformers such as Yan Fu, Kang Youwei, and Zhang Binglin found themselves being labeled "conservatives" for insisting on preserving Chinese tradition. As decisions came to be based more on revolutionary fervor dictated by a belief in progress than on finding a common ground, the moderate position became harder and harder to defend. In this regard, *Quanxue pian* stands out as a plea for moderation before the revolutionary ethos took over China. It serves as a reminder that, a century ago, some Qing officials did try to confront squarely the complexities and ambiguities of modernizing China.

CHAPTER FOUR

The Founding of the Imperial University and the Emergence of Chinese Modernity

Timothy B. Weston

By the end of the sweltering *wuxu* 戊戌 summer of 1898, the radical reformers had either been executed or been forced into exile, and the Empress Dowager Cixi 慈禧 (1835–1908) had overturned the ambitious reform program promulgated by the Guangxu 光緒 emperor (r. 1875–1908), with one significant exception. The Imperial University (Jingshi daxuetang 京師大學堂) was one of the few reform projects to survive Cixi's coup.[1] Even more significant is the fact that the new university, which would be housed in an unoccupied imperial mansion in the heart of the capital just a few minutes' walk from the northern entrance to the Forbidden City, was clearly the brainchild of the radical reformers. Indeed, the regulations for the Imperial University (*daxuetang zhangcheng* 大學堂章程) approved by the Guangxu emperor on July 3, 1898, were prepared by none other than Liang Qichao 梁

I thank Rebecca Karl, Jim Maffie, Tim Oakes, Marcia Yonemoto, Peter Zarrow, and the two anonymous readers for the Harvard University Asia Center for their helpful suggestions. I, of course, bear full responsibility for all weaknesses that remain.

1. Calls for a new imperial university were first made in the aftermath of the Sino-Japanese War of 1894–95, and in 1896 the emperor gave his blessing to the project. However, the university's opening was delayed; serious preparations began only in 1898, after the emperor made the university one of his highest priorities in the June 11, 1898, edict with which he launched the "hundred days of reform." One scholar has calculated that fully a third of that edict addressed the issue of the Imperial University (see Hao Ping 郝平, *Beijing daxue chuangban shishi kaoyuan* 北京大學創辦史實考源 [A study of the historical circumstances of Beijing University's founding] [Beijing: Beijing daxue chubanshe, 1998], p. 174).

啓超 (1873–1929)—to whom Kang Youwei 康有爲 (1858–1927) claimed to have assigned the task because he was too busy.[2]

Scholars of early twentieth-century China writing in English have paid some attention to the university, but most of them have focused on the role of the school in the May Fourth period, when its name had already been changed to National Beijing University 國立北京大學, or Beida 北大.[3] Indeed, because the May Fourth era has long been treated as the moment when Chinese modernity (however imperfectly realized) commenced, Beida—which was at the center of the early phases of the New Culture and May Fourth movements—receives mention in most survey histories and has been the subject of a number of more sustained discussions as well.[4] Discus-

---

2. Kang Youwei is known to have often exaggerated the importance of his role, and his claim should be taken with a grain of salt. I have seen nothing by Liang Qichao to confirm Kang's version of events. See "Kang Youwei ji zhangcheng qicao jingguo" 康有爲記章程 起草經過 (Kang Youwei's record of the process of writing the regulations), collected in Beijing daxue xiaoshi yanjiushi 北京大學校史研究室, ed., Beijing daxue shiliao 北京大 學史料 (Historical materials on Beijing University) (Beijing: Beijing daxue chubanshe, 1992; hereafter cited as BDSL), p. 87. See also Hao, Beijing daxue chuangban shishi kaoyuan, p. 174.

3. The name of the university was changed from Jingshi daxuetang to Guoli Beijing daxue shortly after the 1911 revolution. In addition to my own study, two other English-language studies discuss the Imperial University at significant length. Both are unpublished doctoral dissertations: Renville Clifton Lund, "The Imperial University of Peking" (Ph.D. diss., University of Washington, 1956); and Xiaoqing Diana Chen, "Curricula Development and Academic Professionalization at Peking University, 1898–1937" (Ph.D. diss., University of Chicago, 1993). For my dissertation, see Timothy Bergmann Weston, "Beijing University and Chinese Political Culture, 1898–1920" (Ph.D. diss., University of California, Berkeley, 1995). The two most important studies of the Imperial University in Chinese are Zhuang Jifa 莊吉 發, Jingshi daxuetang 京師大學堂 (Imperial University) (Taibei: Guoli Taiwan daxue, Wenxueyuan, 1970); and Hao, Beijing daxue chuangban shishi kaoyuan.

4. Both Chow Tse-tsung (The May Fourth Movement: Intellectual Revolution in Modern China [Cambridge, Mass.: Harvard University Press, 1964]) and Vera Schwarcz (The Chinese Enlightenment: Intellectuals and the Legacy of the May Fourth Movement of 1919 [Berkeley: University of California Press, 1986]) contribute to the idea that the May Fourth movement signified a profound intellectual break (however incomplete) from the era that came before it, a break that launched China into the modern era. On the other hand, Benjamin Schwartz, Charlotte Furth, and others have questioned the extent to which May Fourth signified a profound intellectual break (see the essays in Benjamin A. Schwartz, ed., Reflections on the May Fourth Movement: A Symposium [Cambridge, Mass: Harvard University, East Asian Research Center, 1972], esp. Furth's "May Fourth in History," pp. 59–68). In addition to the works by Chow and Schwarcz, discussions of May Fourth Beida can also be found in Yeh Wen-hsin, The Alienated Academy: Culture and Politics in Republican China, 1919–1937 (Cambridge, Mass.: Har-

sions of Beida, if they mention the Imperial University at all, tend to say only the most cursory things about it to set the stage for the "main events" that took place at Beijing University in the late 1910s and early 1920s.

But if we move the Imperial University from background to foreground, as I do in this chapter, it becomes clear that the founding of the university in 1898 reflects an outward-opening intellectual and cognitive transformation that had already begun in China and that the epistemological basis of the May Fourth lurch toward Chinese modernity was, in important ways, anticipated at the turn of the century or earlier. As several scholars have argued, and as the present collection seeks to make clear, the extraordinary power and significance granted to the May Fourth period as the moment of transition from the early modern to the modern has discouraged scholars from exploring in full the ways in which China's transition to modernity was well under way in the last several decades of the Qing dynasty.[5] Going further, David Der-wei Wang has recently argued that the May Fourth version of Chinese history repressed the many possible modernities extant in the late Qing period.[6] The founding of the Imperial University both contributed to the turn-of-the-century leap and was an artifact of it.

---

vard University, Council on East Asian Studies, 1990); and Arif Dirlik, *Anarchism in the Chinese Revolution* (Berkeley: University of California Press, 1991).

5. By pointing out the thinness of the English-language historiography on the linkages between intellectual developments in the late Qing and those of the May Fourth era, I in no way mean to suggest that we lack an illuminating body of scholarship on the intellectual history of the late Qing period or that scholars have failed to identify modern developments in the late Qing. Rather, my argument is that the numerous important connections between the 1895–98 period and the May Fourth period have not received their due from scholars. For recent works that do call attention to and shed light on these connections, see Dirlik, *Anarchism in the Chinese Revolution*; Joshua A. Fogel and Peter G. Zarrow, eds., *Imagining the People: Chinese Intellectuals and the Concept of Citizenship, 1890–1920* (Armonk, N.Y.: M. E. Sharpe, 1997); Mary Backus Rankin, "State and Society in Early Republican Politics, 1912–18," in *Reappraising Republican China*, ed. Frederic Wakeman, Jr., and Richard Louis Edmonds, pp. 6–27 (New York: Oxford University Press, 2000); Schwarcz, *The Chinese Enlightenment*; and Peter Zarrow, *Anarchism and Chinese Political Culture* (New York: Columbia University Press, 1990).

6. David Der-wei Wang, *Fin-de-siècle Splendor: Repressed Modernities of Late Qing Fiction, 1849–1911* (Stanford: Stanford University Press, 1997), esp. the introduction and chap. 1. Other examples of recent scholarship that challenge the May Fourth–inflected view of modern Chinese history from different perspectives are Lydia H. Liu, *Translingual Practice: Literature, National Culture, and Translated Modernity—China, 1900–1937* (Stanford: Stanford University Press, 1995); and Yeh Wen-hsin, *Provincial Passages: Culture, Space, and the Origins of Chinese Communism* (Berkeley: University of California Press, 1996).

In the summer of 1898, after approving Liang Qichao's regulations for the new "highest school in the land" (*zuigao xuefu* 最高學府), the Guangxu emperor put his former tutor, Sun Jia'nai 孫家鼐 (1827–1909), a moderate and in 1898 the president of the Board of Works, in charge of the project. People from a wide variety of positions on the politico-ideological spectrum thus contributed to the founding of the Imperial University. It was conceived and designed by radical reformers, overseen by a moderate, and opened under the conservative Empress Dowager after she regained power in September 1898. The widespread backing for the university reveals the near-universal consensus that China had to alter its educational system if it hoped to withstand the imperialist onslaught and that the Qing government needed to direct the change. How it should do this, however, was the subject of much disagreement—education was routinely an area in which contests for political and cultural power were played out.

Education was politicized for two reasons: first, access to power was gained through educational achievements; and second, as a result of this, the dynasty could assert significant control over its servants (as well as all who aspired to be such) through its ability to determine what counted as knowledge. Traditionally, of course, this field of power was structured around and by the civil-service examination system. At the end of the nineteenth century, the viability of that structure was very much in doubt because it was rooted in a Confucian system unable to respond effectively to the problems of the age.[7] Increasing numbers of intellectuals began to accept that China could survive intact only if it adopted some measure of "Western learning," or *xixue* 西學, an omnibus term referring to academic subjects studied in Europe, the United States and, more recently, Japan. In contrast, "Chinese learning," or *zhongxue* 中學, stood for subject matter that either was considered Chinese in origin or was deemed sufficiently familiar by this time to qualify as Chinese.

Throughout the second half of the nineteenth century, intellectuals who believed China had to adopt aspects of Western learning articulated their thoughts according to the *ti-yong* 體用 system. Classically stated by Zhang Zhidong 張之洞 (1837–1909) in his 1898 *Exhortation to Learning* (*Quanxue pian* 勸學篇), that system was based on the idea that both Chinese, or old

---

7. This does not mean that the examination system was entirely rigid or incapable of evolving over time. For a thorough discussion of this subject, see Benjamin A. Elman, *A Cultural History of Civil Examinations in Late Imperial China* (Berkeley: University of California Press, 2000).

(*jiu* 舊), and Western, or new (*xin* 新), learning should be studied but that the former should be viewed as essential (*ti* 體) and the latter merely as practical (*yong* 用): "Chinese history, government, and geography are old learning. Western government, crafts, and history are new learning. The old learning is the fundamental thing; the new learning is for practical use (*ch'iu-hsüeh wei t'i; hsin-hsüeh wei yung* 舊學爲體; 新學爲用)."[8]

Several decades ago, Joseph Levenson argued that the *ti-yong* formulation was the by-product of an intellectual and psychological crisis in China brought about by its encounter with the modern West.[9] Writing in the 1950s and 1960s, Levenson was deeply influenced by the teleology embedded in modernization theory, which conceived of all histories as flowing in essentially the same direction—toward modernity in the Western image. This implied that all premodern civilizations were bound to give way in the face of the logic of modernity. Levenson concluded that the *ti-yong* construct was best understood as an elaborate form of denial born of Chinese intellectuals' driving need to believe that the civilization they knew and loved could never be conquered intellectually. In designating Chinese learning as the essence and Western learning as consisting of useful techniques, Levenson argued, Chinese thinkers like Zhang Zhidong demonstrated how far they had traveled from the true core of Song Confucian principle: "*T'i-yung*, as Chang Chih-tung invoked it, was a vulgarization of a Sung Confucian principle. The traditionalist tried to assure himself that western machines were tame, but when the terms he used for reassurance were so strangely warped from their orthodox meanings, the ravages of western intruders were exemplified, not belied."[10] For Levenson, Zhang Zhidong's use of the *ti-yong* formula "betrays a traditionalist's contribution to the wearing away of tradition."[11] I

---

8. Quoted in William Ayers, *Chang Chih-tung and Educational Reform in China* (Cambridge, Mass.: Harvard University Press, 1971), p. 160.

9. Joseph R. Levenson, *Confucian China and Its Modern Fate: A Trilogy* (Berkeley: University of California Press, 1968), 1: 59–78.

10. Ibid., p. 65. According to Levenson (pp. 68–69), Song thinkers such as Zhu Xi 朱熹 understood *ti* and *yong* in metaphysical terms, as substance and function "jointly defin[ing] one object." Zhang Zhidong's emphasis, on the other hand, was "sociological." Zhang "was concerned not with the nature of things but the nature of cultures, and *t'i* and *yung* were separate in objective embodiment (as they were not for Chu Hsi) and fused only in mind. Man, that is, had something (Chinese) for *t'i* and something (western) for *yung*; while according to Chu Hsi, all 'somethings' had both *t'i* and *yung.*"

11. Ibid., p. 69.

am persuaded that Levenson was correct about the dialectical process at work here and return to the subject from a different perspective below.

In formal logical terms, *ti-yong* was intellectually bankrupt, Levenson declared, and in so doing, he effectively erased it as a subject of serious study. But in researching the founding of the Imperial University, I have found it necessary to revisit the *ti-yong* formulation, since it was, in very explicit terms, the intellectual paradigm on which the university was constructed. Liang Qichao, in the Imperial University regulations he prepared in 1898, for example, gave this explanation of his basic views about the world of knowledge and the purpose of the university: "Chinese learning is the essence, and Western learning is practical (*zhongxue, ti ye, xixue, yong ye* 中學，體也，西學，用也). They complement one another and neither can be ignored; if essence and function are not joined, how will it be possible to develop talent?"[12] Careful inquiry into the role of the *ti-yong* construct during the founding of the Imperial University makes it difficult not to be impressed by Levenson's brilliance, for what one sees, and what I will explain in this chapter, is that Chinese learning, while still thought essential, was forced into a dramatically reduced intellectual role in the university's curriculum in order to survive.

At the same time, however, less encumbered by the assumptions that led Levenson to discuss *ti-yong* thinking primarily as a form of rationalization, I build on his central observation that the popularity of the *ti-yong* problematic in the nineteenth century in itself indicated change and movement within the Chinese intellectual universe. Rather than viewing *ti-yong* as a logically fallacious construct, I stress Levenson's other point, that the *ti-yong* model— its language, logic, and stated goal—helped generate new intellectual possibilities.[13] Not only did it comfort battered psyches, as Levenson argues, but the very process of applying the *ti-yong* formula in actual historical instances allowed those battered psyches to escape their anguish. I am not arguing this with regard to individual thinkers, all of whom of course experienced this period of transformation differently; rather, I will attempt to show that the

---

12. See "Zongli yamen zou ni Jingshi daxuetang zhangcheng" 總理衙門奏擬京師大學堂章程 (The Zongli Yamen's proposed regulations for the Imperial University), in *BDSL*, p. 82.

13. Here I am in agreement with Luke S. K. Kwong ("The T'i-Yung Dichotomy and the Search for Talent in Late-Ch'ing China," *Modern Asian Studies* 27, no. 2 [1993]: 253–79), who has contended that Levenson's interpretation of *ti-yong* is too narrow; Kwong has accused Levenson of "intellectual overkill" on the subject.

ti-yong intellectual model as theory permitted motion and change. Levenson detected this dialectical process at work in Zhang Zhidong's thinking, but he soon leaves the subject behind. As I will argue, one can see the *ti-yong* dialectic at work at the Imperial University's founding, and in that context the model served as the larger frame within which the world of academic knowledge was reclassified. My purpose is not to rehabilitate the *ti-yong* model in order to celebrate it but to observe that it contained many intellectual possibilities. The *ti-yong* formulation may have been a rationalization, but it was also more than that. As an intellectual vehicle, it was full of energy and initiative; it was a means of imagining a new intellectual landscape, not merely a reflection of fear, frustration, and denial. Finally, the *ti-yong* model also enabled creative thinkers to protect themselves from the charge that they were, in their interest in things foreign, being disloyal to Chinese civilization or to the Qing dynasty.[14]

The Significance of the Campaign to Establish a University

In their search for the secrets of the wealth and power of the imperialist countries, Chinese intellectuals tended during the Self-Strengthening decades (1860–95) to focus on technology, with its military and other applications. In the 1860s, scholars inspired by the statecraft (*jingshi* 經世) tradition, such as the Suzhou literatus Feng Guifen 馮桂芬 (1809–74), made use of the *ti-yong* framework when they urged the adoption of the practical skills deployed by Westerners as a means of protecting Chinese civilization from those same Westerners. Although they maintained that moral knowledge should and did remain at the core of civilization, such scholars were prepared to concede that some types of knowledge were worth studying even though they were not based on and could not convey sacred, moral principles. Toward this end, a series of schools—led by the Tongwen guan 同文館 (Interpreters' college) in Beijing and the Guang fangyan guan 廣方言館 (Language college) in Shanghai—were established to train specialists in Western learning. The number of students at those schools was always very small, however, and graduates had a difficult time finding employment within an entrenched bureaucratic system that did not honor men with their skills. It was the shocking defeat by Japan in the war of 1894–95 that led to a profound and widespread shift in thinking on these matters and encouraged

---

14. For another discussion of this point, see ibid., pp. 263–68.

Chinese intellectuals to set about constructing a new approach to the classification and teaching of knowledge.

Driven by that goal, radical reformers launched a campaign to overhaul
China's education system. Among their highest priorities was the founding
of an imperial university in Beijing. Although China had had a "highest
school" in the capital for almost two millennia, the term *daxue* 大學—borrowed from the Japanese *daigaku*—announced that the proposed institution
was to be something new.[15] By seeking to follow Meiji Japan in embracing a
Western institutional model, the reformers were not merely attempting
to establish an institution of learning that they believed would be useful,
they were effectively identifying themselves with modernity and therefore,
they believed, with national wealth and power as well.[16] To the extent
that they were convincing in thus representing their purposes, the reformers
could hope to make themselves acceptable to many who were far more conservative than they, for the goal of a wealthy and powerful China was shared
by people of every political persuasion.

For all its apparent similarities to the *ti-yong* language used by Feng
Guifen and other leaders of the Self-Strengthening movement since the
1860s, the *ti-yong* project of the late 1890s nevertheless rested on a far more
expansive intellectual foundation.[17] This is clear with regard to the campaign
between 1895 and 1898 to establish the Imperial University. Virtually every
official or scholar who memorialized the throne in support of that campaign
found it necessary to explain why, since China already had schools like the

---

15. The term *daxue* is an example of what Lydia H. Liu (*Translingual Practice*, p. 283) refers
to as a "roundtrip neologism." The term originated in China, with a very different meaning. It
was first used to translate "university" by Jesuit missionaries in the seventeenth century, and
in the Meiji era the Japanese employed the term to refer to institutions they established on
the model of the Western university. The Chinese then adopted the term in its new meaning.

16. Liang Qichao acknowledged his heavy reliance on the Japanese school system as a
model. According to Liang, among the texts that had the most influence on the reformers
were Ernst Faber's book on German schools, *Deguo xuexiao* 德國學校, and Timothy Richard's book on the new learning in seven countries, *Qiguo xinxue beiyao* 七國新學備要. See
Chen Pingyuan, "New Education and New Literature: From Imperial University of China to
Peking University" (paper delivered at the "Chinese Modernism" conference, Charles University, Prague, Czech Republic, Aug. 23–27, 1998). On works about foreign education available
in China in the late 1890s, see Sally Borthwick, *Education and Social Change in China* (Stanford:
Hoover Institute Press, 1983), pp. 45–46.

17. For a very useful discussion of the received meanings of the *ti-yong* concept over the
course of Chinese history, see Kwong, "The T'i-Yung Dichotomy."

Tongwen guan devoted to Western learning, it was necessary to found a *daxuetang* 大學堂. Besides pointing to the weak performance of the existing Western learning schools, many of them indicated that they did not accept the rationale for founding these schools. They did not say so in so many words, but it is evident that, along with Yan Fu 嚴復 (1853–1921), the most articulate spokesman for his generation, they believed that rationale was based on overly mechanistic thinking. For example, in 1896 Sun Jia'nai wrote: "The Fuzhou Navy School, the Jiangnan Arsenal, and the Jiangnan Naval Officers and Weapons School are all limited to the teaching of a single skill each; they have had little success at this and fail to [demonstrate an] understanding for the overall situation (*bu ming dati* 不明大體)."[18] Sun's argument was that the existing government schools dedicated to Western learning were founded at a time when there was an insufficient understanding of the first-order intellectual principles underlying the second-order Western subjects (either linguistic or technological) those schools were designed to teach to Chinese students.

Sun Jia'nai was implying that a new way of thinking about knowledge and learning was needed, one that united the various Western disciplines within a single intellectual framework rather than dividing them from one another into hermetically isolated intellectual subspaces. To lead this effort, a new university had to be founded, one whose intellectual reach subsumed the scattered, existing Western-learning schools; at this imperial university all the various foreign languages and practical sciences would be taught (in 1902, in fact, the Tongwen guan was absorbed into the Imperial University). In terms of its offerings, this new school was also to assert in bold terms that Western learning involved not just foreign languages and practical techniques but also the sciences of government, law, history, and so on. Insofar as attitudes toward Western learning were concerned, therefore, at least two substantial shifts in Chinese intellectual life at this time can be discerned in the campaign to establish an imperial university: first, the idea of the university rested on the assumption that Western learning included first-order, theoretical knowledge in addition to second-order, practical learning; and

---

18. See "Sun Jia'nai yifu kaiban Jingshi daxuetang zhe" 孫家鼐議復開辦京師大學堂摺 (Sun Jia'nai's reply to the memorial proposing the founding of an Imperial University), in *BDSL*, p. 23. Sun Jia'nai wrote this in response to a memorial from the official Li Duanfen 李端棻. It is believed that this memorial was composed by Liang Qichao, a relative of Li Duanfen through marriage.

second, that second-order results—practical techniques—could be achieved only through mastery of the fundamental principles that underlay Western learning.

Equally important, however, those who championed an imperial university sought to blend this expanded understanding of Western learning with Chinese learning, which they continued to refer to as *ti*, or essential learning. Pointing to the Japanese case as a negative example, Sun Jia'nai argued: "For five thousand years the spirit of the sages has continued in China . . . [we] absolutely must not do as the Japanese, who had dispensed with their own learning in favor of Western learning."[19] For Sun Jia'nai and the other backers of the university, it was not a question of one learning canceling the other out, for, despite what they believed had happened in Japan, they probably could not even conceive of an intellectual universe shorn of Chinese learning. Such men were now willing to concede that Western learning had something akin to a *ti* of its own, but it was one that could fit within, or alongside, an even more essential Chinese *ti*, so as to form a new whole.

In this way, the campaign to found the university entailed a remarkable intellectual shift toward an expanded and decidedly modern sense of the totality and unity of knowledge. "Modern" because the proposed imperial university was to be a new kind of institution intended to encompass all learning—Chinese and Western, and therefore the entire universe—within its walls and, in so doing, also to organize and control it. This conception of the sum total of human learning excluded the possibility that the non-Chinese and non-Western parts of the world had produced knowledge of any value; the ignorance and chauvinism that this implied should not prevent us from appreciating the receptivity to foreign ideas and ways of organizing knowledge that the founding of the university implied. Although conceived at a time of crisis, the plans for the university bespoke tremendous intellectual ambition, a belief in possibility fueled by a sense of necessity. Accordingly, those who lobbied for the imperial university betrayed a curious mix of self-confidence and insecurity in their vision of the university as a monument that would, simultaneously, enshrine Chinese learning within the new galaxy of knowledge and announce to the world that China deserved to be taken seriously.

In keeping with this idea of the university as monument, the cosmopolitan intellectuals who lobbied for it took for granted that it belonged in Beijing. This was, of course, good politics since they were seeking to persuade

---

19. Ibid., p. 24.

the central government to invest heavily in the project, but it also reflected the nature of their vision. This was to be a capital undertaking, of the utmost importance and significance, an expression of the state's ability to manage knowledge in a modern manner. Time and again the advocates of the university pointed out that the Western powers, and now Japan too, had public universities in their capital cities, a location that implied that foreign governments were committed to higher education and that they were thus gaining influence over and access to new knowledge. The American missionary Gilbert Reid, a strong foreign advocate on behalf of the university with close ties to radical Chinese reformers, was direct on this point: "By establishing a university in the capital it will be possible not only to expand the people's knowledge, and honor the imperial system, but also to raise the country's reputation. . . . If a comprehensive school is founded . . . talent will issue forth every generation, the country will become steadily stronger, and western countries will admire, respect and love [China]."[20] Sun Jia'nai wrote in the same vein the following year: "All the various Western countries have established universities in their capitals; their scale is vast and impressive, the money spent [on them] is abundant, they have several hundreds of teachers and several thousand students." Sun also stressed the importance of locating the university in the center of the capital city, where it could serve as a highly visible symbol of China's cultural greatness.[21] And Liang Qichao, too, made explicit reference to the university as a showcase. The opening line of the university regulations he authored in 1898 stated: "The Imperial University will be the model for the provinces, and all the countries in the world will look upon it respectfully. In scale it must be rich and extensive . . . it must not, because of stinginess, be shabby [in appearance], thereby doing harm to the glorious appearance of the capital."[22]

This notable preoccupation with the university as an emblem of modernity and strength reveals how institutions devoted to the management of

---

20. Li Jiabai 李佳白 (Gilbert Reid), "Ni qing jingshi chuangshi daxuetang yi" 擬請京師創始大學堂議 (A proposal and request that a university be established in the capital), 1895, in *BDSL*, pp. 13–14.

21. "Sun Jia'nai yifu kaiban jingshi daxuetang zhe," in *BDSL*, pp. 23–24.

22. "Zongli yamen zou ni jingshi daxuetang zhangcheng," in *BDSL*, p. 81. When I say that Liang Qichao "authored" the document I use the term loosely, as I do not know exactly how the document—or the 1902 and 1904 versions of the Imperial University regulations—were produced. However, in each case, the person I refer to as the "author" oversaw the document's production and almost certainly approved its content.

knowledge were conceived in political terms, as well as the extent to which the interests of the Qing state were, from the beginning, bound up in the project. Those who wished to see an imperial university founded in the Chinese capital accepted and were seeking to reinforce the imperial government's right to determine what qualified as knowledge. They were calling on the state to assume one of its traditional prerogatives and for it to do so for the purpose of building itself up as a modernizing force in society.[23] The 1898 reforms, including the university, were thoroughly statist in character. This was not merely to be a university located in the capital, but *the* Imperial University, the new creator of intellectual standards and norms, the ultimate and official authority that trumped all educational experiments at the local level. Indeed, the university was envisioned as the metropolitan institution that would oversee the empire's revamped, more centralized education system. Every school in the empire was to be answerable to its head, who in effect was therefore to be chancellor of the Imperial University and the equivalent of a minister of education. As will become evident below, in its founding stages the Imperial University was both an educational institution and a political organization devoted to the expression of dynastic power; in addition to producing talent for the dynasty, it was intended to assist the state in performing its role as custodian and classifier of knowledge.

Arranging the Pieces to Form a New Whole

An effective way to discuss the epistemological transition that occurred in China at the turn of the twentieth century and the manner in which it was embroiled in imperial politics is to study the various organizational plans produced for the Imperial University and approved by the Qing court.[24] Three

---

23. Here the reformers were pushing for significant change for, as Alexander Woodside ("The Divorce Between the Political Center and Educational Creativity in Late Imperial China," in *Education and Society in Late Imperial China, 1600-1900*, ed. Benjamin A. Elman and Alexander Woodside, p. 458 [Berkeley: University of California Press, 1994]) has argued, in late imperial China there was a "divorce between the political center and educational creativity."

24. By "epistemological transition," I mean the substantial change in the way knowledge was understood and classified at this time. For scholarly works in English that treat late Qing trends in epistemology, see Benjamin Schwartz, *In Search of Wealth and Power: Yen Fu and the West* (Cambridge, Mass.: Harvard University Press, 1964); Elman and Woodside, *Education and Society in Late Imperial China*, esp. pt. 3; and Elman, *A Cultural History of Civil Examinations in Late Imperial China*.

such sets of Imperial University regulations (*Jingshi daxuetang zhangcheng* 京師大學堂章程) were produced between 1898 and 1904.[25] In no case were the regulations implemented in full; rather, they represented the ideals of those who devised them.[26] The first, authored by Liang Qichao, was superseded in 1902 by a new document written by Zhang Baixi 張百熙 (1847–1907), then head of the university; the following year, Zhang Baixi's version was in turn replaced by a third set of regulations, whose principal author was Zhang Zhidong. Among other things, these documents laid out taxonomies of knowledge; each successive document was more exhaustively detailed than its predecessor, and each one reflected a different political objective. Indeed, each set of regulations can be understood in relation to the others only by attending to the political circumstances under which it was produced.

Liang Qichao's plan emphasized the need for intellectual breadth and inclusiveness. As noted above, although he referred to Chinese learning as essential (*ti*) and Western learning as useful (*yong*), he nevertheless viewed the two as complements, not as intellectual rivals. According to Liang, "The biggest problem in China is that those who subscribe to Chinese learning do not utter a word about Western learning, whereas those devoted to Western learning completely ignore Chinese learning." He desired to see China evolve a unified but pluralistic language of learning. As he said, if Chinese learning and Western learning "are not combined, their followers will be as irreconcilable as water and fire." Liang's greatest concern was that the continued intellectual standoff between those who favored Chinese learning and those who favored Western learning would make it impossible to cultivate people whose education met the needs of the world in which China found itself. "The two [*ti* and *yong*] need one another," Liang wrote, "[having one] and lacking the other is not acceptable; if both essence and practicality are not attended to, how can talent be produced?"[27]

---

25. I was inspired to compare the three sets of regulations by Hao Ping, who makes a similar comparison in his book *Beijing daxue chuangban shishi kaoyuan*, chap. 8, although in a different way and in order to make a very different argument.

26. For further information about the history of the Imperial University, see Weston, "Beijing University and Chinese Political Culture, 1898–1920," chap. 1.

27. "Zongli yamen zou ni jingshi daxuetang zhangcheng," in *BDSL*, p. 82. In Chapter 3 of this volume Tze-ki Hon makes it clear that Zhang Zhidong, too, was deeply troubled by the divisions within the literati and sought to mend those through the arguments he made in the *Quanxue pian*.

Liang's version of *ti-yong* thinking led him to disavow the idea of a hierarchy between the two traditions of learning. Thus he proposed two principles: first, that Chinese and Western learning should be stressed equally (*Zhongxi bing zhong* 中西并重); and second, that Western learning should be part of what the Imperial University students studied, but not the whole.[28] Consistent with these principles, Liang also urged that the Imperial University establish a massive library of both Chinese and Western books. In making this suggestion he invoked the Four Treasuries (Siku quanshu 四庫全書) project undertaken during the Qianlong reign, an earlier Qing attempt to collect and classify all valuable knowledge in encyclopedic fashion for the purpose of displaying imperial power and achieving control.[29] Like an institutional version of a great encyclopedia, the university Liang envisioned was to encompass the entire world of knowledge. As such, it was marked by the modernist's conceit that the sum total of human learning might be worked into a unified and universally agreed upon whole.

In curricular terms, in their first three years at the Imperial University every student was to be required to master the core subjects of the Classics (*jingxue* 經學); neo-Confucianism (*lixue* 理學); Chinese and foreign historical records (*Zhong wai zhangguxue* 中外掌古學); the ancient noncanonical philosophers (*zhuzixue* 諸子學); elementary mathematics (*chuji suanxue* 初級算學); elementary physics (*chuji gezhexue* 初級格致學); elementary government studies (*chuji zhengzhixue* 初級政治學); elementary geography (*chuji dilixue* 初級地理學); literature (*wenxue* 文學); and physical education (*ticao xue* 體操學). In addition, every student would be required to study English, French, Russian, German, or Japanese during the first three years. After completing that course of study, the student would then select one or two subjects for advanced study from the following list: advanced mathematics (*gaodeng suanxue* 高等算學); advanced physics (*gaodeng gezhexue* 高等格致學); advanced government studies and law (*gaodeng zhengzhixue* 高等政治學 and *falüxue* 法律學); advanced geography and surveying (*gaodeng dilixue* 高等地理學 and *cehuixue* 測繪學); agriculture (*nongxue* 農學); mineralogy (*kuangxue* 礦學); engineering (*gongchengxue* 工程學); commerce (*shangxue* 商學); military science (*bingxue* 兵學); and hygiene and medicine (*weishengxue* 衛生學 and *yixue* 醫學).[30]

---

28. "Zongli yamen zou ni jingshi daxuetang zhangcheng," in *BDSL*, p. 82.

29. Ibid., p. 81.

30. Ibid., p. 82.

Liang Qichao's Imperial University regulations did not spell out in precise terms what each of these fields of study was to entail, but the document did display a crude taxonomy of knowledge in which Chinese learning and Western learning were interwoven. Insofar as it approached the world of knowledge, Liang's Imperial University was to be an entirely new kind of institution, unprecedented in both China and the West. His vision challenged the idea that Western universities were, in the way they accounted for and organized the world of knowledge, the most advanced form of the institution conceivable. There is a clear suggestion here that a synthesis of Chinese and Western learning could result in knowledge more qualitatively powerful than either could offer alone. At the turn of the twentieth century, for one of China's brightest and most creative young thinkers, the rapid "contraction of China from a world into a nation in the world"[31] opened up the possibility of new intellectual combinations even as it threatened old assumptions.

Lost, of course, or well on its way to being lost, was the most basic assumption of all, namely, that Chinese learning not only contained all the essentials (*ti*) of knowledge, but also that those essentials possessed a morally transcendent, sacral power. There is no question that this was a titanic intellectual transition in the happening, one full of loss, even if at this point it was not completely understood as such and was not expected to play out in the fashion that it did. But to the extent that the loss was comprehended, there was also the perception of an opportunity, as I believe Liang Qichao's plan for the Imperial University suggests, and that involved the possibility of redesigning the intellectual universe by expanding the purview of the foreign model of the university to account for all knowledge, Chinese and Western. At this point in time, Liang Qichao clearly did not believe there was only one way to be modern. China was to grow toward the West, but in so doing it did not have to, indeed could not, give up being Chinese.

Like so many of his ideas, Liang Qichao's vision for the Imperial University proved terribly threatening to the conservative powers that be, who were unwilling to countenance the idea that the Chinese intellectual tradition, and by extension the source of their own power, was anything but sacred in nature. Officially at least, both were still sanctioned by heaven's transcendent

---

31. This phrase is Joseph R. Levenson's; quoted in Xiaobing Tang, *Global Space and the Nationalist Discourse of Modernity: The Historical Thinking of Liang Qichao* (Stanford: Stanford University Press, 1996), p. 2.

authority. By the time the Imperial University finally opened in December 1898, the Empress Dowager made sure that Liang's curriculum had been abandoned in favor of one focused far more narrowly on the Confucian classics. Operating with a stopgap curriculum, the Imperial University limped along until the Boxer Rebellion, at which point it was closed down, not to reopen until 1902, after the Qing court had returned from Xi'an to Beijing. Zhang Baixi, a president of the Boards of Works and Punishments, was put in charge[32] and ordered to produce a new set of regulations for the university to replace the one authored by Liang Qichao, which had never been implemented.

Zhang Baixi well understood that foreign countries would use the Qing court's treatment of the Imperial University as a gauge by which to measure the Manchus' newfound dedication to reform: "Now that the court has committed itself to reform in all areas, the principles governing the university should be made very precise, and in scale [the university] should be grand," Zhang wrote, "not merely to please scholars but because all the countries of the world will be watching."[33] Consciousness of the outside world was, of course, extremely high after the attack on and occupation of Beijing, and the chastened Qing court was highly concerned to make wise strategic decisions in the face of increased foreign pressure. This, plus its willingness to think through the problems in a fresh manner, led the court to approve Zhang Baixi's vision of the institution as one that could hold and manage what was considered to be the entire world of knowledge.

In the regulations he authored, Zhang Baixi made no direct reference to the ti-yong idea. Instead, he asserted that the university's ultimate goal was to produce versatile, all-around talent (tongcai 通才) based on comprehensive learning (quanxue 全學), which meant a combination of Chinese and Western learning.[34] Zhang's regulations were far more detailed than Liang Qichao's and contained curricula designed for four different categories of students: those enrolled in the regular university (daxue fenke 大學分科), the preparatory program (yubeike 預備科), the officials' college (shixue guan

---

32. Zhang Baixi replaced Sun Jia'nai, who resigned from the university in 1900.

33. "Zhang Baixi zou chouban Jingshi daxuetang qingxing shu" 張百熙奏籌辦京師 大學堂情形書 (Zhang Baixi's memorial regarding the plans for the Imperial University), in BDSL, pp. 52–55.

34. "Qinding Jingshi daxuetang zhangcheng" 欽定京師大學堂章程 (Imperially ordered Imperial University regulations), 1902, in BDSL, pp. 87–97, esp. p. 87.

仕學館), and the teacher training college (*shifan guan* 師範館).[35] Although the curricula for the officials' and teachers' colleges were tailored to the specific needs of their students, all other students were required to master the preparatory material before going on to specialize at the regular university level, whose opening was to be delayed until the first preparatory class had graduated.[36]

Career tracking began at the preparatory level, as students enrolled in either the government division (*zhengke* 政科) or the skills division (*yike* 藝科). The curricula for those two divisions overlapped somewhat; students in both divisions had to study three years each of ethics (*lunli* 倫理), Chinese and foreign history, a foreign language, mathematics, physics, and physical education.[37] This common area should be considered the indispensable core of Zhang Baixi's curriculum, since its mastery was required of every Imperial University student. Of particular interest to this discussion is the ethics part of the curriculum, because, consistent with the idea of constructing the edifice of knowledge around a Chinese essence, ethics, the category into which Chinese learning was largely placed, was deliberately positioned at the university's intellectual center.

An abbreviated list of the subjects to be taught under ethics—the thought of the sages of the Three Dynasties, Han, and Tang periods, as well as those of the Song, Yuan, and Ming, the *Book of Documents, Book of Songs,*

---

35. The regular university was for advanced study and was based on the Japanese university model; in 1902 there were no students ready to enter it. The three-year preparatory college was designed to give students a basic education that would prepare them for regular university study. The three-year officials' college was for older men who already had civil service examination degrees and now sought an education in Western learning. The teacher-training curriculum was a four-year course of study.

36. Regular university students would specialize in one of the following areas: government, literature, natural science, agricultural science, engineering, commerce, or medicine. Only the literature focus was predominantly weighted toward Chinese learning.

37. The full government division curriculum, in the order listed by Zhang Baixi, was ethics, the Classics, the various schools of the Zhou dynasty, literary works (*cizhang* 詞章), mathematics, Chinese and foreign history, Chinese and foreign geography, foreign language, physics, logic (*mingxue* 名學), law and diplomacy (*faxue* 法學), financial management (*licaixue* 理財學), and physical education. The curriculum for those in the skills division consisted of courses in ethics, Chinese and foreign history, foreign language, mathematics, physics, chemistry (*huaxue* 化學), animal and plant biology (*dong zhiwuxue* 動植物學), geology and mineralogy (*dizhi ji kuangchanxue* 地質及礦產學), drafting (*tuhua* 圖畫), and physical education.

the ancient noncanonical philosophers (*zhuzixue*), the Confucian *Analects*, the *Classic of Filial Piety*, the *Mencius*, the *Examples of Refined Usage* (*Erya* 爾 雅), the *Spring and Autumn Annals*, and the *Book of Changes*—makes it plain that every Imperial University student was expected to be well versed in Chinese learning. Moreover, in classifying these materials under the heading "ethics" Zhang Baixi was clearly implying that Chinese learning was fundamentally concerned with morality, and that the linkage between knowledge and value at the heart of that learning could not and should not be forsaken. Orthodox Chinese ideas about morality were inviolate. At the same time, however, as with Liang Qichao, Zhang did not envision this training as one that would impede open-minded study of Western learning subjects. His concern seems to have been the maintenance of China's cultural literacy and respect for fundamental values, not the furtherance of the hegemony of Chinese learning within the world of knowledge. Chinese moral teachings were to be honored as supreme, but clearly they were not equally applicable to all realms of thought. Furthermore, in giving equal treatment to the ancient noncanonical philosophers, Zhang Baixi was undercutting the assumed absolute supremacy of Confucianism.[38] Operating within a modified *ti-yong* model, then, Zhang Baixi followed Liang Qichao in devising a Chinese-Western curriculum that enshrined a new conception of the world of knowledge. As in Liang's blueprint for the university, the universal relevance of the sacred Classics was clearly in jeopardy in this curriculum, but the importance of Chinese learning was not in doubt.

Indeed, precisely because Zhang Baixi preserved and refined Liang's highly pluralistic approach to knowledge, he may have felt it necessary to distance himself from Liang politically and to prove himself loyal to the regime in power. Within his Imperial University regulations, his effort to do that is most evident in his addition of a section on university rules (*tang gui* 堂 規); every month, the highest officials at the school would lead the entire student body in a study of imperial edicts and ritual observances at the altar to Confucius. In addition, students would observe the Empress Dowager's, the Guangxu emperor's, and Confucius' birthdays.[39] In designing an institu-

---

38. I am indebted to the work of Xiaoqing Lin for drawing out this important point. See Xiaoqing Chen, "Curricula Development and Academic Professionalization at Peking University, 1898–1937," p. 51.

39. "Qinding jingshi daxuetang zhangcheng" (Imperially ordered Imperial University regulations), p. 96.

tional practice in which ritual observance of political loyalty played a central role, Zhang Baixi preserved the concept of sacred value, but he lodged it in political acts as much as if not more than in a set of texts. As the Classics receded in his curriculum, the nation as embodied by the Qing dynasty rose ever more prominently into the sacred space they had formerly dominated.

Nevertheless, at a time when *New Citizen Journal* (*Xinmin congbao* 新民叢報)—which Liang Qichao was publishing in Japan in order to attack the Empress Dowager and her regime and to introduce political ideas from the West—was popular with students at the Imperial University, Zhang Baixi was not able to satisfy nervous conservatives at court that he alone was the right man for the job.[40] As a result, a Mongol Bannerman highly trusted by court conservatives, Rongqing (*jinshi* 進士 1886), was made co-director of the university (and thus also of the empire's educational policies). In the spring of 1903, just after the student-led "Resist Russia movement" (*Ju-E yundong* 拒俄運動) erupted at the Imperial University and all across the country,[41] it was further decreed that another set of Imperial University Regulations be drawn up to replace the one designed by Zhang Baixi and approved by the court the year before. The task of drawing up the third and final set of regulations was officially a joint undertaking between Zhang Baixi, Rongqing, and Zhang Zhidong, but in point of fact Zhang Zhidong was in charge.[42] Zhang Zhidong's revised Imperial University regulations gained imperial approval in early 1904 and remained in force until the end of the dynasty.

Those regulations were conceived as a replacement only for the regular university (*fenke daxue* 分科大學) component of Zhang Baixi's plan; the students in this division were to specialize in one field of study, having already received a broader education in both Chinese and Western subjects at the higher secondary school (*gaodeng xuetang* 高等學堂) level. Zhang Zhi-

---

40. Luo Dunyong 羅惇曧, "Jingshi daxuetang chengli ji" 京師大學堂成立記 (A record of the Imperial University's founding). *Yongyan* 庸言 1, no. 13 (June 1, 1913): *Guowen* 國聞 section, pp. 1–5.

41. Russian troops established a presence in Manchuria at the time of the Boxer Uprising. This was to be temporary, but it soon became clear that Russia had no intention of pulling out its troops and that it sought to develop its position further. On the "Resist Russia" demonstrations at the Imperial University, see Weston, "Beijing University and Chinese Political Culture, 1898–1920," pp. 44–57.

42. Hao, *Beijing daxue chuangban shishi kaoyuan*, pp. 178–80, 198–99.

dong's regulations were far more detailed than those of 1902 and reflect even more clearly that, so far as the court was concerned, the reclassification of knowledge was fraught with political implications. Like Liang Qichao's and Zhang Baixi's renditions, Zhang Zhidong's blueprint for the university indicates a deep commitment to intellectual pluralism, to the blending of Chinese and Western learning. In the provision for a graduate school component (*tongru yuan* 通儒院), Zhang Zhidong's plan in fact represented a significant advance over the earlier versions in terms of a willingness to view knowledge as an ever-changing, invented entity. The Imperial University did not suddenly emerge as a training center for modern-style academic experts in specialized knowledge, but the graduate school was specifically designed to focus on research and therefore was rooted in an understanding that the boundaries of knowledge were always expanding, a concept that struck at the heart of the idea of immutable, divine knowledge.[43] Moreover, the plan was exceedingly precise about which courses would be taught during which year in a student's three-year program of study and for how many hours per week. In that way it reveals a more realistic sense of how much could be taught in a given period of time, as well as a deeper understanding of the Western academic disciplines and how they might be broken down into intellectually and pedagogically workable units than do the 1898 and 1902 plans.

The 1904 blueprint thus presented a refined taxonomy of knowledge. As one would expect from the classic formulator of the *ti-yong* system of thinking, the plan was intended to solidify the status of Chinese learning within that taxonomy. Certainly, there was acute concern with that goal at this politically and culturally sensitive moment, when the campaign to abolish the Confucian-based civil-service examination system was at full throttle. As a leader of that campaign who was deeply committed to the retention of Chinese learning and the maintenance of the Qing dynasty, Zhang Zhidong no doubt sought to demonstrate through his curriculum precisely how the two causes could and should be reconciled. In his statement of the university's primary duty, Zhang linked politics and education in a clear and explicit fashion: "The purpose of [the university] is to promote respect for the impe-

---

43. In the 1902 regulations, Zhang Baixi made passing reference to a graduate training component, but he did not develop the idea in detail. On the discussion of a graduate program in the 1904 regulations, see "Daxuetang zhangcheng" 大學堂章程 (Imperial University regulations), in *BDSL*, pp. 97–129, especially pp. 127–28.

rial will, to set an upstanding and proper direction, and to cultivate all-around talent."[44]

In the 1902 regulations, Zhang Baixi had provided for a specialization in traditional Chinese learning at the regular university level in what he referred to as the Literature Department (*wenxue ke* 文學科). But, as with the rest of the 1902 plan for the regular university component, Zhang Baixi supplied few details (he was far more detailed about the preparatory program and the officials' and teachers' colleges, since those were to open sooner). Even so, it is notable that Zhang Baixi did not assign pride of place to the Literature Department in his crudely sketched plan for the *fenke daxue* portion of the larger Imperial University.

In 1904, by contrast, Zhang Zhidong elaborated at great length on Chinese learning at the very beginning of his plan for this portion of the university, thereby moving it to the top of the list of departments in no uncertain terms. Moreover, whereas Zhang Baixi had assigned most Chinese learning to the Literature Department, Zhang Zhidong assigned it by and large to the Classics Department (*jingxue ke* 經學科). Zhang Zhidong's curriculum also called for sustained and serious study of Chinese materials in the Government and Law and the Literature Departments, but all the texts that Chinese had for thousands of years believed to possess transcendent authority—the *Book of Changes*, the *Book of History*, the *Spring and Autumn Annals*, the *Rituals of Zhou*, the *Book of Rites*, the Confucian *Analects*, the *Mencius*—were to be studied through the Classics Department. In the hands of Liang Qichao and Zhang Baixi, Chinese learning retained an important place to be sure, but the universal relevance of that learning was, at the very least, thrown into doubt. Zhang Zhidong's regulations forcefully sought to clarify exactly how Chinese learning should be taught in a modern university context, and he was direct and clear as to the linkages between that tradition and the Qing dynasty's indisputable right to rule.

Ironically, given that Zhang Zhidong was clearly seeking to give curricular teeth to the idea that Chinese learning constituted the essence (*ti*) within the larger world of knowledge and that by extension the Qing dynasty was the ultimate authority politically and culturally, in clarifying exactly where and how the Classics fit into the intellectual structure of the university, his 1904 regulations reduced the sphere devoted to sacred knowledge. As Tze-ki

---

44. Ibid., p. 97.

Hon suggests in Chapter 3 of this volume, within the limited circle devoted to sacred knowledge Zhang Zhidong was quite rigidly conservative, but by drawing that circle so tightly he allowed himself to be more aggressive and flexible outside it. Indeed, the university he envisioned was a more catholic institution intellectually than those of the West because, like those that Liang Qichao and Zhang Baixi had imagined, the sweep of knowledge it was to include—Chinese *and* Western learning—was greater than that taken in by universities in the imperialist countries.

Classics now was just one department among many in which students could choose to specialize, the others being Government and Law, Literature, Medicine, Natural Sciences, Agricultural Science, Engineering, and Commerce. In classifying the Classics according to the same unit of measure—the department (*ke* 科)—he used to sort those other, Western subjects, Zhang created a taxonomic equivalence between them. Nevertheless, he viewed the Classics Department in special terms, and no doubt those who selected Classics as a field of study could be expected to have a full appreciation of sacred knowledge, or at least of the historical value of that knowledge. As Xiaoqing Lin has observed, the emphasis in Zhang's curriculum on reading the Confucian classics with the help of the *Examples of Refined Usage (Erya)* had the effect of "render[ing] the Confucian Learning Division very much into one of philology or history."[45] This more scientific approach had a desacralizing effect, but it also made it possible for the Classics to become better adapted to life in the brave new world of modernity, wherein all knowledge and the entire Chinese past was soon to be historicized.[46]

The shift from Liang Qichao's blueprint for the university to Zhang Baixi's version and finally to the adoption of Zhang Zhidong's plan in 1904 represented a steady drift toward conservatism, political seniority, and proven loyalty to the Qing dynasty. The fact that each plan was more spe-

---

45. Xiaoqing Chen, "Curricula Development and Academic Professionalization at Peking University, 1898–1937," pp. 60–61.

46. The historicizing movement got much of its early energy from the work of Zhang Binglin 章炳麟 (1869–1935) and was later taken up by scholars heavily influenced by Zhang. One of the most important second-generation figures in this movement was Gu Jiegang 顧頡剛 (1895–1980), a leader of the effort in the 1920s and after to reorganize the national heritage (*zhengli guogu* 整理國故). On Gu's role, see Lawrence A. Schneider, *Ku Chieh-kang and China's New History: Nationalism and the Quest for Alternative Traditions* (Berkeley: University of California Press, 1971).

cific and exhaustive than the previous one indicated both that the university was being built to last and that the Qing state increasingly understood how to assert its power within this new institution through its management of administrative and curricular details. Among other things, this translated into increasingly explicit ritual observances in honor of the Qing dynasty's unassailable political position.

The Imperial University came into being during the ambitious and open-minded hundred days of reform in 1898, but in order to survive its leaders had to learn to tack to the winds of the court's fundamental political and cultural conservatism. Even as the sacred power of the imperial institution was being asserted and reinforced, however, the curricular space allotted to sacred Chinese learning was steadily being reduced in the face of the growing presence in the curriculum of Western learning. The *ti-yong* formulation had clearly enabled dramatic and irrevocable change and thereby served the interests of the reformers. But the change was conceived in such a way as to benefit the conservatives as well, for in its new and more cramped curricular quarters the pursuit of Chinese learning was to be both more focused and more scientific than ever before; this not only prevented its total eclipse but perhaps even assured its continued vitality.

Conclusion

The reclassification of knowledge and learning that I have discussed in this chapter took place *within* the *ti-yong* discursive framework, despite the intellectually restrictive potential of the more conservative interpretations of that model's meanings and purposes. In other words, rather than betraying faulty thinking or revealing to us minds that could not understand or were unwilling to accept the intellectual challenge posed by the modern West, *ti-yong* was a broadly applied conceptual terminology and intellectual project that facilitated the working out of a new epistemology by those who had the creativity and, consciously or not, the will to do so. As I have tried to demonstrate, for Liang Qichao, Zhang Baixi, and Zhang Zhidong, expanding and refining the taxonomy of academic knowledge meant integrating Chinese and Western learning and *ti* and *yong*. Nineteenth-century *ti-yong* thinking was, of course, sparked by the encounter with the West, but it also generated an intellectual energy of its own that enabled Chinese thinkers to demonstrate a significant degree of initiative as they worked out a new relationship to the world of knowledge. Some of those who relied on the construct undoubtedly preferred not to face up to many of its potential ramifications, as Levenson argued, but that did not prevent them from using *ti-yong* to design a new system of knowledge in which Chinese learning became the Classics Department, privileged perhaps, but still just a piece and not the whole.

The founding of the Imperial University took almost a decade, from the shocking defeat of 1895 to the imperial approval of Zhang Zhidong's regulations. By the time the third set of regulations was written and approved in 1904, the radical reformers of 1898 who had played such a decisive role at the beginning of the campaign to establish an imperial university were no longer welcome in Beijing, but the school they envisioned had, to a remarkable extent, become a reality. Although in 1904 the Imperial University was still being built, as a plan it had successfully made its way through a highly complex and rapidly shifting political environment to gain the central government's blessing and promise of future funding. In becoming a reality, the various branches of Western learning were brought together at a single institution in the Chinese capital, where they were combined with Chinese learning. At the highest school in the land, one of the key institutions through which the imperial government hoped to wield intellectual authority over the country in the twentieth century, knowledge had been fundamentally reclassified and expanded. The *ti-yong* framework enabled this not only psychologically but also terminologically—it provided handholds that the founders of the university could use to imagine a new epistemology. In this respect, *ti-yong* might be thought of as the seminal language of Chinese modernity, full of anguished denial to be sure, but also full of movement and possibility.

Moreover, as I have argued, in the process of translating the institution of the university into an imperial Chinese context for the purpose of demonstrating and accelerating China's modernity, the people involved in the founding of the Imperial University envisioned a school that stretched the boundaries of the model they were borrowing. In the very process of seeking to join the process of modernity as defined by the West, in other words, they imagined a significantly different version of modernity. And this distinctively Chinese version of modernity was devised under official auspices during a time that, according to May Fourth leaders and later May Fourth–inflected interpretations of the late Qing period, was intellectually stagnant and inflexible.

Over a decade later, Cai Yuanpei 蔡元培 (1868–1940), one of modern China's most pluralistic thinkers, sketched a vision that calls to mind the different classification schemes outlined in the three sets of Imperial University regulations discussed above. In the introductory statement of a new journal he was helping to launch in 1914, Cai Yuanpei wrote:

This age is one in which the entire world is developing communications. In the past, Chinese people viewed our country as all under heaven, and Westerners likewise thought that Europe was the world. Today things are gradually moving forward; Chinese people already know that there is a so-called Western civilization, and Westerners, even though our country is weak and has learning and customs that they look upon with disfavor, cannot but admit that we constitute part of the world. If there were a worldwide exhibition, our country's products would have to be displayed there; *if there were a university, which made every effort to encompass all the world's teachings, then our language and history would constitute a department*; if there were a large library full of books, then titles from our country would have to be among them; if there were a museum that collected precious specialty items in order to bring humanity's true face to light, then beautiful and ordinary items from our country would have to be gathered there. This is proof that the world has become more integrated.[47]

Two and a half years after writing this, Cai Yuanpei assumed the chancellorship of National Beijing University, formerly the Imperial University. Cai's distinguished tenure at Beida coincided with the New Culture and May Fourth movements, both of which were centered, at least initially, at the highest school in the land, and which, together, are often identified as the foundational moment of Chinese modernity. But as I have attempted to make clear, the May Fourth era was not the first time when the kind of modern and pluralistic sensibility expressed by Cai Yuanpei in 1914 found a home at the highest school in the land. The optimistic vision that Cai articulated of an increasingly global world in which China occupied its rightful place echoed and developed those expressed over a decade earlier by Liang Qichao, Zhang Baixi, and Zhang Zhidong, each in his own way. Moreover, were it not for the efforts that led to the founding of the Imperial University, Cai Yuanpei would have had slightly less reason to believe his vision was already being borne out. Needless to say, he also would not have had a prestigious and national-level platform in the capital from which to make it become even more of a reality.

---

47. Italics added. Cai Yuanpei 蔡元培, "*Xuefeng* zazhi fakan ci" 學風雜志發刊詞 (Foreword for *Winds of Learning*), in *Cai Yuanpei quanji* 蔡元培全集 (Collected works of Cai Yuanpei), ed. Gao Pingshu, 2: 335 (Beijing: Zhonghua shuju, 1988). The journal for which this statement was written never came into being.

CHAPTER FIVE

Placing the Hundred Days: Native-Place Ties and Urban Space

Richard Belsky

Few scholars would contest the notion that the 1895–98 reform movement was a major event in China's national history, but the fact that it was also a major episode in the history of Beijing is generally overlooked. This is unfortunate because the local character of the movement is of considerable historical significance in two fundamental ways. First, the particular characteristics of Beijing so greatly influenced events that the historical trajectory of the movement cannot be fully understood if divorced from the social, spatial, and institutional context of the city. Second, the reform movement and the government's response to it dramatically affected the subsequent development of local relations between state and society and other urban features of Beijing. This chapter addresses both of these subjects and offers a preliminary overview of how Beijing shaped and was shaped by the 1895–98 reforms by looking especially at factors related to urban space and native-place ties in the city.

From 1895 to the suppression of the reform movement in 1898, many key events took place in the capital. Although important developments occurred in the provinces, Beijing served in a real sense as the most important focal point of the reforms. But is the movement's Beijing-centeredness historically significant? After all, the events of 1895–98 were far from unique in this

I thank Philip Kuhn, Li Qiao, members of the Columbia University Seminar on Modern China, the editors of this volume, and two anonymous reviewers of the manuscript for the Harvard University Asia Center for their helpful comments on earlier versions of this chapter.

regard; to some degree all late imperial matters of state took place mainly in the capital. Must these reform-related developments be considered necessarily *of* the capital just because they were enacted *in* the capital?

The usual answer to this question is "no." The urban context of the city beyond the palace and bureaucratic offices is generally considered largely irrelevant to what happened during the hundred days. Yet there are two reasons to question this assumption. First, the significance of the Beijing context to late imperial political decisions has been too readily disregarded in general. More work is needed in this area, but James M. Polachek's work on the debates surrounding Opium War policy and the significance of such activities as the formation of poetry societies in the Southern City by scholar-officials in Beijing is a notable step toward an approach that incorporates the local context of the capital in its consideration of late imperial political dynamics.[1] Second, the 1895–98 reform movement demands a fuller consideration of the Beijing context, primarily because a new mix of lower bureaucratic and unranked elites, such as examination candidates and lower-level metropolitan officials, emerged as an unprecedentedly influential political force at this time. As I hope to show here, the actions of this group were greatly shaped by the particular urban ecology of Beijing.

I focus especially on the influence of the patterning of urban space and the unique institutionalization of native-place ties in the capital. By "urban space," I mean not only the physical topography of the city but also the structure of social space. As we shall see, the residences of the Han scholar-bureaucrats that dominated the movement were not evenly distributed over the whole area of the city but were concentrated in a specific ward. The density of their residence there facilitated the exchange of information and the assembling of activists that were essential features of the movement. The actions of the reform advocates were further influenced and facilitated by the way native-place ties were institutionalized in the capital. By "institutionalization," I refer both to the co-opting of native-place ties by the imperial government through its regulations governing subject-initiated interactions with it and to the extraordinary proliferation of corporately administered native-place lodges (*huiguan* 會館). Both the regulations and the scholar-official character of the lodges were unique to the capital, and both profoundly shaped the course of events.

---

1. James M. Polachek, *The Inner Opium War* (Cambridge, Mass.: Harvard University, Council on East Asian Studies, 1992).

After examining the ways these characteristic features of Beijing shaped the events of 1895–98, I examine how the reforms in turn shaped the city, by once again focusing on matters of space and native-place institutions. Indeed, the new uses found after 1898 for the considerable space offered by the hundreds of native-place lodges in the capital were among the notable legacies of the movement. I focus on two such functional changes: the establishment of lodge-based schools and the use of lodge spaces such as opera halls and meeting rooms to convene explicitly political assemblies—a practice that began in the 1895–98 period and continued thereafter. The second trend in turn provoked the growing regulation and penetration of the lodges by the state that transformed the nature of state-society interactions in the capital.

Spatial Characteristics of Beijing: The Inner and Outer Cities

In the late nineteenth century, Beijing proper—the intramural area of the city—comprised two adjacent but discrete walled areas referred to as the Inner City (nei cheng 內城) and Outer City (wai cheng 外城). The Outer City was bordered on the north by the southern wall of the Inner City and extended two and a half miles further south. The Inner City was somewhat larger than the Outer City overall, although the walls of the latter extended approximately a third of a mile further to the west and east on each side.[2] Access between the two "cities" was restricted to three gates built into the wall that divided them. From west to east these were named the Xuanwu 宣武, Zhengyang 正陽, and Chongwen 崇文 gates.

Physically and spatially the two "cities" differed dramatically. Symbolic and actual representations of governmental authority were concentrated in the Inner City—the imperial palace; the bell and clock towers; governmental offices and official institutions of learning; the altars to the sun, the moon, the earth, and so on. The Outer City, on the other hand, possessed little that directly reflected imperial authority beyond the imperial altars to heaven and to agriculture. Even the layout of the streets reflected the divergence in the character of the two "cities." In contrast to the orderly checker-

---

2. The Inner City occupied an area of 35.5 km² (13.7 mi²); the Outer City, about 26 km² (10.03 mi²); see Chen Zhengxiang (Chen Cheng-siang) 陳正祥, *Beijing de dushi fazhan* 北京的都市發展 (The metropolitan development of Beijing), Research Report no. 73 (Hong Kong: Chinese University of Hong Kong, Graduate School, Geographical Research Center, 1974), p. 24.

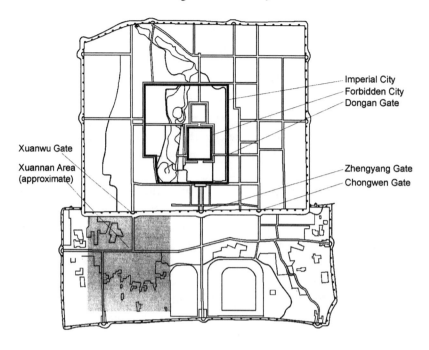

Imperial City
Forbidden City
Dongan Gate

Xuanwu Gate

Xuannan Area
(approximate)

Zhengyang Gate
Chongwen Gate

Late Qing Beijing

board of Inner City streets, those of the Outer City ran in a jumble (preserved to this day) of forks, bends, and irregular angles that often corre-
sponded only vaguely to the cardinal directions.

The Inner and Outer Cities differed in more than the character of their
physical form. One such factor, which considerably influenced the reform
movement, was the amount of interest taken by the state in the administration and policing of the two areas. Relatively tighter control was maintained
over the Inner City.[3] Social control in the Outer City was to a much greater
degree (though by no means entirely) left in the hands of traditional corporate organizations such as guilds and native-place lodges. This greater
autonomy was an important reason so much of the reform moment activity
occurred in the Outer City.

---

3. See Alison Jean Dray-Novey, "Policing Imperial Peking: The Ch'ing Gendarmie, 1650–
1850" (Ph.D. diss., Harvard University, 1981); and idem, "Spatial Order and Police in Imperial
Beijing," *Journal of Asian Studies* 52 (1993): 885–922.

The two areas also differed dramatically in social composition. The most notable discrepancy was a sharply drawn ethnic division resulting from a policy imposed on the city in 1648, four years after the establishment of Manchu rule, that forbade Han Chinese to reside within the Inner City walls.[4] The prohibition was not officially rescinded until 1905.[5] However, by the 1890s, although the spatial separation of the ethnic groups still greatly affected the social character of the city, the policy was no longer quite so strictly enforced, and the authorities tolerated a certain amount of Han residence in the Inner City.

Relaxation of the segregation policy began in the mid-eighteenth century when the court began to bestow Inner City residential compounds on eminent Han officials as reward for particularly meritorious service to the dynasty. The descendents of these specially favored officials were allowed to continue to live in these compounds; this created a small but growing number of Han residents in the Inner City. Increased acceptance of limited Han residence in the Inner City during the late nineteenth century was further reflected in the establishment there of a dozen or so native-place lodges, typically referred to as "examination lodges" (*shiguan* 試館), that catered exclusively to Han examination candidates.[6]

---

4. For a translation of this edict, dated Oct. 5, 1648, see Frederic Wakeman, Jr., *The Great Enterprise: Manchu Reconstruction of Imperial Order in Seventeenth-Century China* (Berkeley: University of California Press, 1985), 1: 147–48.

5. Fang Biao 方彪, *Beijing jianshi* 北京簡史 (A short history of Beijing) (Beijing: Yanshan chubanshe, 1995), p. 59.

6. Examples include the (Anhui) Luzhou shiguan established by Li Hongzhang and his brother Li Hanzhang in 1870 (*Xuxiu Luzhou fu zhi* 續修盧州府志 [The revised Luzhou prefecture gazetteer; 1885] 17.81b; Beitu jinshi zu 北圖金石組, ed., *Beijing tushuguan cang Zhongguo lidai shike taben huibian* 北京圖書館藏中國歷代石刻拓本匯編 [Collected Chinese historical stelae housed in the Beijing Library] [Beijing, 1991], 84: 133); the (Anhui) Chizhou shiguan established in 1882 (Li Jingming 李景銘, comp., *Anhui huiguan zhi* 安徽會館志 [The gazetteer of Anhui native-place lodges in Beijing] [Beijing, 1943], *juan* 4 [n.p.]); and the (Hunan) Shanhua shiguan established in 1887 (Gong Zhenxiang 龔鎮湘, ed. and comp., *Shanhua guan zhi* 善化館志 [The Shanhua native-place lodge gazetteer] [Shanhua: 1888], 1.6a–8b; this property was bought from a Manchu bannerman, see ibid., 1.10a–b). Other inner-city lodges that appear to have been established in the late nineteenth century but whose exact establishment date in unknown include the (Anhui) Sizhou shiguan, (Anhui) Tongcheng shiguan, (Jiangsu) Yijing shiguan; (Shandong) Shandong shiguan; (Yunnan) Yunzheng shiguan; (Zhejiang) Hangjun shiguan; (Zhejiang) Ningbo shiguan (Richard Belsky, "Beijing Scholar-Official Native-Place Lodges: The Social and Political Evolution of

In practice, select Han visitors to the capital were also able to temporarily reside in the Inner City. Indeed, the leading figures of the 1895–98 events offer examples of the options available to Han scholar-officials who sought temporary accommodations there. For example, Manchus could and did occasionally invite Han acquaintances to stay with them; Kang Youwei 康有爲 (1858–1927) stayed at the Inner City residence of the Manchu nobleman Shengyu 盛昱 (1850–1900) on several occasions before 1898.[7] Temples provided another form of temporary lodging for scholar-officials in the Inner City. Kang Youwei again provides an example of this; on several periods of sojourn in the capital, he stayed at an Inner City temple called the Gold Roof Temple (Jinding si 金頂寺).[8] In fact, the location of one of the most famous and disputed incidents of the "hundred days" reflects this practice. Tan Sitong's 譚嗣同 (1865–98) meeting with Yuan Shikai 袁世凱 (1859–1916), during which Tan tried to persuade the general to lead a military strike against the Empress Dowager and the conservative minister Rong Lu 榮祿 (1836–1903), occurred in the Fa Hua Temple (Fahua si 法華寺), where Yuan was temporarily quartered, just to the east of the Dong'an 東安 gate of the Imperial City.[9]

Huiguan in China's Capital City" [Ph.D. diss., Harvard University, 1997], "Appendix Three: Beijing Native-Place Lodges During the Late Qing and Republican Periods").

7. Kang Youwei, "Chronological Autobiography of K'ang Yu-wei," in Jung-Pang Lo, ed. and trans., *K'ang Yu-Wei: A Biography and a Symposium* (Tucson: University of Arizona Press, 1967), p. 61. For biographical information on Shengyu, see Arthur Hummel, ed., *Eminent Chinese of the Ch'ing Period (1644–1912)* (Washington, D.C.: Government Printing Office, 1944), pp. 648–50.

8. For references to the temple, see Kang Youwei, "Chronological Autobiography," pp. 61, 63, 126. The location of the temple has been something of a mystery over the years, since Kang's description of its location is vague. For an intriguing and largely convincing solution to the mystery, see Zhou Yumin 周育民, "Kang Yuwei yusuo Jinding miao kao" 康有爲寓所金頂廟考 (An investigation of the Golden Roof Temple where Kang Youwei resided), in Lin Keguang 林克光 et al., eds., *Jindai jinghua shiji* 近代京華史跡 (Historical traces of modern Beijing) (Beijing: Zhongguo renmin daxue chubanshe, 1985). Zhou identifies the temple as a long-since abandoned temple to Lord Guan (Guan Di 關帝) located on Shaojiu hutong near the Dong'an Gate on the east side of the imperial city.

9. Ding Wenjiang 丁文江, *Liang Qichao nianpu changbian* 梁啓超年譜長篇 (Chronological biography of Liang Qichao), ed. Zhao Fengdian 趙豐田 (Shanghai: Shanghai renmin chubanshe, 1983), pp. 141–42. For a succinct treatment of what was discussed at the disputed meeting and confirmation that Tan did indeed propose to strike against Rong Lu and the Empress Dowager, see Young-Tsu Wong, "Revisionism Reconsidered: Kang Youwei and the Reform Movement of 1898," *Journal of Asian Studies* 51 (1992): 535–38.

Even so, Han residence in the Inner City remained limited, and the overwhelming majority of Han residents of Beijing lived in the Outer City. The population was not uniformly distributed across that area, however. Open spaces extended in a swath along the periphery of the Outer City just within the western, southern, and eastern walls. Although seemingly abandoned, much of that peripheral area was occupied by charitable graveyards serving the sojourning native-place communities of Beijing. Most of the population of the Outer City resided in the more centrally located area to the south of the three gates that provided access to the Inner City. A distinct pattern of spatially expressed social bifurcation was clearly evident within the Han population of the Outer City, too. In this case, the division had no legal origins since it was based on occupational specialization rather than ethnicity. In the eastern half of the densely settled area that extended south between the Zhengyang and Chongwen gates thrived a bustling commercial district dominated by merchants and tradesmen. By contrast the area (popularly known as Xuannan 宣南) to the south of the Xuanwu gate was primarily the center of scholar-official residence and activity.

The existence of two distinct areas dominated, respectively, by scholar-officials and merchants conforms roughly to a model of urban ecology originally proposed by G. W. Skinner in which such spatially discrete nuclei characterize late imperial Chinese cities.[10] The scholar-official nucleus in the Xuannan area developed in the mid-eighteenth century. By that time the area boasted not only a thick concentration of scholar-gentry residences and native-place lodges but also bookstores and cultural curio shops such as those famously located in the heart of the Xuannan area around the site of the old imperial roof-tile kiln, Liuli chang 琉璃廠. As we shall see below, the high concentration in this ward of scholar-officials greatly affected the development of the reform movement. To properly appreciate the ways in which it did so, we must first not only consider the size and density of the

---

10. G. William Skinner, "Introduction: Urban Social Structure in Ch'ing China," in idem, ed., *The City in Late Imperial China* (Stanford: Stanford University Press, 1977), pp. 521–51. Note that although Skinner correctly intuited the existence of a "gentry" nucleus in Beijing, he misjudged where it was located, placing it not in the Xuannan ward but in the eastern third of the Inner City. For a critical review of Skinner's piece and a discussion of the historical formation of a scholar-official nucleus in the Xuannan ward, see Richard Belsky, "The 'Urban Ecology' of Late-Imperial Beijing Reconsidered: The Transformation of Social Space in China's Late Imperial Capital City," *Journal of Urban History* 27, no. 1 (Nov. 2000): 54–72.

scholar-official population in that area but also examine the sojourning nature of that community.

Tongxiang *Connections*

One shared characteristic of the scholar-official and merchant areas in the Outer City was that both were composed predominantly of sojourners. Propelled by the greater opportunities for trade and labor in urban areas, widespread domestic migration was a pervasive fact of late imperial urban life. Cities throughout China boasted large numbers of those who identified themselves and were legally registered as natives of other regions (although such "sojourners" may not have been born in their home region and may well have spent most if not all of their lives outside it). Sojourners dominated many of the merchant and craft trades of Beijing. The native-place imprint on the structure of Beijing's late imperial economy is attested by the plethora of merchant and craft "guilds" and merchant *huiguan* in the central and eastern sections of the Outer City that represented tradesmen from regions throughout the empire.[11]

Beijing's position at the top of the bureaucratic central-place hierarchy of Chinese cities ensured that to a much greater degree than was true elsewhere large numbers of scholar-official sojourners were a constant presence.[12]

---

11. Among the most comprehensive works on the craft and commercial guilds of Beijing are Niida Noboru 仁井田陞, [*Niida Noboru hakushi shū*] *Pekin kōshō girudo shiryōshū* 仁井田陞博士輯北京工商資ギルド料集 (Source materials on the guilds of Beijing compiled by Dr. Niida Noboru), ed. and annot. Saeki Yūichi 佐伯有一 and Tanaka Issei 田中一成 (Tokyo: Tōkyō daigaku, Tōyō bunka kenkyūjo, Tōyōgaku bunken sentā, 1975–83); John Stewart Burgess, *The Guilds of Peking* (New York: Columbia University Press, 1928); and Li Hua 李華, ed., *Ming-Qing yilai Beijing gongshang huiguan beike xuan bian* 明清以來北京工商會館碑刻選編 (A selection of stelae from the handicraft and merchant lodges of Ming and Qing Beijing) (Beijing: Wenwu chubanshe, 1980). For a preliminary treatment of the relationship between native-place origins and the organization of craft and commercial guilds, see Niida Noboru, "The Industrial and Commercial Guilds of Peking and Religion and Fellow-Countrysmanship as Elements of Their Coherence," trans. M. Elder, *Folklore Studies* 9 (1950): 179–206. Many craft and commercial guilds were not organized along specifically native-place lines.

12. The Beijing example nicely confirms William Rowe's observation that we should expect a greater "socioeconomic dominance by nonlocals . . . in cities ranked higher in the hierarchy of central place in China" because of "a greater orientation of the city to . . . [a] broader geographic scale" ("Introduction," in Linda Cooke Johnson, ed., *Cities of Jiangnan in Late Imperial China* [Albany: State University of New York Press, 1993], p. 10).

Proper administration of the empire required tens of thousands of officials, bureaucrats, and clerks drawn from across the realm. This sojourner bureaucracy consisted of officials who tended to be posted in the capital for long periods of time, often for their entire professional careers. The capital also attracted large numbers of scholar-officials who did not serve in the metropolitan bureaucracy, although most members of this group stayed for shorter periods of time. Provincial-level officials were required to have an imperial audience every few years. Expectant officials came in hope of appointment to government positions, and thousands of examination candidates periodically poured into the capital to take part in the metropolitan civil-service examinations, as well as those for Shuntian 順天 prefecture (which passed candidates at a significantly higher rate than examinations held in the provincial capitals).

As is well known, late imperial Chinese society was greatly shaped by particularistic relationships based on shared personal qualities, such as membership in the same lineage, successful participation in the same civil-service examination (*tongnian* 同年), and a shared place of origin (*tongxiang* 同鄉). In Beijing, the *tongxiang* or shared native-place relationship most permeated social and political action. No other tie was more widely relied on or sought out. This sensitivity to native-place ties was promoted by the fact that, to a far greater degree than obtained elsewhere, *tongxiang* relationships in the capital not only channeled social interaction but also enabled official access and governmental decisions. Native-place ties served to facilitate a multidirectional flow of information and influence between center and region. Provincial elites used *tongxiang* ties to sway administrative decisions made in the capital, and metropolitan officials used them to affect and coordinate local administration in their native place.[13] Scholar-official elites universally recognized native-place ties as one of the most valuable sources of social capital in China's political center. Although important everywhere in the Chinese world, *tongxiang* consciousness was unusually evident in Beijing.

The special efficacy of *tongxiang* relations in Beijing was both reflected and promoted by the fact that the compatriot relationship was officially vested with an element of mutual responsibility to a degree far exceeding that found in other cities. This was institutionally manifested in the man-

---

13. Belsky, "Beijing Scholar-Official Native-Place Lodges," chap 4, "The Articulation of Regional Interests in Beijing: The Role of Huiguan During the Late Qing," pp. 201–28.

dated use of documents of guaranty called "chopped bonds" (*yinjie* 印結).[14]
Yinjie could be issued only by officials serving in Beijing who shared a common native place with those who sought the guaranty.[15] The *yinjie* attested to the proper family background and examination credentials of the person to whom it was issued and affirmed his native-place registration.[16] The official who signed the bond was held accountable for his client. If the person proved not to be who he claimed, or if, aided by the bond, he engaged in inappropriate activity, the official was deemed to share responsibility. Precedents regarding the punishments meted out to officials who inappropriately or incorrectly stood bond were numerous and detailed.[17] Chopped bonds were required of all those seeking to accomplish any of a multitude of official actions in the capital, such as the purchase of rank, appointment to public office, and permission to attend the Shuntian prefectural examination.[18]

---

14. The *Cihai* dictionary defines "*yinjie*" as a type of certificate issued as a guaranty by government officials. The certificate was referred to as "*jie*," and those which had been chopped, or affixed with an official stamp, were known as "*yinjie*" (*Cihai* 辭海, 1-vol. ed. [Hong Kong: Zhonghua shuju, 1988], p. 225). See also Li Pengnian 李鵬年 et al., eds., *Qingdai liubu chengyu cidian* 清代六部成語詞典 (A dictionary of phrases associated with the six boards of the Qing period) (Tianjin: Tianjin renmin chubanshe, 1990), p. 41, for a more detailed description. E-tu Zen Sun translates the term as "sealed bond of guaranty"; see *Ch'ing Administrative Terms: A Translation of the Terminology of the Six Boards with Explanatory Notes* (Cambridge, Mass.: Harvard University Press, 1961), p. 25.

15. Ordinarily only officials of the sixth rank and above were entitled to issue *yinjie*, but officials of lower rank could do so if no fellow-provincial officials of that level were then serving in the capital. See *Qing huidian shi li* 清會典事例 (Collected statutes and substatutes of the Qing) (1899; reprinted—Beijing: Zhonghua shuju, 1991), *juan* 115, 2: 483. The precedent for the exception cited here was dated 1800 and dealt specifically with guarantees required by examination candidates, although one suspects that the "rule of analogy" would have allowed this principle to be applied in all cases requiring the use of *yinjie*.

16. For a sample *yinjie* form, see Huang Liuhong 黃六鴻, *Fu hui quan shu* 福惠全書 (Beijing, 1893 [originally published 1694]), 1.22. All such sample forms were excluded from the English translation of this work by Djang Chu, *A Complete Book Concerning Happiness and Benevolence: A Manual for Local Magistrates in Seventeenth-Century China* (Tucson: University of Arizona Press, 1984). Djang translates the term as "a reference letter from an official in the capital," which somewhat misses the formality and the degree of responsibility conferred upon the issuer; see, e.g., p. 86.

17. *Qing huidian shi li, juan* 115, 2: 482–85, gives precedents related to the inappropriate issuance of guarantees.

18. For more on this and other aspects of the *yinjie* bond, see Belsky, "Beijing Scholar-Official Native-Place Lodges," pp. 230–37.

Failure to obtain the proper chopped bond could conversely prove an obstacle to achieving the desired government action.

Mutual accountability in the capital for *tongxiang* compatriots was not limited to the acquisition of the chopped bonds alone. The sense that native-place groups of scholar-officials in Beijing were responsible for the actions of others from their home area encouraged such groups to take steps toward policing their own. This explains why during Kang Youwei's visit to the capital in 1888–89, his compatriots from his home county of Nanhai sought to expel Kang from Beijing so that they would not be implicated by his unorthodox public proclamations.[19]

The Scholar-Official Native-Place Lodges (Huiguan) of Xuannan

As the center of Han scholar-official residence, the Xuannan ward contained numerous private residential compounds of notable officials and an unparalleled number of native-place lodges. By the 1890s, Beijing boasted nearly 400 separately administered lodges by even the most conservative reckoning. The Beijing lodges were distinguished not only by their number but by their character as well. *Huiguan* in other cities tended to serve and be operated by sojourning merchants and/or tradesmen. In Beijing, however, no more than 15 percent or so of native-place lodges served a similar socio-economic niche.[20] Instead, the great majority served the huge numbers of scholar-officials who gravitated to the capital. Many even specifically excluded merchants. Scholar-official *huiguan* filled the streets of the Xuannan ward. Hardly a street or lane of any size did not have some number of them, often with the walls of one lodge compound abutting the walls of another. This unusual concentration of scholar-official *huiguan* proved to be an integral element in the development of the reform movement.

Almost every central figure in the reform movement lived in or was closely associated with a native-place lodge while he was in the capital. Al-

---

19. Wang Qing 王青, *Qimeng yu nahan* 啓蒙與吶喊 (Enlightenment and the call to arms) (Beijing: Yanshan chubanshe, 1998), pp. 60–61. Kang attributed the friction between him and his Nanhai county compatriots to his refusal to pay several high-ranking officials from Nanhai the courtesy calls customarily expected of junior compatriots when visiting the capital; see Kang Youwei, "Chronological Autobiography," p. 46.

20. The pre-eminent Chinese scholar on the Beijing merchant *huiguan*, Li Hua (*Ming-Qing yilai Beijing gongshang huiguan beike xuan bian*, p. 20), estimated that no more than 14 percent of the 392 late Qing Beijing lodges he identified served merchants and artisans.

though Kang Youwei occasionally resided briefly in the Inner City, his primary residence in Beijing was the (Guangdong) Nanhai huiguan 南海會館 on Mishi hutong 米市胡同. Liang Qichao 梁啓超 (1873–1929) stayed in the (Guangdong) Xinhui huiguan 新會會館 on Fenfang Liuli jie 粉坊琉璃街. Tan Sitong resided in the Liuyang huiguan 瀏陽會館 on Kudui hutong 庫堆胡同. Lin Xu 林旭 (1875–98) and Yang Rui 楊銳 (1857–98) also maintained close ties to their native-place lodges. The identification of these men with their lodges is revealed in the titles they bestowed on the collections of their personal writings. Kang's collection of poetry, *Han man fang ji* 汗漫舫集; Tan Sitong's *Mang cang cang zhai ji* 莽蒼蒼齋集; Liang Qichao's *Yinbingshi heji* 飲冰室合集; and Yang Shenxiu's 楊深秀 (1848–98) *Xue xu sheng tang shichao* 雪虛聲堂詩鈔 all took their names from courtyards in the Beijing native-place lodges where they resided.[21]

The historical significance of the lodges lies not merely in the fact that so many influential figures of the reform movement lived in and identified with them; rather, many of the most pivotal events of the movement also occurred within native-place lodge compounds (as I discuss below). To the limited extent that the literature has recognized a native-place connection to the reform movement, the connection has not been sufficiently analyzed or its import fully appreciated. There are various reasons for this oversight, but it is at least in part because the reformist activities that took place in the lodges were in no case undertaken in the name of the lodges. *Huiguan* did not operate as explicit corporate participants in this movement. Reformers met in lodge meeting halls and delivered addresses from lodge opera stages, but they did not walk out on the "public stage" as representatives of this or that lodge. However, much more was involved here than just the use of value-neutral space by participants in a cause unrelated to the lodges or the native-place ties they represented. To see more clearly what was involved, we need to examine the nature of lodge space and familiarize ourselves with the

---

21. For Kang's description of moving into the courtyard and his bestowal of the poetic name on it, see Kang Youwei, "Chronological Autobiography," p. 47; and Wei Jingzhao 韋經照, "Nanhai huiguan chunqiu" 南海會館春秋 (History of the Nanhai native-place lodge), in Lin Keguang et al., *Jindai Jinghua shiji*, pp. 269–76; on Tan Sitong, see Tong Xun 佟洵, "Liuyang huiguan mang cangcang zhai" 瀏陽會館莽蒼蒼齋 (The Mang cangcang studio of the Liuyang native-place lodge) in Lin Keguang et al., *Jindai Jinghua shiji*, pp. 277–86; on Liang Qichao and Yang Shenxiu, see Hu Chunhuan 胡春煥 and Bai Hequn 白鶴群, *Beijing de huiguan* 北京的會館 (The native-place lodges of Beijing) (Beijing: Zhongguo jingji chubanshe, 1994), pp. 70–71 and 196, respectively.

numerous and mutually reinforcing ways native-place ties engendered, directed, and constrained reform movement activity. To do that, we need to consider the particular spatial and native-place context of the capital.

The Reform Movement and the Beijing Urban Context

The degree to which the particular characteristics of Beijing influenced the development of the reform movement can be seen in the early reform-related activities of scholar-officials who petitioned the government regarding the Sino-Japanese War of 1894–95. During this formative period of the reform movement, Beijing's particular urban context influenced events in three primary ways. First, the extraordinary concentration of scholar-officials in the Xuannan ward facilitated the exchange of information within that group and promoted collective action. Second, the pervasive *tongxiang* consciousness that permeated Beijing, the overwhelmingly *tongxiang* nature of scholar-official residence in the Xuannan ward imposed by the native-place lodges there, and the official policies mandating compatriot mutual accountability in petitions submitted to the state combined to ensure that much of the public action in the course of the reform movement was undertaken by groups defined by shared native-place origins. And, third, the spatial character of the hundreds of scholar-official native-place lodges in the Xuannan ward and the relative absence of state supervision granted by their status as recognized corporate entities facilitated the holding of the new style of political meetings that were essential elements of the reform movement.

The most famous event associated with the upsurge in scholar-official protest against the war policy was the 1895 "Petitioning of the Emperor by the Examination Candidates" ("Gongche shangshu" 公車上書).[22] This incident arose in response to the humiliating conditions the Qing state was forced to accept as part of the Treaty of Shimonoseki, the treaty that brought the Sino-Japanese War to a conclusion. Word of the proposed settlement reached Beijing in late April 1895, just as thousands of candidates were in the capital to take the examinations. When news of the unprece-

---

22. The term *gongche* was widely used in late imperial texts as a term for examination candidates. Scholars disagree about the proper pronunciation of the term, with some insisting that the proper pronunciation is *gongju*. Since an informal canvassing of Chinese scholars revealed no consensus on this point, I have followed the pronunciation given in two authoritative Chinese dictionaries, the *Hanyu da cidian* 漢語大詞典 (Shanghai: Hanyu da cidian chubanshe, 1990) and *Cihai*.

dented concessions granted a foreign power (and former tributary) reached the thousands of idle, idealistic, and ambitious examination candidates assembled in the capital, who were already stressed because of the examinations, it proved to be incendiary.

The most celebrated petition submitted by examination candidates was that signed on April 30, 1895, by 1,300 or so candidates from all eighteen provinces. The candidates gathered at Songyun an 松筠庵, a courtyard area in the heart of the Xuannan ward maintained as a shrine to the sixteenth-century official Yang Jisheng 楊繼盛. Yang had been martyred for his strong opposition to the policy of appeasement of the Mongols. His shrine resonated with obvious symbolism for those opposed to the 1895 peace treaty. The candidates who gathered there signed their names to a petition drafted by Kang Youwei that called for a resumption of the fighting, the transfer of the capital to the interior, and other measures of reform and resistance. The Songyun an petition expressed the will of those normally excluded from voicing an opinion on governmental affairs and served, in turn, as a model for popular protest for many years thereafter. It was, moreover, just one in a series of group petitions submitted by scholar-officials regarding war policy.

Over eighty examination candidates from Guangdong and Hunan, organized in part by Liang Qichao, submitted petitions on April 22, eight days before the Songyun an meeting.[23] According to Kang Youwei, that action inspired other groups of provincial candidates to submit petitions as well.[24] Less widely appreciated is the fact that protests, petitions, and calls for the reform of the war policy began much earlier and emerged from a wider social-professional base than Kang indicates. The writings of the prominent reformist official Wen Tingshi 文廷式 (1856–1904), for example, make clear that similar efforts to remonstrate with the government over war policy began not among examination candidates but among low-ranking metropolitan officials as early as September 1894. The officials drew up joint petitions advocating measures such as placing Prince Gong in charge of the war

---

23. According to the records of the censorate, four petitions related to the war were submitted that day, one signed by 81 Guangdong natives, and three petitions signed by a total of 120 Hunan natives. See Lin Keguang 林克光, *Gexinpai juren Kang Youwei* 革新派巨人康有為 (Giant of the reform faction, Kang Youwei) (Beijing: Zhongguo renmin daxue chubanshe, 1990), p. 133.

24. Kang Youwei, "Chronological Autobiography," p. 64.

effort and entering into an alliance with England to strengthen China's hand against Japan.[25] Later, groups of low-level metropolitan officials signed and submitted more petitions, including three by groups of Hanlin scholars, one signed by 56 secretaries in the Zongli yamen, and another signed by 156 members of the Grand Secretariat.[26]

The actions of these bureaucratic remonstrators in late 1894 and early 1895 is particularly relevant to this chapter's focus on the connection between the unique characteristics of Beijing and the historical development of the reform movement. First, the pool of thousands of metropolitan officials resident in Beijing from which the first protesters emerged was a social-professional group, found on this scale nowhere else. Second, the emergence of this early protest trend was clearly facilitated by the dense congregation of metropolitan officials in the Xuannan area. And third, those involved took advantage of uniquely plentiful space in native-place lodges to meet and or-ganize. Wen Tingshi, for example, in his record of the events leading to the submission of petitions in which he was involved, describes groups meeting in several different *huiguan* locations, including the Zhejiang Provincial Huiguan and the (Jiangxi) Xiegong ci 謝公祠.[27]

In late April and early May 1895, as the terms of the proposed treaty were made known, the protest movement entered a new stage. The number of petitions submitted by low-ranking metropolitan officials and unranked ex-amination candidates suddenly jumped in number. In fact, a total of 32 sepa-rate petitions were presented to the censorate by groups of examination can-didates and metropolitan officials between April 22 and May 5, 1895.[28] Indeed, approximately 3,000 candidates overall put their names to these pe-titions, bringing the total number of signatures including those affixed to the Songyun an petition to well over 4,000. The submission of the petitions was accompanied by a tumultuous popular protest that arguably may be consid-ered a harbinger of the student-led protests against government policy that so marked the twentieth century. Beginning on April 22, 1895, examination

---

25. Wen Tingshi 文廷式, *Wen Tingshi ji* 文廷式集 (Collected works of Wen Tingshi) (Beijing: Zhonghua shuju, 1993), p. 1495. Prince Gong had been cashiered in 1884. He was in-deed called back in 1894 and placed in charge of the Zongli yamen and the Board of Admi-ralty to direct the war against Japan.

26. Luke S. K. Kwong, *A Mosaic of the Hundred Days: Personalities, Politics and Ideas of 1898* (Cambridge, Mass.: Harvard University, Council on East Asian Studies, 1984), p. 73.

27. Wen, *Wen Tingshi ji*, p. 1495.

28. Lin Keguang, *Gexinpai juren Kang Youwei*, pp. 132–35.

candidates and other scholar-officials gathered outside the censorate to demonstrate their opposition to the treaty. The protests continued every other day after that for the rest of the month (the censors reported to the court on alternate days, and the protests matched their schedule). During these demonstrations, it was said that the street in front of the censorate filled with carts and horses, and the throngs of scholars voicing their views were so tightly assembled that not even "sunlight could pass between them."[29]

The unique institutionalization of *tongxiang* relations in Beijing is reflected in the striking *tongxiang* character of the movement and its expression through the petitions. With the exception of the Songyun an petition, all the others were submitted by groups of candidates from a single province. What accounts for this? The fact that the candidates were living, socializing, and meeting in their native-place lodges was certainly one factor. One can imagine how effectively the spirit of protest must have caught on among the candidates as news of the events circulated through each of the native-place lodges. The proximity to *tongxiang* fellows provided by the lodges certainly contributed to the group expression of opinion, but there was more at work than physical proximity. The candidates surely conceived of themselves as representing their shared region of origin as they submitted petitions. A certain degree of native-place rivalry may also have stimulated the submission of petitions, as the candidates strove to demonstrate the moral indignation of their respective home regions at a time when examinees from other regions were doing the same thing.

The omnipresent influence of compatriot ties was present even in the Songyun an event. Although candidates from every province signed the petition, they signed in blocs of provincial groups. Moreover, the space used to organize the signing had native-place ties as well. Across the street from the Songyun an stood the Songyun caotang 嵩雲草堂, a hall with a capacity of 200–300 people. That site was the main building of the (Zhili) Zhongzhou huiguan 中州會館. According to a retrospective account by an eyewitness, because the thousand-plus candidates who gathered for the mass signing

---

29. Hushang yuanshi laoren 滬上袁時老人, "Xu" 序 (Foreword), in *Gongche shangshu ji* 公車上書記 (Record of the petitions submitted by the examination candidates) (Shanghai: Shiyin shuju, 1895); cited in Kong Xiangji 孔祥吉, *Kang Youwei bianfa zouyi yanjiu* 康有爲變法奏議研究 (A study of Kang Youwei's reform memorials) (Shenyang: Liaoning jiaoyu chubanshe, 1988), pp. 80–81.

could not fit into the small Songyun an, the candidates actually assembled at both the Songyun an and the Songyun caotang to sign the petition and then met outside the Xuanwu Gate and proceeded to the censorate from there.[30] Even the Songyun an may have possessed a *tongxiang* connection to Zhili compatriots in the capital. It was certainly administered by Hebei sojourners in later years, although whether a connection existed in 1898 is not clear.[31]

The unique system of native-place mutual accountability imposed through the *yinjie* system was another factor of crucial importance in determining the *tongxiang* structure of the protests. According to Qing statutes, examination candidates were not entitled to submit their views directly to the throne. Acceptance of the petitions by the censorate was contingent on the protesters' receiving the proper chopped-bond guaranty from compatriot metropolitan officials. This rule helps to explain why of the 32 known petitions submitted at that time, the only one the censorate refused to accept and transmit to the throne was the one associated with the Songyun an gathering. In fact, the refusal of the censorate to accept this petition has long been something of a mystery. According to Kang Youwei, censorate officials "refused to accept the petition, stating that the imperial seal had already been affixed [to documents accepting the peace treaty], and they could not be canceled."[32] However, Kong Xiangji, using the Grand Council archives and other materials, has shown that Kang Youwei was wrong.[33] In fact, fifteen other similar petitions were accepted by the censorate on May 2, the very day that Kang claimed the Songyun an petition was presented. In noting the reasons for the acceptance of the other petitions, the officials at the

---

30. Ye Zufu 葉祖孚, *Beijing Fengqing zatan* 北京風情雜談 (Miscellaneous comments on the customs of Beijing) (Beijing: Zhongguo chengshi chubanshe, 1995), pp. 116–17. For background on the Songyun caotang, see Lin Keguang 林克光, "Beijing Qiangxuehui yizhi" 北京強學會遺址 (The original site of the Beijing Society for the Study of Self-strengthening), in idem et al., eds., *Jindai jinghua shiji*, pp. 257–76. For background on the Zhongzhou huiguan (later renamed the Henan huiguan and referred to such in this work) see Hu Chunhuan and Bai Hequn, *Beijing de huiguan*, pp. 216–18.

31. For background information on the Songyun an, see Lin Keguang 林克光, "Songyun an yu 'Gongche shangshu'" 松筠庵與公車上書 (The Songyun an and the petitions submitted by the examination candidates), in idem et al., eds., *Jindai jinghua shiji*, p. 255.

32. Kang Youwei, "Chronological Autobiography," p. 65.

33. Kong Xiangji 孔祥吉, *Wuxu weixin yundong xintan* 戊戌維新運動新談 (A new look at the 1898 reform movement) (Changsha: Hunan renmin chubanshe, 1988), pp. 10–11. The imperial seal was not affixed until May 3.

censorate explained to the court: "Within each of these petitions there are some imperfections. However, in consideration of the important and urgent nature of this matter, and as these functionaries and examination candidates, and so on, have all obtained chopped bonds from their *tongxiang* metropolitan officials . . . we do not dare to keep them from your attention."[34]

However, Kong Xiangji has convincingly argued that the Songyun an petition was not submitted to the censorate on May 2, as Kang Youwei remembered, but on May 4. It is possible that the challenge of securing *yinjie* for all the provinces represented in that document resulted in its submission without the proper paperwork, for we know that other petitions were submitted and accepted on that day and the next.[35] It thus seems that it was largely because of the multiprovincial origins of the signers of the Songyun an petition (rather than the timing or the content of the text) that it was not passed on to the emperor. This would explain why the censorate accepted Kang's "Third Petition to the Emperor" a few weeks later, even though in content the document was largely a version of the Songyun an petition. Indeed, as the censors passed that document to the emperor, they noted among the most important reasons for their doing so was that Kang had acquired the proper chopped bonds from his *tongxiang* metropolitan officials.[36]

Native-Place Lodges and the Formation of Political Societies

The hundreds of native-place lodges in Beijing were essential to the sudden outbreak of new forms of mass action undertaken by the examination candidates and low-ranking metropolitan bureaucrats in the spring of 1895. The role of the lodges was noted at the time: when some government officials decided to put an end to the movement, they targeted the Xuannan native-place lodges. In the final days of the protests, a close associate of the grand councilor Sun Yuwen 孫毓汶 (1833–99) was dispatched to make a round of the native-place lodges in the Xuannan ward in order to intimidate the candidates.[37] Sun's representative was successful; many candidates withdrew

---

34. Zhongguo shixue hui 中國史學會, *Zhong-Ri zhanzheng* 中日戰爭 (The Sino-Japanese War) (Shanghai: Xin jinshi chubanshe, 1956), 4: 58; cited in Kong Xiangji, *Wuxu weixin yundong xintan*, p. 11.

35. Kong Xiangji, *Wuxu weixin yundong xintan*, p. 14.

36. Ibid., p. 43.

37. Kang Youwei, "Chronological Autobiography," p. 65. For a thumbnail biography of Sun Yuwen, see Hummel, *Eminent Chinese of the Ch'ing Period*, p. 685.

their support for the petitions, and in the end the signing of the treaty by the emperor deprived the movement of an issue to protest.

The role of the native-place lodges in the reform movement was far from over, however. One of the most significant developments leading to the 1898 reform movement was the founding of study societies that brought scholar-officials together in a new form of political association in order to discuss and advocate reforms. The first of these societies was the Qiangxuehui 強學 會 (Society for the study of self-strengthening). Founded in Beijing in October 1895, it was closed by the government only five months later for violating the Qing ban on the founding of private societies.[38] Despite its short life, the society proved tremendously influential. Later study societies were founded in other cities (including the Southern Qiangxuehui, the influential off-shoot of the Beijing society founded in Shanghai), but it was no accident that the earliest reform society was founded in Beijing. Nor was it an accident that its meetings were held on lodge grounds, since the degree of autonomy from state control traditionally accorded corporately adminis-tered space provided the necessary breathing room for this new form of soci-ety to take hold. As Kang Youwei later recorded, "If the societies had first been organized in the provinces, they would have been checked by the local officials. Therefore it [was] necessary to organize a society of scholars and officials in the capital first."[39]

The Qiangxuehui was not organized along native-place lines, but it was closely associated with two of the capital's native-place lodges. One was the Anhui huiguan 安徽會館, where the powerful official Sun Jia'nai 孫家鼐 (1827–1909), who hailed from Anhui, made space available for the society's meetings.[40] The other site was the Songyun caotang in the Zhongzhou huiguan, which had earlier served as a meeting place for the candidates in-volved in the Sungyun an petition to the emperor.[41]

Two years after the Qiangxuehui was disbanded, the capital once again witnessed the establishment by scholar-officials of a new group of political

38. Hao Chang, "Intellectual Change and the Reform Movement," *Cambridge History of China*, vol. II, pt. II, *The Late Ch'ing, 1800–1911*, ed. Denis Twitchett and John K. Fairbank (Cambridge, Eng.: Cambridge University Press, 1980), pp. 293–95.

39. Kang Youwei, "Chronological Autobiography," p. 71.

40. Lin Keguang, "Beijing Qiangxuehui yizhi," pp. 263–64.

41. Kang Youwei, "Chronological Autobiography," p. 72; see also Liang Qichao 梁啓超, *Wuxu zhengbian ji* 戊戌政變記 (Record of the 1898 reforms) (Shanghai, 1936), p. 126.

societies. Founded on the eve of the hundred days of reform, these societies mobilized scholar-officials in Beijing to engage publicly in the advocacy of reform and represented a vital step in the creation of a groundswell of elite opinion for a change in state policy. The particular urban characteristics of Beijing were especially apparent in the *tongxiang* organization of many of the societies and in the reliance of the societies on the native-place lodges of Xuannan to provide space not only big enough for their gatherings but also somewhat shielded from state observation and control.

These elements are clearly reflected in Kang Youwei's description of the establishment of the earliest of these societies:

At this time I wanted to revive the former activities of the Society for the Study of Self-Strengthening (Qiangxuehui); and so as my first step, I organized a society of my fellow scholars from Guangdong which, when it was formally established at a meeting of more than twenty of my friends at the Nanhai huiguan on the thirteenth day of the twelfth month (January 5, 1898), came to be known as the Guangdong Study Society (Yuexuehui 粵學會).[42]

Two months after the founding of the Yuexuehui, other reform activists established provincial-based groups. The Sichuan Study Society (Shuxuehui 蜀學會), for example, was founded by in the Sichuan huiguan 四川會館 at Piku ying 皮庫營 by Sichuanese scholar-officials under the direction of Yang Rui and Liu Guangdi 劉光第 (1859–98), both of whom were eventually martyred for their roles in the reforms.[43] Another official, Lin Xu, also later executed for his role in the reforms, founded the Fujian Study Society (Minxuehui 閩學會) in the Fujian huiguan 福建會館.[44] Among other provincial study groups established on the grounds of their respective native-place lodges were the Zhejiang Study Society (Zhexuehui 浙學會) and the Shaanxi-Shanxi Study Society (Shaanxuehui 陝學會).

---

42. Kang Youwei, "Chronological Autobiography," pp. 79–80. I have substituted the term *huiguan* for the term "club" used in the original translation, and I have converted the transliteration to pinyin spellings.

43. See Liang Qichao 梁啓超, "*Yinbingshi wenji*" 飲冰室文集 (Collected works from the Ice-Drinker's Studio), in Zhongguo shixue hui 中國史學會, ed., *Wuxu bianfa* 戊戌變法 (The 1898 reforms) (Shanghai: Shanghai renmin chubanshe, 1957), 4: 64–65. Yang Rui is given most of the credit for forming the society, but Liu was also involved; see Liu Guangdi 劉光第, *Liu Guangdi ji* 劉光第集 (Collected works of Liu Guangdi) (Beijing: Zhonghua shuju, 1986), p. 456.

44. Liang, "Yinbingshi wenji," p. 56.

Kang Youwei clearly recognized the potential role of the native-place lodges in serving as instruments for organizing the candidates and scholar-officials of the capital. Early in 1898 he sought to enlist the help of the court in re-creating the lodges as centers not only for scholar-official gatherings but also for propagating the latest knowledge gathered from abroad. As Kang later recorded in his chronological autobiography:

Since the *huiguan* are places where officials in the capital often congregate and since I wished to take advantage of their presence there to guide them, I drafted a memorial, which I handed to the provincial censor, Chen Qizhang, to submit, requesting that the Zongli yamen and the Tongwen guan (College of Foreign Languages) distribute books to the various *huiguan* for perusal by officials of the capital. A decree was issued ordering that this proposal be carried out.[45]

Despite Kang's claim, there is no evidence that a decree was issued. Nevertheless, Kang's proposal underscores the importance of the lodges as meeting places for the scholar-gentry in the capital. It also represents a fascinating vision of how the lodges might have been employed in the reform project and suggests an imagined cooperation between the state and these independently established corporate bodies. Kang's suggestion that the government keep *huiguan* libraries stocked with the latest translations of materials from abroad would have linked state and lodge in an effort to keep the capital's educated elite informed as a means to advance reform.

Although Kang's proposal was never acted on, a project of another kind soon emerged in Beijing, once again with close ties to the lodges. In April 1898 the most influential study society, the Protect the Country Society (Baoguohui 保國會), was established.[46] Organized along countrywide

---

45. Kang Youwei, "Chronological Autobiography," pp. 79–80. Indeed, the memorial was submitted by Chen on Feb. 19, 1898 (GX 24.1.29). Entitled "Qing jiang yiyin geguo tushu ban'gei gexue geguan pian" 請將譯印各國圖書頒給各學各館片 (Memorial requesting printed translations of foreign books to be distributed to schools and lodges), it may be found in Kong Xiangji 孔祥吉, ed., *Jiuwang tucun de lantu: Kang Youwei bianfa zouyi ji zheng* 救亡圖存的藍圖：康有爲變法奏議輯證 (A blueprint for salvation and survival: the reform memorials of Kang Youwei collected and authenticated) (Taibei: Lianhe baoxi wenhua, 1998), pp. 21–22; see also *Qing shi lu* 清實錄, 57.424 (GX 24.1.29). As the title of the memorial makes clear, the emphasis was on the distribution to the lodges of translated works from abroad.

46. Although often translated as the "Protect the Nation Society," the sense of *guo* here surely does not correspond entirely to "nation" as *guo* would later come to be understood. By

rather than provincial lines, it nevertheless also utilized Xuannan area native-place lodges for its meetings. Over 400 scholar-officials attended the founding meeting, held on April 12, 1898, in the Yuedong huiguan 粵東會館, one of two provincial-level *huiguan* representing Guangdong. Kang addressed the crowd from the Yuedong huiguan's impressive stage in a rousing speech that touched on a range of reform proposals.[47] The Baoguohui met only three times before disbanding in the face of mounting criticism. After the first meeting, Kang was refused permission to use the Yuedong huiguan by his powerful fellow-provincial Xu Yingkui 許應騤 (d. 1903), the president of the Board of Rites, but the final meetings of the society met in other native-place lodges in the Xuannan ward.[48] The second meeting, on April 15, 1898, was held in the Songyun caotang. The third meeting was held at the Guizhou huiguan 貴州會館 and attracted about a hundred people.[49] The establishment of the Baoguohui, which had built on the previous founding of the various provincial study societies, led in turn to the founding of still more provincial societies in the capital, such as the Protect Yunnan Society (Bao-Dian hui 保滇會), the Protect Zhejiang Society (Bao-Zhe hui 保浙會), and the Protect Sichuan Society (Bao-Chuan hui 保川會).

It was no accident that the events of the early months of 1898, much like the petitions, protests, and meetings held in the capital three years before, coincided with the influx into the capital of thousands of examination candidates preparing to take the triennial examinations. Kang Youwei portrayed a direct link between this inpouring of candidates to Beijing and his founding of the Baoguohui: "Many provincial graduates were at this time gathered in the capital, and among them were many talented men. I therefore wished to give expression to the sentiment of the entire nation."[50]

---

the same token, by 1898 its meaning had just as assuredly evolved beyond the earlier sense of "dynasty." Thus I render it as "country" here.

47. Hu Sijing 胡思敬, "Wuxu lü shuang lu" 戊戌履霜錄 (A record of walking on thin ice in 1898), in Zhongguo shixue hui, *Wuxu bian fa* 1: 374–75.

48. Xu was a native of Panyu county in Guangdong. Reference to his forbidding Kang to make further use of the provincial *huiguan* is found in the memorial submitted by Xu on June 22, 1898 (GX 24.5.4); see Dai Yi 戴逸 et al., eds., *Wuxu bairi zhi* 戊戌百日志 (Chronicle of the hundred days of 1898) (Beijing: Yanshan chubanshe, 1998), pp. 71–73; see Kwong, *A Mosaic of the Hundred Days*, pp. 184–87, for discussion of the context of this memorial.

49. Kang Youwei, "Chronological Autobiography," p. 90.

50. Ibid., p. 89.

Soon after the Baoguohui was pressured to cease its meetings, Kang and others were able to direct this timely convergence of the talented and politically aware to pressure the court publicly. Sparked by the defilement of a Confucian temple by German soldiers in Shandong, hundreds of candidates emulated the petition movement of 1895 by submitting petitions and demonstrating outside the gates of the censorate in May 1898. This group action is sometimes referred to as the "Second Petitioning of the Emperor by the Examination Candidates" ("Di'erci gongche shangshu" 第二次公車上書).[51] As before, the petitions and demonstrations were organized largely along native-place lines. One of the initial petitions was signed by 369 candidates from Fujian under the direction of Lin Xu; 165 candidates from Hubei signed another one; 43 from Hunan signed another; candidates from Jiangsu quickly followed with one of their own.[52] The movement culminated with a single petition signed by 830 candidates from all the provinces, but there can be little doubt that this important mass action on the eve of the hundred days could not have taken place without the unique set of circumstances afforded by the capital, the Xuannan ward, and the hundreds of native-place lodges there.

The importance of native-place lodges as residences and meeting places for those involved in the reforms persisted to the end of the movement. Following the Empress Dowager's coup d'état, soldiers arrested several of the principal activists in their *huiguan* residences. Kang Youwei's younger brother, Kang Guangren 康光仁 (1867–98), was arrested in the Nanhai huiguan on Mishi hutong, Tan Sitong waited for his arrest in the Liuyang huiguan on Kudui hutong, and Yang Shenxiu was taken into custody from his courtyard in the (Shanxi) Wenxi huiguan 聞喜會館 on Ganlüshi hutong 趕驢市胡同.

How the Reforms Reshaped Beijing

When the Guangxu emperor began to issue his sweeping series of edicts in early June 1898, the dynamics of reform fundamentally shifted. Once the emperor adopted the reform program, forces at play within the court, the upper ranks of government, and the military largely dictated events. During the hundred days, the impetus for reform emanated from the government

51. Kong Xiangji, *Wuxu weixin yundong xintan*, pp. 315–42.
52. Ibid., pp. 319–20.

rather than from the lanes and lodges of the capital. Moreover, with the conclusion of the imperial examinations, the candidates' return to their respective native places depleted the *hutong* 胡同–based movement that had so characterized earlier efforts. Beijing's urban context exerted less influence than it did in the period leading up to the emperor's decision to throw his authority behind the reform program. The intimate connection between Beijing and the reform movement was by no means terminated, however. Some measures proposed during the hundred days concerned Beijing, and although only some were enacted, the rise and fall of the reform policies greatly affected the capital.

Reform of metropolitan institutions was a constant if not central theme of the movement throughout. One intended reform that never was implemented involved the capital's roads. Although the Roadway Office (Jiedao ting 街道聽) long established under the superintendence of the police censors of Beijing was charged with "the maintenance, in good order, of the streets of the Outer City," the capital's roads were notoriously poor.[53] As one popular local couplet humorously put it:

> When the wind is calm, there is three feet of dust;
> When the rain falls, the whole street is mud.[54]

Correcting this situation had been on the agenda of key reform activists for several years. In 1895 Kang Youwei had arranged for a memorial requesting road repair to be submitted on his behalf, and in 1896 Wen Tingshi petitioned the court asking that the streets and drainage ditches of the capital be repaired.[55] According to Kang, an edict was issued authorizing the repair, but in the end only a small section of roadway in the Xuannan area was repaired.[56] The issue resurfaced during the hundred days, and the emperor once again issued an edict decrying that the streets were filled with mud and the canals and waterways blocked with obstructions. He called on the appropriate authorities to investigate and correct the problems.[57] As before,

---

53. H. S. Brunnert and V. V. Hagelstrom, *Present Day Political Organization of China* (Fuzhou, 1911; reprinted—Taipei, Ch'eng Wen, 1978), p. 378.

54. Chen Zongfan 陳宗蕃, ed. *Yandu congkao* 燕都叢考 (Compendium on Beijing) (Beijing: Beijing guji chubanshe, 1991), p. 163.

55. Wen, *Wen Tingshi ji*, pp. 91–92.

56. Kang Youwei, "Chronological Autobiography," pp. 68–69.

57. Dai Yi et al., *Wuxu bairi zhi*, p. 402. The edict was issued on Sept. 5, 1898 (GX 24.7.20).

however, little appears to have been accomplished after the edict was issued; indeed, it is a testament to the limits of imperial power that the emperor could not even fix the streets of his own capital. The emperor was still fielding requests to repair the streets of Beijing on the ninety-fifth day of the hundred days.[58]

Another aborted reformist idea involved Beijing's status as the capital. Contemporaries often referred to the city as the empire's "pre-eminent place" (*shoushan zhi chu* 首善之處). No single phrase better described Beijing's position at the pinnacle of China's urban hierarchy. Ironically, only days after the emperor had used the phrase in the edict calling for repair of the capital's streets, Kang Youwei submitted a memorial that would have fundamentally undermined Beijing's claim to pre-eminence and would have transformed the city in other ways as well. Kang recommended the removal of the imperial capital from Beijing.[59] Kang's proposal may have partially been inspired by a desire to move the court away from what he perceived to be a base of conservative interests, but it also reflected an old platform of his—he had first called for transferring the capital inland during the Sino-Japanese War as one measure by which China could continue to resist the Japanese. Kang's 1898 proposal expanded on that theme by listing the many ways in which Beijing had proved less than an ideal capital. According to Kang, Beijing was too far north and therefore difficult to travel to; its climate was too dry and cold; its blowing sands obstructed one's vision, and so on. Kang proposed constructing a new capital in the Jiangnan region and creating a system of nine subsidiary capitals. Beijing would have been one of this new set of subsidiary capitals, along with Guangzhou, Wuchang, Lhasa, and Urumqi (Dihua), and other cities.

Kang's visionary—though impractical—proposal was not adopted, and Beijing was spared the sweeping changes that would have resulted. But the origins of other more modest but important changes can be directly traced to this period. There were, for example, substantial developments in the educational infrastructure of the city. Educational reform was one of the principal objects of the decrees issued during the hundred days. The most notable consequence of these efforts was the establishment of the Imperial University, the progenitor of Beijing University, as well as the eventual

---

58. Ibid., p. 512; see also p. 526; *Qing shi lu*, Sept. 13, 1898 (GX 24.7.28).

59. Dai Yi et al., *Wuxu bairi zhi*, pp. 425–29. The memorial was submitted on Sept. 5, 1898 (GX 24.7.20).

abandonment of the entire imperial examination system (the latter, of course, not enacted until 1905, although first ordered in 1898). Less widely recognized, however, is that the hundred days also proved a turning point in the character of primary and secondary education in the capital. Here, too, there was a strong link to the scholar-official native-place institutions of the capital. Prior to 1898, education of children resident in Beijing was largely left to tutors independently hired by families and lineages. During the 1898 reform period, this began to change.

The eminent official Sun Jia'nai had earlier served as personal tutor of the Guangxu emperor. Beginning in 1896, the emperor had entrusted Sun with various reforms relating to education, including the abortive 1896 attempt to establish a university in the capital. When during the course of the hundred days efforts to establish the university were revived, Sun was again at the heart of them, and he became the university's first president.[60] Although Sun is best known for his involvement in the establishment of what would become Beijing University, he also played a role in the founding of Beijing's primary and grade schools.

In late July 1898, a memorial submitted to the emperor requested that Sun be placed in charge of deliberations and decisions regarding the establishment of primary and middle schools in the capital.[61] Sun shortly responded with a memorial of his own recommending elementary and middle schools in the capital for local commoners, as well as for the sons of metropolitan officials and other sojourning scholar-officials.[62] Sun followed this with another memorial five days later suggesting that the primary and middle school reforms should be undertaken in conjunction with the efforts to establish the university.[63]

In the end, this top-down approach to the establishment of primary and middle schools did not succeed. However, a number of grade schools with direct ties to the reform movement were set up around this time. On September 17, 1898, an expectant second-class secretary in the Board of Revenue submitted a memorial requesting the metropolitan officials of the various

---

60. These and other activities related to education undertaken by Sun are well related in Hummel, *Eminent Chinese of the Ch'ing Period*, pp. 673–775.

61. *Qing shi lu*, July 24, 1898 (GX 24.6.6); Dai Yi et al., *Wuxu bairi zhi*, p. 226.

62. Dai Yi et al., *Wuxu bairi zhi*, p. 256. The memorial was recorded on Aug. 4, 1898 (GX 24.6.17).

63. Ibid., p. 265. The memorial was recorded on Aug. 8, 1898 (GX 24.6.22).

provinces be instructed to establish primary schools and middle schools in their native-place lodges.[64] Within a decade or so, *huiguan*-run schools had come to occupy a major niche in primary and secondary education in the capital.

In the early years of the twentieth century, spurred by the abolition of the examination system and the perceived need for a new effective means of educating China's youth, educational reform swept through China. Richard Orb has demonstrated the leading role of Zhili province, which surrounded Beijing, in the implementation of educational reform in the waning years of the Qing dynasty.[65] Orb did not specifically examine Beijing, but the residents of the capital made impressive efforts in educational reform. Once again, the strong native-place social structure of the capital contributed to and informed these developments. According to a 1909 police report that focused exclusively on Beijing, 250 new-style schools had been established in Beijing by that time. These were categorized at the time as private (*sili* 私立), official (*guanli* 官立), or public (*gongli* 公立). The "official" schools were established by the state, and the "public" schools were established through the collective efforts of social groups without state support (in today's parlance they might be called "nonprofit community schools"). Of the nineteen schools categorized as public schools, fifteen were operated by and on behalf of provincial sojourning communities in the capital. One such school, the Sichuan School (Shuxuetang 蜀學堂), had been established by Yang Rui (one of the "Six Martyrs" of 1898) in the Sichuan huiguan on Piku ying. Indeed, in recognition of his efforts on behalf of the school and in response to a memorial submitted by Sun Jia'nai, the emperor issued an edict in encouragement of Yang's efforts.[66]

The 1909 police report did not record all the schools known to have been established by sojourning communities in Beijing. Among those excluded were the Yunnan School, which was set up on the premises of the Yunnan

---

64. Ibid., 563. The memorial was recorded on Sept. 17, 1898 (GX 24.7.2).

65. Richard A. Orb, "Chihli Academies and Other Schools in the Late Qing: An Institutional Survey," in *Reform in Nineteenth Century China*, ed. Paul A. Cohen and John E. Schrecker (Cambridge, Mass.: Harvard University, East Asian Research Center, 1976), pp. 231–40.

66. Dai Yi et al., *Wuxu bairi zhi*, p. 586. Sun's memorial was recorded on Sept. 19, 1898 (GX 24.8.4); see also *Qing shi lu*, 57.597 (GX 24.8.4).

xin'guan 雲南新館 on Zhuchao jie 珠巢街 shortly after 1898.[67] Also overlooked was the Zhili School established in 1898 and still operating into the 1930s.[68]

Given the overall numbers of new schools established in Beijing in the last years of the dynasty, the number of schools organized along native-place lines may appear to have been a negligible part of the new trend. In fact, however, they represented a disproportionate amount of the educational investment in the capital, even if only the fifteen schools recorded in the 1909 police report are taken into consideration. Established to educate the children of sojourner communities, these schools benefited from the well-established methods of fund-raising for such community causes. These schools were among the best endowed of all the new schools in the capital. The total registered income of all categories of schools in the report was 380,303 *liang* of silver; the provincial schools accounted for 156,040 *liang*, or just over 40 percent of the total. The value of the reported assets of the provincial schools is even more impressive—414,389 *liang* out of a total 667,501 *liang* for all schools in Beijing.[69] According to the report, the *tongxiang* schools possessed over 60 percent of all school-owned assets in Beijing.

Beijing was surely as affected by the events of 1895–98 as any other single place. Some reform proposals aimed at Beijing, such as Kang Youwei's suggestion that the capital be moved, were never even seriously considered. Even more modest proposals, such as those calling for the repair of the capital's roadways, which were picked up by the emperor, had only limited impact. On the other hand, educational reforms were to prove to have lasting consequences. The establishment of what would become Beijing University is a good example, as is the eventual abolition of the imperial examinations. Modest reform measures made their influence felt as well, as is seen in the trend to establish primary and secondary schools in the city. Among the most fundamental consequences of the reforms on the

---

67. Jian Enpei 簡恩霈, "Yunnan ren zai Beijing" 雲南人在北京 (Yunnan natives in Beijing), *Yandu* 1, no. 22 (1989): 47–48.

68. Zhang Xiaoxin 張孝訢, "Beiping huiguan diaocha" 北平會館調查 (Investigation of the native-place lodges of Beiping) (unpublished graduation thesis, Yenching University, Sociology Department, 1936), pp. 54b–59.

69. First Historical Archives of China, Board of the Administration of the People (Minzheng bu).

city, however, was the transformation in the nature of the meeting spaces in the native-place lodges of Xuannan, and a related shift toward state penetration of such space.

Native-Place Space After 1898

As we have seen, the native-place lodges in the capital became centers of provincially organized political networking and organization during the 1895–98 reform movement. At the same time, the meeting halls and spacious opera stages found in the more prominent lodges increasingly became venues for explicitly political meetings and public speeches that cut across native-place lines. Native-place lodges were not, of course, the only arenas for politically charged events in the years following the reform. But the lodges provided an important form of such space, both because of the extensive space they occupied and because they benefited from what David Strand has called a "modicum of protection" that led the authorities to refrain from attacking corporate bodies directly.[70] Such relative insulation from state intrusion stemmed from both the location of the lodges in the Outer City (and the less intrusive police presence there) and, in Strand's words, "a tradition of corporate self-regulation," which accorded the *huiguan* an added measure of autonomy.[71]

What began in 1894–95 with meetings of lower-level metropolitan bureaucrats and examination candidates to protest war policies expanded into further meetings and the establishment of political "study societies" in the years that followed. Native-place lodge space was increasingly used for political activities after 1898. This trend was especially pronounced in the years from the eve of the 1911 revolution through the May Fourth period. A detailed examination of this phenomenon lies outside the parameters of this chapter, but a few representative examples of such meetings will illustrate the point. In the last year of the empire, for example, representatives from the various provinces attended a meeting in the Hunan huiguan 湖南會館 advocating the convening of a parliament in conjunction with the establish-

---

70. David Strand, *"Civil Society" and "Public Sphere" in Modern China: A Perspective on Popular Movements in Beijing, 1919–1989.* Durham, N.C.: Duke University, Asian/Pacific Studies Institute, 1990, p. 11.

71. Ibid.

ment of a new constitution.[72] The transformation in the political functions of native-place lodges became even more apparent after the republic was founded. Sun Yat-sen 孫逸仙 (1866–1925) was a frequent visitor to the capital's native-place lodges at this time. In the summer of 1912, during his second trip to Beijing, Sun delivered public speeches at the (Anhui) Anqing huiguan 安慶會館, the (Guangdong) Yuedong huiguan, and the (Guangdong) Xiangshan huiguan 香山會館.[73] Over the years, Sun Yat-sen also delivered a number of political speeches to audiences at the (Hunan-Hubei) Huguang huiguan 湖廣會館, at Hufang qiao 虎坊橋 in the heart of the Xuannan ward.[74]

A number of political parties and political societies were formed in the native-place lodges of Xuannan in this period as well. Among them were the Military Study Society (Wuxue she 武學社) founded in the Hunan huiguan in 1912, and the Administering Virtue Society (Zhengdehui 政德會) founded in the Sichuan huiguan in 1913.[75] That same year the Greater China Party (Dazhongdang 大中黨) and the Society for the Establishment of a Constitution (Xianfa qicheng hui 憲法期成會) were founded in the Sichuan huiguan and the Anqing huiguan, respectively.[76] No doubt the most notable of such party foundings was that of the Nationalist Party (Guomindang 國民黨) in August 1912. The new party was created from the merger of a reorganized Tongmeng hui 同盟會 and with several smaller parties in preparation for the first national elections to be held in December

---

72. First Historical Archives of China, Board of the Administration of the People (Minzheng bu), #30, Jingzheng ci, Xingzheng jingwu ke, "Minzheng bu deng guangyu jingshi baozhi, jicha ji tianceng zheng jing zhi xiangyin de wenjian."

73. Wu Zhezheng 吳哲征, "Huiguan" 會館, in Zhongguo renmin zhengzhi xieshang huiyi 中國人民政治協商會議, Beijing shi weiyuanhui 北京市委員會, Wenshi ziliao yanjiu weiyuanhui 文史資料研究委員會, ed., Beijing wangshi tan 北京往事談 (Chats on Beijing's history) (Beijing: Beijing chubanshe, 1990) p. 90. Sun's speech in the Anqing huiguan was recorded in the Zhengzong aiguo newspaper of Sept. 4, 1912; a portion is excerpted in Hu Chunhuan and Bai Hequn, Beijing de huiguan, p. 283.

74. Wang Canchi 王燦熾, "Sun Zhongshan yu Beijing Huguang huiguan" 孫中山與北京湖廣會館 (Sun Yat-sen and the Huguang huiguan in Beijing), in Beijing shi duiwai wenhua jiaoliu xiehui 北京適對外文化交流協會 et al., eds., Beijing Huguang huiguan zhi gao 北京湖廣會館志稿 (Draft gazetteer of the Huguang huiguan in Beijing) (Beijing, 1994), pp. 29–54.

75. Beijing dang'an shiliao 1995, no. 3, pp. 6–19; 1990, no. 1, pp. 4–7.

76. Ibid., 1990, no. 2, pp. 2–9; 1990, no. 3, pp. 21–29.

of that year. The Nationalist Party was founded at a public meeting organized by Huang Xing 黃興 (1873–1916) and held in the Huguang huiguan,[77]
which had one of the grandest and most spacious opera stages in the capital.
During the Republican period, this stage was increasingly used for gatherings featuring public speakers. One such occasion occurred in 1916 when
Liang Qichao and Cai Yuanpei 蔡元培 (1867–1940) debated each other
publicly there.[78]

Native-place lodges played a key role in the May Fourth Movement as
well. Among the many political activities held around that time, it is worth
mentioning the founding of the Young China Study Association in the
(Zhejiang, Ningbo) Yinxian huiguan 鄞縣會館 on Pen'er hutong 盆儿胡
同.[79] David Strand has noted that huiguan facilities played an important role
as a place to organize the May Fourth demonstrations in 1919 and as a
place of refuge when the soldiers were brought out.[80] In the years that
followed, the lodges continued to serve as favored places for political organization. The young Mao Zedong 毛澤東 (1893–1976), for example, delivered
a speech rousing his compatriots to expel the warlord Zhang Jingyao 張
敬堯 (1880–1933) from their home province in the Hunan huiguan.[81] As
late as 1925, Communist party activists founded in the (Sichuan) Tong-
chuan huiguan 潼川會館 the Light of the Catalpa Society (Ziguangshe 梓
光社) and the Catalpa Light Journal dedicated to the propagation of Marxist
ideas.[82]

The growing use of huiguan facilities for politically charged events, however, led the state to interact with them in new ways. Previous tolerance of

---

77. Recognition of this meeting re-emerged over the past few years, largely in conjunction
with municipal efforts to renovate the Huguang huiguan as a museum of and performance
site for Chinese opera. Articles in the Beijing ribao 北京日報 of Sept. 26, 1992, and the Beijing
wanbao 北京晚報 of Sept. 26, 1992, first redirected attention to this meeting. See also Hu
Chunhuan and Bai Hequn, Beijing de huiguan, pp. 161–63.

78. Beijing Municipal Archives, J181.

79. Wu Zhezheng, "Huiguan," p. 89.

80. Strand, "Civil Society," pp. 10–11.

81. Mao gave his speech on February 7, 1920. A plaque commemorating the event hangs
on the outside wall of the original Hunan huiguan compound on Lan Man hutong (formerly
Lan Mian hutong) in the Xuannan district.

82. Hu Chunhuan and Bai Hequn, Beijing de huiguan, p. 229. The catalpa tree was a common symbol of one's native place.

corporate autonomy increasingly lost out to new forms of state penetration and control of the lodges. Just as the initial rise in political activity within *huiguan* predated the establishment of the republic, so, too, did the emergence of an increased state sensitivity toward these activities. In the years following the fall of the ancien régime, the new municipal government progressed from observation to increasing control and regulation. As early as 1915, the municipal government issued detailed organizational regulations and instructed all *huiguan* in the city to adopt them. Subsequent government directives dictated precise administrative structures, procedures for elections by secret ballots, and even membership criteria. *Huiguan* were instructed (and appear, by and large, to have complied) to adopt regulations that established an elected board of governors and a director who would assume legal responsibility for the lodge—an incentive, naturally, for those who ran such lodges to keep them free of punishable activities. *Huiguan* were required to open their doors to all of their regional compatriots of good character, including women (who had been excluded under traditional rules), and prohibited from admitting the usual disreputable suspects, such as opium smokers, gamblers, those who engaged prostitutes, and those with contagious diseases. Socially disruptive activities were also prohibited. Subsequently, the government ordered all lodges to provide a list of administrative personnel to the police and the municipal social bureau of the municipal government each year and to register all lodgers with the authorities on an ongoing basis. Lodges were also instructed to give prior notice to the authorities of any meetings or gatherings to be held on their premises.[83]

The space available in native-place lodges was increasingly put to new uses during the early twentieth century, including, most notably, overtly political activities. The government's response greatly affected relations between the municipal government and traditional corporate bodies and altered relations between the state and society more broadly. Seen from this perspective, the decision of the new communist government to disband all native-place lodges and nationalize (or "municipalize") their property in the

---

83. Documents reflecting the successive regulations issued by the municipal government during the Republican period are found scattered throughout the holdings on *huiguan* in the Beijing Municipal Archive; a selection of 30 such orders can be found in Beijing shi dang'an guan 北京市檔案館, ed., *Beijing huiguan dang'an shiliao* 北京會館檔案史料 (Historical archival materials on native-place lodges in Beijing) (Beijing: Beijing chubanshe, 1997), pp. 1–67.

early 1950s did not reflect communist dynamics alone. In a sense, this action was the culmination of a pattern of increasing state control over the lodges that began in the years following 1898.

Conclusion

In this chapter, I have sought both to show how the particular social ecology of Beijing helped direct the course of political history and to detail the impact of those political events on local society. The 1895–98 reform movement was inextricably linked to urban institutions uniquely characteristic of Beijing. If not for the triennial examinations, which periodically attracted thousands of examination candidates, or the presence of the imperial government, which employed many thousand low-ranking officials, the movement would have been deprived of the social-professional base from which so many of its activists emerged. If not for the scholar-official "nucleus" located in the Xuannan ward, the movement could not have benefited from the ready transmission of information and the ease of organization afforded by the concentration of so many potential activists in a single area. If it were not for the existence of hundreds of native-place lodges dedicated exclusively to the use of scholar-officials, the movement would have lacked the centrally located, relatively autonomous meeting places provided by lodge opera stages and meeting halls. The reform as we know it could not have taken place anywhere but Beijing because it was so profoundly influenced by the institutions of that city.

By the same token, the reform movement, which was to prove such a pivotal event in China's modern national history, exerted a profound effect on the social character of the capital in surprising ways. Some of the effects, such as the establishment of schools operated by native-place organizations, resulted from conscious reform initiatives. Some effects, such as the increasing penetration by the state of the native-place lodges, resulted from the governmental reaction to the transformation in the uses of corporately administered space. By focusing on the social and cultural factors specific to the urban context in which the events unfolded, we can begin to formulate an urban-historical approach to major political events. Admittedly, this approach cannot reveal the deeper forces behind the movement, nor can it even wholly address the profound changes that transformed the city in the years following 1898. Even those aspects of urban change that possessed clear roots in the reform movement, such as education and state-society relations, were also profoundly affected by other forces, most notably those associated with the New Policies during the last years of the Qing. However, by highlighting the roles of urban space and native place in the 1895–98 reform movement, hitherto overlooked factors that profoundly shaped events emerge more clearly. This approach also illuminates previously unnoted consequences of a movement more commonly remembered for what it failed to achieve than for the real (if sometimes unintended) impacts it had.

CHAPTER SIX

Reforming the Feminine: Female Literacy and the Legacy of 1898

Joan Judge

The "literacy myth," as Harvey Graff calls it, posits a causal and uncomplicated relationship between literacy and progress, mass reading knowledge and the modern. Chinese reformers of the 1898 period bought into this myth.[1] Faced with a profound political and cultural crisis, the reformers drew a direct link between national strengthening and the expansion of popular literacy in general and female literacy in particular. Women's education thus became one variable in their formula for nationalist utilitarianism.[2]

An examination of the reformist legacy demonstrates, however, that the relationship between female literacy and the national project did not correspond to some neat social science equation. Rather, it was both product and generator of complex processes of cultural, social, and political change. New and often contested interpretations of the cultural meaning of female literacy arose in the late Qing as new spheres of knowledge were validated from the late 1870s, as the centuries-old civil service examination was replaced by a system of modern schools beginning in 1901, and as female education was

1. Harvey J. Graff, *The Literacy Myth: Literacy and Social Structure in the Nineteenth-Century City* (New York: Academic Press, 1979); idem, *The Legacies of Literacy: Continuities and Contradictions in Western Culture and Society* (Bloomington: Indiana University Press, 1987).

2. The term "nationalist utilitarianism" is taken from Alexander Woodside's discussion of how the reformists of the 1898 period viewed popular literacy as a basis of wealth and power; see his "Real and Imagined Continuities in the Chinese Struggle for Literacy," in *Education and Modernization: The Chinese Experience*, ed. Ruth Hayhoe, pp. 38–39 (New York: Pergamon Press, 1992).

formally sanctioned in 1907 for the first time in China's history. At the same time, notions of the political function of female literacy were debated as conceptions of the nation, citizenship, and society evolved and were integrated into competing political agendas. These changing views of female literacy became potent symbols in a broader process of re-evaluating what one might call "literacy capital"—varying levels of reading knowledge that provided differing degrees of access to history, prestige, wealth, and power. The reformists made a key contribution to this process by devaluing the elitist version of female cultural literacy then in place in favor of a more broadly based, instrumentalist, political literacy.

This chapter explores the often contradictory legacy of the 1898 reform movement in both establishing and limiting the value of female literacy capital in the late Qing. In examining this legacy, I analyze two specific bodies of sources: writings from the 1898 period (1896–99) on the issue of female literacy, which were almost exclusively written by men, and the essays of Chinese female overseas students who traveled to Japan shortly after the failure of the hundred days.[3] This second group of essays is valuable in assessing the 1898 legacy for two reasons. First, as the Chinese scholar Luo Suwen 羅蘇文 has argued, the reformist ideals thwarted by the September 1898 coup first came to fruition in the context of overseas study in Japan early in the twentieth century.[4] And second, these essays are among the few extant examples of women's writing from this period.

In examining these two bodies of sources, I attempt to link the discursive construction of the social to the social construction of discourse; to explore how these discourses on female literacy prescribed, circumscribed, and defined women's social and political roles, and how social positions and interests in turn helped determine the content of these discourses. The reformist

---

3. For a detailed account of the history of Chinese female overseas study in Japan, see Ishii Yōko 石井洋子, "Shingai kakumei ki no ryū-Nichi joshi gakusei" 辛亥革命期の留日女子學生 (Female overseas students in Japan at the time of the 1911 revolution), *Shiron* 36 (1983): 31–54; Sun Shiyue 孫石月, *Zhongguo jindai nüzi liuxue shi* 中國近代女子留學史 (The history of overseas study by Chinese women) (Beijing: Zhongguo heping chubanshe, 1995); Guo Changying 郭常英 and Su Xiaohuan 蘇曉環, "Jindai Zhongguo nüzi liuxue tanxi" 近代中國女子留學探析 (An analysis of modern Chinese overseas study), *Shixue yuekan* 3 (1991): 57–63, 56; Xie Zhangfa 謝長法, "Qingmo de liu-Ri nüxuesheng" 清末的留日女學生 (Overseas female students in Japan in the late Qing), *Jindaishi yanjiu* 2, no. 86 (1995): 272–79.

4. Luo Suwen 羅蘇文, *Nüxing yu jindai Zhongguo shehui* 女性與近代中國社會 (Women and modern Chinese society) (Shanghai: Renmin chubanshe, 1996), p. 473.

elites of 1898 tied the practice of literacy to normative practices of womanhood. Although their objective was to teach women literacy skills, they concurrently advanced a social discourse that defined feminine behavioral norms and duties of family production and reproduction. The writing women who published in overseas journals were both practitioners of the literacy skills promoted by the reformists and the creators of their own discourse on the function and meaning of female reading knowledge. An examination of their essays reveals how these women deployed literacy in potentially subversive ways that male reformers had not anticipated. In contrast to the leaders of the 1898 reform movement, their calls for female learning generally aimed to eliminate rather than to enforce women's familiar daily duties, to alter rather than maintain existing gender arrangements. There are, however, remarkable similarities in the terms and the scope of the ideologies of literacy found in the two groups of sources, both of which are overwhelmed by the perceived urgency of the national project. It is only in the transcendence of this call to nationalism, I will argue, that a new female subjectivity begins to emerge through the articulation of an alternative paradigm of literacy.

The Context for Reassessing Female Literacy: 1898 and Post-1898

More than half a century elapsed between the opening of the first missionary school for female Chinese students in Ningbo in 1844 and the establishment of the first Chinese-run school for the education of girls and women in Shanghai in June 1898. Before this and other independent Chinese schools could be founded, promoters of women's learning recognized the need to raise public awareness of the importance of female education.

This process began in the early 1890s in essays by Song Shu 宋恕 (1862–1910), Zheng Guanying 鄭觀應 (1842–1922), and others. In 1891, for example, Song put forward what would become a familiar argument for the education of girls and women in the age of nationalism and social Darwinism: China's rates of literacy were far behind those of countries of the white race and even other countries of the yellow race. Among the white race, according to Song, the ratio of female to male literacy was nine to ten; in Asia, Japan was the most literate of yellow races (Song does not give a figure), and even India had a 4 percent literacy rate for women. In China, however, only 1 percent of males were literate, and only one in 40,000 females. Song's figures for literacy for China are so below the mark that he was clearly exaggerating in order to make his point.[5] In order to improve literacy rates in China, Song advised imitating Japan in instituting compulsory education for all children between the ages of six and thirteen. Although the Japanese Education Act of 1872 stipulated that elementary education would be co-educational, however, Song insisted that schools for Chinese girls be separate from those for boys.[6]

The majority of the reformist writings studied in this chapter were penned after Song's essay, in the period immediately preceding and following the hundred days. They were written by individuals directly involved in promoting the complex of institutions tied to the promotion of female literacy: schools for girls and women, anti-footbinding societies, study societies, and new-style journals. Most of these texts were written by men, most notably Yan Fu 嚴復 (1853–1921), Liang Qichao 梁啓超 (1873–1929), and Jing Yuanshan 經元善, and by one woman, Kang Tongwei 康同薇, the daughter of Kang Youwei 康有為 (1858–1927).[7]

All these authors worked from the premise that women were inherently intelligent and educable. They argued, however, that women had squandered their talents in recent centuries for two primary reasons. First, the traditional ethical teachings (*zhengjiao* 政教) restricted women's access to learning and thereby consigned them to superficial and idle lives. Women thus became mere playthings preoccupied with making up their faces, binding their feet, and piercing their ears. They lacked any knowledge of the seriousness of affairs beyond the inner chambers and remained passive even in

---

5. It has been estimated that in China in the 1800s, 30–40 percent of males were literate and 2–10 percent of females; see Evelyn Rawski, *Education and Popular Literacy in Ch'ing China* (Ann Arbor: University of Michigan Press, 1989), p. 140.

6. Song Shu 宋恕, "Biantong pian—kaihua zhang disi" 變通篇・開化章第四 (Essay on adaptation: fourth essay on the civilizing process), in *Liuzhai beiyi* 六齋卑議, pp. 18–19; reprinted in Zhu Youhuan 朱有瓛, ed., *Zhongguo jindai xuezhi shiliao* 中國近代學制史料 (Historical materials on the modern Chinese educational system; hereafter cited as *XZSL*), in *Jiaoyu kexue congshu* 教育科學叢書 1986, 1, no. 2: 865. For a discussion of Song's views on women, see Bao Jialin 鮑家麟, "Song Shu de funü sixiang" 宋恕的婦女思想 (Song Shu's views on women), in *Zhongguo funü shi lunji sanji* 中國婦女史三集 (Materials on the history of Chinese women, no. 3), ed. Bao Jialin, pp. 163–82 (Taipei: Daoxiang chubanshe, 1988).

7. I cannot, within the scope of this chapter, analyze all writings from this period that touch on women's issues. I do not, for example, discuss Tan Sitong's very interesting ideas on the unity of the sexes. For some discussion of Tan's thinking on gender in this period, see, e.g., Yamazaki Jun'ichi 山崎純一, "Shinmatsu henpōron dankai no joshi dōtokuron to kyōiku ron" 清末變法論段階の女子道德論と教育論 (The late Qing reform discourse on female ethics and female education), *Chūgoku koten kenkyū*, Dec. 17, 1970, pp. 10–12.

the face of disaster.[8] The second reason for the dissipation of female talent lay in the proclivity of the small percentage of women who were literate to become consumed by worthless poetic indulgences. Not only was this inclination a waste of their skills, but it also damaged their moral standing. The reformists' objectives in promoting education for girls and women were thus twofold: to identify and discourage past literary practices that degraded women's literacy, and to align the course of female literacy with the national project.

Commitment to national reform drove these authors' concern with women's issues. Their writings thus provide an example of how social and political interests construct gender—in this case, how different stakes in the debate over nationalism gave rise to distinct images of China's ideal "new woman." This was not the first time in Chinese history that male elites debated the definition and scope of women's learning as an extension of their own political and cultural concerns. One example is the famous controversy between Zhang Xuecheng 章學誠 (1738–1801) and Yuan Mei 袁枚 (1716–98) in the eighteenth century.[9] The late Qing was, however, the first time that such discussions contributed to the official publication of regulations for women's schools and to a documented increase in the number of girls and women receiving formal schooling. It was also the first time that women publicly joined the debate.

The most prominent forum for this new female participation in deliberations of national importance in the late Qing was overseas student journals published in Japan and widely read in China proper. Young women who went to Japan to study beginning in the first years of the twentieth century had the opportunity not only to write for but also to actually found their own journals—some ten such journals were published by Chinese women in Tokyo between 1903 and 1911. These women appropriated the new print genre of political journals to their own purposes even more effectively than their male counterparts. Whereas there was only one female overseas stu-

---

8. See, e.g., Yan Fu 嚴复, *Lun Hushang chuangxing nüxuetang* 論滬上創興女學堂 (The establishment of schools for girls and women in Shanghai), in *Wanxing wenxuan* 晚清文選, pp. 695–97; reprinted in *XZSL* 1, no. 2, pp. 880–81; and Jing Yuanshan 經元善, "Quan nüzi dushu shuo" 勸女子讀書說 (Exhortation to females to study), in *Juyi chuji* 居易初集, 1899, no. 1: 39–40; reprinted in *XZSL* 1, no. 2, p. 882.

9. On this high Qing controversy, see Susan Mann, *Precious Records: Women in China's Long Eighteenth Century* (Stanford: Stanford University Press, 1997), pp. 83–94.

dent for every 40 males in Japan, there was one women's journal to every ten men's journals.[10] The first of these women's journals was Chen Xiefen's 陳 擷芬 (1883–1923) *Nüxue bao* 女學報 (Journal of women's studies), which was first established in Shanghai and published in Tokyo from the fourth issue in October 1903.[11] Another of the more influential journals was *Tianyi* 天義 (Natural justice), a bimonthly edited by the anarchist He Zhen 何震, wife of Liu Shipei 劉師培 (1884–1919), which appeared from June 1907 to 1908.[12]

In addition to publishing their own journals, female students also contributed articles to the main overseas student journals published in Japan, such as the following monthlies, all published in Tokyo: *Hubei xuesheng jie* 湖北學生界 (Hubei students), founded by overseas students from Hubei in January of 1903 with a run of eight issues; *Zhejiang chao* 浙江潮 (Tides of Zhejiang), published for ten issues between February and December 1903; and *Jiangsu* 江蘇, which appeared from April 27, 1903, to March 17, 1904, for ten issues. *Jiangsu* became the most important platform for female overseas students. In addition to including occasional articles on issues concerning the female population, a special women's section in issues four to six included three or four articles each written by and for women.

A reading of the essays from the 1898 period on female literacy gives some sense of the context within which the women who wrote for these overseas journals operated: the expectations they encountered, and the representations they either battled or conformed to. In turn, these writings by female overseas students reveal how the discourse of 1898 opened up new possibilities for Chinese women. In calling for the development of female schools run and staffed exclusively by Chinese women, for example, the reformist program tacitly encouraged study abroad, since China lacked the means to train the necessary teachers and administrators. The experience of study abroad

---

10. Ishii, "Shingai kakumei ki no ryū-Nichi joshi gakusei," p. 46.

11. Sun Shiyue, *Zhongguo jindai nüzi liuxue shi*, p. 110; Charlotte L. Beahan, "Feminism and Nationalism in the Chinese Women's Press, 1902–1911," *Modern China* 1, no. 4 (Oct. 1975): 389–90.

12. Sun Shiyue, *Zhongguo jindai nüzi liuxue shi*, pp. 11–12; Jacqueline Nivard, "Bibliographie de la presse féminine chinoise, 1898–1949," *Etudes chinoises* 5, nos. 1–2 (Spring–autumn 1986): 185–236. On *Tianyi*, see Ono Kazuko, *Chinese Women in a Century of Revolution, 1850–1950*, ed. Joshua Fogel (Stanford: Stanford University Press, 1989), pp. 66–69; and Peter Zarrow, "He Zhen and Anarcho-Feminism in China," *Journal of Asian Studies* 47 (Nov 1988).

in turn led to the emergence of concrete arenas—like overseas publications—in which not only the pedagogical skills but also the subjectivities and politics of late Qing women could develop.

Cultural and Political Literacy

In both the 1898 and the post-1898 discourses, the new female literacy was defined as political rather than cultural, a key component in the modern nationalist project that was itself defined against China's centuries-old literate tradition. Without denying the contribution of learned women to this tradition, neither the reformists nor the overseas women writers sought to build on their legacy. Instead, both called for a radical break with the cultural world of the talented women (cainü 才女) of the past and described this world in starkly disparaging terms, portraying the women writers who inhabited it as useless, self-indulgent, and solipsistic. The representation of modern Chinese women as having no usable or redeemable past that characterizes twentieth-century Chinese writing on gender is thus, I would argue, not a legacy of May Fourth cultural iconoclasm, as is commonly assumed, but of the 1898-period nationalist utilitarianism.

Implicit in the reformists' discourse on the meaning of female literacy is what appears to be a profound cultural anxiety about women as inheritors and producers of a literary tradition and a shared subjectivity. Only talented women of the distant and idealized classical past are celebrated as exemplars of what talented women could achieve in an age of moral stability. Jing Yuanshan, for example, stated that literate women had existed in China from ancient times, and he held that half the poems in the Shijing 詩經 (Book of odes) were written by women of a modest social background.[13] Kang Tongwei also reached into antiquity to find feminine exemplars. She praised the daughter of the classical scholar Fu Sheng 伏勝 of the Western Han, Ms. Fu 伏女, for example, for her ability to transmit the Classics.[14] More recent female literary luminaries from the Tang Dynasty on, however, were written out of history in the reformists' essays. With ties to this more immediate legacy of literate women ignored or severed, late Qing women

---

13. Jing Yuanshan, "Quan nüzi dushu," p. 882.

14. Kang Tongwei 康同薇, "Nüxue libi shuo" 女學利弊說 (The advantages and disadvantages of education for girls and women), Zhixin bao 知新報 52 (May 11, 1898); reprinted in XZSL 1, no. 2, p. 878.

were deprived of past or current cultural capital and discouraged from becoming members of a historical, literary female community.

These efforts to redefine the value and content of a feminine literary legacy were not so much a reflection of the reformists' views on women, however, as one component in their broader project of re-evaluating the meaning of literacy capital and reassessing the Chinese literate tradition. Women writers of the recent past came to function as a metonym for all that was obsolete and degraded in that tradition, and the passionate offensive against them was an attack on the perceived backwardness of the "old culture." Since these reformist writers themselves had a complex relationship to that culture—they were trained in its values and bound by its referents—it was perhaps easier for them to speak their critique of it through an indictment of the *cainü*.

Liang Qichao included such a critique in the influential section on female education, "Lun nüxue" 論女學 (On female education), in his famous 1896–97 essay "Bianfa tongyi" 變法通議 (General discussion of reform). This treatise put forward four separate but related justifications for women's education as a key component of national strengthening. In his discussion of the second of these justifications, Liang sought to refute the long-standing view—held, he argued, by dimwitted scholars (*maoru* 瞀儒)—that only women who lacked talent were virtuous (*wucaibiande* 無才便德).[15] Liang argued that it was not female talent per se that was problematic, but the uses to which it had conventionally been put. "Those who were called talented women in the past," he wrote, "were capable of doing nothing more than accumulating volumes of poems on the sadness of spring and the pain of parting, chanting about the sun and the moon, and toying with images of the flowers and the grass."[16] Yan Fu, while not writing as detailed an indictment

---

15. Although the origins of this saying have been dated to the Song, it and several variations did not appear until the seventeenth century; see Chen Dongyuan 陳東原, *Zhongguo funü shenghuo shi* 中國婦女生活史 (A history of the lives of Chinese women) (Shanghai: Shangwu yinshuguan, 1928; reprinted, 1937), pp. 188–202; also cited in Dorothy Ko, "Pursuing Talent and Virture: Education and Women's Culture in Seventeenth- and Eighteenth-Century China," *Late Imperial China* 13, no. 1 (1992): 9. According to Ko (p. 9), this saying, often reiterated in the sixteenth and seventeenth centuries, construes talents and virtues as mutually exclusive and suggests that an advanced literary and cultural education was detrimental to a woman's moral cultivation.

16. Liang Qichao 梁啓超, "Lun nüxue" 論女學 (On female education), in *Yinbingshi heji, wenji*, 飲冰室合集，文集, 1: 37–44; reprinted in *XZSL* 1, no. 2, p. 870.

of the *cainü*, concurred with Liang's view that women's talents had been misused in recent centuries. He claimed that of the 10 to 20 percent of Chinese women who were literate, only one or two were truly cultured (*zhishu* 知書). Their abilities were squandered, however, on crude exegeses of literary works.[17]

This discourse on the role of female literacy could be interpreted as an effort by male elites to preserve their near-monopoly on cultural and literacy capital by limiting the amount of such capital that Chinese women could claim as their own. However, Kang Tongwei shared the male reformists' disdain for the past achievements of literary women. Although she lamented how shameful it was for a nation to belittle the importance of female literacy and how the absence of formalized female education in China made it the object of foreign ridicule, she herself wrote disparagingly of how women had used their literary abilities in the past. She attributed the widely held conviction that only untalented women were virtuous to the common practice among learned women of privileging intellectual achievements and brilliance of mind (*caihua* 才華) over virtuous conduct. These women immodestly flaunted their own abilities, Kang maintained, and their inappropriate behavior instilled in men the fear that even slightly literate women would become "hens who would rule the morning" and dominate the household. These men therefore attempted to limit their wives' and daughters' access to learning and deemed the preparation of food and wine to be the only worthy female activities.

In addition to criticizing the immodest behavior of the *cainü*, Kang also questioned the substance of the writings of talented women. The most refined of these women, she wrote, "wallow in their own compositions of sentimental prose-poems set to music (*ci* 詞) and descriptive prose interspersed with verse (*fu* 賦)." Although the sound of lamentation filled the inner chambers, their poems on the spring flowers and the fall moon yielded nothing but confusion. Women of less refined talents immersed themselves not in *ci* and *fu* but in novels and rhymed stories chanted to music (*tanci* 彈詞). The fathers and brothers of these women of varying talents feared that such literary indulgences would divert women from following the Way. They therefore prohibited their daughters and wives from engaging in any literary activity. Although Kang considered such restrictions excessive and equated them with gouging out the eyes of the nearsighted or cutting off the

---

17. Yan Fu, *Lun Hushang chuangxing nüxuetang*, p. 880.

feet of the lame, she was nonetheless as contemptuous as men were of the specific literary practices in which women had chosen to engage.[18]

Like the writings of Kang Tongwei, the essays of overseas students in Japan demonstrate that the indictment of the *cainü* was not only a gendered but, more important, a politicized discourse that was first articulated in the 1898 period and resonated well into the twentieth century. Women committed to the same modernist ideology as the creators of the reformist discourse devalued the feminine literary heritage in their writings, often in language that was more passionately critical and more openly nationalistic than that of their 1898 predecessors. Rather than claim cultural capital by identifying themselves with accomplished women writers of the past, the overseas female students derided their literary forebears as selfish traitors to the pursuit of a collective good. Instead, they called for the validation of a new female literacy that was defined in nationalist terms and against past written traditions.

One of these overseas writers was He Xiangning 何香凝 (1878–1972). Among the earliest group of female students to travel to Japan, in 1905 He became the first woman to join Sun Yat-sen's (1866–1925) Tongmenghui 同盟會 (Revolutionary Alliance). In an article that appeared in the journal *Jiangsu* in 1903, she criticized literate women of the past for indulging their emotions rather than serving the nation. Not only was her critique redolent of the 1898-period writings, but it was directly derivative: some 32 characters of her essay plagiarized Kang's description of upper-class women wallowing in *ci* and *fu*. He pushed her argument further than Kang, however, by criticizing the *cainü* not only for their emotional verbiage but for their lack of patriotism. These women were so infatuated with poetry that they "did not know what the nation was," she lamented. Only when national tragedy touched their own bodies did they react. As an example of this embodied nationalism, she cited the alleged suicide of 1,100 women of good families who were raped when the Joint Expeditionary Forces entered Beijing in 1901.[19]

Female overseas students who were members of the Gongaihui 共愛會 (Humanitarian association), an organization with a political and feminist agenda founded in Tokyo on April 8, 1903, expressed similar views. In an es-

---

18. Kang Tongwei, "Nüxue libi shuo," p. 878.

19. He Xiangning 何香凝, "Jinggao wo tongbao jiemei" 敬告我同胞姊妹 (A warning for my sister compatriots), *Jiangsu*, no. 4 (June 25, 1903), p. 144.

say in *Jiangsu*, they wrote that literate women with poetic sensibilities were one with the illiterate. Chinese women in the past were either illiterate and "stupid as beans," they claimed, or literate and capable of nothing more than "discoursing on the spring flowers and the autumn moon, chanting poems in a sing-song voice, and writing ditties in order to express and find comfort in their own feelings."[20] Women who devoted their talents to the nonlyrical tradition were considered to be equally ridiculous and irresponsible. Wang Lian 王蓮, a student who arrived in Japan from Hubei in September 1902, described how motivated women of the past "read the Classics when they were young and perused novels or Tang poetry when they were older" and were thus deemed to be exceptional individuals. But such learning lacked all relevance. "In these Chinese classics and novels," Wang asked, "besides the depiction of loyal subjects, filial sons, hated husbands, and spurned wives, where is there any discussion of patriotism?" What is the value of a literary tradition that offers only rejected and tragic figures as models, like the character Cui Yingying 崔鶯鶯 from *Xixiang ji* 西廂記 (The story of the western wing) or Lin Daiyu 林黛玉 of *Honglou meng* 紅樓夢 (Dream of the red chamber)? If these are literate women, how can China claim it has ever had female education? In the end, Wang maintained, "Our literate sisters are the same or even worse than illiterate ones." It was this situation that had given rise to the common saying that "only a woman without talent is blessed."[21]

In formulating their new conceptions of female literacy, the 1898 essayists and the female overseas students not only called for a radical break with feminine cultural literacy of the past but also elided the crucial role women had played as bearers of culture within the family. From the Han to the Qing dynasties, women of the upper classes had played a crucial role in passing classical teachings to their sons through a tradition known as *jiaxue* 家學 (family learning). In the Song, a dynasty not renowned for enlightened views on women, many mothers of the educated class taught their sons and daughters to read and introduced them to the elementary texts that would serve as the foundation of a classical education. The same was true in the

---

20. "Gongaihui tongren quan liuxue qi" 共愛會同人勸留學啟 (Members of the Humanitarian Association exhort overseas study), *Jiangsu*, no. 6 (Sept. 1903): 160.

21. Wang Lian 王蓮, "Tongxianghui jishi: Hubei zhi bu" 同鄉會紀事湖北之部 (Record of same-place association meeting, section on Hubei), *Hubei xuesheng jie*, no. 2 (Feb. 1903): 114. For a discussion of Cui and Dai, see Ann Waltner, "On Not Becoming a Heroine: Lin Dai-yu and Cui Ying-ying," *Signs: Journal of Women in Culture and Society* 15, no. 1 (1989): 61–78.

seventeenth century and the high Qing.[22] This legacy—including the classic examples of Mencius' and Ouyang Xiu's 歐陽修 mothers educating their sons—was completely overlooked, however, by Liang Qichao, Jing Yuanshan, Kang Tongwei, and the overseas female students. In another essay by members of the Gongaihui, for example, female overseas students argued that the level of women's education in China was historically so low that mothers were in no way fit to educate their own children. "Whereas in Europe and America, children learn their habits from their mothers," the essay stated, "in China, the mother's level of knowledge is even lower than that of her children."[23] The omission of any reference to the *jiaxue* tradition may be attributed to the elite status and small numbers of the women transmitters of family learning. However, it is more likely that it was another reflection of the perceived need to establish a radical break with the cultural past in the late Qing in order to create a new nationalist present.

The new meaning of women's literacy as put forward by both the 1898 reformists and the female overseas students was thus disassociated from the realms of classical prose, poetic fancy, and family traditions of learning and then harnessed to the needs of the nationalist project. Whereas in the past women's literary talents had been admired as a haven independent from the heartless male intellectual world and distant from politics, in the late Qing female literacy was to be almost exclusively in the service of a new politics. This new female literacy became a powerful symbol of a new Chinese epistemology in the late nineteenth and early twentieth centuries, operating as a signpost of the spirit and objectives of the Western-style "new learning," just as the *cainü* of the recent past had become a metonym for all that was whimsical and outmoded in the literate tradition. Yan Fu summed up the objectives of this new epistemology by explaining that China's young women had to do more than study the texts of the ancients (*dushu* 讀書) if they were to compete in the new global context of the late nineteenth century. In order to become the equals of their Western counterparts in up-

---

22. On the Song, see Patricia Buckley Ebrey, *The Inner Quarters: Marriage and the Lives of Chinese Women in the Sung Period* (Berkeley: University of California Press, 1993), pp. 185–86; on, e.g., Gu Ruopu 顧若璞 (1592–ca. 1681) of the seventeenth century, see Dorothy Ko, *Teachers of the Inner Chambers: Women and Culture in Seventeenth-Century China* (Stanford: Stanford University Press, 1994), pp. 237–40; on the high Qing, see Mann, *Precious Records*, pp. 101–8.

23. "Gongaihui tongren quan liuxue qi," p. 160.

rightness and strength, Yan wrote, it was imperative that they leave past teachings behind, become well-versed in contemporary writings, and develop their knowledge of the times (*yueshi* 閱世). The true challenge of female instruction, according to reformists like Yan, lay in educating women to become citizens and patriots, or, more commonly, mothers of China's new citizens and patriots.

Instrumental and Empowering Literacy

The distinction between women as citizens and as mothers of citizens was an important one in the late Qing.[24] It marked one of the fundamental differences between the discourses on female literacy by the reformists and by the overseas women writers. Whereas the reformists emphasized women's embodied but indirect link to the nation as economic producers and mothers of citizens, the women writers expressed the need for women to cultivate the abilities of autonomous national actors. This difference reflects, in part, the different social positions from which these discourses were constructed: whereas the reformists spoke prescriptively for women, the overseas writers wrote exhortatively as women. It also reflects the important transition from discourse to experience that took place from the late 1890s to the early twentieth century, from Shanghai and Beijing to Tokyo, as the reformists' objectives concerning the new female literacy were translated into the practice of everyday life.

Liang Qichao's "Lun nüxue" defined different facets of the indirect relationship between women and the nation. Establishing what would become a common trope in later essays on women's education from Yan Fu through the revolutionaries in the early twentieth century, Liang claimed that women had to be transformed from parasites to producers, from helpless creatures who lived off the labor of their fathers or their husbands to economically independent individuals. Ignoring the important role women played in the family economy,[25] Liang thus established a link between female illiteracy and

---

24. Joan Judge, "Citizens or Mothers of Citizens? Gender and the Meaning of Modern Chinese Citizenship," in *Changing Meanings of Citizenship in Modern China*, ed. Elizabeth Perry and Merle Goldman. Harvard Contemporary China Series. Cambridge, Mass.: Harvard University Press, forthcoming.

25. On women's work in the late imperial period, see Francesca Bray, *Technology and Gender: Fabrics of Power in Late Imperial* China (Berkeley: University of California Press, 1997), pp. 173–272; on the high Qing see Mann, *Precious Records*, pp. 143–77.

national poverty.[26] Yan Fu took this argument one step further, obliquely tying female literacy to the risk of colonization. Men incapable of bearing the burden of providing for their entire families would be forced, he claimed, to submit to others in order to ensure their own, and their families', survival.[27]

The second common reformist trope that established an indirect link between the female and the nation represented women as the moral and biological source of both the country and the race. Again, the reformists elided relevant aspects of the historical record—in this case the Chinese precedent of family learning passed on by women (*jiaxue*) discussed above— in order to represent female literacy as a new, transformative value that would enable China to enter the world of modern nation-states. Liang, and later Jing Yuanshan, looked to the West rather than to the Chinese past in legitimizing the need to educate women as mothers of China's future citizens. Jing claimed, for example, that in the West, mothers were responsible for 70 percent of their children's elementary education, friends for another 20 percent, and teachers for only 10 percent.[28] Kang Tongwei also argued that mothers, rather than teachers, should play the central role in the education of their children because they alone could cultivate the innate goodness in their offspring.[29] The 1898 reformists thus advocated training women in the principles and pedagogical methods that would enable them to instruct their sons and daughters and consequently improve the quality of China's elementary-level education.[30]

Since women were also the biological source of China's future patriots, the reformists advocated that they be not only intellectually but also physically fit to play their new role. They called for both the development of physical education programs for women and the end of footbinding. The reformists claimed the nation was weak because its men were weak, its men were weak because their mothers were weak, and their mothers were weak because they had bound feet. A number of reformers were actively involved in programs designed to strengthen China's women physically in the late

---

26. Liang Qichao, "Lun nüxue," pp. 869–70.

27. Yan Fu, *Lun Hushang chuangxing nüxuetang*, p. 880.

28. Jing Yuanshan, "Zhi Zheng Yang Dong sanjun lun ban nügongxue shu" 致鄭楊董三君辦女恭學書 (To Messieurs Zheng, Yang, and Dong concerning public schools for girls and women), in *Juyi chuji* 居易初集, 1899, no. 1: 19–20; reprinted in *XZSL* 1, no. 2, p. 881.

29. Kang Tongwei, "Nüxue libi shuo," p. 877.

30. Liang Qichao, "Lun nüxue," pp. 871–72.

nineteenth century. Kang Youwei founded the first Chinese-initiated anti-footbinding society, and his daughter Kang Tongwei had natural feet. In 1897 Liang Qichao organized an association to abolish footbinding.[31]

These anti-footbinding initiatives continued in the early twentieth century. Although the numbers of women who unbound their feed in the 1898 era were small—even Kang Tongwei was scorned by her own relatives—it had become common practice for female overseas students in Japan just a few years later. Shimoda Utako 下田歌子, the founder of the Jissen jogakkō 實踐女學校 (Practical women's school) in Tokyo, where the greatest number of Chinese female overseas students were educated in the early twentieth century, demanded, for example, that all women who attended her school unbind their feet.[32] In contrast to the reformists—and to Shimoda—however, the female overseas students did not exclusively tie anti-footbinding to national strengthening. Rather, they directly linked the latter to female literacy and the development of women as thinking national subjects. A recurrent trope in their writings identified the illiterate female as a dolled-up toy with pierced ears and bound feet. These physical practices, and particularly footbinding, were juxtaposed to book learning for males: boys enrolled in school, embarking on their intellectual and public careers, at the same age as girls bound their feet in a symbolic retreat from public life.[33] According to Chen Yan'an 陳彥安, another of the early overseas students, whereas "young boys are educated even if they are poor," females of all social classes were more preoccupied with "piercing their ears, binding their feet, and making up their faces to look like playthings."[34] Wang Lian also identified pierced ears and bound feet as the prime impediments to female education. These forms of physical mutilation were like "torture meted out to

---

31. Ono, *Chinese Women in a Century of Revolution*, p. 32.

32. "Riben Dongya nüxuexiao fushu Zhongguo nüzi liuxuesheng sucheng shifan xuetang zhangcheng" 日本東亞女學校附屬中國女子留學生速成師範學堂章程 (Regulations for the Chinese female overseas students short-term normal school, an addition to the Japanese East Asian Female School), *Dongfang zazhi* 2, no. 6; reprinted in *Jindai Zhongguo nüquan yundong shiliao, 1842–1911* 近代中國女權運動史料 (Historical materials on the early modern Chinese women's rights movement, 1842–1911), ed. Li Youning 李又寧 and Zhang Yufa 張玉法, 2: 1258–67 (Taibei: Zhuanji wenxue, 1975).

33. See Ko, *Teachers of the Inner Chambers*, p. 149; Wendy Larson, *Women and Writing in Modern China*, (Stanford: Stanford University Press, 1998), p. 77.

34. Chen Yan'an 陳彥安, "Quan nüzi liuxue shuo" 勸女子留學說 (Exhortation for female overseas study), *Jiangsu* 3 (June 1903): 155.

criminals," and debilitated women to the point that they lacked the energy and the will to study.[35] Wang described the painful process of unbinding her own feet in an overseas student journal and explained how it released her to pursue learning for the nation. Once her toes gradually relaxed, she was finally able to walk—wearing Western socks and leather shoes—the twelve or thirteen *li* (about four miles) to and from school each day with no trouble at all.[36]

Wang's linking of unbinding her feet to her personal growth rather than to national development underlines one of the fundamental differences between the views of these women writers and those of the reformists on the subject of women's education. The overseas writers' actual practice as literate subjects provides another example of how they went beyond the prescriptive reformist discourse in applying their literacy skills. Whereas reformists like Yan Fu had encouraged young women to read contemporary writings in order to gain knowledge of current events, female students in Tokyo used the new medium of overseas journals not to attain a mediated and abstract experience of the social world but to directly comment on it and attempt to shape it through their own writing. They posited a new understanding of female literacy as a means of enabling women to become independent national actors, rather than passive—but informed—mothers of citizens.

The consensus among women writing for these publications was that educating themselves for the nation was their highest calling. They drew a direct link between women's learning and the national project: female knowledge would not be merely for the nation, as the male reform discourse on female literacy maintained, but of the nation; not a necessary precondition for the strengthening of China, but a means of empowering women to participate personally in the national struggle.

Wang Lian described how her experience as an overseas student in Japan opened her eyes to the meaning of nationalism and the inextricable link between women and the nation. Back in China, Wang wrote:

I did not understand what a nation was or what the importance of female education was. Then when I went to Japan, I often heard people talk about the nation. After asking several questions, I finally began to understand . . . when people unite they form a family, when families unite they form a nation. All people belong to a nation,

---

35. Wang Lian, "Tongxianghui jishi: Hubei zhi bu," p. 114.
36. Ibid., p. 115.

and all must make the nation their own. This means females are also part of the nation. One must act for the nation in order to be worthy of self-respect.

Wang warned that if women passed responsibility for the nation off on men, this would be the beginning of national disaster. Men would in turn pass responsibility off on the emperor, the emperor on officials, and the officials, who would be overwhelmed, would then be forced to extort and exploit the people. If women were to prevent the situation from deteriorating, they had to be educated: literacy was the key link between women and their new national roles. If women did not understand national matters, Wang asserted, "they must study books and read newspapers. If their bodies are weak, they must unbind their feet and become active. If women become stronger and more intelligent, then the nation will become stronger and more advanced."[37] Chen Yan'an agreed that women needed to apprehend the importance and meaning of national politics. "Women are ignorant," she wrote, "because they are isolated in the inner chambers. Just as one cannot realize the height of Taishan without first climbing a mountain or the depth of the sea without physically going to the ocean, without exposure to the world and education women have no way of knowing how strong the foreign nations are and how weak China is."[38]

Although this new epistemology for women would be driven by national aspirations, it would also be bound by national concerns. The pursuit of pure knowledge was secondary; learning for the nation was primary. A woman writing under the name Yi Qin 憶琴 explained that a new form of education was necessary for the new age. By focusing on the nation, this new learning would redefine the mode and meaning of heroism. If Ban Zhao 班昭 (ca. 49–120), the famous literata who had served the emperor by completing her brother's work on the *Han History*, lived today, Yi Qin wrote, she "would transfer her love of the sovereign to love of the nation." If Ti Ying 緹縈, a devoted daughter who had saved her father from a cruel punishment, were to come to life again, she "would transmute her love of her father into love of her compatriots." Such women would be the equals of men in their "ambition and their ardor" and in their ability to "bear daggers to defend the nation." They would not necessarily be their intellectual equals, however: even these radical women continued to construct pure knowledge as primar-

---

37. Ibid.
38. Chen Yan'an, "Quan nüzi liuxue shuo," p. 155.

ily masculine. "Although their understanding of the written and spoken language may be inferior to men's," Yi Qin claimed, women can still become reliable patriots. This, she wrote, "is understood by those who promote female education," a statement that implies the standard for women's learning would be national activism, not intellectual achievement.[39]

The new Chinese woman was thus called on by these overseas writers to cultivate political rather than cultural literacy, to pursue learning for the nation rather than for the self. Although the pursuit of pure knowledge was not a priority, it was, nonetheless, on the agendas of certain of the women writers. This was less true of the writings of the 1898 reformists. A few of the 1898-period texts did suggest that women should be educated in order to develop their potential as human beings: Yan Fu explained in his essay on the establishment of women's schools that education separated humans from beasts, and Jing Yuanshan maintained that the "two strokes of the character for people (ren 人) have the meaning of left and right, yin and yang," and therefore it was not right to call males "people" but not females, or to require males to study when they reach boyhood but not young girls who reached a comparable age.[40] However, all these reformist authors ended their appeals for women's education by linking women to broader national objectives: they were to be educated as conveyers of modernity rather than modern subjects, as mothers of citizens rather than as citizens.

In contrast, a few of the overseas female writers directly addressed the need for women to increase their intellectual and not just their instrumental literacy in order to become autonomous social and political actors. He Zhen, the female anarchist writing in *Tianyi*, was one of the rare authors who did not appropriate the nationalist-based rationale for the development of female literacy. Instead, she condemned both nationalism and militarism for contributing to the subjugation of women and ridiculed her female compatriots for holding up China's historical martial heroines as exemplars. He collapsed nationalism into all other male discourses and saw them as aimed at producing and reproducing gender inequality.

In a historically and conceptually sophisticated essay, He explained how the male monopoly on literacy capital had had profound social and cultural

---

39. Yi Qin 憶琴, "Lun Zhongguo nüzi zhi qiantu, xu" 論中國女子之前途，續 (The future of Chinese females, continued), *Jiangsu*, no. 5 (Aug. 1903): 130.

40. Yan Fu, *Lun Hushang chuangxing nüxuetang*, p. 880; Jing Yuanshan, "Quan nüzi dushu," p. 882.

ramifications for women. She described how knowledge was power, and how, from the ancient Three Dynasties period, men had been able to dictate all social norms and laws by controlling the dominant discourse. From the Qin and the Han dynasties on, learning was in the hands of Confucians who were renowned, He claimed, for their misogyny: the great Confucian teacher Mencius divorced his wife—following the custom introduced by Confucius himself—on the grounds that she had not greeted him properly on his return home one day. Twisting words and forcing interpretations to advance their selfish interest, later Confucians—like the authors of the Later Han text *Baihu tong* 白虎通 (Discussions in the White Tiger Hall)—established the principles of a social universe that was designed to oppress women. They declared that when Heaven created humanity, it favored males. Therefore anything associated with the masculine *yang* was good and anything associated with the feminine *yin* was bad, a view that ensured the female's subordinate status and justified a system that allowed one man to have several wives. Realizing women might not accept this position of inferiority, they created the discourse of submission in which it was the woman's responsibility to be faithful to one husband all her life. Knowing that some wives would protest such an arrangement, they gave women duties but no rights and prohibited them from leaving their husbands, remarrying, or expressing jealousy. Until women were able to access, develop, and use knowledge themselves, He argued, they would be condemned to subordination.[41]

Other women writers who called for women's right to pursue pure knowledge also took issue with Confucian ideology, which continued to be implicitly upheld in the 1898 essays. Most specifically, the overseas female writers opposed the privileging of duties over knowledge and manual over intellectual labor as the hallmark of female achievement. "Chinese emphasize the importance of women learning handicrafts and de-emphasize the importance of knowledge," members of the Gongaihui wrote. As a result, their own generation of women lacked the literacy skills necessary to convey their deepest convictions. "Although we have the ambition to write, we have great difficulty making our brushes express our meaning," they lamented. "And although we have the ambition to lecture, our mouths are incapable of uttering what is at the bottom of our hearts." In an effort to overcome this legacy and advance their own knowledge, they formed a study group. And in

---

41. Zhen Shu 震述 (pseud. of He Zhen), "Nüzi fuchou lun" 女子復仇倫 (Female's revenge) *Tianyi* 3: 17–20.

order to include all their female compatriots in this quest for learning, they called for the elimination of the absurd teaching that only a woman without talent was virtuous and the abandonment of the woman's duty to prepare food and wine.[42]

Chen Yiyi 陳以益, a fellow traveler of women radicals in Tokyo, where he founded his own journal, wrote that it was essential to educate women to become independent human beings rather than good wives and wise mothers. He claimed that much progress had been made in China in terms of education of girls and women and gender relations. However, he wrote, "although we have warded off the tiger at the front door, the fox has slipped in the back. In the name of the Japanese ideology of good wives and wise mothers," Chinese girls today are educated only to become high-level slaves, the "literate maidservants of their husbands and sons. Alas! This so-called women's learning is only for the sake of men!" Chen went on to explain that "whereas education for males includes all kinds of specializations, females only receive a general education." This refusal to provide specialized education for females was part of an effort to keep women from taking part in the literate human community. "Males and females are both members of humankind," Chen asserted, "and therefore should receive the same level of education. . . . Then equality and equal rights would no longer be empty words, and it would be possible for women's education and women's rights to develop."[43]

Conclusion

A number of different conceptions of reading knowledge coexisted historically in China, from classical to functional, from official to household literacy. In the late nineteenth and early twentieth centuries, however, conceptions of literacy became increasingly complex, as they were gendered and

---

42. "Zhu Gongaihui zhi qiantu" 祝共愛會之前途 (Celebration of the future of the 911 Humanitarian Association), *Jiangsu* 6, p. 162.

43. Chen Yiyi 陳以益, "Nanzun nübei yu xianmuliangqi" 男尊女卑與賢母良妻 (The view that males are superior to females and "good wives and wise mothers"), *Nübao* 1, no. 2 [1909]; reprinted in *XZSL* 2, no. 2: 681–83. Although represented in some secondary writings as a female (e.g., Nivard, "Bibliographie de la presse féminine chinoise, 1898–1949," p. 222), Chen was a male. A close friend of Qiu Jin's, he was a supporter of women's issues; see Sun Shiyue, *Zhongguo jindai nüzi liuxue shi*, p. 295. I thank Amy Dooling for questioning my assumption that Chen was female.

politicized in conjunction with the project of modernization. The reformists of the 1898 period initiated this process by drawing a sharp distinction between an obsolete classical literacy and a dynamic new civic literacy, between narrow ancient book learning and global contemporary understanding, between the sterile, male scholarly tradition and a vital female knowledge for the nation. In so doing, they redefined the meaning of literacy capital, establishing a fundamental distinction between cultural and political literacy that would mark cultural politics well into the twentieth century.

A new ideology of female literacy was integral to the reformists' reevaluation of Chinese literacy capital and reassessment of the Chinese literate tradition. One component in their broader agenda of national strengthening, this ideology both heralded the expansion of female literacy and advanced new strategies for its containment. The reformists defined women's learning as learning for the nation and through its children, merging past preoccupations with familism with a new concern for nationalism, balancing new opportunities for epistemic gain with newly constraining modes of patriotic behavior. This ideology left a complex legacy, which first unfolded in the context of the early twentieth-century overseas experience in Japan. Female overseas students and practitioners of this new literacy—the first generation of Chinese women with a public political voice—attempted to counter the restrictions imposed by the reformists on women's literacy by claiming that the objective of women's learning should be the cultivation of a direct and empowering knowledge of the nation, rather than the fulfillment of moral and biological duties for the nation. Their calls for a new feminine epistemology remained, however, bound by the national project. Overtly challenging the traditional privileging of manual over intellectual labor, socially functional over politically meaningful literacy, these women were nonetheless complicit in the stabilizing discourse of political utilitarianism. Their impassioned rejection of past expressions of feminine subjectivity manifested their submersion of selfhood in the pursuit of nationhood and marked the first phase in a broader cultural critique that would inform radical politics throughout the twentieth century.[44]

---

44. Leftist critics of women writers in the 1920s and 1930s and Communists in the following decades would continue to criticize the feminine literary voice for its lack of social commitment, realism, and patriotic fervor, for its excessive individualism and subjectivity. On the leftist critique of the 1920s and 1930s, see Larson, *Women and Writing in Modern China*, pp. 140–46, 165, 170–72. For a fuller discussion of these issues, see Joan Judge, "Talent, Virtue,

The social condition of this new female literacy did, however, open a brief moment in the late Qing when the transcendence of this new political utilitarianism seemed possible and demonstrates how historical ruptures can emerge from the most constraining of discourses. The voices of the women who advocated the pursuit of pure knowledge, empowering knowledge, and autonomous knowledge may have had few resonances in a century that increasingly sacrificed individual subjectivities to the collective. Nonetheless, these women writers were among the first in modern China to recognize the ambiguities and contradictions in, and the potentially coercive nature of, the "literacy myth."

---

and the Nation: Chinese Nationalisms and Female Subjectivities in the Early-Twentieth Century," *American Historical Review*, June 2001, pp. 765–803.

CHAPTER SEVEN
Naming the First 'New Woman'
Hu Ying

[The labor of historiography] . . . promotes a selection between what can be understood and what must be forgotten in order to obtain the representation of a present intelligibility.

—Michel de Certeau

In 1897, Liang Qichao 梁啓超 (1873–1929) published the biography of a Ms Kang Aide 康愛德 in *Shiwu bao* 時務報 (The Chinese progress).[1] Unlike the subjects of his other biographies of Chinese and Western luminaries, Ms Kang was at the time an obscure figure from the small town of Jiujiang 九江 in Jiangxi. Although long since forgotten, for a brief period before and during the 1898 reforms, her name became synonymous with the "new citizen" of China and, more specifically, with the new Chinese woman.

The case of Kang Aide is interesting because of her apparent centrality as well as her hidden marginality to the project(s) of modernity. Her case illustrates a peculiar historical paradox: the term "woman" was endowed with tremendous representational power during this period, but the existence and intelligibility of the concept were predicated on what was forgotten about

Part of this research was funded by the Chiang Ching-kuo Foundation for International Scholarly Exchange. I thank the staff at the General Commission on Archives and History of the United Methodist Church, the Bentley Historical Library at the University of Michigan, and the Library at Northwestern University for making available crucial archival material for this paper. My gratitude goes to Francesca Bray, Gail Hershatter, Joan Judge, Angela Leung, Susan Mann, and Harriet Zurndorfer for critiquing earlier versions of this paper and to Theodore Huters, Xiaobing Tang, and Weili Ye for answering my queries. An earlier version of this paper was published in *Nan nü* in 2001.

1. Liang Qichao, "Ji Jiangxi Kang nüshi" 記江西康女士, in idem, *Yinbing shi heji: wenji* 飲冰室合集文集 (Shanghai: Zhonghua shuju, 1936), 1: 119–20.

"women," that is to say, both her predecessors who were dismissed as "traditional" as well as elements in her that were deemed less than modern. Through the case of Kang Aide, this chapter traces the enactment of modernity at a particular historical moment, an enactment fraught with ambiguity and often contested at the very moment of its conception.

Indeed, even Kang Aide's name became a locus of dispute. Missionary publications hailed her as "a daughter of Confucius" and emphasized that her surname was Kong. In her own writings, she used the name Ida Kahn in English and Kang Cheng 康成 in Chinese. Different names, competing genealogies, conflicting interpretations—she was clearly a figure in whom others found different meanings.[2] Each act of naming tells a distinctive story about Kang Aide and assigns her to a different group. Liang Qichao's exemplar of the new woman, the missionaries' Western-educated descendent of Confucius, a woman capable of telling her own stories—each version of her personal history implies a different version of the larger history. The 1898 reform period was a pivotal one in modern Chinese history, and these names create origin stories that become a part of modern myths, with different configurations of tradition and modernity and different roles for China and the West.[3]

---

2. *Ann Arbor News*, Apr. 22, 1948, in which Ida Kahn (Kang Aide) and Mary Stone (Shi Meiyu) were described as "the first Chinese women graduates of University of Michigan" and "the first and only medical doctors in an area of five million Chinese" (University of Michigan, Bentley Historical Library, necrology file of Ida Kahn). In the early part of this chapter, I use Liang Qichao's formulation of her name for the sake of clarity; later in the paper, I switch to the other two names in accordance with the context.

3. In reading these different versions of her story—the reformers', the missionaries', and Kang's own—this chapter does not aim to answer the complex historical question of the role of missionaries in China's modernization, which is the subject of a great deal of scholarship presented in a variety of interpretive frames. The major figures of the reform movement that are typically the subjects of previous studies on missionary influence were more or less educated in the traditional literati milieu but influenced by Western ideas, wielding influence from major cities at home or abroad. See Max Weber, *The Religion of China* (Glencoe, Ill.: Free Press, 1951 [1915–20]); Joseph Levenson, *Confucian China and Its Modern Fate*, vol. 1, *The Problem of Intellectual Continuity* (Berkeley: University of California Press, 1958); John K. Fairbank, ed., *The Missionary Enterprise in China and America* (Cambridge, Mass.: Harvard University Press, 1974); and Paul Cohen, *China and Christianity: The Missionary Movement and the Growth of Chinese Anti-foreignism, 1860–1870* (Cambridge, Mass.: Harvard University Press, 1963). For a recent reappraisal of Weber, see Wang Hui 汪暉, "Weibo yu Zhongguo xiandaixing wenti" 韋伯與中國現代性問題, *Xueren* 6 (1994): 381–424. For a critical reflection on American models of Chinese history writing, see Cohen, *Discovering History in China: American Historical*

As a primary way of signifying difference, gender was becoming a potent metaphor. The status of women, as we shall presently see, was intimately linked to the representation of history, as the image of the traditional woman was closely associated with the past, and that of the modern woman rhetorically wedded to the model of progress.[4] The discourse of history, critics have recently argued, necessarily suppresses other stories; that is to say, the intelligibility of history is predicated on what is repressed and forgotten.[5] Gender figures prominently in the narrativization of history, and its intelligibility also depends on what is forgotten. Building on this framework,

---

Writing on the Recent Chinese Past (New York: Columbia University Press, 1984). One of the main issues in this debate concerns the role of Christianity in Western modernity and whether Confucianism in China was able to perform a similar role. Much effort has been directed toward determining how the literati "wrenched free from the old culture" (Cohen, *China and Christianity*). In the case of Ida Kahn (Kang Cheng), as we shall see, because of her marginal status with regard to Confucian high culture, no particular "wrenching" was necessary. Nonetheless, her relationships to Christianity and Confucianism were full of a different kind of complexity.

4. My argument builds on a new body of scholarship on gender in the nationalist discourse of twentieth-century China. See, among others, Prasenjit Duara, "The Regime of Authenticity: Timelessness, Gender, and National History in Modern China," *History and Theory* 37, no. 4 (1998): 287–308; Christina K. Gilmartin, "Gender, Political Culture, and Women's Mobilization in the Chinese Nationalist Revolution, 1924–1927," in idem, Gail Hershatter, Lisa Rofel, and Tyrene White, eds., *Engendering China: Women, Culture, and the State* (Cambridge, Mass.: Harvard University Press, 1994); Gail Hershatter, *Dangerous Pleasures: Prostitution and Modernity in Twentieth-Century Shanghai* (Berkeley: University of California Press, 1997); and Meng Yue, "Female Images and National Myth," in Tani Barlow, ed., *Gender Politics in Modern China* (Durham: Duke University Press, 1993). This scholarship demonstrates that the woman figured prominently as an object of nationalist discourse and is made to signify variously as "the national exemplar" who embodies "the eternal Chinese civilizational virtues" (Duara), as a source of authority to legitimize or delegitimize a political party (Gilmartin), as a symbol of the health of the nation (Hershatter), and as the authentic political identity of the Chinese Communist Party (Meng).

5. Michel Foucault and Michel de Certeau have made this issue central in their critique of historiography, Foucault in positioning discursivity in relation to an eliminated other, and de Certeau in furthering the investigation of areas formerly consigned to silence or set outside of the frame of history. See Foucault, *The Archeology of Knowledge* (London: Tavistock Publishers, 1972); and Certeau, *The Writing of History* (New York: Columbia University Press, 1988). Closer to the China field, Prasenjit Duara, in his recent study of modern Chinese history, has also argued that the formation of the national identity was such that "other identifications and alternatives, often incipient narratives of the nation are repressed and obscured" (Duara, *Rescuing History from the Nation: Questioning Narratives of Modern China* [Chicago: University of Chicago Press, 1995], p. 16).

this chapter argues that the 1898 reforms originated a particular and gendered version of tradition in an effort to produce and enact a particular and gendered version of modernity. This version of history would be further elaborated, canonized, and ossified in the May Fourth restatement of Chinese history and continued into much of the twentieth century.

Redefinition of Knowledge Through the Cainü

The familiar and monolithic image of benighted traditional womanhood was not a creation of the May Fourth and New Culture movement. Rather, its origins can be traced to the 1898 reformers and further still to the missionaries, whose castigations of traditional Chinese womanhood were prominent among a host of other critiques of the Chinese culture.

The American missionary Young J. Allen (1836–1907), of the Southern Methodist Episcopal Church, for example, cited "the woman's place" in the West as a demonstration of higher civilization. Known to his readers by his Chinese name, Lin Lezhi 林樂知, Allen was one of the most active missionaries in China in the latter half of the nineteenth century, and his crusade for political reform was quite influential.[6] *Wanguo gongbao* 萬國公報 (The Chinese globe magazine), which Allen edited, is said to have "penetrated to every quarter of China" in the late nineteenth century.[7] After the Sino-Japanese War of 1894–95, Allen's critique of Chinese cultural practices intensified, chief among which was the status of women.[8] In the preface to his

---

6. For Allen's earlier career and his publishing endeavors before the 1898 reform period, see Adrian A. Bennett, *Missionary Journalist in China: Young J. Allen and His Magazines, 1860–1883* (Athens: University of Georgia Press, 1983). For missionary influence on the late Qing reformists, see Paul Cohen, "Littoral and Hinterland in Nineteenth Century China: The 'Christian' reformers," in Fairbank, *The Missionary Enterprise in China and America*, pp. 579–80; and Wang Lixin 王立新, *Meiguo chuanjiaoshi yu wan Qing Zhongguo xiandaihua* 美國傳教士與晚清中國現代化 (American missionaries and Chinese modernization in the late Qing) (Tianjin: Tianjin renmin chubanshe, 1997).

7. For a detailed discussion of the ambivalent relationship between missionaries and Liang Qichao, see Chi-yun Chen, "Liang Ch'i-ch'ao's 'Missionary Education': A Case Study of Missionary Influence on the Reformers," *Papers on China* (Cambridge, Mass.: Harvard University) 16 (1962): 66–125. Liang Qichao apparently acted as Timothy Richard's Chinese secretary for a brief period during 1895 and favored his works over those of Young J. Allen, whom he met once. See Wang Shuhuai 王樹槐, *Wairen yu wuxu bianfa* 外人與戊戌變法 (Foreigners and the 1898 reforms) (Shanghai: Shanghai shudian, 1998 [1980]), p. 51.

8. Wang Shuhuai, *Wairen yu wuxu bianfa*, pp. 72–73.

ten-volume *Quandi wudazhou nüsu tongkao* 全地五大洲女俗通考 (A survey of female customs on the five continents), Allen explained:

This book employs the status of women and their treatment in every country as the yardstick for judging the degree of civilization of each culture. This is why it is titled *A Survey of Female Customs* and otherwise known as *The Evaluation of All Civilizations, Ancient and Modern*. Readers of this book will be able to assess the true place of Chinese civilization themselves.[9]

Extrapolating from his tripartite scheme of "uncivilized people" (Africans), "people of some civilization" (Egyptians and peoples of Asia Minor), and "people of modern civilization" (Europeans and Americans), Allen argues that "no country can ever hope to flourish without elevating and educating its women."[10] Not unusually for his time, Allen couches his "lifelong championing of women's education and equality" in the language of colonialism, with the West as the indisputable standard for cultural comparison. "Woman" becomes a metonym for progress and provides a crucial justification for the colonialists' "civilizing mission."

Although the imperialist overtones of his writing no doubt occasioned ambivalence in some of his Chinese readers, Allen's basic assumption was not disputed. Adopting Allen's yardstick of the status of women but rephrasing it to suit his own reform agenda, Liang Qichao correlated women's education with the strength of the nation. In his *General Discussion on Reform* (*Bianfa tongyi* 變法通議), one chapter of which is devoted to women's learning, Liang wrote: "When I try to deduce the deepest underlying reason for the weakness of a nation, it always starts from the lack of education for women."[11] What lies behind this argument is a particular image of the traditional woman—"ignorant, apathetic, sequestered," in Liang Qichao's words.

---

9. Lin Lezhi (Young John Allen), *Wanguo gongbao*, Aug. 29, 1904; reprinted in *Jindai Zhongguo nüquan yundong shiliao, 1842–1911* 近代中國女權運動史料, ed. Li Yuning 李又寧 and Chang Yufa 張玉法, 2: 824. (Taibei: Zhuanji wenxue, 1975).

10. This is a typical application of the famous dictum by Charles Fourier that the emancipation of women is the index of the general emancipation of an age. Pressed into the service of colonialism, "age" became "civilization." This idea still has some currency in China, as contemporary scholars continue to employ the same language. See Wang Lixin, *Meiguo chuanjiaoshi yu wanqing Zhongguo xiandaihua*, chap. 4. For a critique of this line of argument, see Joan Kelly, "Did Women Have a Renaissance?" in idem, *Women, History and Theory: The Essays of Joan Kelly* (Chicago: University of Chicago Press, 1984).

11. Liang, "Lun nüxue" 論女學, in *Yinbing shi heji: wenji*, 1: 37–44. This essay was originally published in 1897 in *Shiwu bao*, a few issues earlier than his biography of Kang.

However, one particular group of women presented difficulties for this reductive picture: elite women who were highly literate. Liang conceded that indeed there were women "who had even composed several volumes of poems": "What was called the talented woman (*cainü* 才女) in ancient times was the woman who waxed lyrical about the wind and the moon (*pifeng muoyue* 批風抹月), the flowers and the grass (*nianhua nongcao* 拈花弄草), the woman who toyed with ditties lamenting spring and bemoaning separation (*shangchun xibie* 傷春惜別)."[12] In order to dismiss *all* women, including the *cainü*, as "ignorant," what Liang Qichao's essay has had to accomplish is an epistemological re-definition of *xue* 學, learning. Thus, he summarily concluded: "Now this sort of thing really cannot be called learning at all." Later in the essay, Liang gave two explicit reasons for dismissing the accomplishments of the traditional *cainü*. First, the image of *cainü* is closely associated with the privileged minority born into literati-gentry families, whereas the modern nation demands popular education for all its (mothers of) citizens. Second, the talent of the traditional *cainü* is "useless," since it is closely tied to traditional high culture and therefore far from the practical learning needed for the advancement of modern China.

Still, something has to account for the emotional excess between the lines of Liang Qichao's dismissal and disdain. This excess, which not only marked Liang's discussion of the *cainü* here and elsewhere but became infectious and ever more intensified in the writings of new-style women and men in years to come,[13] may be attributed to "a decision to be different from the past."[14] What we witness, then, is a conscious effort to transform the meaning of knowledge and its relationship with politics, as the writing of history accomplishes an act of division, a separation of the present from the past. For Liang, the woman poet represents more than herself or women writers as a group; she becomes a figure for bad poets in general and, even more abstractly, for the lyrical tradition as a whole, here represented as sentimental

---

12. Ibid., 1: 39.

13. Liang Qichao's critique of the *cainü* typically functions as a foil to the image of the new woman, as demonstrated in the following section of this chapter. Joan Judge, in her well-documented study of female literacy of this period in this volume, also points to the escalating critique of the *cainü* as an important legacy of the 1898 reform movement. Indeed, the very wording of this critique is suspiciously similar to Liang's, though more emotionally vehement; one critic even concluded: "Our literate sisters are the same or even worse than illiterate ones" (quoted in Judge's chapter; see p. 168).

14. Certeau, *The Writing of History*, p. 36.

and flaccid—the *cainü* as metonym of a feminized cultural tradition leading to the emasculation of the national fiber. The cure is the "martial" or "colonizing" spirit exalted by Liang.[15] The discourse of tradition and modernity then becomes implicitly gendered, with the past coded as feminine and the future as masculine. This does not mean that women poets per se become the inheritors of the past but that a tradition is represented in gendered terms, in that it is at once embodied (by the women poets) and at the same time abstracted (metaphorically effete). Similarly, as we will see below, the coding of the modern as masculine does not mean that the woman does not figure in its construction; rather, the narrative of the modern becomes saturated with metaphors of masculinity.

Thus, with one powerful rhetorical flourish, Liang Qichao buries both the traditional *cainü* and the traditional high culture represented by the *cainü*. This tradition is now consigned to the "past," not to mention a distant past.[16] And the past, once named as such, establishes the crux of current time and thus enables the enactment of the modern. The burial of the *cainü* heralds the birth of the new woman, who is first introduced by Liang Qichao himself. She is Dr. Kang Aide, the first new woman knowledgeable in Western medicine—the modern *cai* par excellence.

To set the stage for the introduction of the new woman, it turns out that two *cainü* are required. At the beginning of the biography before the protagonist makes her entrance, Liang Qichao laments how "very few women among the two hundred million women of the empire are literate and able to compose a few trifling poems on wind and moon, flowers and grass."[17] He proceeds to account, and repudiate, the achievements of two other Chinese women, both very much in the model of *cainü*: Liang Duan 梁端, a mid-nineteenth-century scholar who redacted and annotated the classic *Biogra-*

---

15. In his study of Liang Qichao and the poetic revolution in the volume, Xiaobing Tang demonstrates that Liang's rhetoric in discussing the poetic revolution is suffused with the metaphor of colonization, with its accompanying images of aggressive incorporation and vigorous expansion.

16. In practice, Liang Qichao himself was by no means consistent in the rejection of tradition or traditional high culture. (And for that matter, nor were many of the May Fourth advocates of literary revolution.) Indeed, it appears that the rhetoric of a radical break with tradition need not be consistent with practice to effect its primary objective, namely, to serve as a springboard for the enactment of the modern.

17. Liang, "Ji Jiangxi Kang nüshi," 1: 119 (hereafter cited in the text).

phies of Women (*Lienü zhuan* 列女傳), and the prolific classical scholar Wang Zhaoyuan 王照圓 (1763–1851), who edited and annotated various ancient texts including *Biographies of Transcendents* (*Liexian zhuan* 列仙傳) and *Biographies of Women*, in addition to composing volumes of poetry and essays on poetics. These are recent *cainü* whose achievements were well within the tradition of female learning and whose works were available during Liang Qichao's time; indeed, in the case of Wang Zhaoyuan, her learning rested squarely within the classical scholarship tradition of the Qing, so much so that she was widely considered a *Hanxue* 漢學 expert and several of her works bear notes in the vermilion ink of the Guangxu emperor.[18] Liang Qichao grants these women writers grudging recognition for "having read a few classical texts and being able to write," if only because "there have been so very few of them throughout the empire." In the final analysis, however, Liang proclaims their learning "not real learning," much as he did earlier in the chapter on women's education.

Following this brief cataloging of the meager achievements of women, Liang reaches his dire conclusion, "Without [true] learning, one cannot know the way. With a mass of two hundred million ignorant people, there can be no nation." At this point, the text abruptly changes direction. Liang (referring to himself in the historical third person) dramatically highlights the entry of a different model of womanhood, in contrast to the traditional *cainü*: "Since Liang Qichao holds this view and worries about the country, Zou Linghan 鄒凌瀚 implores him to speak of Ms Kang."[19] (Zou Linghan was Liang Qichao's source of information about Kang Aide and makes only a fleeting appearance.) The very first appearance of the modern woman is inextricably linked with the nation or, more precisely, with anxiety over the

---

18. For sources on Liang Duan, see Hu Wenkai 胡文楷, ed., *Lidai funü zhuzuo kao* 歷代婦女著作考 (Shanghai: Guji chubanshe, 1985 [1957]), p. 544. For sources on Wang Zhaoyuan, see ibid., pp. 242–45; Liang Yizhen 梁乙眞, *Qingdai funü wenxueshi* 清代婦女文學史 (Taibei: Zhonghua shuju, 1958), pp. 205–8; and Harriet Zurndorfer, "Wang Zhaoyuan," in Clara Wing-Chung Ho, ed., *Biographical Dictionary of Chinese Women: The Qing Dynasty (1644–1911)* (New York: M. E. Sharpe, 1998), pp. 227–30. For a recent study of Wang, see Harriet Zurndorfer, "How to Be a Good Wife and a Good Scholar at the Same Time," in Léon Vandermeersch, ed., *La Société civile face à l'état dans la traditions chinoise, japonaise, coréene et vietnamienne* (Paris: Ecole française d'Extrême Orient, 1994), pp. 249–70.

19. Zou Linghan was from Jiangxi province, where Kang was practicing medicine. For a brief biography of Zuo, see Chen Yutang 陳玉堂, *Zhongguo jinxiandai renwu minghao dacidian* 中國近現代人物名號大辭典 (Shanghai: Zhejiang guji chubanshe, 1993), p. 395.

fate of the nation.[20] Indeed, the anxiety over the future of the nation signals a level of performativity on the part of Liang Qichao, since it provides the necessary emotional context for the narrative of Kang's story. This is the point at which Liang switches from the first person to the third person; the third-person speaker with his worries about the nation becomes the foundation for a position that will authorize itself later to speak in the guise of total objectivity.

Af-filiation to Global Modernity

Liang Qichao paid special attention to two elements in Kang's life: her status as an orphan and the graduation ceremony at the University of Michigan at which she received a medical degree. Not coincidentally, both elements underline Liang's effort to portray China's entry into global modernity.

In Liang's biography, Kang Aide's parents died when she was very young. Hao Geju (Gertrude Howe), an American traveler in China, met Kang and "appreciated her intelligence and pitied her poverty." Howe adopted Kang and took her to America at the age of nine. Kang Aide then went through the American educational system, "mastering several languages, as well as subjects like cosmology, geography, mathematics, physics, chemistry." She eventually obtained a medical degree and came back to serve her country.

Personal as the genre of biography may seem to be, ultimately, it is not the individual that interests Liang, but the Chinese female citizen:

Although I do not know Ms Kang personally, I imagine that her native intelligence and capabilities must not be greatly different from ordinary people's. Had she not lost her parents and become an orphan, had she not meet Hao Geju and gone with

---

20. The term Liang Qichao uses is *tianxia* 天下, which he, like several of his contemporaries, sometimes employed interchangeably with *guojia* 國家 or *guo* during this period. Whether the term *tianxia* carries overtones of the nation-state is a matter of scholarly debate. Based on his study of Liang Qichao, Joseph Levenson first posited the distinction between the two terms and argued that the turn of the twentieth century marked a transition from culturalism to nationalism; see Levenson, *Liang Qichao and the Mind of Modern China*, 2d ed. (Cambridge, Mass.: Harvard University Press, 1959). This restricted model of nationalism has recently been subjected to a scholarly critique; see Prasenjit Duara, *Rescuing History from the Nation*, pp. 56–57; and Theodore Huters, "Appropriations: Another Look at Yan Fu and Western Ideas," *Xueren* 9 (1996): 296–355. Following this line of inquiry, I assume the term *tianxia* as used during this period includes key aspects of nationalism, especially the awareness of the nation-state as the ultimate goal of the community in the face of challenges posed by other nation-states.

her to America, had she not studied at the University of Michigan, then today she would be just as ignorant, apathetic, sequestered—no different from ordinary women. (1: 120)

What makes Kang different from ordinary Chinese women, as Liang sees it, is her paradoxical good fortune in being orphaned, which made it possible for her to be adopted by an American and benefit from a modern educational system. By thus playing up the adoption plot, Liang replaces the filiation of family with filiation of global modernity.[21]

Another element on which Liang Qichao lavishes elaborate and detailed description is the graduation ceremony at the University of Michigan, which in effect provides the stage for the confrontation of the particular (the Chinese) with the universal (the modern West). The university itself is described as being situated in "one of the largest metropolises of the country" and having "more than a thousand students, including those from a dozen foreign countries and alien races." On to this cosmopolitan stage stepped Kang Aide and her friend Shi Meiyu 石美玉 (Mary Stone, 1872–1954), two among the more than one hundred graduates that day:

Ms Kang carried herself with great dignity. Wearing Chinese clothing and with carefully measured square-steps (*jubu* 矩步), she solemnly (*ranran qu* 冉冉 趨, lit. "with mincing rapid gait") ascended the stairs to the stage. . . . Westerners are used to denigrating the Chinese, comparing us to barbarians. When the two of them approached, their costumes greatly different from the rest of the crowd, their diploma of the first grade, the best one could get in the system, all the professors and officials, whether of the school or visiting from elsewhere, were amazed by their unusual manners. They all stood up with great solemnity, bowing with respect [to the two Chinese graduates]. Inside and outside the gate, thousands of students from more than ten countries formed a wall of spectators, and they all applauded and sighed with admiration. (1: 119)[22]

---

21. For the use of adoption plot in late Qing fiction, see my *Tales of Translation: Composing the New Woman in China, 1899–1918* (Stanford: Stanford University Press, 2000), pp. 121–26.

22. Liang's description of the graduation ceremony, minus his ritualistic rhetoric, is corroborated by a contemporary report in the *China Medical Missionary Journal*, 10, no. 4 (Dec. 1896): 181–84. The report registers the surprise of university authorities that the graduation papers of the "little foreigners were among the best that were presented." The report also mentions that "in the procession of over four hundred graduates," the two young women, in their "native dress," were met with applause. I am grateful to Angela Leung for sharing this information with me.

Strikingly, the language with which Liang describes the walk of the two
Chinese women resonates with ritual propriety. The stock phrases "carefully
measured square-steps" and "mincing rapid gait" are closely associated with
the correct comportment of literati-officials in public office and loaded with
connotations of individual outward appearance and its public consequences.
Since correct ritual behavior often functioned as an index of class distinction, the very language of Liang's description confers on the two Chinese
women membership in the ranks of male literati, at the time still arguably
the identity Liang and most of his readers would have claimed for themselves. This ritual performance, furthermore, is conducted in front of an
audience sharply delineated for maximum contrast; the two women are portrayed as representing China in front of the other students and faculty, the
"wall of spectators" from "more than ten countries," forming a veritable
United Nations. The portrayal of the graduation ceremony thus involves a
kind of double gaze: seeing the other seeing the self. This foreign other, who
"used to denigrate the Chinese," is confronted with the "unusual manners" of
the two Chinese graduates and persuaded to welcome them as equals. The
textual emphasis on the surprised response from the audience highlights the
"difference" presumably embodied by the two Chinese women. Of course,
the manners are unusual only to the imagined spectators, not to Liang's
contemporary readers, to whom the graduation ceremony must have resem-
bled the ceremonies surrounding the passing of the imperial examination.[23]
It is, then, the acting-out of literati ritual in front of alien others that makes
the graduation ceremony an event worthy of historical record. What it performs is the drama of China's entry into the global universal, a significant
ritual moment imaginatively staged at the University of Michigan.

　　Yet, what is elided in this grand act of history-making is the alterity of
the real subject, two traces of which we find in other historical records: her
gender and her missionary background. In their ritual performance, the two
graduates are said to be clothed in "Chinese costume," presumably in concert
with their "carefully measured square-steps" and the ritually correct "mincing gait." But in fact, the dress was Chinese *women's* clothing and indicated
both their nationality and their gender.[24] The irony of Liang's historical nar-

---

　　23. For detailed description of the Qing ceremony of *changming* 唱名, see Ichisada Miya-
zaki, *China's Examination Hell: The Civil Service Examinations of Imperial China* (New Haven:
Yale University Press, 1981), pp. 83–86.

　　24. In several Qing *tanci* 彈詞 women impersonate men and pass the palace examination;
they are always represented as in disguise and wearing male garb; see Siao-chen Hu, "Literary

rative is that the representatives of the new China only appear to follow literati rituals but are in fact female impostors who share little of the elite male
literati culture. Another trace of Kang's alterity is her strong missionary
background. In Liang Qichao's biography, Kang's adoptive mother, Gertrude Howe (1847–1928), is "the daughter of an American scholar-official,"
an identification that resonates with the representation of Kang conducting
herself as though she were a member of the literati-official class. In Liang's
account, Howe is a Victorian globe-trotter, who happens to meet the orphaned Kang while traveling through China and subsequently spirits her off
to America. In fact, Howe came to China as a missionary of the Methodist
Episcopal Church in 1872 and had been working off and on in China for
more than twenty years when Liang wrote this essay.[25]

"A Daughter of Confucius": The Missionary Portrait

In the National Archive of the United Methodist Church, there is a file under
the name Ida Kahn, complete with medical records, curriculum vitae, news
clippings, turn-of-the-century photographic portraits (both in traditional
Chinese gowns and in Victorian dresses), recommendation letters for mission
grants produced on early typewriters, and a lithographic print of Gertrude
Howe's obituary, in Chinese by Kang Cheng, the Chinese name used by
Kang Aide or Ida Kahn.[26] Similar files exist at the Bentley Historical Library

---

Tanci: A Woman's Tradition of Narrative in Verse" (Ph.D. diss., Harvard University, 1994).
This was apparently something that Kang and her friend Shi Meiyu expressly did not want
to do. The dresses were specially ordered from China for the occasion, contrary to the usual
practice of the two women, who dressed in the Western style of the time (General Commission on Archives and History, the United Methodist Church, file on Mary Stone).

25. It is not impossible that Liang Qichao was unaware of the history behind the story of
Kang Aide, but two factors militate against his ignorance. Although Liang's information is
secondhand, his informant, Zuo Linghan, interviewed Gertrude Howe about Kang Aide. It
would be highly unlikely that Zuo was not aware of the strong missionary presence surrounding this story. The second and more likely factor is Liang's own effort to separate
Western knowledge from Christianity. In his "Xixue shumu biao" 西學書目表, published in
1897, the same year as his biography of Kang Aide, Liang assiduously avoided including works
on Christianity except for two titles, which were included for their historical value (see Zhi-
xuezhai congshu 治學齋叢書 [1896], preface, 3b–4). For a discussion of Liang's conscious
separation of Western learning from Christianity, see also Chi-yun Chen, "Liang Ch'i-ch'ao's
'Missionary Education,'" pp. 111–12.

26. General Commission on Archives and History, the United Methodist Church, Drew
University, N.J., Personal file on Ida Kahn. For brief accounts of Kahn's medical career, see

at the University of Michigan and at the archive department of the Library at
Northwestern University. From these fragments there emerges an image of a
woman quite different from that produced by Liang Qichao.

A rough biographical chronology of Ida Kahn can be pieced together
from the files. She was born in 1873 in Jiujiang, Jiangxi, to a family that already had five girls. Two months after she was born, her parents failed in an
attempt to betroth the girl infant because her astrological signs were incom-
patible with those of the would-be groom. An acquaintance who worked as a
Chinese-language teacher for American missionaries suggested to the family
that they have the infant adopted by his employer Gertrude Howe, who had
only recently come to Jiujiang and had opened a school for girls in January of
that year. The school at the time had two pupils. Howe adopted the infant
and gave her the name Ida Kahn, which sounded like her Chinese name. In
time, Howe would adopt three other girls.[27] Except for one year of travel in
America and Japan in 1883, they stayed in China until 1892, when Howe
took Ida, then nineteen years old, Shi Meiyu, and three boys to the United
States for college education. Four years later, the two young women graduated from the University of Michigan with medical degrees. For the next
thirty-odd years, Ida Kahn worked as a self-supporting missionary doctor in
Nanchang, while her adoptive mother helped with the hospital work and
preached in the missionary school. Between 1909 and 1911, Ida Kahn returned to the United States and acquired a bachelor's degree in English literature from Northwestern University. She never married, although some of
her adoptive siblings did. In the winter of 1928, Gertrude Howe died in
Nanchang; Ida Kahn wrote a moving obituary in Chinese. Two years later,
Kahn herself passed away.

Two features in the missionary portrait of Ida Kahn are striking: the
continued fascination with Kahn's natal family and the erasure of her relationship with the reformers. They highlight the meanings the missionary

---

K. Chimin Wong and Lien-teh Wu, *History of Chinese Medicine, Being a Chronicle of Medical
Happenings in China from Ancient Times to the Present Period* (Shanghai: National Quarantine
Service, 1936). For a historical study of Chinese women overseas students, see Ye Weili, "Nü
Liuxuesheng: The Story of American-Educated Chinese Women, 1880s–1920s," *Modern
China* 20, no. 3 (1994): 315–46.

27. Mary Stone, "Miss Gertrude Howe," in the file on Gertrude Howe, General Commission on Archives and History, the United Methodist Church. All the other girls adopted by
Howe (Fanny, Belle, and Julia) took her last name. Ida Kahn appears to be the only exception.

portrait ascribes to tradition and femininity, meanings radically different from those ascribed by Liang Qichao.

In a featured article published in *The Christian Advocate* on October 15, 1914, Fletcher Brockman, the general secretary of the National YMCA of China, wrote of his impressions of Dr. Kahn's hospital. The title of the piece is "A Daughter of Confucius." This appellation apparently derives from the author's conversation with Gertrude Howe, who described Kahn's natal family as "a good one, named Con, or, as it is pronounced in this dialect, Kahn, direct descendants of Confucius."[28] A letter of recommendation written by a Dr. J. G. Vaughan, who worked in another hospital in Nanchang for four years, also devotes a paragraph to this issue of the surname:

> The name of Dr. Kahn is well known throughout Kiangsi [Jiangxi] Province and by the intellectual leaders of China. She belongs to the Kong family and the name Kahn is an Americanization of the Chinese character, which would more properly be spelled Kong. This is the family of Confucius and although for several generations no doubt her immediate relatives have been in the province of Kiangsi yet she justly claims relation to the family of China's greatest sage, the great Confucius.[29]

Similarly, biographies of Ida Kahn by officers of the Women's Foreign Missionary Society never fail to mention her "highly respected family" and its "direct descent from Confucius." One biography published after her death even appends "Kung" directly after her English surname, as if to correct five decades of mispronunciations.[30]

In this account of Kahn's early life, there is, however, a significant rupture that problematizes the genealogical story: the family's willingness to relinquish the baby girl when she was barely two months old. In fact, according to Gertrude Howe, Ida Kahn was adopted in part to prevent her natal fam-

---

28. Newspaper clipping: Fletcher S. Brockman, "A Daughter of Confucius," General Commission on Archives and History, the United Methodist Church.

29. The letter on file is produced on a typewriter and was written in late 1911 or early 1912, since it refers to Burton's *Notable Women of Modern China* (1912) as forthcoming. General Commission on Archives and History, the United Methodist Church.

30. "Dr. Kahn–Nanchang, China," by Amy Clifford Lewis, secretary of General Office, Women's Foreign Missionary Society, New York City, *Christian Advocate*, June 30, 1932. Another article simply titled "Ida Kahn, MD" by Bessie F. Merrill, also of the Women's Foreign Missionary Society, appears in *Adventure in Faith*. General Commission on Archives and History, the United Methodist Church.

ily from claiming her back when she reached productive age.[31] The plan worked: in none of the accounts is there any indication that Howe or Kahn had any contact with the natal family.[32] Thus there is a definite rupture in the "direct descent" story; more important, the rupture is what provides the beginning of Kahn's life as a Chinese Christian. Typically, the missionary articles attribute this to either superstition ("yet it was a family that followed the advice of a blind fortune-teller") or poverty ("a sixth [daughter] meant one more to provide rice for, which was impossible"). Implicitly, then, several different and conflicting meanings were attributed to "China's greatest sage, the great Confucius."

Gertrude Howe's stress on the "good" family of Ida Kahn may be attributed to two historical considerations, both of which have to do with class. One consideration harks back to the formation of what was called the "middling classes" in nineteenth-century America, in which religious piety was one of the key building blocks.[33] Presenting her daughter as a Chinese Christian of good family, more or less like the middling classes at home, no doubt recommended her favorably to someone like Fletcher Brockman. Another, perhaps more important, consideration may be the nineteenth-century history of Chinese Christian converts, who had the reputation of coming from the lowest classes of society. Indeed, one missionary account relates how, even in the first decade of the twentieth century, a member of the gentry attempted to lure Kahn away from the church by telling her that her missionary associations did not reflect well on her since the "lower class

31. Adoption of Chinese children by missionaries was common practice at the time and was often informal, with the relationship variously defined. The more common practice was to have the adopted children brought up in the families of Chinese Christians, financially sponsored by the missionaries; see Jane Hunter, *The Gospel of Gentility: American Missionary Women in Turn-of-the-Century China* (New Haven: Yale University Press, 1984), p. 192. Howe, however, not only departed from this racially segregationist practice by having the Chinese children live with her but went so far as to move into a Chinese house with her adopted children.

32. Concern about the adoptee returning to the natal family has always been central in the practice of adoption; see Ann Waltner's analysis of adoption across different surnames in late imperial China in *Getting an Heir: Adoption and the Construction of Kinship in Late Imperial China* (Honolulu: University of Hawaii Press, 1990).

33. For discussions of religious revival and the formation of the middling classes, see Barbara L. Epstein, *The Politics of Domesticity: Women, Evangelism and Temperance in Nineteenth-Century America* (Middletown, Conn.: Wesleyan University Press, 1981).

joins the church for pecuniary good."[34] Because Kahn's lowly family background is rather typical of nineteenth-century Christian converts, the claim of direct descent from Confucius is an attempt at erasure, whether conscious or not, of a piece of the missionary history that by the early twentieth century was increasingly being censured.[35] An unwanted daughter from a destitute family, a marginal figure in Chinese society, was transformed into someone who could "justly claim relation to the family of China's greatest sage," the epicenter of the Chinese tradition.

This fascination with Kahn's pedigree may be attributed to the peculiar workings of missionary cultural logic: that of difference and that of analogy. By emphasizing her well-known and prestigious surname, these stories build on the image of gentility and good old tradition, an analogy to the image of middle-class home and church that renders the foreign familiar. At the same time, the "unbroken pedigree" establishes Ida Kahn as genuinely Chinese—racially pure and therefore different from her adoptive mother. Marked off by her illustrious surname, Kahn is represented as difference, despite her Christian faith and her largely American education. In her similarity, she is intelligible and even sympathetic as a member of the missionary family. In her difference, the "daughter of Confucius" is an authentic representative of the Chinese tradition.

But the image of tradition, in both its concrete form and its abstract rendition, is filled with ambiguity. Tradition, as represented by Ida Kahn's prestigious surname, is at times seen as being in a state of decay, poverty-stricken ("a sixth [daughter] meant one more to provide rice for, which was impossible") and superstitious ("yet it was a family that followed the advice of a blind fortune-teller"). Cultural tradition could be easily recast into the limitations of Chinese civilization, which only Christianity can help remedy. A biography of Gertrude Howe, published for the Women's Foreign Missionary Society, mentions that Kahn "objected to [the placement of] any

---

34. Brockman, "A Daughter of Confucius," p. 2.

35. On the low social standing of Christian converts in the nineteenth century, see Paul Cohen, "Christian Missions and Their Impact to 1900," in *The Cambridge History of China*, vol. 10, pt. I, *Late Qing, 1800–1911*, ed. John K. Fairbank (Cambridge, Eng.: Cambridge University Press, 1978), pp. 558–59. By the turn of the century, the situation had changed significantly. Missionary reports routinely boasted of increasing numbers of "paying students"; see Margaret E. Burton, *The Education of Women in China* (New York: Fleming H. Revell, 1911), pp. 77–99. By 1906, missionary boards ruled against official adoption of Chinese children (Hunter, *The Gospel of Gentility*, p. 192).

tablets, Confucian or other," in the government-sponsored school in which she was asked to teach.[36] That a "daughter of Confucius" should be the one to object to Confucian tablets exposes the inherent contradictions in the many meanings of "Confucius" and the Chinese tradition that it represents. As an easily recognizable name for class and pedigree, the surname Kung is highlighted and lauded; as a sign of culture heritage, it is rendered as destitute and decadent; as a symbol of religious belief, it is represented as heathen and must therefore be repudiated by its heirs.[37]

Another historical fact lies buried in the missionary fascination with Ida Kahn's surname: her relationship with the reform movement represented by, among others, Liang Qichao. That "the name of Dr. Kahn is well known throughout Kiangsi [Jiangxi] Province and by the intellectual leaders of China" is readily recognized in missionary records. But her reputation is attributed to her prestigious surname, rather than to any connection with the reformers.

According to Gertrude Howe, a few months after she and Kahn returned to China in 1898, a Mr. Wen and a Mr. Tseo, described as local gentry leaning toward reform, called on them. Mr. Tseo is Zou Linghan, Liang Qichao's informant. Once convinced of Kahn's achievement, they borrowed her diploma and had it hung up on the wall of a recently founded "Anti-Footbinding Society," so that "the two hundred thousand women of China would see what a woman can achieve."[38] Later, when someone in Mr. Tseo's family was gravely ill, Ida Kahn was sent for; the patient's eventual recovery was crucial in the establishment of Dr. Kahn's reputation in the region. In this portrait, the reformers' meeting with Ida Kahn is represented as serendipitous and beneficial in promoting her fledgling career as a physician. In a 1905 letter to *The Alumnus* magazine of the University of Michigan, Kahn herself struck a neutral note: "There is a reform party in China now ready to

---

36. General Commission on Archives and History, the United Methodist Church, file on Gertrude Howe.

37. For debate on the issue of idolatry/Confucianism among missionaries, see Kwang-Ching Liu, *American Missionaries in China: Papers from Harvard Seminars* (Cambridge, Mass.: Harvard University Press, 1966); and Wang Lixin, *Meiguo chuanjiaoshi yu wanqing Zhongguo xiandaihua*, pp. 40–45.

38. General Commission on Archives and History, the United Methodist Church, file on Gertrude Howe.

seize upon almost any means for the improvement of the country."[39] In later accounts by missionaries, however, the "local gentry" were increasingly portrayed in less favorable light, sometimes as unenlightened heathens whose main function was to test the steadfastness of the young doctor's Christian faith. This is especially the case with letters of recommendation, which were written to secure funding from the mission board of the Methodist Church for Kahn's work in China. A letter written by Bishop Lewis on her behalf thus declares: "The gentry offered to support her hospital very generously if she would discontinue its connection with the church. This she steadfastly refused to do and they have therefore not been so generous to her."[40]

Thus, any connection with the reformers is erased in missionary accounts, just as in Liang Qichao's biography, Kahn's missionary background is buried. The missionary records paint her as securely rooted in the tradition of China, if only as a guarantee of her good family; the reformists portray her education as thoroughly American and Kahn herself as the very embodiment of modern citizenship. Just as her Christianity is represented as entirely compatible with her Confucian descent in the missionary portrayal, in Liang's biography, there is no sense of conflict between her traditional literati demeanor and her modern American education. The relationship between the reformers and the missionaries in the late Qing was complex and fraught with ambivalence on both sides.[41] Kahn, sometimes the poster girl of the reformers, sometimes that of the missionaries, is thus a figure caught between two powerful discourses, each with its own formulation of Chinese tradition and its own vision of modernity.

---

39. Bentley Historical Library, the University of Michigan, necrology file of Ida Kahn.

40. Bishop Lewis, June 8, 1917. General Commission on Archives and History, the United Methodist Church, file on Ida Kahn. Bishop Lewis's account is contradicted by another account by Bishop J. W. Bashford, who ten years earlier had written, "The gentry of Nanchang . . . have bought and presented to us five acres of ground inside the city wall and have raised 5,000 or 6,000 teals for the erection of a hospital on these grounds, in return for our sending to them Dr. Ida Kahn, a Chinese woman educated in America and a graduate of the medical department of the University of Michigan" (Bentley Historical Library, University of Michigan, necrology file of Ida Kahn). There is also a slippage of meaning between "reformers" and "local gentry."

41. See Cohen, "Christian Missions and Their Impact to 1900," pp. 559–72. What is important to note here is the potential alliance between the gentry/reformers and missionaries on a local level around the time of the 1898 reforms, an alliance that the reformers and missionaries alike apparently rejected.

"An Amazon in Cathay": Recasting Gender and Class

As a counterpoint to the stories that others tell about her, Kahn's own writings, a short story and an obituary/biography of her adoptive mother, give us glimpses of her reflections on the major issues of her day, such as race, gender, and the nation. Despite her apparently conservative stance, her version of history contests the dominant discourse of nationalism and modernity. Where the dominant discourse singles out the family as the basis for women's role in modernization, her stories stress a collective female community outside the conventional family; where the dominant discourse employs a racialized language of nationalism, her heroines espouse an antiracist internationalism and eschew an unproblematized nationalism/patriotism. Her vantage point in contesting the dominant discourse may be a powerful consciousness of her own marginal position in the Chinese society.

One period in Kahn's life that does not fit neatly into either the reformist portrait of the modern woman / citizen of the nation or the missionary portrait of "a story of thrilling interest" of self-sacrifice and service to God. After a dozen years as a medical missionary, Kahn spent a two-year furlough at Northwestern University and obtained a bachelor's degree in English literature in 1911. She came back to Nanchang to find her hospital crowded with wounded soldiers from the revolutionary war. A few months later, in 1912, she published "An Amazon in Cathay," a short story of eight closely printed pages published as a pamphlet by the Women's Foreign Missionary Society in Boston.[42] A fictional account of the lives of two young Chinese women in the midst of the Republican revolution, it is layered with personal ambivalence, generic conventions, and the hesitancy of an amateur fiction writer trying her hand in a language that is both her mother tongue and a foreign one.

The short story, written in flawless English, is part sentimental fiction, part religious tract. It is set in 1911, during the tumultuous days of the revolution. In an ancient household, two branches of the family are headed by widowed mothers, each with a daughter. The younger widow "had fortunately been persuaded to go to the woman's school at the Mission in Kiu-

---

42. "An Amazon in Cathay," by Ida Kahn, MD (1912; hereafter cited in the text). The pamphlet was priced at two cents. Publications from the Women's Foreign Missionary Society follow the spirit of the founding father of the Methodist Church John Wesley in his stress on the printing press as an aid to the wide dissemination of religious literature.

kiang [Jiujiang]," historically the school headed by Gertrude Howe herself. The narrative focus is exclusively on the female half of the household, for although there are apparently several sons, they are inconsequential in the plot development. Hoying, the daughter of the younger widow, had been a nurse in a missionary hospital when "the sudden revolution drove the young girl home." This is when the two branches of the family come into conflict. Curiously, the conflict is initially represented in terms of different tastes:

The country girl [Pearl] was struck by the beauty and culture of her city cousin [Hoying]. Not that she could not claim herself to be pretty, for both were good-looking according to the Chinese standard. Both had heavy masses of dark hair, but while the country cousin wore hers tightly coiled and covered with gold pins and artificial flowers, the other's was loosely coiled and decorated only with a green jade-stone lotus bud and a large pearl set in the heart of a blossom and placed in the center of the coil. (p. 4)

The passage goes on to describe the different colors of their costumes, the city cousin in clothes "exquisite in their soft tints," the country cousin "delighted to wear the brightest of hues." Colors, hairstyles, and fashions, apparently trivial details of personal taste, nonetheless carry significance as indicators of social difference, distinguishing what is legitimate (the cultured and refined) from what is not (the ignorant and coarse).

Continuing along the same lines of contrasts between the two young cousins, the narrative develops its central concern: the correct behavior for women in a time of national crisis. Should women participate in public service and, more precisely, national revolution? Pearl, the country cousin, is tormented by this question:

How envious she was of her cousin's learning and culture! The thought of her cousin's work in the hospital inspired her with admiration. What would she not give to be able to serve her country in some way? The thought preyed upon her mind until actually her face began to lose its rosy contour of health. Everyone was talking of patriotism until her very heart was sick. (p. 5)

Like a young heroine in a sentimental novel, the country cousin appears quite lovesick, except that her beloved is the country and she yearns for patriotic service.

Under the banner of patriotism, Pearl joins the female Dare-to-Die (Gansi dui 敢死隊) band, later referred to in the story as the "Amazon Corps." It is significant that the term "Amazon" is substituted as a functional equivalent for the more literal translation of the Chinese *gansi dui*. There is

something not quite "equivalent" in the translation: the original Chinese
term has no connotation of gender, whereas "Amazon" is pointedly gender-
inflected, with unfeminine or even antifeminine connotations. If the previous discussion of taste serves to distinguish the approved style of femininity
from its opposite, then the clear rejection of the Amazon archetype further
delineates the boundaries of femininity itself. Hoying, the city cousin, de-
cides to stay at home at a time of war. She attempts to persuade "the mistaken one" by arguing that Pearl "was untrained and had not the necessary
strength." What prevents the well-trained and capable Hoying from serving
can be nothing other than the constraints of femininity.

The Amazon role dictates that Pearl be stripped of her outward markers
of femininity. She dons masculine dress and has her "beautiful tresses"
clipped, not, the story notes, without shedding tears in private. Pearl's decline into that well-known Victorian creature, the Fallen Woman, is pre-
cipitous. Once she is at the front and comes into contact with "the Chinese
native soldiery," she encounters barbarism in the extreme, an encounter that
makes her wonder whether it is "necessary to become a cannibal in order to
be a patriot." Then the inevitable happens: "unchaperoned and unprotected,"
Pearl "suffered personal persecution"—the author's euphemism for rape.
There follow many attempts at suicide, highly reminiscent of both the sentimental novel in the English-American tradition and the biographies of
virtuous women in the Chinese tradition. At this point, the story switches
from the mode of sentimental fiction to that of religious conversion.
Through prayers to "her cousin's God," Pearl is removed to a missionary
hospital, where her cousin nurses her back to life. Pearl is converted to
Christianity and studies at the missionary school, just as her cousin has before her. The story ends with the young woman cheered by the thought
"that the God of the Christians despised not 'even the least of these little
ones'" and that this God "will teach [her] to serve [her] country in a way
that is worthy." Thus, thanks to divine intervention, the story does not end
in tragedy. The fate of the Fallen Woman is not unavoidable.[43] Not only is

---

43. Typically, in the tradition of the sentimental novel, the cast includes the persecuted
(seduced) heroine, the glittering rake, and the faithful confidante. In its earlier incarnation,
the sentimental novel often set up the dichotomy of the fallen woman against the pure
woman. This dichotomy would later translate into an internal dichotomy: the pure and fallen
woman in one. In addition there are the notorious amount of tears, an abundance of sensibility, and didactic purpose for moral reform. See Herbert Ross Brown, *The Sentimental Novel in*

"her cousin's God" particularly merciful, but he appears to respond directly to the sincere prayers of a woman. Although invoked to support a rather conservative code of behavior for women, in averting the hand of tragedy, this god represents a gender-inflected power that would have been considered out of bounds for traditional literati and reformists alike.[44]

What is Pearl's mistake, the beginning of her fall? It is not so much patriotism, since God as the ultimate authority implicitly endorses service to the country. Nor is there any problem with women serving their nation, since the aspiration to service itself is never condemned. Although the author does not explicitly indicate her own political stance, it is possible to deduce her aversion to the violence of revolution from her mention of soldiery and cannibalism in the same breath. More interesting, however, is that this aversion is expressed primarily from a gendered perspective, for the outcome of the story indicates that the unworthy way of service involves the negation of oneself as a woman. It is the denial of one's gender identity that leads to the catastrophic mistake in the fictional text.[45]

Most strikingly, Pearl's mistake is registered on her body, first through the erasure of her female identity (the donning of male costume, the cutting of her hair) and then through the assault on her as female (the experience of rape). To judge from the depiction of the totally alien "native" soldiery Pearl encounters at the front, it appears that the national identity that presumably binds Pearl with the soldiers is not nearly as strong as the sexual difference

---

America, 1789–1860 (New York: Pageant Books, 1959); and George Watt, *The Fallen Woman in the Nineteenth-Century English Novel* (London: Croom Helm, 1984).

44. This rendition of the savior is strikingly reminiscent of certain forms of traditional popular religion. In a study of one such religious cult, Kenneth Pomeranz observes that "no matter how orthodox the ends for which [the goddess] Bixia Yuanjun was usually invoked, the powers she represented were in many ways dangerous" (see Pomeranz, "Power, Gender, and Pluralism in the Cult of the Goddess of Taishan," in *Culture and State in Chinese History: Conventions, Accommodations, and Critique*, ed. Theodore Huters, R. Bin Wong, and Pauline Yu, p. 185 [Stanford: Stanford University Press, 1997]).

45. Within the Methodist Evangelical Church, there has been a long-standing debate over the prioritization of the "Three-fold Cord of the Gospel": medical, evangelical, and educational endeavors. The debate concerns the relative importance of saving bodies (medical work) and souls (evangelical work). Although the conversion at the end of Ida Kahn's story appears to resolve the conflicting priorities, the stress on Pearl's female body registers her heightened awareness of gender identity. It appears that this issue was not easily resolved in the lives and works of either Ida Kahn or Mary Stone; see Margaret Burton, *Notable Women of Modern China* (New York: Fleming H. Revell, 1912), pp. 126–60, 169–82.

that divides them. Indeed, the identity of the enemy the soldiers and the "Amazons" are fighting against is never made clear in the story. As far as Pearl is concerned, and as far as the fictional structure goes, the enemy is none other than her male compatriots. Patriotism at this point undergoes a radical redefinition with regard to the woman, as her body is made to register her gendered identity, an identity so marginalized that it marks her as an alien in her own nation.

Hardly the powerful Amazon that the title of the story would have us assume, Pearl does share with the mythical archetype an attempt to transcend the gender barrier on the war front, a mistaken attempt as the story clearly indicates. What is wrong with the Amazon figure, the narrative outcome tells us, is the crossing of the gender line.[46] At once supportive of women's education, of the acquisition of professions as well as patriotic service, the story sets a definite limit for its young women protagonists, beyond which lies an abyss. The Amazon, greeted by "the music of the band and the cheering of the crowd," is far from a figure of female empowerment; rather, she is seen as a false promise of liberation, a public spectacle without much practical substance, and a temptation that easily leads to a fall from social respectability.

Before and during the Republican revolution, there were, of course, a number of women who in fact did don men's clothing and fight on the revolutionary front. Those iconoclastic figures are still featured in books on the history of twentieth-century China. Qiu Jin 秋瑾 (1875–1907), who was executed for her revolutionary activities four years before Ida Kahn's story was written, was well known for such brazen behavior as riding a horse in public while dressed in male attire. Zhang Zhujun 張竹君 (1879–?), a missionary-educated doctor like Kahn and famous for her work with the Red Cross during the 1911 revolution, was also known for donning men's clothing when paying outpatient visits.[47] Read against this historical backdrop,

---

46. The gender line itself, however, is not always such a clear-cut matter. Hunter (*The Gospel of Gentility*, p. 181) argues convincingly that "beginning conservatively, [the women missionaries] found themselves offering a radical social alternative to Chinese women," which included professional career, single life, and the possibility of a life outside the family. This ambiguous gender line thus has the potential of opening up space for negotiation, as I will argue below.

47. For primary sources on the two women, see Li Yuning and Chang Yufa, *Jindai Zhongguo nüquan yundong shiliao, 1842–1911*.

Kahn's fictional account of a fallen Amazon may be interpreted in several different ways.

In the first reading, it is a conservative rejection of women heroines like Qiu Jin and Zhang Zhujun, who are found lacking when measured against standards of Victorian gentility. In this reading, Kahn's conservatism may be a reflection of her keenly felt position of marginality within her natal culture, both as an unwanted infant and as a Christian convert, a marginality that must have generated a strong sense of precariousness. Unlike women of elite background such as Qiu Jin, Kahn could not easily ally herself "in class terms with those elite men who claimed to be the primary legitimate agents of China's national sociopolitical practice."[48] Indeed, her awareness of marginality is underscored by the main attribute of "the God of the Christians," who "despised not 'even the least of these little ones,'" the abandoned, the rejected, and the fallen.

In the second reading, the clear narrative rejection of the iconoclastic heroine and the attendant public glamour may also be understood as Ida Kahn's active intervention in the Grand History in which she found herself. Not so long before, Kahn herself had been met with "the music of the band and the cheering of the crowd" when she first returned from America with her medical degree and was made an exemplar of modern womanhood by prominent reformers like Liang Qichao. Having grown up on the margins of Chinese society, Ida Kahn suddenly found herself at the center of public attention, as an exception to benighted Chinese womanhood and in the league of male literati-*cum*-modern-intellectuals. Her rewriting of history rejects this image of the token enlightened woman. It is significantly a story about women and about their response to their marginal status as woman in the grand history of the nation.

Indeed, even as the figure of the Amazon is critiqued in the story, there is an affinity between the mythic figure and the women depicted in the fictional narrative: both belong to close-knit female communities that derive their power in large measure from their closeness. Notwithstanding the requisite torrents of tears found in a sentimental novel, the focus of the fictional narrative is the community of women, which in the end proves as powerful as a

---

48. Rebecca Karl's chapter in this volume, pp. 221–22. For discussion of the dual identification of the elite woman, both with the subordinate category of "women" (and the broader term "people") and also with elite men, see the chapter by Karl in this volume. Kahn in fact came from "the people."

band of mythical Amazons. It is the resuscitating hand of Hoying that gives Pearl the will to live, as much against her own apathy as against powerful literary and cultural conventions: those of women's biographies in China (in which the sullied female is lauded for seeking death) and those of the Victorian novels of the Fallen Woman (who is so irrevocably fallen that her life is usually considered not worth living). Although the definition of correct feminine behavior in "An Amazon in Cathay" may owe its origin to Victorian gentility, the story can also be read as a narrative about the power of the female community in a time of great political turmoil and historical change.

Ideal Womanhood: What Does Family Have to Do with It

When we examine another of Kahn's writings, the obituary/biography of her adopted mother, Gertrude Howe, it is evident that Ida Kahn, or Kang Cheng as she calls herself here, was thoroughly dedicated to just such a community in her own life. In celebrating this female community, the obituary implicitly contests the family-oriented tenor of the dominant discourse at the time, which defines the woman, figuratively and literally, as the "mother of the citizen" and which legitimates the family as the only site of female agency.[49]

The obituary clearly indicates the extraordinary care that Kang took over the details of her mother's funeral ceremony, with a portrait of Howe flanked by the Chinese and American flags.[50] Most remarkable is the sense of a close-knit family in this obituary of a woman who died in a foreign land and without a conventional family. The list on the front page of the obituary of the names of the surviving family members indicates a full and prosperous line of descendents: the names of Howe's four adoptive daughters (buxiaonü 不孝女, "unfilial daughters," as convention dictates they be described), and below these the names of four "grand-daughters" from the daughters' side, wai sunnü 外孫女. So strong is the sense of a female community that it is as if a matriarch had died within the loving fold of her family after a long and fruitful life.[51] At the same time, by conducting an important family ritual,

---

49. See the chapters by Judge and Karl in this volume for the close connection between family and gender in the discourse of both male and female reformers.

50. Kang Cheng, "Fu" 訃 and "Hao nüshi lilüe" 昊女士歷略; General Commission on Archives and History, the United Methodist Church.

51. The concern for creating a woman's identity and respectability through family was important both for the Chinese and American contexts. Jane Hunter (The Gospel of Gentility,

Kang Cheng herself, a woman without a conventional family of her own, is represented as the pillar of a prosperous female community, her missionary community providing her with a powerful alternative to the conventional female role as wife and mother.[52]

In addition to her adoptive family, Gertrude Howe's natal family also gets considerable attention in the biography. Significantly, Kang stresses that Howe's father was a prominent abolitionist in America and that Gertrude "inherited the spirit of her father's work." This is consistent with Kang's repeated stress that throughout her life Gertrude Howe "had no use for the concept of race." Historically, the Methodist Church was deeply involved in the American Civil War. Women's missionary work especially gained momentum in conjunction with abolition: the correlation between the biblical arguments in support of women's work ("female reform") and against slavery (abolitionism) strengthened both causes.[53] Indeed, it was

---

chap. 3, "Single Women and Mission Community") argues that for single missionary women, family "signifies legitimacy and even sanity." There were alternative models of family in the form of collective women's residences. Howe's route of creating a family with her Chinese adoptive children appears to be the road less traveled. On the other hand, such honoring of one's adoptive parent is deeply rooted in traditional Chinese practice; as Francesca Bray has pointed out, "biological motherhood was less binding . . . than social motherhood," which was increasingly defined by the education of the young in Late Imperial China (see Bray, *Technology and Gender: Fabrics of Power in Late Imperial China* [Berkeley: University of California Press, 1997], p. 281). Alien as Gertrude Howe may have seemed within the traditional social fabric of rural China, as an adoptive parent who educated her daughters, she was squarely within the tradition of a "social mother."

52. In offering an alternative, the missionary community thus added one more powerful recourse to the long tradition of women's resistance to marriage. For other means of marriage resistance, such as Buddhism and a successful career in the silk industry, see Margery Topley, "Marriage Resistance in Rural Kwangtung," in *Women in Chinese Society*, ed. Margery Wolf and Roxane Witke, pp. 67–88 (Stanford: Stanford University Press, 1975); and Waltner, *Getting an Heir.*

53. Before and during the American Civil War, slavery was often used as an analogy and model for the oppression of women in speeches by famous suffragists such as Elizabeth Cady Stanton and Susan B. Anthony. There was also a powerful though brief coalition between the abolitionists and suffragists until the 1868 split. It is interesting to note, especially in light of Karl's chapter in this volume, that some of the reasons that suffragists employed against the so-called Negro's Hour were elitist in addition to being racist. For the religious basis for abolition and women's suffrage, see Mary D. Pellauer, *Toward a Tradition of Feminist Theology: The Religious Social Thought of Elizabeth Cady Stanton, Susan B. Anthony, and Anna Howard Shaw* (New York: Carson, 1991). For the coalition and later split between the abolitionists and suffragists, see Elizabeth Griffith, *In Her Own Right: The Life of Elizabeth Cady Stanton* (New York:

soon after the Civil War that the Women's Foreign Missionary Society was formed (1870); Gertrude Howe became one of the first missionaries to China (1873) under its auspices.

By stressing the link between Howe's abolitionist background and her lifelong work in China, Kang voiced a personal echo to the global consciousness common in late Qing and early Republican China. Attesting to this newly emerged consciousness were the many impassioned responses to Lin Shu's 林紓 (1852–1924) 1901 translation of *Uncle Tom's Cabin*, responses that compared the life of the black slaves with that of the Chinese immigrant workers in America and noted the sorry fate of those whose nations are weak or defeated.[54] Simultaneously, the popular "rating" of races complacently ranked the "yellow race" above the "black race."[55] Incidentally, this social Darwinist sentiment perhaps introduced only a new racialized vocabulary to the sinocentrism that most Chinese espoused. Indeed, we get a glimpse of it in Liang Qichao's biography of Kang Aide, cited above, in which he expresses indignation at "Westerners . . . [comparing] us to barbarians (*tufan* 土番)." The indignation no doubt reflects the new global consciousness; more precisely, it comes from a new geopolitical scheme, in which the West equates us (the Han Chinese) with them, the *tufan*, the barbarians. The indignation, in other words, comes from an inversion of the ranking system. Between these competing models of the world, Kang clearly endorses the antiracist model by emphasizing her maternal heritage of abolitionism. Rather than a naïve gesture of Christian goodwill, this choice demonstrates Kang's conscious construction of an ethical system that crosses national and racial boundaries, an ethics that is registered in an internationalized family, whose spirit of abolition she has inherited well.[56]

Oxford University Press, 1984); and Kathleen Barry, *Susan B. Anthony: A Biography* (New York: New York University Press, 1988).

54. Harriet Beecher Stowe's *Uncle Tom's Cabin* was translated by Lin Shu under the Chinese title *Heinu yutian lu* 黑奴吁天錄. It soon became one of the two most popular Western novels of the time. See Ma Zuyi 馬祖毅, *Zhongguo fanyi jianshi—wusi yiqian bufen* 中國翻譯簡史：五四以前部分 (Beijing: Zhongguo duiwai chuban, 1984), pp. 299–300. For a discussion of the connection of slavery with the status of women, see Karl's chapter in this volume.

55. For the prevailing racialized discourse of the period, see Frank Dikötter, *The Discourse of Race in Modern China* (Stanford: Stanford University Press, 1992), pp. 97–123.

56. In paying tribute to her adoptive mother's family lineage, Kang was also operating within traditional practice. As Arthur Wolf and Chieh-shan Huang have argued, adoption in late imperial China was always "a means by which families manipulate their composition to . . . achieve long-term goals" (p. 57), the central one of which is the maintenance of the ances-

Yet another example of antiracist practice is stressed in Gertrude Howe's own life, and this time in a practice that she introduced in the education of her adoptive daughters: she taught them English. This method of rearing her adoptive daughters was a serious departure from conventional missionary practice in the nineteenth century, and apparently Howe was much criticized by fellow missionaries for it.[57] The common practice in the missionary schools of the 1870s and 1880s was to primarily focus on the Gospel and Bible stories and to eschew liberal arts education as practiced in the West. The argument for not teaching English to Chinese Christian converts or adoptive children was that it would "distract . . . students from the worship of the Lord."[58] Although the rationale may have been religious, the teaching of European languages to non-European peoples was often determined not so much by the needs of religious practice as by the goals of imperialist projects. The teaching of French by the missionaries in the Congo in the late nineteenth to early twentieth centuries, for example, was carefully rationed. It was in part dictated by utilitarian concerns of labor supervision and in part

---

tral line; see Wolf and Huang, *Marriage and Adoption in China, 1845–1945* (Stanford: Stanford University Press, 1980). Understood within this tradition, Kang's lineage would logically be that of Howe and her family. Where her practice departs from tradition lies in gender and race: that ancestral line is usually understood as patrilineal, and cross-surname adoption in this case is stretched to cross-racial adoption.

57. Kang's biography is a bit vague on this point, noting only that Howe was squeezed out of her position at Mulberry School in 1883. Another account by Bessie F. Merrill makes it clear that "Miss Howe was frequently criticized for the methods of training used with these girls, so when Ida was about thirteen, Miss Howe thought it wise to change her surroundings" (see "Ida Kahn, M.D.," in *Adventurers in Faith*; see also Mary Stone, "Miss Gertrude Howe," United Methodist Church, General Commission on Archives and History, file on Gertrude Howe).

58. Ida B. Lewis points out that it is owing to the pressures from "progressive Chinese who demanded 'new educational methods, including the study of English'" that the subject began to be taught "as somewhat of an experiment" in the mid-1880s in a few schools; see Lewis, *The Education of Girls in China* (New York: Columbia University, Teachers College, 1919), pp. 20–21. Jane Hunter (*The Gospel of Gentility*, p. 9) documents that only in the 1910s did English begin to be taught in most of the missionary schools; by the 1920s, it had become a requisite subject as the missionary schools increasingly courted wealthy families and turned themselves into finishing schools for well-to-do young ladies. Howe's insistence that her daughters be taught English was thus at least three decades ahead of the general practice. In later missionary biographies of Gertrude Howe and in the obituary written by Ida Kahn, this departure from common practice is duly noted but is typically interpreted as evidence of independent thinking and strength of character.

designed to prevent free communication between speakers of French and African languages.[59] Seen in this context, Howe's transgression was a serious departure from the practices of her church and prevailing imperialist ideology. As Kang recalled in this biography, Howe went so far as to proclaim that knowing English was more important than knowing mathematics for her girls, because it would open up the world for them.[60] Rejecting the instrumentalist education that "native converts" were to receive, Howe extended to her daughters and her students linguistic access to the world and therefore symbolically access to universalist ideals of the Enlightenment.

It is also significant that in this obituary the author signs her name as Kang Cheng in Chinese, using neither the transliteration of her English name, Kang Aide, which Liang Qichao had made famous, nor the surname Kong (Con or Kung in missionary records) of her reputed Confucian descent. It is hard to imagine that she was unaware of both stories. We do not know her reasons for rejecting these other names, but what is clear from her biography of Gertrude Howe is that she was a woman deeply rooted in the community of her family, profession, and belief, a woman fully conscious of her ability to tell her own story, not to mention to name herself. Her biography of her adoptive mother is a portrayal of an ideal woman, "loving God as she loved people," independent in her thinking even when that meant defying the rules of her church, "paying no mind to fortuitous compliments nor being unduly affected by criticism from those who demand perfection according to their own agenda."[61]

One of the most powerful of late Qing discourses was that of national reform; in pursuing this objective, Liang Qichao in effect buried the tradition of female writing and turned Kang Aide, arguably a figure of anomaly and difference, into a central image of modernity by carefully erasing her alterity. Another discourse with much currency at the time was that of the missionaries, who were intent on their own version of modernity for the Chinese

---

59. See Johannes Fabian, *Language and Colonial Power: The Appropriation of Swahili in the Former Belgian Congo, 1880–1938* (Berkeley: University of California Press, 1986), chaps. 4–6.

60. Kang Cheng (Ida Kahn), "Hao nüshi lilüe," p. 4.

61. Ibid., p. 5. There is evidence to suggest that in her own conduct, Kang was not unlike her mother in her independent thinking. In an article on self-supporting medical missionary work, for example, Kang argues for "something different in form, but not in principle, from what He did in a different land under far different circumstances one thousand and nine hundred and more years ago" (*China Medical Missionary Journal*, 19, no. 6 [Nov. 1905]: 226).

through evangelization. For them, Ida Kahn was the epitome of missionary success story, her alleged Confucian descent made to signify her essential Chineseness. There reformers' and missionaries' discourses overlapped, for example in their portrayals of the traditional Chinese woman; there is also much disagreement over the specific version of modernity China was to pursue. Hence the apparent need for both sides to distance themselves from each other resulted ultimately in the burial of their historical connection. It is precisely their concerted effort to efface their connection that accounts for the many names of our heroine, who existed precisely at the intersection of two powerful but different discourses of history.

Framed by these two grand versions of history, each telling of Kang's personal story selects elements that can be understood only by erasing other elements. To return to the quotation of Michel de Certeau that appears as the epigraph for this chapter, the question becomes: If the writing of history entails burying certain elements of the past, what happens to the forgotten? Certeau's answer is that they inevitably resurface:

Whatever this new understanding of the past holds to be irrelevant—shards created by the selection of materials, remainders left aside by an explication—comes back, despite everything, on the edges of discourse or in its rifts and crannies: "resistances," "survivals," or delays discreetly perturb the pretty order of a line of "progress" or a system of interpretation.[62]

In the case under investigation, the "shards" reappear in two forms: obliquely in certain oxymoronic configurations from the two powerful discourses, and more directly, in Kang's own writings. Liang Qichao's female literata/nationalist representing China at the University of Michigan is surely as odd a figure as the missionary portrait of the female-heir-to-Confucius-turned-model-Christian. The oddity of these figures belies the fact that Kang's various "identities" were produced by language saturated with ideologies and, specifically, the act of naming. The very oddity at the edges of discourse signals the return of the repressed and messes up the "pretty order" of the two systems of interpretation.

In Kang's own writings, the shards of the past come back in the shape of a subtle resistance that perturbs "the line of 'progress.'" It is evident that her relationships with both reformists and missionaries were complicated, that she was at once central and marginal to each. Even more marginal is her

---

62. Certeau, *The Writing of History*, p. 4.

connection to Confucian high culture. Despite her arguably spurious surname, Kang was born into a poor family without the privilege of a traditional education; thus, the *cainü* and their poetry were far from being part of
her heritage. By the same token, Kang was at best marginal to the literati-
official culture, even when recast on Liang's international stage. High culture
in the form of *wen* 文 therefore could never have been her source of authority, as it was for the *cainü* and the literati alike. Nor could she claim a class
alliance with male reformers, as most prominent women did at the time.
Although her identity was no doubt closely bound up with the missionary
community, it is evident from her biography of Gertrude Howe that the in-
ternationalist, antiracist model could at times justify resistance to the practices of the church. Most important, Kang was consciously resistant to nationalist discourse; its model of the female revolutionary was anathema to
her self-perception and her gender ideology. Specifically, Kang registered her
resistance to the nationalist discourse and its mode of history writing by inserting the body, concrete and female.

Much as Kang may be an anomaly in her own time, her career prefigures
important elements for the generation of women writers and professionals of
the May Fourth era. Like Kang, many of them were educated in missionary
schools, influenced by Western culture, and, above all, brought up on a
model of femininity that by definition differed from the traditional one.[63]
Like Kang, many were cut off from the long tradition of the *cainü*; again like
Kang, many juggled multiple identities.[64] Even though the woman figured
prominently and repeatedly in nationalist discourse in years to come, some
women writers treated the nationalist agenda with ambivalence even as they
themselves became identified with it. Xiao Hong 蕭紅 (1911–42), to take a
famous example, registered her profound ambivalence toward nationalism

---

63. By the first decade of the twentieth century, missionary schools had gradually become
reputable, and gentry families began sending their daughters to them. Thus, the next generation of missionary-educated Chinese women often came from more privileged backgrounds
than Kang's; see Hunter, *The Gospel of Gentility*, pp. 233–34.

64. See, e.g., Emily Honig's study of one such woman, Deng Yuzhi (1900–?), a generation
or so later than Kang. As Emily Honig points out, "Defining, juggling, and sometimes manipulating the Christian, communist and feminist elements of her identity was a major theme
in [Deng's] career" (Honig, "Christianity, Feminism, and Communism: The Life and Times
of Deng Yuzhi [Cora Deng]," in *In Expanding the Boundaries of Women's History: Essays on
Women in the Third World*, ed. Cheryl Johnson-Odim and Margaret Strobel, p. 122 [Bloom-
ington: Indiana University Press, 1992]).

during the anti-Japanese war by exhuming the body, specifically marked as female, much as Kang had in her fictional account of the Republican revolution thirty years earlier. In her novel, *Shengsi chang* 生死場 (The field of life and death), the much-used trope of the raped woman in nationalist discourse is stood on its head as the woman, having escaped being raped by the Japanese soldiers, is then raped by a Chinese man. As Lydia Liu points out succinctly in her study of Xiao Hong, "The author's refusal to sublimate or displace the female body leads to a gendered position that intervenes in a nationalist discourse the novel seemingly establishes but in actuality subverts. Nationalism comes across as a profoundly patriarchal ideology."[65] Speaking essentially, then, these women writers thus inscribe a radical alterity in their response to history-making, an alterity that resists the totalizing discourse of nationalism and refuses to be subsumed by Grand History.

---

65. Lydia H. Liu, "The Female Body and Nationalist Discourse: Manchuria in Xiao Hong's *Field of Life and Death*," in *Body, Subject and Power in China*, ed. Angela Zito and Tani E. Barlow, p. 174 (Chicago: University of Chicago Press, 1994).

CHAPTER EIGHT
'Slavery,' Citizenship, and Gender in Late Qing China's Global Context
Rebecca E. Karl

This chapter addresses broad historical and historiographical questions about the relationship between gender and nation that were first systematically raised in the post-1898 period in China. It presents an exploration of a historical problematic rather than an exhaustive account of any one facet of the questions raised, and its inquiry is premised on skepticism toward the two most prominent historiographical encapsulations of gender issues in the late Qing period. The first is the notion that ready-made nationalist discourses on "women" instrumentalized women in the name of a male-defined "nation" project and hence blocked women's subjectivity.[1] The second is the retrospective gender discourses of the May Fourth (1919–1920s) period that represented women as ahistorical victims of China's past. In a general sense, then, the chapter explores ways of recasting the analytical and historical relationship between gender and nation away from the teleological functionalisms assumed in historical narratives that see "women" as having a poten-

I thank Peter Zarrow for organizing the original AAS panels for which I wrote the first version of this essay and for agreeing to co-edit the current volume. In addition, I acknowledge the editorial efforts of Marilyn Young on previous drafts of this essay. I am grateful to Benjamin Elman for his helpful comments at the AAS panel, as well as to Dorothy Ko and the two anonymous readers for Harvard University Asia Center for further comments that forced me to focus my arguments more closely.

1. Here, I understand subjectivity not to be a reified objective category, but rather, as Georg Lukács notes, a "force that transforms facts into processes" (cited in Kathi Weeks, *Constituting Feminist Subjects* [Ithaca: Cornell University Press, 1998], p. 96).

tially pure or autonomous "female" subjectivity that is inevitably betrayed by the "nation" and by "men" or that present the May Fourth period as the culmination of an inevitable historical march toward female liberation.

The specific historical problematic addressed here has two primary aspects. On the one hand, I ask how women came to be discursively contained by the notion of "slavery" as a way to delimit female access to the political realm in the newly conceptualized Chinese nation; and on the other hand, I analyze how, simultaneously, the notion of "slavery" was deployed to argue for very different sociopolitical visions. The historical issue, I argue, was in large part centered on the contested position of the family as a sociopolitico-economic unit within new national imaginaries. Further, this issue is best illumined by connecting the late Qing emergence of "women-as-slaves" (*nüzi wei nuli* 女子爲奴隸) as a sociopolitical topos to the early twentieth-century global context of imperialist modernity, from within which the intertwined discourses of "nation," "citizenship," "slavery," and "women" first arose. The first sections of the chapter clear some historical ground; the latter sections open a more substantive—albeit still sketchy—discussion of the specific problem of "slavery" and the family.

Historiographical and Historical Problems

At first glance, it appears paradoxical that in the late Qing, at the very moment when women were becoming more visible—as political subjects, discursive objects, cultural producers, and urban economic actors, among others—one dominant way of referring to them, and in which they referred to themselves, was via a trope of enslavement: *nüzi wei nuli*. Few scholars have explored the emergence of this locution, even though it is a striking one.[2] It is, of course, well established that women emerged as a concern of late Qing nationalists[3] and that a few elite women participated in this discourse in

---

2. At most, it is noted that the translation of John Stuart Mill's work on women, in which he refers prominently to women's historical roles as slaves, was influential; there is no doubt that Mill's work had a great impact, but simply stating that begs the question of why this discursive mode and historical understanding became so widely adopted in China.

3. See, e.g., Ono Kazuko, *Women in a Century of Revolution, 1850–1950*, trans. Joshua Fogel (Stanford: Stanford University Press, 1989); Alison R. Drucker, "The Influence of Western Women on the Anti-Footbinding Movement, 1840–1911," in *Women in China: Current Directions in Historical Scholarship*, ed. Richard W. Guisso and Stanley Johannesen, pp. 179–200 (Youngstown, N.Y.: Philo Press, 1981); Charlotte Beahan, "In the Public Eye: Women in

ways mostly complementary to male-nationalist debates.[4] It is also widely agreed that by the May Fourth period women were consistently equated metaphorically with China's subjugation, as both the nation and women came to be construed as "victims" of history.[5] Analysis has, until recently, therefore sought to reveal the truth of the enslaving and victimizing forces of family/patriarchy and to link this truth to the metaphorical-discursive use of woman as a signifier for China's actual or imminent enslavement—to the West, Japan, and/or the Manchu Qing dynasty.

In the past decade, however, the May Fourth origins of the narrative of victimization and oppression, a narrative that connected an oppressed servile woman to the Chinese nation in a tightly woven symbolic that presented a history of unremitting female subjugation, have been exposed.[6] These revi-

---

Early Twentieth-Century China," in *Women in China: Current Directions in Historical Scholarship*, ed. Richard W. Guisso and Stanley Johannesen, pp. 218–28 (Youngstown, N.Y.: Philo Press, 1981); idem, "Feminism and Nationalism in the Chinese Women's Press, 1902–1911," *Modern China* 1, no. 4 (Oct. 1975): 379–416; Sally Borthwick, "Changing Concepts of the Role of Women from the Late Qing to the May Fourth Period," in *Ideal and Reality: Social and Political Change in Modern China, 1860–1949*, ed. David Pong and Edmund S. K. Fung, pp. 63–91 (Lanham, Md.: University Press of America, 1985).

   4. As Tani Barlow ("Theorizing Woman: *Funü, Guojia, Jiating* [Chinese Women, Chinese State, Chinese Family]," in *Scattered Hegemonies: Postmodernity and Transnational Feminist Practices*, ed. Inderpal Grewal and Caren Kaplan, pp. 173–96 [Minneapolis: University of Minnesota Press, 1994], p. 179) summarizes: "Late-Confucian women sought liberty on 'nationalist' grounds," and the flourishing of women's journals at the time "contributed to what rapidly emerged as 'myths of the nation.'" For a different view, see Joan Judge's chapter in this volume.

   5. Rey Chow (*Chinese Woman and Modernity: The Politics of Reading Between East and West* [Minneapolis: University of Minnesota Press, 1991], pp. 5–9) persuasively argues that the servile Chinese woman became a primary symbol of the impotent Chinese nation dominated by masculine foreign powers intent on raping it. See also idem, "'It's You, and Not Me': Domination and 'Othering' in Theorizing the 'Third World,'" in *Coming to Terms: Feminism, Theory, Politics*, ed. Elizabeth Weed, pp. 152–61 (New York: Routledge 1989).

   6. Rey Chow notes that this linkage is so accepted that "even [contemporary] Chinese scholars critical of the Orientalist lapses of Western writers are just as committed [as Western scholars] to the view of Chinese women's history as 'a history of enslavement'" (cited in Dorothy Ko, *Teachers of the Inner Chambers: Women and Culture in Seventeenth Century China* [Stanford: Stanford University Press, 1994], p. 3). Susan Mann (*Precious Records: Woman in China's Long Eighteenth Century* [Stanford: Stanford University Press, 1997], p. 8) has succinctly summarized the historiographical problem: "Retrospective views of the Qing period, as seen from the vantage point of 20th-century reformers and revolutionaries, lump it together with the Ming as a 'feudal' or 'traditional' era when Chinese women were the oppressed subjects of

sionist analyses have offered persuasive evidence not of unchanging stagnation but of vitality and change in women's roles in the society, economy, and cultural production of late imperial (seventeenth and eighteenth century) China.[7] Even in the revisionist accounts, however, the late Qing disappears from view—curiously so, since the late Qing is when the accumulated silences and accumulated changes came to be articulated and debated openly for the first time.[8]

The point of departure for this chapter is to ask why slavery became the representational trope of choice in the late Qing—a choice that was later transformed into the May Fourth "women-as-victim" narrative (although the lines of this transformation were hardly direct). I argue that the rise of the slavery trope (with its meanings of dependence, servitude, and unpaid

---

a Confucian patriarchy. . . . Far from being an era of unremitting female oppression, the Ming and Qing periods were dynamic and diverse centuries of social, political, and economic change with profound consequences for gender relations in China."

7. There is, however, no consensus on the degree, the scope, the direction, or even the sources of change and vitality. See Paul Ropp, "The Seeds of Change: Reflections on the Condition of Women in the Early and Mid Ch'ing," *Signs* 2, no. 1 (Aug. 1976): 5–23; William Rowe, "Women and the Family in Mid-Qing Social Thought: The Case of Chen Hongmou," *Late Imperial China* 13, no. 2 (Dec. 1992): 1–41; Kathryn Bernhardt, "A Ming-Qing Transition in Chinese Women's History? The Perspective from Law," in *Remapping China: Fissures in Historical Terrain*, ed. Gail Hershatter, Emily Honig, Jonathan Lippman, and Randall Stross, pp. 42–58 (Stanford: Stanford University Press, 1996); Hill Gates, *China's Motor: A Thousand Years of Petty Capitalism* (Ithaca: Cornell University Press, 1996); and Mann, *Precious Records*.

8. In Chinese history as seen from the vantage of the May Fourth, the disappearance of the late Qing moment is strikingly reflected and reproduced in most recent U.S. scholarship on Chinese gender issues. For example, Christina Gilmartin, Gail Hershatter, Lisa Rofel, and Tyrene White, eds., *Engendering China: Women, Culture and the State* (Cambridge, Mass.: Harvard University Press, 1994), includes essays on the Ming through the mid-Qing (1800), and then on the May Fourth through the Maoist and post-Maoist periods; the late Qing (nineteenth and early twentieth centuries) is nowhere represented. See also Lü Tonglin, ed., *Gender and Sexuality in Twentieth-Century Chinese Literature* (Albany: State University of New York Press, 1993); Tani Barlow, ed., *Gender Politics in Modern China: Writing and Feminism* (Durham: Duke University Press, 1993); Angela Zito and Tani Barlow, eds., *Body, Subject & Power in China* (Chicago: University of Chicago Press, 1994)—all of which construe China's twentieth century as beginning with the May Fourth. One exception is the anthology edited by Amy Dooling and Kris Torgeson, *Writing Women in Modern China: An Anthology of Women's Literature from the Early Twentieth Century* (New York: Columbia University Press, 1998), which makes a cogent argument for beginning China's twentieth century with the late Qing.

labor) as a way of understanding and defining the relationship among women, family, and nation needs to be anchored more explicitly in the context of an emerging global consciousness. That is, it cannot be treated as the expected outcome of the recognition and critique of an unequal social structure as seen through the lens of an already-constituted nationalism. Indeed, such an epiphenomenal treatment ignores the historical processes through which nationalism and gender discourses—or, national and gender subjectivities—came to constitute one another. It also conceals the numerous gaps within and between the two types of discourses or subjectivities and proposes a female subjectivity that stands outside the historical practices that constitute it. As a first step in establishing this argument, the next two sections analyze the slavery trope in order to explore the links between each of its components and historically specific discourses.

Establishing Terms and Contexts:
"Slavery" and "Citizenship"

After the Qing defeat in the Sino-Japanese War of 1895, the dynasty's political system came under increasing pressure. By summer 1898, a small but influential group of elite men attempted to reorient the way sociopolitical power operated in the polity; they submitted proposals for institutional reform intended to open the field of state politics to a wider segment of elite men than allowed for by the civil-service examinations. They hoped that such reforms would make the dynasty more open and efficient in dealing with foreign threats, internal economic development, and social dislocation.[9] Aimed at saving the dynasty by reforming aspects of it, the 1898 reform movement (*wuxu bianfa* 戊戌變法) was crushed in the Empress Dowager Cixi's 慈禧 coup d'état in September 1898. This pushed pressures for sociopolitical transformation into new and more radical directions and inaugurated a far-reaching rethinking of the premises on which the polity was organized.

At exactly the same moment as Chinese critics of their nation's internal power arrangements were finding a voice and language with which to press their new visions, various nationalist or anticolonial movements erupted around the world—in the Philippines, South Africa, India, Poland, and

---

9. For some of these issues, see Peter Zarrow's chapter in this volume.

elsewhere. These struggles not only helped Chinese critics to understand the modern world as a global system constituted by fundamental inequality and unevenness but also brought to their attention the critiques of that system emanating from its ostensibly weakest points: the non-Western world. Indeed, many Chinese intellectuals quickly linked China's situation—both internal and external—to these critiques and practices in an effort to analyze the universal and particular features of China's problems. Struggles in the non-Western majority of the world thus contributed to the formulation of new concepts and languages of imperialism, colonialism, nationalism, and modernity through which both global and local processes could be articulated and understood.[10]

One of the most ubiquitous new locutions/concepts to emerge from this process was "slave(s) of a lost [subjugated] country" (*wangguo nu* 亡國奴), an old term whose meaning was substantively altered after 1898.[11] For centuries, *wangguo nu* had denoted a civil servant who, upon the fall of the dynasty he served, shifted his loyalties and service to the new state. *Wangguo* thus indicated a dynastic change, and *wangguo nu* an official who served as a "slave" to the imperial state, no matter who controlled it. After 1898, with the growing awareness of the patterns of nineteenth-century imperialism and global disparities, *wangguo nu* increasingly came to be used as a general term for imperialized or colonized *peoples*—and *wangguo* itself came to denote a national condition of being colonized by a foreign power. As the prominent late Qing intellectual and later co-founder of the Chinese Communist Party, Chen Duxiu 陳獨秀, summarized this new understanding in 1904:

Historically, when the surname of our emperor changed, we called this *wangguo* . . . but this is merely a change of dynasties, it cannot be called "*wangguo*." Not only are *wangguo* and dynastic changes not the same, but *wangguo* does not even require a change of dynasties. It just requires that the territory, vested economic interests, and

---

10. For an extended discussion of this topic, see Rebecca E. Karl, *Staging the World: Chinese Nationalism at the Turn of the Twentieth Century* (Durham: Duke University Press, 2002).

11. As several readers have pointed out, "lost country" as a translation for *wangguo* is imperfect at best; *wang* 亡 can mean, among other things, lost, perished, destroyed, conquered. The suggested alternative is "subjugated." However, given the finality of *wang* in the late Qing, "subjugated" seems tame and indeed more properly a translation for the later *bei yapo minzu/renmin* 被壓迫民族/人民 (oppressed/subjugated peoples) that became popular in the 1920s.

sovereignty of the nation be seized and occupied by others. . . . This is when there is true *wangguo*.[12]

Increasingly, then, after 1898 *wangguo* and *wangguo nu* emphasized the threatened condition of the nation (not merely the state) and its people; and these concepts were deployed not as exclusive critiques of state servants or dynastic failings, but as a reflection of the deep anxiety and terror raised by the threatened loss of political/economic sovereignty and the "enslavement" of the "national people" (*guomin* 國民). Indeed, "national people" now also began to emerge as a sovereign concept, particularly as the conceptual antithesis of colonized slaves (*nu* 奴). In the process, the notion of slavery—as a globally structured condition—moved along with "nation" and "people" to the forefront of sociopolitical analysis and discourse. In an explicit counterposing of *wangguo nu* and *guomin*, Liang Qichao 梁啓超, one of the most eloquent of the late Qing generation of critical intellectuals, lamented in 1901 that the "slavishness" (*nuxing* 奴性) of China's officials and its people was the greatest barrier to the formation of the national citizenry (*guomin*) he deemed necessary for China's successful transition from its compromised condition to nation-statehood.[13] Liang's allusion to "slavishness" cannot be understood as equivalent to May Fourth writers' (notably Lu Xun's 魯迅) narrow use of the term as a critical description of the Chinese "national character." For Liang, "slavishness" represents the nation's compromised territorial and economic independence; in contrast to the slave, the citizen is active rather than passive, proactive in civic duty rather than reactively obedient to the state's dictates, patriotic toward the collective nation rather than parochially loyal to family-clan, and so on. Many late Qing intellectuals, in common with Liang, noted that in the modern imperialist era, it was not merely the state that was lost, but also the people (*min* 民) and sometimes the race (*zhong* 種). It was, in fact, the simultaneity of these (threatened)

---

12. Chen Duxiu 陳獨秀, "Wangguo pian" 亡國篇 (An essay on *wangguo*), *Anhui suhua bao* 安徽俗話報, no. 8 (July 27, 1904); reprinted in idem, *Chen Duxiu zhuzuo xuan* 陳獨秀著作選 (Selected important works of Chen Duxiu), 1: 67–85 (Shanghai: Renmin chubanshe, 1993).

13. Liang Qichao 梁啓超, "Zhongguo jiruo suyuan lun" 中國積弱溯源論 (On tracing China's accumulated weaknesses), in idem, *Yinbingshi wenji* 飲冰室文集 (Collected essays from the Ice-Drinker's Studio) (Taipei: Zhonghua shuju, 1982; hereafter cited as *YBSWJ*), juan 5: 12–42; quotation on p. 18 (originally published in *Qingyi bao* 清義報, nos. 77–84 [Apr. 29, 1901]).

losses that defined modernity, for Liang Qichao as for many others of his generation.[14]

Although much of the invocation of *wangguo* in these years designated loss (*wang*) as the fate of the state (*guo* 國), there was a powerful subtext, in which the loss of state was the very condition that permitted and promoted the people's rise to political activity. To forestall or reverse this loss, the people had to be mobilized, even if that meant leaving the state behind. In short, it was by separating the loss of state from the potential destruction of the people that "the people" as a topos of a new politics could emerge. Indeed, in the immediate aftermath of the 1898 reform movement and in the context of his advocacy of a creative and open politics to replace the ritualized and enclosed dynastic system of bureaucratic politics, Liang Qichao wrote that a political concept of the national people needed to be simultaneously created and mobilized by inculcating a new awareness among the populace of the relationship between the state and the people.

The Chinese people do not even know there is such a thing as a national people (*guomin*). For several thousand years, there have been the two words *guo* 國 and *jia* 家 (state, family), but I have never heard the two words *guo min* (state, people) uttered. . . . *Guojia* 國家 is when one family (*jia*) owns the state (*guo*) as private property. . . . *Guomin* connotes that the state (*guo*) belongs to the people (*min*) as public property. . . . This is then called a "national people."[15]

Liang's distinction—terminological and conceptual—turns on word combinations: *guo* as state, *jia* as family, and *min* as people, where *guojia* is the family-state (or dynasty) and *guomin* the national people (a term, which, at least by 1902, was understood as a "citizenry").[16] In *guomin*, the state is

---

14. For a good statement of this equation for Liang, see his *Xinmin shuo* 新民說 (On the new citizen), esp. chap. 2, "Lun xinmin wei jinri Zhongguo diyi jiwu" 論新民爲今日中國第一急務 (The most urgent tasks for the new citizen in today's China), in idem, *Yinbingshi zhuanji* 飲冰室傳集 (Collected works from the Ice-Drinker's Studio) (Shanghai: Zhongguo shuju), juan 4: 1–80, in which he noted that the "national imperialism" of his era was much different from the empires of old.

15. "Lun jinshi guomin jingzheng zhi dashi ji Zhongguo qiantu" 論今時國民競爭之大勢與中國前途 (On recent trends in the competition between national peoples and China's future), originally published in *Qingyi bao* 清義報, no. 30 (Oct. 15, 1899); reprinted in *YBSWJ*, juan 4: 56–61; quotation on pp. 56–57.

16. For Liang's concept of "citizenry," see Hao Chang, *Liang Ch'i-ch'ao and Intellectual Transition in China, 1890–1907* (Cambridge, Mass.: Harvard University Press, 1971), chap. 6.

explicitly reconstituted as the state of the people and not of the family (dynasty) or its civil servants, and the *min* is cast as the national people, whose relationship to the state is in turn considerably more abstract and much less passive than loyalty to a dynastic or clan "family." I will return below to the significance of Liang's unlinking of the family-state nexus in his rearticulation of the conditions for the creation of a citizenry, since the repositioning of the family within this nexus is crucial for understanding women's particular relationship to the politics of a transformed nation. For the moment, suffice it to note that the introduction and spread of the concept of *guomin* after 1898—by Liang and increasingly by others—was almost instantly counterposed conceptually and discursively to *wangguo nu*. Thus, in its deployment in the internal political and the global imperialist contexts, (*wangguo*) *nu*'s terminological and conceptual opposite was *guomin*, now understood both as the reconceived citizenry within a particular nation, and as one national people among other national peoples in the context of a multinational world. Much of the debate in late Qing intellectual circles revolved around the issues of who constituted the *guomin* and how. Not the least of these debates was over the role of women as citizens.

Gender and Politics: "Women," "Slavery," and "the People"

As Dorothy Ko and others have argued, before the late Qing, the gender system as a foundational structure of Chinese society had "proved to be flexible enough to survive" change and had hitherto not been subjected to a systemic political critique.[17] After 1898, however, China's unequal gender system came to be seen not only as part of the internal structures of sociopolitical power, signification, and economic participation—all now under attack—but also as a contributing factor in the blocking in China of the very trend toward popular revolutionary struggle that the non-West was demon-

---

17. Dorothy Ko, *Teachers of the Inner Chamber*, pp. 125, 9. For the argument that the gender system survived *because* of and not despite the changes, see Gates, *China's Motor*; see also Mann, *Precious Records*; Francesca Bray, *Technology and Gender: Fabrics of Power in Late Imperial China* (Berkeley: University of California Press, 1997); and Patricia Ebrey, *The Inner Quarters: Marriage and the Lives of Chinese Women in the Sung Period* (Berkeley: University of California Press, 1993).

strating to be essential to overcoming national enslavement.[18] This produced a contradiction. By the post-1898 period, with the struggles of non-Western peoples to reclaim sovereignty from the imperialists and with the increasingly sharp critiques of the structures and systems of political power in China, "the people" emerged positively as the abstract objects of a new national politics capable of transforming society. At the same time, however, they also came to be viewed negatively (particularly after the Boxer Rebellion of 1900–1901) as suspicious subject-agents of a "primitive" (*yeman* 野蠻) politics that needed to be contained and channeled by elites.[19] What is noteworthy for the purposes of this chapter is that, as "the people" emerged as a new political topos—both negatively and positively—"women," too, were interpellated as political beings, albeit contradictorily as well.[20]

"The people," "women," and sometimes the Chinese nation were articulated in terms of "slavery" and "loss" (an additional factor is that, by the early 1900s Han Chinese were also increasingly being designated "slaves" of the Manchu rulers). Yet these "enslavements" were not completely commensurate with one another. In general, women, by virtue of their newly recognized and newly articulated subordinated social position, were often identified as constituent parts of "the people" (those ambiguous objects of elites' programs of containment and transformation). Yet *elite* women, through their writings and activities in the newly politicized realms of journalism and education, identified themselves not merely as objects of others' activity but also as proper subject-agents of both politics and social transformation. Hence, while beginning to identify themselves as part of the newly recognized socially subordinated category "women," a component of the broader category of subordinated people, *elite* women also allied themselves in class terms with those elite men who claimed to be the primary legitimate agents

---

18. For more on this issue, see Rebecca E. Karl, "The Everyday and Gender in Early-Twentieth-Century China," paper delivered at the "Materializing Modernity" workshop, University of Washington, Sept.–Oct. 2000.

19. For intellectual discourses on "the people" and "society," see Hao Chang, *Chinese Intellectuals in Crisis: Search for Order and Meaning* (Berkeley: University of California Press, 1987); and Arif Dirlik, *Anarchism in the Chinese Revolution* (Berkeley: University of California Press, 1991), chap. 2. For "the people" as subject-agents of a new politics, see Roxann Prazniak, *Of Camel Kings and Other Things: Rural Rebels Against Modernity in Late-Imperial China* (Lanham, Md.: Rowman & Littlefield, 1999).

20. Dooling and Torgeson, *Writing Women*, p. 7.

of China's national sociopolitical practice. This dual identification—as subordinated and elite at the same time—introduced profound disjunctures into the emerging articulation of the relationship between the nation and political-social agency, particularly as such articulations pertained to the debates over the meaning of citizenship, slavery, and women.

In gender terms, these contradictions led to a redefining of the family among elite females as the site of *their* access to the realm of the political, to citizenship, and thus to the transformed realm of the public or the social.[21] In class terms, these same contradictions led both to an identification of women with "the people" in universal nationalist discourse and to an appeal by elite women for their *particular* suitability for citizenship above and before the "ignorant" masses themselves—on the basis not of gender or general peoplehood but of eliteness.[22] Here, the redefinition of women and the family within the context of politics—articulated in the opposed terms of slaves and of citizens—became an argument for the fundamental realignment of the relationship between the family and the state in a restructured conceptualization of the nation. This elite contestation over the position of the family—notwithstanding the sharp critiques of that institution at the time—stands in stark contrast to the outright rejection of the family by male and female radical elites in the 1920s as nothing more than the site of women's (and men's) sociopolitical and personal victimization and oppression. More immediately, in the late Qing, this reclaiming of the family by some participants in the debate also contrasts with the efforts of male nationalists to sunder the conceptual nexus between family and state loyalty, which was part of their attempt, as we saw with Liang Qichao, to conceptualize how to produce a new loyalty to the nation that transcended both the existing dy-

---

21. Not to a reified domestic cultural ("private" or "family") sphere that served to *contain* women from the public, as Partha Chatterjee (*The Nation and Its Fragments: Colonial and Postcolonial Histories* [Princeton: Princeton University Press, 1993], chap. 6) has suggested for Indian women. For an argument diametrically opposed to the one I am constructing here, see Joan Judge's contribution to this volume.

22. In a sense, this split between elite women and the people in terms of citizenship in China recalls the initial alliances American feminists made with abolitionists in the pre–Civil War period, only to drop racial equality as a platform once white women had been locked out of the political realm by the fourteenth and fifteenth amendments recognizing black men, but not black or white women, as voting citizens. For a discussion that suggested this line of inquiry to me, see Louise Michelle Newman, *White Women's Rights: The Racial Origins of Feminism in the United States* (London: Oxford University Press, 1999).

nastic state and the enclosed realm of the family (clan). It also contrasts with the contemporary reclaiming of family by Japanese women that tied the family quite directly to the needs of the Meiji state.[23]

I return in the conclusion of this chapter to the contrast with the May Fourth. The remainder of the essay is concerned first with exploring how the gender-nation nexus was discursively articulated—through what sorts of language strategies—and, second, with how this nexus was positioned at the turn of the twentieth century through the conflicted positioning of the family as a site of economic productivity. I take the strategic deployment of the new locution "woman-as-slave" as both emblematic and symptomatic of the discursive contours and strategic social emplotment of this contradiction and conflict, and I suggest that this trope referred both to a new articulation by elite women of their experiences of patriarchal family structures and to a gendered difference in the ways men and women proposed to actualize the sociopolitical role of women in terms of a supposedly universal national citizenship. I conclude—as I began—that this difference becomes visible only when we call "slavery" into question, for only in such a perspective can the centrifugal repositioning of gender be released from a functional analysis, in which family, polity, and the global are separately conceived as *a priori* enclosed systems.

Making the Links: Women as Slaves and
Slaves of a Lost Country

The July 30, 1906, issue of *Beijing Women's News* (*Beijing nübao* 北京女報) published a short story entitled "Tuobi feiren" 託庇非人 (Seeking protection from an unworthy person),[24] a title that recalls the phrase *shoutuo feiren* 受託非人, or "to seek protection from [that is, to marry] the wrong man."[25]

---

23. On this, see Joan Judge's contribution to this volume.

24. "Tuobi feiren" 託庇非人 (Seeking protection from an unworthy person). *Beijing nübao* 北京女報, no. 334 (June 30, 1906): n.p. The *Beijing Women's News* was the first daily newspaper in the world written for women that had a woman as editor. It began publication in 1905, with financial support from the Empress Dowager Cixi, and was edited by Rang Ranyun, a Manchu lady of the court. The journal was generally concerned with women's education, and its primary audience was Manchu court ladies. For more on the journal, see Beahan, "Feminism and Nationalism in the Chinese Women's Press"; and Mary Wright, *China in Revolution: The First Phase, 1900–1913* (New Haven: Yale University Press, 1970), p. 34.

25. I thank Dorothy Ko for pointing this out to me.

The story tells of the female writer-narrator's encounter with a peacock one hot summer's day:

It was really hot; insects buzzed everywhere; sweat ran in rivulets. At noon, I moved a bamboo cot under the cool shade of a large locust tree and lay down to take a nap. In my left hand I held a palm-leaf fan; in my right hand, I held a copy of *The History of the Destruction of Poland* (*Bolan miewang shi* 波 蘭 滅 亡 史). I planned to use the book to lull myself to sleep, but . . . the more I read, the less sleepy I was. . . . Reading that book, I first became angry, then sad, then scared.

A cool breeze wafts across the stillness, and the narrator finally closes her eyes. Suddenly, she hears a noise, and looking up into the locust tree, she sees a resplendent peacock perched on a branch. Puzzled, she asks the bird what he is doing; somberly, he replies that he is melancholy, for although his feathers are prized as symbols of high rank among the powerful, he is treated as if he were the most ordinary of creatures.

Annoyed at the peacock's complaints, the narrator lashes out:

In the beginning, when man put you in a cage to honor you, you could have rejected his empty praise and summoned a bit of independent spirit. . . . But you accepted . . . his protection. Yet man was never of the same species and family as you (*ta benlai gen ni bushi tongzhong tongzu* 他本來跟你不是同種同族). . . . He was only taking advantage of you . . . to decorate his house and [to offer you] as a gift. In the end, he trampled you underfoot. [And] when those who were originally of the same race as you (*gen ni tongzhong de* 跟你同種的) saw you dependent on foreigners (*tuobi wairen* 託庇外人), they cut off relations with you. No one would acknowledge that they were of the same kind as you (*gen ni tonglei* 跟你同類). Whom do you hate? Should you not hate yourself?[26]

After listening to these harsh words, the peacock departs, and the narrator immediately records the marvelous episode in her notebook, ending with the assertion: "Some people [might] say that I was dreaming; but even if I were, it is true. Truth can be illusory."

This brief story concisely raises a number of interpretive problems. First, there is the matter of the story's title and the shift in the phrasing that appears in the text. The title, "Tuobi feiren," cognitively and linguistically suggests a critique of female dependence in marriage and family relations; yet it also suggests a link to the phrase *tuobi wairen* (seeking protection from

---

26. "Tuobi feiren," n.p.

foreigners), a phrase used later in the text. Because the peacock is male and his feathers are used to denote bureaucratic rank, the title also suggests a critique of bureaucratic dependence in the political realm. The text places the peacock—through the vocabulary of caging and decoration—in the feminized position of being "kept," a link that suggests the intertwined family and political realms of dependent loyalty or patriarchy. However, as the narrator directs her wrath at the bird, her accusation of *tuobi wairen* marks the bird not only as a dependent, feminized prisoner of family and a cultural-political prisoner of a hierarchical dynastic polity but also as a representative of the dynasty's "imprisonment" to foreigners. This association of dependence on the family, the state, and the foreign powers triply disempowers the bird. The three dependencies form a tight conceptual whole.

Second, yet complicating the above, in berating the peacock, the narrator deploys the languages of "sameness" and "difference"—in terms of kind, species, race, type—in a play on the ambiguities of the compound linguistic terms and their referents. I have highlighted the ambiguity in my translation by rendering *tongzhong tongzu* through a biological phrase, "same species and same family," to catch the indicated opposition between the human and the animal realms; this opposition also corresponds textually to the opposition between the male and female realms. In the second passage, *tongzhong* is paired with *wairen* ("foreigners" or "outsiders"), and I have accordingly rendered *tongzhong* as "same race" to signal its placement in the cultural-political realm of global and national difference and the Social Darwinian discourse on inequality.[27] Finally, *tonglei* at the end is rendered in an ambiguous biological-social categorization as "same kind," in which *lei* can be understood as a subclassification of *zhong* (understood either as biological species or as so-

---

27. Because this journal was edited and primarily read by Manchu court ladies, it is less likely that the *tongzhong/wairen* opposition would indicate the Han-Manchu split, even though by 1906, *tongzhong* was frequently deployed in Han Chinese revolutionary discourse to indicate the racial and thus national "otherness" of the Manchus. For an analysis of *tongzhong* as Han-Manchu racial otherness, see Rebecca E. Karl, "Creating Asia: China in the World at the Beginning of the Twentieth Century," *American Historical Review* 103, no. 4 (Oct. 1998): 1096–118. For an analysis of *tongzhong* as a global concept, see idem, "Race, Ethnos, History in China at the Turn of the Twentieth Century," in *Philosophies of Race and Ethnicity*, ed. Peter Osborne and Stella Sandford (London: Athlone Press, forthcoming 2002); and idem, "Staging the World in Late-Qing China: Globe, Race, and Nation in a 1904 Beijing Opera," *Identities: Global Studies in Culture and Power* 6, no. 4 (Winter 2000): 551–606.

ciohistorical race).[28] The ambiguity of these overlapping fields of signification and their juxtaposition with the gendered languages of decoration, objects of exchange, gifts, status, and fetishization of beauty render opaque
how the story's narrator-author understands the relationships of race, gender, ethnicity, nationality, polity, and the global. If one throws in the dream
context—revealed truth? mere illusion? or indistinguishable and thus mutually constitutive of one another?—the story becomes impervious to a transparent reading.

One way to make sense of these overlapping and contradictory fields is to
relate them specifically to the global space indicated by the story's central
prop—the book entitled *The History of the Destruction of Poland*. As I have
detailed elsewhere, "Poland," as metaphor and history, haunted the late
Qing discourse on politics and the global.[29] Without reiterating those arguments, I note here only that the story's illusory (real?) peacock appears as the
globally illusory (real?) truth of "Poland": that is, "Poland" as simultaneously
present as a nation-spirit haunting the world, as it were, yet also absent by
virtue of its disappearance from world maps by the nineteenth century. In
other words, just as "Poland" exists as an illusion of the past and present and
also as a recuperable sign for a future of nationalist struggle, the peacock also
exists not only as a dream of a past and present of dependence but also as the
potential for a different future. The story thus appropriates the "Poland"
sign—ubiquitous in late Qing essays of almost every ideological stripe—in
which "Poland" signifies that which is "lost" (*wang*) or absent, as well as that
which is recoverable in the future. The story then deploys that image or sign
to illumine the multiple fault lines of power, absence, and presence in the
global, national, and family arenas to rearticulate relationships among them.

Specifically, Poland's history, invoked in late Qing essays to point to the
modern era of imperialism in which a state is overtaken from the inside
(weak government) and from the outside (rapacious foreigners) and its people enslaved to stronger powers, helps expose, through juxtaposition to the
peacock, multiple anxious spheres of social, political, and global hierarchies
and dependencies. These interlocking spheres identify the (now-questioned)
link between the intertwined dependencies of family, dynastic, and global

---

28. Compare this to Frank Dikötter's (*The Discourse of Race in Modern China* [Stanford:
Stanford University Press, 1993], p. viii) claim that all these terms can be equally rendered by
the concept "race."

29. See Karl, "Staging the World in Late-Qing China."

orders. The peacock story can thus be seen at once as a reflection on the space of nation, polity, and family from the trapped perspective of the caged prisoner (the peacock), as a sharp critique of the prisoner's own complicities in the production of his/her irrelevance (loss) and servitude, and as an incomplete proposal for altering the intertwined relationships of dependence that block the future. For the purposes of the present discussion, what is noteworthy about this story, then, is that it articulates concisely the more general way in which, in essays of the time, the images of slavery and dependence in the global and domestic realms were used to reflect explicitly on each other.

Another example of this nexus from a different political direction—after all, the *Beijing nübao* was a relatively conservative journal published at the Qing court—is from the pen of the prominent journalist and intellectual Chen Xiefen 陳擷芬. In 1904, Chen wrote about a multifaceted "crisis in the women's world" (*nüjie zhi kewei* 女界之可危). In this essay, she connected *wangguo*—in its multiple forms—and female enslavement in the family through a complex analysis of the intersection between crises in the modern global world and the women's world. Indeed, for Chen, as for the author of the peacock story, it is the global crisis that helps illumine and make visible the crisis in the women's world.

Alas! What kind of age is the present? Our nation (*guo*) is no more, and our race (*zhong*) is about to perish. . . . Can we allow ourselves to become slaves of a lost country (*wangguo nu*)—can we willingly become an India or a Poland? . . . Today, when our nation is already subjugated and our whole race is in peril of becoming slaves held in common by every land, these men [i.e., Chinese men] who have called themselves "honorable" can indeed be ashamed! We women have been their slaves for several thousand years. How can we still remain blindly unaware and follow them, thereby becoming slaves of those enslaved by foreign races [i.e., by the Manchus and Westerners]? . . . In the future, they [our fellow countrymen] may be willing to become slaves like the people of Poland or India, but I fear that even this will be impossible.[30]

The shifting meaning of the "we" is crucial in this essay. In connecting China to Poland and India in the modern global space of *wangguo*, Chen illumined the national crisis of China by invoking a "we" of the nation—itself constituted by its position in the world as a nation/people that, like India

---

30. Chen Xiefen, "Crisis in the Women's World," trans. in Dooling and Torgeson, *Writing Women in Modern China*, pp. 83, 84, 85 (translation slightly altered).

and Poland, is beset by outside powers. Yet, she simultaneously narrowed the space of the "we" to a subjectively identified Chinese race-people and thereby opened a gap between the political state (Manchu Qing) and the race-people (Han Chinese). That gap allows her to further narrow the space of the "we" from the larger race-people to "women," whom, she asserts, are doubly enslaved (or even triply so)—to men and to foreigners, and as Hans to Manchus.

In a sense, then, Chen Xiefen illuminated gendered enslavement (women to men) through the other types of slavery; at the same time, she also demonstrated a deep anxiety that the male preoccupation with China's enslavement to foreigners would facilitate the reconcealment of the gendered enslavement of women to men. In other words, her linking of female enslavement to *wangguo nu* makes gendered slavery concrete and visible by naturalizing female enslavement through a now-accepted correlation to a global imperialist situation of subjugated (enslaved) peoples. Yet she also split the *wangguo* from the *nu*, as it were, by inserting "women" (*nü*) into the middle of that construction to prevent the disappearance of women into "nation." In the end, rather than draw a straight line through the multiple spheres that points to a new female subjectivity through nationalism alone, Chen evokes the threat of the disappearance of the "we" of the nation/people-race in the *wangguo* context as paralleling the danger that an exclusive focus on *wangguo* slavery could be used to conceal and thus leave intact the space of female enslavement. On my reading, she writes explicitly against such a concealment.

For Chen, then, "slavery" offered a term through which, in Clifford Geertz's words, she could "grasp the nature of distress and *relate* it to the wider world."[31] It was also a term through which she could materially *connect* women to a much-discussed modern global situation without losing a specifically gendered form in the generalized invocation. As with the peacock story, Chen's resolution to this situation is not clear, for, at the time, none of the institutional frameworks or sociopolitical relations of national transformation had been fully worked out, within either China or the regime of global modernity. As such, gaps in the illusion of national solidarity and homogeneity—signaled by the uneasy fit of "women"—remained apparent, just as the ways to close those gaps remained elusive.

---

31. Clifford Geertz, *The Interpretation of Cultures* (New York: Basic Books, 1973), p. 105.

Nevertheless, it is evident that Chen and the author-narrator of the peacock story—just two of many possible examples[32]—were positioned and positioned themselves in particular ways within the growing move toward a desired national integration. Their eliteness—class affiliations—led them to a certain consciousness about their situation as "women" and as "Chinese" (whether this was specified as Han or not), even as their femaleness—or gendered position—presented obstacles to actualizing this consciousness in real terms. Thus, it may well be true in a general sense that, in Tani Barlow's words, "late-Confucian women sought liberty on 'nationalist' grounds" which "contributed to what rapidly emerged as 'myths of the nation.'"[33] Yet, it is probably more accurate to note that "women" were not necessarily seeking "liberty" in exclusively nationalist terms, even though they were clearly nationalists of one type or another and even though they clearly were drawing on the same vocabulary of nationalism as men. These were languages through which they articulated their particular desire for political and social space.

In short, then, in the vexed situation of imperialist modernity, elite women did not resist or oppose the proposed processes of national integration—the discourse on unity and sovereignty in opposition to foreign usurpation and corrupt dynastic rule—nor should they retrospectively be expected to have done so.[34] Yet, nor were women completely complicit in the dominant nationalist discourse on what the process of national integration entailed. Rather, they often articulated a mode of national integration that included an explicit connection between the hierarchical family and dynastic orders and the global hierarchy of imperialism in order to illumine and claim

---

32. There are countless examples of this tendency in essays in *Zhongguo xin nüjie* 中國新女界, *Nüzi shijie* 女子世界, or any of the other late Qing women's journals. The issue is pervasive. I have focused on a close reading of several essays because, aside from considerations of brevity, they seem to raise the issues most pointedly while providing a good sense of how the discursive construction was ubiquitous across otherwise relatively tense political lines.

33. Barlow, "Theorizing Woman," p. 179.

34. A huge literature and filmography is currently building about the betrayal of women by nation—for China as for most other non-Western countries; it has become very fashionable to read "betrayal" back into the anti-imperialist/anticolonial moments of nationalism and thus to indict nationalism *tout court*. This practice, it strikes me, is not only antihistorical but politically reactionary. Part of the larger project of which this chapter forms a part is aimed at disputing these positions.

a specific space for themselves as subjects in the new Chinese nation.[35] Ambivalent as both Chen and the peacock story's author might be about the future prospects of women and the nation—autonomously and in relation to each other—it was by relating gendered "slavery" and its consequences for the Chinese polity to the global enslavement of peoples and nations through an appropriation of the *wangguo nu* figure that they inserted women into the very center of not only the new narrative of China's historical loss[36] but also the modern global arena of struggle through which this loss might be recuperated.

Indeed, as most activist women recognized, in the global realm the right to be sovereign was to be won through collective struggle, just as in the national realm women would have to struggle to win the status of political and social agents.[37] In China—as in many other places, Western and non-Western alike—the claim to the right to political agency came to rest on education, or on that which would render a person fit for citizenship. A 1904 essay for *Nüzi shijie* 女子世界 (Women's world) indicates the problem for elite women of achieving political and social status and uses the same tactic of splitting *wangguo* from *nu* used by Chen Xiefen. The pseudonymous author wrote: "It is said that the reason for the loss of state (*wangguo*) is the very same as the reason for the perishing of the people/race (*wangzhong* 亡 種)."[38] After noting that *wangguo* and *wangzhong* are not the same, the author continued:

35. I am currently engaged in research to substantiate this point more explicitly.

36. This is true regardless of whether that loss was said to reside in the Ming-Qing transition or in the current era of imperialism.

37. For an illuminating discussion of how "humanity," "citizenship," and "rights" are achieved statuses within polities and within Enlightenment philosophy more generally, see Yanni Kotsonis, "A European Experience: Human Rights and Citizenship in Revolutionary Russia," in *Human Rights and Revolutions*, ed. J. Wasserstrom, L. Hunt, and M. Young, pp. 99–112 (Lanham, Md.: Rowman & Littlefield, 2000). As Kotsonis (p. 100) remarks, "Human rights and its pair, citizenship, were not about claiming an inherent right . . . but about the achievement of a status and the attainment of qualities that would admit one to political society, civil society, and indeed, full humanity."

38. Zhu Zhuang 竹庄, "Lun Zhongguo nüxue buxing zhi hai" 論中國女學不興之害 (On the evil consequences of undeveloped women's education), *Nüzi shijie* 女子世界, no. 3 (Mar. 17, 1904); reprinted in *Xinhai geming qianshinianjian shilun xuanji* 辛亥革命前十年間時 論選集 (Selected articles on current events from the decade preceding the Xinhai Revolution), ed. Zhang Dan 張枏 and Wang Renzhi 王忍之, 1: pt. II, p. 924 (Beijing: Sanlian shudian, 1978).

I have heard that the brown people of the Nanyang [Southern Seas], the red people of the Americas, and the indigenous primitives (*tufan* 土 藩) of Taiwan have all but declined and vanished and that the lost peoples of India and Poland (*Yindu, Bolan wangguo zhi min* 印 度 波 蘭 亡 國 之 民) are also daily becoming more [enslaved]. Yet, the disaster of *wangguo* is not the same as the pain of the perishing of a people (*wangguo zhi huo, da buru wangzhong zhi can ye* 亡 國 之 禍 大 不 如 亡 種 之 慘 也)! It can, however, be said to be the origin of the so-called perishing of a people.[39]

Here, the author distinguished between the fate of the browns, reds, and primitives, who were generally believed not to have had strong family or political structures and who had thus been easily destroyed as peoples and polities by invaders and colonizers, and the situation in Poland and India, in which the state was lost, but the people remained—albeit daily more enslaved. This distinction allows the author to make another: in those cases in which the loss of state does not necessarily presage the destruction of the people, there is still space for the creation of a new politics. This space, the author said, is visible if one understands one thing: "If you look hard enough, how can we not blame the disaster of our *wangguo* on women?" Indeed, the author blamed women for China's *wangguo*, because "women are the mothers of the national people / citizenry (*guomin zhi mu* 國 民 之 母), and they are the source of the race (*zhongzu suo youlai ye* 種 族 所 由 來 也)." Chinese women's failure to be mothers of citizens has led to *wangguo*; but, by the same token, women are also the only ones who can prevent *wangzhong* (the destruction of the people/race) by immediately taking up this task seriously.

The centrality of women to *wangguo* is based, in the author's view, on the proposition that women are at the center of the production and reproduction of the people and the race (both *zhong*) from within the structures of family. By inserting women into the middle of the *wangguo/wangzhong* nexus, indeed by splitting the inevitability of this link, the author implied that the only way to forestall the destruction of the Chinese race in the context of the loss of state was to admit and foster the central role of women in producing citizens.[40] Women's future centrality to this realm, as well as the reasons for

---

39. Ibid.

40. Although many scholars have read this as a concession—insofar as such a position appears to reduce women to the function of motherhood and domesticity—I am considerably less convinced, particularly when we take the global context into consideration. On this, also see Joan Judge's contribution to this volume as well as her forthcoming work.

their past failings in this regard, was emphasized by pointing to a lack of education in general as the central factor in any people's decline and destruction, and thus to education as the hope for women's political revival and for the nation's survival. The family thus becomes "political" in a wholly different way than it had previously been. Significantly, both the lack of and the desire for education was linked to the political centrality of the family by situating education within the family. I will return to this education-family-politics connection in a moment.

First, these linkages helped define a place for women in the emerging rearticulation of sociopolitical power in China. By connecting female enslavement to the demonstrated consequences of global imperialism, women persuasively proclaimed their relevance to nation and elaborated new social roles for themselves. As I have suggested, many late Qing essayists did this increasingly by appropriating and rearticulating the problem of the loss of the state as a problem of regenerating the people—in effect, arrogating to themselves (and taking away from the state) the responsibility for producing the citizenry. In this way, they were able to specify the inherent genderedness of all political and social space.[41] Two problems immediately arose with this rearticulated sphere of politics: it was tied to the family, as that structure was to be redefined; and it was premised on a class blindness that invoked gender sameness ("women") while reinscribing class difference.

National Integration and Social Subjection:
Family, Gender, Class, Nation

From the beginning of the emergence of modern nationalism in late Qing China, the efficient political and economic integration of the population into a new whole consumed the philosophical energy and practical activity of many intellectuals, women and men alike, as well as of government officials and local activists. As we have seen, in the political logic and language of na-

---

41. Much as the discourse on late Qing Chinese women as producers of citizens seems to mimic, or even follow, that of Meiji era Japanese women, these historical parallels need to be carefully considered. At the minimum, it needs to be recognized that the Meiji state, however much it may have been resisted, was nevertheless a strong state, and Japanese feminist articulations of potential sites for their participation in state projects from within the context of family were thus situated very differently—ideologically and structurally—from the discussion of late Qing Chinese women, who were dealing with a much more fluid and unstable situation. Thus, although the appeal to family *appears* similar, it was situated quite differently.

tional integration, "slave" was most often counterposed to "citizen," and for women, integration was to take place primarily within the family as mothers of citizens. Yet, with reference to the economic logic of national integration, the obverse of "slave"—unpaid family laborer—was a producer of national (not family) wealth, or a wage worker. In the ongoing discussion of the political and the economic during the post-1898 period, the incorporation and integration of women loomed large for many nationalists, and clearly economic logic and the political logic of the family clashed. Whereas for elite women creating a political space through the family was crucial, for elite men it was initially the incipient economic logic of national integration that pushed women into the spotlight.

In 1898, Liang Qichao anxiously wrote, "Out of two hundred million women, every one is a consumer, not one is a producer. Because they cannot support themselves, but depend on others for their support, men keep them like dogs and horses or slaves."[42] Similarly, Zhang Zhidong 張之洞, a major Qing official, publicly advocated that women's place was in the factory.[43] Liang was to repeat his call for wage-paying work for women frequently during the late Qing period; he even proposed that the new-style women's education concentrate more on productive activities (spinning, weaving) than on literary pursuits.[44] In these and many other cases, one major reason male nationalists saw women as enslaved was economic. By using the new tools of modern liberal-bourgeois economic logic—which made a clear distinction between wage labor and domestic labor—male nationalists often split consumption from production. In this model, women were confined to the role of (family) consumer and conceived as nonproducers. This made "slavery" into an economic system that contained women's labor and productivity within the family while denying it to the nation. The discourse and activism of male nationalists consequently focused on incorporating women as producers into the proposed national sphere.

---

42. Liang Qichao 梁啓超, "Lun nüxue" 論女學 (On women's education), in *Jindai Zhongguo nüquan yundong shiliao* 近代中國女權運動史料 (Source materials on the women's movement in modern China), ed. Li Youning 李又寧 and Zhang Yufa 張玉法, p. 550 (Taibei: Zhuanji wenxue she, 1975).

43. Cited in Borthwick, "Changing Concepts of the Role of Women," p. 74.

44. Borthwick, "Changing Concepts of the Role of Women," pp. 73–75; also see Liang's 1904 essay, "Lun nügong" 論女工 (On women's work), *Dongfang zazhi* 1, no. 8 (Oct. 1904): 108–12.

Sally Borthwick has pointed out that this argument was advanced by elite men, who were basically blind to the fact that nonelite women labored very hard both in elite households and in their fields and homes as vital producers.[45] Blind they may have been to these types of female productive activities, yet it was precisely *not* the family-based economy that male nationalists were proposing as the cornerstone of the new national economy.[46] For Liang just as much as for Qing bureaucrats and provincial entrepreneurs, the desired direction for economic change, national integration, and wealth accumulation was semi-capitalist production—factories and large agricultural production units.[47] Male nationalist rhetoric on the economic enslavement of women thus reflected not so much ignorance (willful or otherwise) about nonelite women's productive work as a rejection of the particular mode of production that this family-contained labor and family-based economy represented.[48]

A certain disjuncture was thus introduced from the beginning into the male nationalists' lamentations over women's enslavement in economic terms. What they sought was women's participation in a mode of production that would sustain a nation-based economy, and this led many to dismiss the specific forms of family production that formed the major sphere for female economic activity. At the same time, male lamentations over female enslavement—nonproductivity, in other words—were read by the very stratum of women whose eliteness was in fact premised on their own nonproductivity as well as the nonproductive labor and high social status of their male kin. Ironically, although some elite women reclaimed the family as a form or site of cultural and political agency for themselves and for "women" in general, they almost never reclaimed the family as a site of economic productivity—or, at least not for themselves.

Of course, some women, such as Qiu Jin 秋瑾 and He Zhen 何震, seized on the problem of female economic dependence on men and their

---

45. Borthwick, "Changing Concepts of the Role of Women," p. 73.

46. For indications on how productive *nügong* 女工 (women's work) discourses were turned into culturalist *nügong* (womanly work) discourses by the Qing dynasty, see Bray, *Technology and Gender*, pt. II.

47. For one example of such transitions, see the discussion in Kathy LeMons Walker, *Chinese Modernity and the Peasant Path* (Stanford: Stanford University Press, 1999), pt. II.

48. One need not accept completely Hill Gates's (*China's Motor*) argument on a thousand years of petty capitalism in China to appreciate her discussion of the essential resilience of the family-based economy through all trends and efforts to reconfigure it.

families to promote female economic independence. Yet, theirs was an advocacy premised on women as *individuals*, not on women as agents of national
economies. For example, Qiu Jin, in a short story written in 1905–7, depicted
one female character, who, in the midst of a lamentation about her impending arranged marriage, protests against the entrapment of elite women by
evil husbands. She (Qiu / her character) notes:

> If you are of the lower classes, you can always go out to work as a servant to make a
> living and avoid this horrid treatment, but if you are of the upper classes, a single
> move out the door requires a sedan chair and maids to accompany you. These
> women know little of the outside world and have no skills with which to make a
> living. And, of course, it's impossible for an upper-class woman to find employment
> as a maid.[49]

Here, Qiu suggested that lower-class women are freer than upper-class
women, by virtue of their opportunities for remunerated work, even if in the
realm of "servitude."[50] Whereas elite women are labeled "slaves," the remunerated labor of lower-class female servants is construed as personal freedom—wage labor. At the same time as Qiu was writing, the anarchist He
Zhen was promoting economic self-sufficiency as the basis for female—or
indeed more general social—liberation. Being an anarchist, her advocacy was
hardly aimed at enhancing state and national power or national integration;
rather she wanted to promote the ability of women and people in general as
individuals to resist both the patriarchal family and state authority.[51]

More usually, however, when elite women wrote about slavery, they
rarely addressed national economic issues or economic productivity. Rather,
"slavery" pointed to the cultural, patriarchal structures of family relations
and to political agency; and, in referring to themselves either as *wangguo nu*
or as "horse and cow slaves" (*nüzi wei nuli niuma* 女子為奴隸牛馬), they
appropriated metaphors of servitude mostly to illumine their own social and
cultural enslavement to the family. For them, the transformation of the *elite*
family became a fundamental step in claiming political agency.

---

49. See Qiu Jin, "Excerpts from *Stones of the Jingwei Bird*," trans. in Dooling and Torgeson,
Writing Women of Modern China, p. 67.

50. Compare this depiction to, e.g., Lu Xun's paradigmatic May Fourth story, "New
Year's Sacrifice," in which the protagonist, Xianglin Sao, is trapped in wage labor by her family, gender, and class situation, none of which is construed as "liberating" in the least.

51. For He Zhen, see Peter Zarrow, *Anarchism and Chinese Political Culture* (New York:
Columbia University Press, 1990), chap. 6.

By the same token, elite women's focus on recuperating the family and on
the relationship between the family and the nation was at odds—in economic, no less than in political terms—with the attempts of male nationalists to separate the family from the nation, a separation deemed essential to
fostering a national consciousness among the people at large and to promoting a nationally integrated economy. Liang Qichao, while perhaps the
most eloquent writer, was certainly not the only one at the time to distinguish citizenship and nation from the family and to argue that the creation
and mobilization of citizenship were crucial to the transformation of China
into a unified national polity. In 1904 Chen Duxiu lamented that the Chinese people "know only the family, they don't know the nation. In our
China, the family system is the most developed in the whole world." He
then compared the Chinese to the Jews, a paradigmatic example for Chen of
those who knew only the family and consequently lost their state and nation:

In the past, there was a state (*guo*) called the Jewish state (*youtai guo* 猶太國), and it
was located in West Asia. But because the Jewish people knew only the family and
didn't know the nation, they ignored national affairs, and the nation gradually declined. In the end, Turkey destroyed them. Today, the Jews wander in the East and in
the West, with no nation to return to; they are the objects of other people's prejudices
and insults. Simply because they have no state to protect them, they must silently en-
dure, swallow [these insults], and be tortured by others. . . . We Chinese have the
same disease as the Jews of knowing only the family and not knowing the nation.[52]

This "family disease" was one that Chen, Liang, and many other male
nationalists hoped the Chinese would overcome.[53] For many male intellectuals, then, family and nation increasingly became opposed categories. Whatever the particular content each invested in the concepts of "citizen" or
"nation," most firmly believed that creating a proper citizenry—in political
no less than in economic terms—was ineluctably linked to transforming
family ties into national ties.[54]

---

52. Chen Duxiu 陳獨秀, "Wangguo de yuanyin (yi)" 亡國的原因(一) (The reasons for
wangguo, pt. 1); reprinted in idem, *Chen Duxiu zhuzuo xuan*, 1: 82.

53. Clearly, some of this lament emerged from the ongoing abuses being suffered by Chinese laborers in the United States, news of which was plastered across the journals of the
time.

54. In the late Qing, Sun Yat-sen, for example, posited a complete incompatibility between the ideologies of clan and nation; Tan Sitong, too, in elevating the friend-friend relationship to centrality in his revisioning of social relations in China at the turn of the century,

One primary mode of doing so, they said, was to raise the people's cultural level through the enhancement of popular education, so as to make them fit for political, or at least for efficient social, subjection to the nation.[55] In this regard, as we have seen, the noted lack of education among the people at large was also reflected in discussions of the low level of education among women. This failing was designated, by men and women alike, as a primary reason for the historical subjugation and lowly position of women.[56] Indeed, it was through this argument that women as a social category were closely identified with the category of the people. This identification was based not on social status (in a sociological sense)—not in elite/nonelite terms—but on a putative common ignorance. And it was precisely the relationship drawn between education and fitness for citizenship that then dovetailed with elite women's arguments about their cultural and political enslavement and about their central role within the family to educate and produce citizens. In other words, elite women turned education for the nation, the nationalist argument advanced for the people in general, into an argument for the transformation of the family through female education and thus for the closer knitting of family to nation via the trope of "mothers of citizens" (*guomin zhi mu*). And it was this nexus that helped introduce a contested family-nation relationship into nationalist discourse and that contributed to the muddiness of feminist political programs at the time.

----

implicitly posited the incompatibility between the hierarchical relationships of family and the desired equality of nation.

55. The educational argument was not only an oppositional intellectual position; it was one promoted by Qing officials and a host of local elites and entrepreneurs who were vigorously setting up schools at the time in their own localities; however, separation of the state and family was anathema to Qing supporters and local elites alike. For local elites and education, see Mary Rankin, *Elite Activism and Political Transformation in China* (Stanford: Stanford University Press, 1986); Marianne Bastide, *Aspects de la réforme de l'enseignement en Chine au début du xxᵉ siècle* (Paris: Mouton & Co., 1971); Sally Borthwick, *Education and Social Change in China: The Beginnings of the Modern Era* (Stanford: Hoover Institution Press, 1983); Paul Bailey, *Reform the People: Changing Attitudes Towards Popular Education in Early Twentieth Century China* (Edinburgh: Edinburgh University Press, 1990).

56. For general discussions of this linkage, see Ono, *Women in a Century of Revolution*, chap. 2; Sun Shiyue 孫石月, *Zhongguo jindai nüzi liuxueshi* 中國近代女子留學史 (A history of modern Chinese women students abroad) (Beijing: Zhongguo heping chubanshe, 1995), chaps. 4–5; and Lü Meiyi 呂美頤 and Zheng Yongfu 鄭永福, *Zhongguo funü yundong, 1840–1921* 中國婦女運動 (The Chinese women's movement: 1840–1921) (Zhengzhou: Henan renmin chubanshe, 1990).

In seizing on the education argument and proclaiming themselves mothers of citizens, women focused their attention on the family practices that kept them physically weak (footbinding), housebound (culturalist patriarchy), and uneducated (with ignorance defining female virtue). As we saw above, they identified this female situation as the wellspring not only of "the people's" ignorance but of the decline of the nation itself.[57] Thus, even as male nationalists were trying to separate the family from the nation conceptually in the political and economic spheres, elite women were reclaiming the intimate connection between family and nation in cultural and political terms, so as to position themselves centrally as political actors (albeit thus neglecting the economic issues). In making these claims, a gap opened in nationalist discourse between the analytical priorities of transforming state-society relations as a whole and redefining the *structural* relations between family (women) and nation.

It is important to remember that the family of which elite women spoke was implicitly the elite family, which was able to educate its offspring. This was the concrete and known structure of their life experience through which they came to claim oppression and a subjectivity as "women." For male elites, however, the family appears as an almost abstract category that blocked the equally abstract people from performing their political and economic responsibilities to the nation. As such, the result of these disjunctures was that, for male nationalists, women's lack of education and fitness for citizenship bound them to the larger category of the people, who were to be freed from the family, even while the elite women producing the rhetoric of family-citizenship-education conceived of education as taking place within the family and thus tied themselves more fully to the family. This gap—between women and the people vis-à-vis the family as a political or economic unit—opened the possibility for the distancing of the social category "women" (now, implicitly elite women) from "the people" (implicitly the masses). Moreover, because the women producing the rhetoric were elites, there was

---

57. As Xia Xiaohong (夏曉虹, Wan Qing wenren funü guan 晚清文人婦女觀 [Elite views of women in the late Qing] [Beijing: Zuojia chubanshe, 1995]) has exhaustively documented, "mothers of citizens" arguments were themselves highly contested at the time. This contestation, while having real consequences in terms of political positioning among various female and male activists, does not negate my general point here.

resentment that men were understood as legitimate agents of politics by virtue of being men, whereas they, as women, needed to prove their 'fitness' for politics.[58]

Indeed, as a 1904 essay in *Nüzi shijie* argued, women's lack of education affected every sphere of life: individual, family, society, nation. Yet, this was not peculiar to women; the lack of education among the vast majority of men also influenced every sphere of the nation's life. Claiming that the strength of a people determined the strength of the nation, the author noted (rather idealistically) that in strong countries, there "is not one useless person," whereas in China, not only were 200 million women ignorant and useless due to lack of education, but the vast majority of men were as well: "Of 200 million men," she noted, "there are only a few who are completely qualified to be citizens."[59] The educational deficiencies foregrounded here reveal a split between male claims on citizenship—based either on the abstract people-race category or on elite maleness—and elite women's claims on citizenship as educated elite women. If education were truly the criterion for citizenship, most men ("people") would be unfit for it. Thus, women, to press their own claims when education became the determinant of suitability for national participation, readily transformed citizenship into a class-based political logic, even as citizenship continued to be articulated in the singular categories of "the people" and the nation. Even as they advocated a unified nation that took the people seriously and universal education as a central factor in making a proper citizenry out of the people, they staked a particular claim to fitness for citizenship apart from the people based on their social eliteness, their access to education, and the potential malleability of their own family situations. Transforming the nature of the elite patriarchal family into a new basis for female citizenship through educational access and opportunity began at this point to take analytical and practical priority over transforming elite-nonelite relations in general. The social, political, economic, and class differentiations concealed by an appeal to the nation were thus also inscribed almost immediately in gender terms as well.

Elite women were quite vigorous in producing this argument, although they were not the only ones to do so. (In this sense, it is probably more accu-

---

58. Indeed, when women and unpropertied men were locked out of political participation after the 1911 revolution, women took up the suffragist battle in gender terms alone, not in class terms.

59. "Lun Zhongguo nüxue buxing zhi hai," p. 924.

rate to label this a particular type of feminist position.) Indeed, the logic and process of this position is elegantly and succinctly demonstrated in an essay by Ding Chuwo 丁初我, the (male) editor of *Nüzi shijie*.[60] As Ding noted in early 1904, "The eighteenth and nineteenth centuries in Europe were the world of revolutions for bourgeois rights (*junquan geming shijie* 君權革命世界); the twentieth century will be the world of revolutions for women's rights. . . . And yet, women's rights and people's rights are directly linked; there is no distance between them." Having established the intimate connection between women's and people's rights and between the European nineteenth century and the global twentieth century, Ding gives priority to women's rights. "When speaking of the relative importance of male and female revolutions, then female revolution is in reality infinitely more urgent"[61]—a priority he asserts through a logic of family and motherhood: "If one wishes to create a nation, one must create a family; if one wishes to give birth to citizens, one must give birth to girls." The rest of the essay is devoted to a discussion of the necessity for a "female family revolution" that is premised on the structure of elite families, in which economically nonproductive girls are nevertheless politically suitable citizens.[62]

A gender sameness that masked a class separation was similarly and succinctly implied in a speech by Xie Zhen 謝震, principal of a girl's school in Shanghai, who spoke in 1909 on citizenship to an audience of female students. The speech was reprinted in *Nübao* 女報 (The national women's journal), a Shanghai-based paper, and in the *Beijing Women's News*, both less politically progressive than Ding Chuwo's *Women's World*. Xie concluded her speech by noting that "I don't think we can only blame the government [for China's troubles]," for:

Our Chinese people don't have the capacity for self-rule: they have no sense of civic duty (*gonggong xin* 公共心). Myriad matters are thrown aside as wasteful, while immediate small matters of profit and advantage are daily contested and rile their hearts. How are they qualified to be citizens? (*Nali you guomin zige ne?* 那里有國民資格呢)

---

60. Ding has usually been identified as a woman; he was, however, in fact a man. For the confusions and the substantiation, see Xia Xiaohong, *Wan Qing wenren funü guan*, p. 35.

61. "Nüzi jiating geming shuo" 女子家庭革命說 (On female family revolution), *Nüzi shijie* 女子世界, no. 4 (Apr. 16, 1904); reprinted in *Xinhai geming qianshinianjian shilun xuanji*, ed. Zhang Dan and Wang Renzhi, p. 926.

62. Ibid.

As for us women, we are accustomed to being slaves in a male society and are not particularly valued or utilized. Yet, even though things are now this way, there are no difficult problems in the world that cannot be solved if one puts one's mind to it. We must all strive to do this. . . . Cannot our glorious history begin again with women? You may look to the great women of China's past to take heart for the struggle.[63]

Xie, like Ding and others, separated "our Chinese people" from "us women." The referent of "people" is the mass of men, and of "us women" her elite female audience. Indeed, Xie's solution to the question of women's fitness for participation in national politics was to posit the (elite) woman as the prototypical universal citizen of a new China and to propose that women could join the national struggle by rediscovering their heroic sisters from history. Among other things, this formulation exposes a gender and class gap in the supposed unitary identity of nation and citizenship, and the tensions between the people, women, and citizenship are revealed by Xie's purposeful evocation of the people and her simultaneous denial of their fitness for citizenship, as well as by her claim of citizenship for elite women based on their recoverable historical ties to women heroes of the past.

To sum up, the question of female participation in the emerging nation, when phrased in terms of fitness for citizenship, led to several discursive and practical problems for elite women. To protect their claims as elites, they often found resolutions to their contradictory identification with "the people" in distinctions that implicitly served to separate them—as elites and as women—from the larger category of the male-gendered, lower-class generic term "people." The exploitation of this contradiction was possible (and not particularly noticeable) at the time because, at the point when women were first interpellated as political agents, the juridical, economic, and political meanings of the nation itself were unclear. Even so, it nevertheless became quite apparent that women were to be incorporated into the nation in a fashion quite different from that used for men; similarly the people and the elites were joined to the nation in quite different ways. Thus, to cope with their identification with the people at large—deemed by elite men and

---

63. Xie Zhen 謝震, "Lishi tan" 歷史譚 (Chatting about history), *Nü bao* 女報, no. 1 (Jan. 22, 1909). This was a reprint of a speech that Xie gave at the Aihua nüxuexiao 愛華女學校 (China patriotic girl's school). The journal in which it appeared was published under the editorial guidance of Chen Yiyi 陳以益.

women unfit for citizenship because of their lack of education—elite women increasingly came to link themselves politically and socially more closely not to the people but to the elite stratum of men to whom citizenship was assumed to pertain, even while they (along with the elite men) continued to use the rhetoric of the people to speak of the nation and of national integration. By the same token, elite women's site of political agency was the reclaimed space of the family—the site of their "slavery"—or, more precisely, the institution from which the people needed to be weaned, an institution rejected by male nationalists as a site of politics and nationally integrative economics.[64] The contradictions inherent in these differential claims—effectively concealed by the 1911 revolution and the political chaos that followed—exploded anew in the abortive suffragist movements immediately following the revolution and then most forcefully in the May Fourth period.

Conclusion

The struggles over citizenship in late Qing China proceeded through a vexed gender/class differentiation, within which elite women took up the problem of their "enslavement" to the family (though distancing themselves initially from the economic logic of this enslavement), while at the same time differentiating themselves from the unenlightened enslavement of the people in political terms.[65] When they appropriated "enslavement" as a gendered locution and generalized it to cover their distance from the people through claims on citizenship rights and political participation in the new nation in class terms, arguments for female political agency were rendered visible by linking the category of female enslavement to the colonized global space of "slaves of lost countries." I have argued that it is by noting the reference to

---

64. The family was soon reified by male politicians and nationalists in an explicit effort to contain women's citizenship claims and roles in the new nation. Although this took place most explicitly after 1911 and the toppling of the dynasty, I would argue that it was in part the late Qing elite women's own promotion of the family as the rightful site of female political agency that helped provide the discursive legitimation upon which the post-1911 male reifications and containments drew. This is the topic of a different inquiry, however.

65. Elite women's anxieties about the gender politics of nation, of course, were quite prescient: the new Republican government quickly legislated against women's suffrage and political rights once the national parliament began meeting.

this latter space that the various fault lines in women's discourse on their place in the new Chinese polity at the time become apparent.

To return to the peacock story, it is now possible to see that the unstable appropriation of a newly glimpsed global context (signaled by the book on Poland) established a global and a local historical condition for an articulation of the woman-as-slave. Indeed, it suggests how the widespread interiorization of a colonial discourse on China contributed to the particular articulation of women in terms of enslavement and why this articulation gained such explosive popularity across otherwise sharp ideological and political divides. Although it is certainly no coincidence that the trope arose at that time, the phenomenon does need to be explained historically. And rather than trace the rise of the "woman-as-slave" locution either to an exclusively internal recognition of Confucian social structure prompted by Western missionary critiques or to objectivist recognitions of China's lack vis-à-vis the West, or even to the influence of John Stuart Mill's work on women—as important as all of these might have been—I have drawn particular attention to the mutual constitution of women's discourses on their enslavement and discourses on global colonization.

By placing slavery in an early twentieth-century context that includes a consciousness of imperialism, colonialism, geopolitics, and uneven global modernity—all signaled by *wangguo*—we can see that "slave" had an ambiguous connotation: it reflected and gave voice to both the promise and the anxiety over possibilities for transformation in late Qing China, a promise and an anxiety that are broadly characteristic of the post-1898 period in general. Indeed, what appears through this locution is a series of gaps in the emerging relationship between nationalism and citizenship—between men and women, and between elite women and men of different classes—gaps that, while often rhetorically and historiographically concealed through a discourse of woman and nation as singular categories, actually helped produce implicit sociopolitical differentiation. Moreover, in the late Qing, when nation and imperialism were linked into an interwoven and yet still loosely understood structural totality—at the moment when the components of a participatory mode of politics in terms of citizenship overlapped with the pursuit of regimes of integrative social subjection in terms of nation—these gaps appear as ruptures. These ruptures effectively worked to differentiate the proposed polity in class and gender terms and to expose the rifts in a supposedly homogeneous national solution to politics and economy,[66] even as this differentiation was being effectively concealed by the rhetoric and urgency of the national situation.

Finally, in the post-1911 period, and particularly in the New Culture / May Fourth periods, the issues of family, state, citizenship, nation, and imperialism—which first aired in the post-1898 period but which as yet had not hardened into hegemonic axioms[67]—were reworked into more rigid formulations and relationships. In these reworkings, the basis for women's liberation from slavery and victimization could rest only on liberation *from* the family (not *within* it). The link between women and nation—and the basis for the so-called betrayal of victimized women by the nation—was thus in part established in the May Fourth period on a fundamental misrecognition of the historical, discursive, and, most important, the *flexible* origins of slavery as a discourse of gendered political positioning in the uneven late Qing global context of imperialist modernity. This misrecognition—as passionately lived as it was—combined with the 1920s and 1930s commoditization of life in urban centers of China, which reinstantiated the family as the site of bourgeois commodified consumption (not production). This combination in turn helped produce a new set of contradictions that strongly resemble the theoretical and lived gender conundrums visible in present-day China, with the reintroduction of commodity culture and global capitalism into new formulations of "national salvation."

---

66. The abandonment of the dynasty by local entrepreneurial elites in, e.g., the Rights Recovery movement through the last years of the Qing indicates that the process of social subjection in terms of capital was well under way; women's participation in these movements was considerable. See Beahan, "In the Public Eye," esp. pp. 222–27.

67. For the importance of historically transitional periods as moments of transparency, see Karatani Kojin, *The Origins of Japanese Literature*, trans. Brett de Bary (Durham: Duke University Press, 1993).

CHAPTER NINE

'Poetic Revolution,' Colonization, and Form
at the Beginning of Modern Chinese Literature
Xiaobing Tang

On December 20, 1899, after having been in political exile for more than
a year in Tokyo, Liang Qichao 梁啓超 (1873–1929) left Japan for the
United States. Although the trip had been arranged by overseas supporters
of the besieged Guangxu emperor, Liang was as interested in North America as in the royalist campaign to restore the emperor. Since his arrival in Japan, the renowned spokesperson for reform had immersed himself in reading about politics and history and found himself more and more inclined to
the idea of a republican government, one enviable example of which was the
United States. However, still loyal to the emperor and to the possibility of
orderly and effective reform, Liang could not fully identify with the revolutionary cause championed by Sun Yat-sen 孫中山 (1866–1925). Nonetheless, he was genuinely excited about his trip to the New World, "the moth-
erland of republicanism." It was during this period that Liang Qichao began
to be preoccupied with the questions of governmental form and of implementing and sustaining the reform program. As I have examined elsewhere,[1]
between 1899 and 1903 Liang developed an intense interest in constitutional
monarchy, statism, and republicanism as differently determined, historical
models.

On the same day that Liang began his trans-Pacific journey, the Qing
court issued yet another edict authorizing the arrest or even the assassina-

---

1. Xiaobing Tang, *Global Space and the Nationalist Discourse of Modernity: The Historical
Thinking of Liang Qichao* (Stanford: Stanford University Press, 1996), pp. 80–116.

tion of Kang Youwei 康有爲 (1858–1927) and Liang Qichao.[2] Aware of the
manhunt and the very real danger to his life, Liang was traveling on the
passport of his Japanese friend Kashiwabara Buntarō 柏原文太郎 (1869–
1936). After being seen off by a dozen associates and students, Liang found
himself all alone and decided to keep a diary during his trip, as he had on
previous journeys. As he began to put his thoughts in writing, the fact that
he had to travel under a borrowed identity must have been a poignant reminder of his situation. The rare moment of quiet and solitude nonetheless
allowed him a chance to reflect on his turbulent life since the heady days of
the summer of 1898. He had developed, he wrote at the beginning of the diary, in three stages. Brought up as a "content and innocent man of the vil-
lage," he had grown into a "man of the nation" only after he had traveled
across the country and been caught in the great global tides of the nineteenth century. Now he would gradually metamorphose into a man of the
world: "Born into the nation, one cannot but be a man of the nation; born
into the world, one cannot but be a man of the world" (22: 185).[3] It was his
escape to Japan, "the most advanced Asian country that has established constitutionalism," that compelled him to learn how to be a man of the nation;
his journey to America, "the most advanced country that has established a
republican government in the world," would teach him how to be a man of
the world (22: 185). Ready to learn to be a national subject and a cosmopolitan (or world citizen) at the same time, Liang was evidently overwhelmed by
the enormity of the task at hand and named his diary *Hanman lu* 漢漫錄
(Records of vastness). He also thought that *Ban jiushi lu* 半九十錄 (Ninety-
as-half-of-a-hundred records) would serve as an appropriate title because he
needed a great deal of resolve and caution to finish the last part of an imaginary one-hundred-mile journey (22: 185).

The first entry in *Records of Vastness*, which would later be renamed
Xiaweiyi youji 夏威夷遊記 (Travels to Hawaii), is conspicuously dated

---

2. Ding Wenjiang 丁文江 and Zhao Fengtian 趙豐田, eds., *Liang Qichao nianpu changbian*
梁啓超年譜長編 (Chronological biography of Liang Qichao) (Shanghai: Shanghai renmin
chubanshe, 1983), p. 194; Tang Zhijun 湯志鈞, *Wuxu bianfa renwuzhuan gao* 戊戌變法人物
傳稿 (Draft biographies of people involved in the 1898 reforms), 2d ed., 2: 827–29 (Beijing:
Zhonghua shuju, 1982).

3. Page references are to *Xiaweiyi youji* (Travels to Hawaii), in Liang Qichao 梁啓超, *Yinbingshi heji: zhuanji* 飲冰室合集專集 (Collected writings from the Ice-Drinker's Studio: collected works), vol. 22 (Shanghai: China Books, 1936); hereafter volume and page numbers are
cited in the text.

"December 19 according to the Western calendar (the seventeenth day of the eleventh month in the Chinese calendar)." After giving these two dates, Liang explained that it made sense to adopt the Western calendar because he was traveling to a place where the traditional Chinese calendar was not observed. The new temporal framework made him more acutely aware of moving into a new historical and geopolitical reality. The first entry therefore is mostly about his nostalgia for Tokyo as he was heading to Yokohama in preparation to sail across the Pacific. The prospect of leaving Japan, even though he expected to be gone only temporarily, made Liang realize how deeply attached he had become to this country, "a second homeland" that had offered him spiritual support and nourishment. He already began to miss his friends and comrades and reminisced fondly about the projects that they had undertaken or were about to embark on.

Great anticipation and intense homesickness combined to elevate Liang Qichao into an unusually poetic mood, despite the seasickness that began soon after the ship left Yokohama. Since childhood, Liang had been particularly afraid of traveling on the water. Reduced to curling up in bed for the first few days, Liang nonetheless felt enough inspiration to compose classical-style regulated verse to keep himself "amused" (22: 189). Of the thirty-odd poems that came to him during this period, he would later collect 26 under the collective title "Zhuangbie" 壯別 (Heroic farewell); the central topics of this collection are declarations of will and determination, reminiscences of friendship, and observations on history.

During these agitated but profoundly solitary days (only two missionaries on board could converse with him, and they spoke a northern dialect unfamiliar to Liang), Liang Qichao also organized his thoughts on the question of writing a new kind of poetry that would correspond to his contemporary world. In his view, a revolutionary age was sweeping across the land, and poetry would not be exempted from change: "In short unless there is a poetic revolution (*shijie geming* 詩界革命) in China, poetry will near its end" (22: 190–91).[4] Scholars have commented on the significance of this proposal: al-

---

4. Two days after outlining his theory for a poetic revolution, Liang decided to "give up" his addiction to poetry. He reasoned that by nature he was not a poet, but in the past few days, as if drunken or entranced, he had indulged himself in poeticizing at the great expense of all other matters. This sudden obsession was laughable, and he resolved not to let himself become one of those parrot-poets that he had always detested. After forming this resolution, Liang neatly transcribed his recent poems as a memorial to this bout of self-expression. Yet

though it supplied a theoretical justification for the creative practices of the young generation of reform-minded literati Chinese (Xia Zengyou 夏曾佑 [1863–1924], Tan Sitong 譚嗣同 [1865–98], Qiu Fengjia 丘逢甲 [1864–1912]), it was also the first of a series of genre revolutions that Liang Qichao would advocate and even put into practice. It preceded his call for a "new fiction" by well over one year and offered a more systematic program than the "stylistic revolution" that he had envisioned earlier.[5] As one critic points out, Liang's notion of "a poetic revolution" established for the first time a comprehensive conception of "Chinese poetry" and introduced a radically new system of reference—European poetry.[6] In other words, by introducing a different tradition as the equal of Chinese poetry, Liang succeeded in bringing to the tradition of Chinese poetry a conceptual coherence and identity. The question that I tackle in this chapter is the relationship between Liang Qichao's proposal for a "poetic revolution" and Chen Duxiu's 陳獨秀 (1879–1942) proposal for a "literary revolution," which presumably ushered in a new age, namely, the May Fourth period. In the process, I will examine the discursive paradigm that underlies Liang's notion of a "poetic revolution."

What engendered Liang's call for a new poetry was a modern global imaginary that he increasingly came to appreciate after his arrival in Japan. Lamenting that native poetic conventions yielded nothing but hackneyed

---

such poetic outbursts would be repeated at several critical points throughout Liang Qichao's eventful life, especially in the early years after his return to China in 1912 (see Xia Xiaohong 夏曉虹, *Jueshi yu chuanshi: Liang Qichao de wenxue daolu* 覺世與傳世：梁啓超的文學道路 [Enlightenment and permanence: the literary career of Liang Qichao] [Shanghai: Shanghai renmin chubanshe, 1991], pp. 160–61). In fact, poetry writing remained a vital emotive release for Liang throughout his life.

5. See ibid., pp. 161–64; Chen Jianhua 陳建華, "Wan Qing 'shijie geming' de fasheng shijian ji tichangzhe kaobian" 晚清 "詩界革命" 的發生時間及提倡者考辨 (An examination of the duration of the "poetic revolution" in the late Qing and its promoters), *Zhongguo gudian wenxue congkao* 1 (1985): 321–40; idem, "Wan Qing 'shijie geming' shengshuai shishi kao" 晚清 "詩界革命" 盛衰史實考 (An examination of the historical facts concerning the rise and fall of the "poetic revolution" during the late Qing), *Fujian luntan: wenshizhe ban* 3 (1987): 74–80; and Zhao Shenxiu 趙慎修, "Lun wan Qing de wenxue biange" 論晚清的文學變革 (On the literary reforms during the late Qing), *Wenxue yichan* 2 (1989): 41–48.

6. Zhao Shenxiu 趙慎修, "Chengxian qihou de 'shijie geming'" 承先啓後的 "詩界革命" (On the transitional "poetic revolution"), in *Zhongguo jindai wenxue baiti* 中國近代文學百題 (One hundred topics in modern Chinese literature), ed. Chinese Academy of Social Sciences, Institute for Literature, pp. 65–68 (Beijing: Zhongguo guoji guangbo chubanshe, 1989).

phrases and images, he called on his contemporaries to explore new colonies and territories of poetic composition:

In the present age, it would be a different story if one chose not to poeticize, but if one does write poetry, one cannot but emulate Columbus and Magellan. This is the same situation as in Europe. When its land was exhausted and a stage of overproduction was reached, people had to seek new territories in America and along the coast of the Pacific. (22: 189)

The need for poetic innovation is not by itself modern or even unusual, given the long Chinese tradition of honoring poets who strove for unique and surprising expressions. Yet in explicitly comparing poetic innovation to modern colonization on a global scale, Liang not only promoted adventurousness as a positive quality underlying both enterprises, but, more important, also rendered a new poetry a historical necessity that is both demonstrated and corroborated on a material and geopolitical level. The writing of poetry becomes parallel to economic production and ought to follow the same logic of incessant innovation and territorial expansion. No longer construed as a disinterested aesthetic exercise or private musing, poetic practice is now revealed to be parallel to the socioeconomic enterprise of appropriating and colonizing the new and the unknown.

Obviously, at this juncture, Liang regarded European colonization with a moral or world-historical neutrality to which he did not adhere when writing in other contexts. His admiration for the individual modern discoverers of the New World was unqualified; yet he could warn urgently of the danger that the foreign powers would divide and annex China. This unspoken conflict between hero worship and self-conception or self-interest reflects a fundamental condition of the modern world that Liang grappled with on many levels: namely, the incongruity between an overarching, rationalistic justification of modernity and the local, immediate experiences of the consequences of modernity. A grand world-historical overview allowed Liang to see in the European tendency to colonize a basic operating logic of the modernizing, capital-driven world system. Continents are discovered, conquered, and colonized because of the continual economic need in Europe to develop a world market; similarly, new poetry has to be created because the existing resources of vocabulary and imagery are overused and exhausted. The inner dynamics or maturation of a given productive system makes the aggressive pursuit of both new poetry and new territory equally unavoidable. Colonization therefore becomes a general practice that leads to the strongest form of self-affirmation and reproduction.

Indeed, underpinning Liang's conception of a poetic revolution is a notion of colonization, which, I wish to emphasize, does not acknowledge the destructive exploitation of the colonized as victim or even as subaltern. The reason may be that for Liang Qichao colonization was not exclusively a European practice; nor was its object confined to the non-European sphere. Rather, colonization was a modernizing enterprise justified by the powerful capitalist mode of production as much as by the then-prevalent social Darwinian discourse, which functioned as the universal law and principle of historical progress. For Liang, colonization was not merely a process that imposed deprivation and uniformity. On the contrary, it inevitably instituted migration, hybridization, and cross-fertilization on an unprecedented, global scale. What Liang celebrated therefore was not so much the system of colonization or its ideological justification as the cultural traffic and permutations that modern colonization effectuated. This euphoric vision of emancipatory globalization allowed him to speak as the subject and agent, rather than as the object or target, of purposeful colonization. The transformation engendered by colonization would affirm his flexible (and thereby reflective) subjecthood through his active engagement with heterogeneity. As we will see, Liang Qichao imagined European culture and intellectual systems being colonized and appropriated to enrich the Chinese poetic tradition.

In this context, it is interesting to note that in Liang's time the term zhimin 殖民 (the modern Chinese translation of "colonization") did not have the negative connotation that it would acquire over the course of the twentieth century. (The root meaning of the verb zhi is amazingly close to the Latin word colere [to cultivate, to inhabit], the source of the English verb "to colonize." The Chinese word specifically describes the act of farming, growing, and then reproducing. Another meaning of the verb zhi is to engage in commerce or exchange.) At the turn of the twentieth century, zhimin had a wide range of meanings, one of which was "adventures in an exotic land." For instance, beginning with the thirty-fourth issue in January 1900, Liang's political journal Qingyi bao 清議報 (The China discussion) featured a column called "Zhimin zazu" 殖民雜俎 (Colonization miscellany) that reported not only on the abuses suffered by Chinese laborers in the United States but also on unusual and exciting events abroad, such as a red rain in Jilong, Taiwan, and local customs among the aborigines in the South Pacific (see the thirty-fifth issue). In 1903, Liang published a brief historical account of eight great colonizers in Chinese history in *Xinmin congbao* 新民叢報 (New citizen journal).[7]

The justification of a new poetry as analogous to colonization was particularly felicitous to Liang Qichao because it was based on territorial metaphors. The realm of poetic imagination (*shi zhi jingjie* 詩之境界), according to him, had been completely partitioned by servile parrot-poets over the preceding thousand years. As a result, a poetic Columbus or Magellan would first have to discover a new realm of the imagination, in the same way that a new territory is discovered, claimed, and assimilated. The first goal for a new poetry is therefore the creation of a new content. The second is to employ new terms and expressions that must be incorporated into, or agree with, the "classical style of the ancients." This "classical style of the ancients" in fact constitutes a third standard that governs the first two. Anyone who can accomplish these tasks, promises Liang, can expect to become "the king of poetry in twentieth-century China" (22: 189). Implied in this aspiration is also the radical notion of "twentieth-century Chinese poetry," which was the harbinger of a series of contemporary pronouncements on a new historical entity—"twentieth-century Chinese fiction"—which, according to Chen Pingyuan,[8] marked the self-conscious modernization of the native narrative tradition. However, in a cautionary note, which reveals Liang's territorial thinking to be largely Earth-centered, he warned that if exotic phrases and expressions were not tamed by the classical style, they would look like strange animals plucked directly from Jupiter or Venus. "Gorgeous they might be, but how preposterous they would appear!" (22: 189).

The poetic imagination that Liang advocated as the most important component in a new poetry is therefore a conceptual colony in the making. It is an outward extension that is both discontinuous with and yet supplementary to the existing system of meaning and signification. During the Song and Ming periods, wrote Liang, poets succeeded in expanding poetic diction and imagery by skillfully incorporating elements from Indian Buddhism. "Yet today this imagination is already an old world. To change this situation, one must turn to Europe. The imagination developed in Europe

---

7. *Xinmin congbao*, reprinted in 17 vols. (Taipei: Yiwen, 1966), 8: 1–5.
8. Chen Pingyuan 陳平原, *Ershi shiji Zhongguo xiaoshuo shi* 二十世紀中國小說史 (History of twentieth-century Chinese fiction), vol. 1, 1897–1916 (Beijing: Peking University Press, 1989), pp. 23–25.

and expressions found there are rich and extraordinary. Once in possession of them, one will be able to triumph over all ages and encompass everything" (22: 189). "Twentieth-century Chinese poetry" depends on aggressive incorporation and cannibalization. The innovative new poet is an omnivorous cosmopolitan instead of a purist, much less a defender of some putative native essence or heritage. Poetry is here largely a medium for expressing new ideas and concepts; its success in fashioning a new, albeit initially shocking, vocabulary will ensure its value in the contemporary, discovery-oriented world. Among his contemporaries, Liang singled out Huang Zunxian 黃遵 憲 (1848–1905) as the most ingenious in creating a "new kingdom" (xin guo 新國). He believed that several of Huang's poems embodied a "thoroughly European imagination," even though they contain few new words or expressions. Huang Zunxian's aversion to novel terminology, explained Liang, owed much to the poet's emphasis on the integrity of classical style and form, which determined his approach to resolving the constant conflict between "new expressions and old style" (22: 189). The refreshing and radical "European imagination" that Liang found in Huang apparently constitutes the new poetic content/continent that the poet colonizes for the sake of extending his poetic vision and capacity. Modern Europe, in this instance, can and ought to be subjected to colonization, because it supplies the space into which traditional Chinese poetic discourse can expand.

Two years later, Liang Qichao would speak even more enthusiastically of Huang Zunxian's achievements and hail some of his poems as the best representatives of the "poetic revolution."[9] Of all contemporary poets, in Liang's opinion, Huang Zunxian was the most outstanding in "welding new ideas onto old style."[10] As early as 1896 and 1897, Liang had had a chance to keep a manuscript copy of Huang's collection *Renjing lu shi* 人境廬詩 (Poems from the hut in the human world) for over two months and perused it several

---

9. Liang Qichao, *Yinbingshi shihua* 飲冰室詩話 (Poetic commentary from the Ice-drinker's Studio), comp. Shu Wu 舒蕪 (Beijing: Renmin wenxue chubanshe, 1982), p. 43; see Chen Jianhua, "Wan Qing 'shijie geming' yu piping de wenhua jiaolü—Liang Qichao, Hu Shi yu 'geming' de liangzhong hanyi" 晚清"詩界革命"與批評的文化焦慮—梁啓超，胡適與"革命"的兩種含義 (Cultural anxieties of the late Qing "poetic revolution" and its criticism: Liang Qichao, Hu Shi, and the two meanings of "revolution"), in *Chinese Literary Criticism of the Ch'ing Period (1644–1911)*, ed. John C. Y. Wang, pp. 220–21 (Hong Kong: Hong Kong University Press, 1993).

10. Liang Qichao, *Yinbingshi shihua*, p. 2.

times.[11] In his preface to the collection, written in the summer of 1891, Huang had made a series of statements about his poetry, the central ethos of which is his claim to a historical subjectivity. After acknowledging the difficulty of freeing himself of the bonds of the past, Huang wrote, "Yet, I have always believed that there is a world beyond poetry and a human being within poetry. If the world today is different from that of old, why should the human being be the same as that in the old days?"[12] This statement agrees with his 1861 declaration "My hand writes what my mouth speaks / How can antiquity be a constraint!" Yet Huang also put much emphasis on "cultivating a style" and vowed to draw not only from all the great masters from Tang and Song but also from less recognized poets of recent times.[13] "The key is to not lose my own poetic style. It is true that in doing so I may not measure up to the ancients; however, I will at least be able to establish myself as a distinct poet."[14] Huang's succinct preface amounted to an incipient defense of a poetry that would engage the historical present. It affirmed poetic creativity and significance based on the poet's historical consciousness and situation. Hence, his belief that the colloquialisms and vulgar expressions that he introduced into his poetry will be revered as classic treasures by future generations.

In reflecting on the implications of a "poetic revolution," Liang was more interested in his contemporaries' capacity to inject new terms and concepts into their poems. He marveled at one poet's adroitness at employing, all within one poem, the Japanese translations of such Western notions as "the republic," "a representative," "liberty," and "equal rights." Yet such a semantic *tour de force* does not by itself form a coherent poetic voice or style, and Liang

---

11. Ibid. The recent discovery of an early copy of Huang Zunxian's *Renjing lu shi* shows that Liang Qichao and Xia Zengyou wrote a preface and a postscript, respectively, for the volume; see Zhang Yongfang 張永芳, "Shilun 'xin shi'" 試論 "新詩" (On "new poetry"), *Wenxue yichan* 4 (1982): 136n5.

12. Jian Yizhi 簡夷之, ed., *Zhongguo jindai wenlun xuan* 中國近代文論選 (Selections from early modern Chinese literary criticism) (Beijing: Renmin wenxue chubanshe, 1962), 1: 169; Kirk A. Denton, ed., *Modern Chinese Literary Thought: Writings on Literature, 1893–1945* (Stanford: Stanford University Press. 1996), p. 69.

13. For a recent discussion of Huang Zunxian's poetry, see J. D. Schmidt, *Within the Human Realm: The Poetry of Huang Zunxian, 1848–1905* (Cambridge, Eng.: Cambridge University Press, 1994).

14. Jian Yizhi, *Zhongguo jindai wenlun xuan*, 1: 169; Denton, *Modern Chinese Literary Thought*, p. 70.

made it clear that when his friends Xia Zengyou and Tan Sitong studded
their poems with abstruse and exotic expressions culled from various
sources, they stopped being poets altogether. He laughed at himself for following their example and crafting a poem that required lengthy annotation
for it to be understood. Occasional successes aside, Liang saw little sign of a
"true European spirit and thought" in contemporary poetry. The reason,
commented Liang, was that much more than crude and fragmented borrowing needed to be imported. At this, he pledged: "Although I am not a
poet, I will devote my energies to introducing European spirit and thought
so that poetic material will be provided for the future" (22: 190). The "poetic
material" (*shiliao* 詩料) that Liang was determined to import from Europe
resembles the raw material of an exploitative colonial economy, and the implied materiality and transportability of ideas and intellectual concepts underlies his proposal for a poetic revolution. Three days after writing down
his thoughts about the poetic revolution, Liang was engrossed by Tokutomi
Sohō's 德富蘇峰 (1863–1957) *The Future Japan*; what Tokutomi had
achieved, according to Liang, was precisely to introduce "European and
Western ideas into the Japanese language" and initiate a new literary field.
"Should there be a literary revolution in China," noted Liang, "it will have to
begin with the same approach" (22: 191).[15]

The future of poetry thus depended on reinvigorating a native tradition
by appropriating new material, in short, by replenishing it through productive colonization. More important, the revolution in poetry Liang envisioned
would generate a new content largely through an existing form that, as demonstrated in Huang Zunxian's and others' poetry, encompassed a great variety of styles and conventions and could be made to accommodate new
themes and ideas. Such a revolution was imminent because, in Liang's view,
the conditions for a general revolution were ripening day by day. It would
not be long before a Chinese Columbus or Magellan was born. "All of what I
cited above are signs of the development of a revolutionary force, and poetry
is but a small indication thereof" (22: 191). Obviously, the conception of a
poetic revolution embodies some fundamental paradigms of contemporary
reformist thinking. It also reveals aspects of Liang Qichao's political orienta-

---

15. According to Nakamura Tadayuki (quoted in Lin Mingde 林明德, "Liang Qichao de
sanwen licheng" 梁啓超的散文歷程 [The development of Liang Qichao's essay], *Gudian
wenxue* [Taipei] 11 [1993]: 264), Liang Qichao developed a close friendship with the modern
Japanese writer and was determined to become a Chinese Tokutomi.

tion in the wake of the aborted 1898 reforms. As I hope to show in this chapter, the aftermath of the 1898 political reforms should be taken as the self-conscious beginning of the dominant modes of literary production in the twentieth century, in which the concepts of a "poetic revolution" and a "twentieth-century Chinese poetry" were instrumental. The advocacy of a modern-style fiction by Yan Fu 嚴復 (1853–1921) and Liang Qichao may have preceded the call for a poetic revolution by a few critical years, but the programmatic approach to a new poetic language and imagination would prove much more foundational for the development of a new literature in modern China, including the project of "new fiction" launched by Liang in 1902.

There is little doubt that the use of the term *revolution* in this context reflects the radicalization of Liang's thinking from 1898 to 1902, when a millenarian destructionism became a central theme of his voluminous writings and the chief cause of disagreement between himself and his mentor Kang Youwei. Although his references to a "revolutionary condition" and a "revolutionary force" were vague, by linking his call for a new poetry to an impending historical transformation, Liang evidently envisioned the creation of a comprehensive revolutionary movement and culture.[16] Poetry was now charged with a mission and expected to be part of the larger historical unfolding or moment. "Poetic revolution" made poetry writing a serious social and intellectual commitment, and the role of poets was to usher in a new age and new imagination. This elevation of poetry writing prepared the way for the ideas of a "stylistic revolution" and a "revolution in fiction" that Liang Qichao would soon propose. Through a revolutionary transformation, which Liang until 1902 regarded as a noble and heroic enterprise mandated by modernity,[17] poetry, fiction, and writing in general would contribute to the new life. The historical vision and axiomatic paradigm established through the concept of a "poetic revolution" would continue in different forms and guises throughout a large part of the twentieth century. The most salient factor in this new conception of poetry and literature in general was the desire to infuse artistic practice or sensibility with social relevance, to overcome the traditional separation of aesthetic self-cultivation from collective engagement. This ethos was to beset literary discourse in twentieth-

---

16. See Chen Jianhua, "Wan Qing 'shijie geming' yu piping de wenhua jiaolü," pp. 218–19.
17. See Xiaobing Tang, *Global Space and the Nationalist Discourse of Modernity*, pp. 104–5.

century China, if only because the continual social upheavals and reconfigurations radically redefined the status and self-conception of the poet.

This continuity between Liang Qichao's call for a "poetic revolution" and future revolutionary ideologies of literature and arts is better acknowledged in earlier histories of modern Chinese literature, when the rigid ideological division between early/recent modern (*jindai* 近代) and modern (*xiandai* 現代) was yet to be instituted. The division of modern Chinese literature into *jindai* and *xiandai* reflects a political discourse of legitimacy and claims of historical agency and authority. Writing a literary or cultural history that challenges this periodization would necessarily entail the retelling of a story of origins and sources of identity. In the brief *Zhongguo jindai wenxue zhi bianqian* 中國近代文學之變遷 (The transformation of modern Chinese literature; 1929), an early historiographical effort that has subsequently found few echoes, Chen Zizhan 陳子展 traced the origins of modern Chinese literature to the failed political reforms of 1898 and to Liang's proposal for a "poetic revolution." According to Chen, one foundation for the May Fourth literary revolution is Liang Qichao's and his comrades' call for a "poetic revolution." (However, Chen seems to have confused the scattered poetic experiments of Tan Sitong, Xia Zengyou, and Liang himself with Liang's more systematic program for the "poetic revolution."[18] The same confusion appears in Hu Shi's 胡適 [1891–1962] groundbreaking *Wushinian lai Zhongguo zhi wenxue* 五十年來中國之文學 [Chinese literature in the past fifty years; 1923]).[19] In describing the factors contributing to the development of the poetic revolution, Chen Zizhan believed that the proposed abolition of the eight-legged essay and the poetry requirement in the civil-service examinations was as crucial as the impact of foreign ideas.[20]

In his influential *Chinese Literature in the Past Fifty Years*, Hu Shi saw a radical break between the late Qing and 1917, when his own proposal for lit-

---

18. See Chen Zizhan 陳子展, *Zhongguo jindai wenxue zhi bianqian* 中國近代文學之變遷 (The transformation of modern Chinese literature) (Shanghai: China Books, 1929), pp. 7–9.

19. See Zhang Yongfang, "Shilun 'xin shi'"; and Chen Jianhua, "Wan Qing 'shijie geming' yu piping de wenhua jiaolü," pp. 222–23.

20. Chen Zizhan, *Zhongguo jindai wenxue zhi bianqian*, pp. 3–5. Wu Wenqi 吳文祺 (*Jin bainian lai de Zhongguo wenyi sixiang* 近百年來的中國文藝思想 [Chinese literary thought in the past 100 years] [1941; reprinted—Taipei: Congwen shudian, 1971], pp. 23–32), in his overview of Chinese literary thinking from around 1840 to 1925, adopted the same view and suggested that the failure of the political reform movement did not diminish Kang Youwei's and Liang Qichao's impact on literary developments.

erary reforms led to Chen Duxiu's (1917) call for a general "literary revolution." Hu Shi characterized the preceding half-century as a period during which classical Chinese literature experienced its final and slow demise, despite efforts to make an outmoded literature relevant and practical to the new age. The movement for a "literary revolution" in 1917, according to him, was truly revolutionary because it affirmed the living, vernacular language as its resource and justification, and it was bound to be successful because it was a purposeful movement with specific proposals.[21] Hu Shi's historical narrative became the canonical version of the development of modern Chinese literature. This should be of little surprise given the pioneering role played by Hu Shi in the May Fourth era, which has since become the central moment in modern Chinese history.

Indeed, the historical significance of Liang Qichao's proposal for a poetic revolution raises many interesting questions that may profitably be examined in connection with Chen Duxiu's call for a literary revolution in 1917. With the creation, in the inaugural issue of Liang's *New Citizen Journal*, of a poetry forum called "Echoes of Poetic Tidal Waves" ("Shijie chaoyin ji" 詩界潮音集), the movement to renovate Chinese poetry attracted more than forty authors who contributed over 500 poems between 1902 and 1907. The first poem that appeared in this forum is Liang's own irrepressibly exuberant and fantasy-filled "Song of the Pacific in the Twentieth Century," written halfway through his journey to Hawaii. While tracing the origins of the new literature of the May Fourth era, Zhou Zuoren 周作人 (1885–1967) commented that Liang Qichao and his comrades "created a condition ripe for the literary revolution." There is ample evidence that the earlier poetic revolution was a spiritual forerunner of the literary revolution, especially if we adopt an evolutionary view of literary history and development.[22] Not surprisingly, the new poetry that Liang promoted has usually been represented as a transitional stage that led to the May Fourth literary revolution.[23] Yet

---

21. Hu Shi 胡適, *Wushinian lai Zhongguo zhi wenxue* 五十年來中國之文學 (Chinese literature in the past fifty years) (1923); reprinted in *Hu Shi xueshu wenji: xin wenxue yundong* 胡適學術文集: 新文學運動 (Scholarly essays by Hu Shi: the new literature movement), ed. Jiang Yihua 姜義華, pp. 94–160 (Beijing: Zhonghua shuju, 1993), pp. 96–97.

22. See, e.g., Wu Wenqi, *Jin bainian lai de Zhongguo wenyi sixiang*.

23. See Helmut Martin, "A Transitional Concept of Chinese Literature 1897–1917: Liang Ch'i Ch'ao on Poetry-Reform, Historical Drama and the Political Novel," *Oriens Extremus* 20 (1973): esp. pp. 206–8; Lü Meisheng 呂美生, "Shilun wan Qing 'shijie geming' de yiyi" 試論晚清"詩界革命"的意義 (On the significance of the "poetic revolution" of the late Qing),

between these two separate calls for a revolution there was also a world of difference, most notably in the imaginary relationship to Europe, which reflects an altered self-image and conception. A shared intellectual genealogy should not obscure the historical conditions that prompted Liang Qichao and Chen Duxiu to advocate their respective visions of a new poetry or literature. It may ultimately be misleading to suggest that Liang's poetic revolution was a prerequisite for Chen Duxiu's literary revolution. Different logics and concerns underlie these two separate historical moments, especially in regard to the dialectics of form and content. In other words, the differences in literary conceptions between 1899 and 1917 should not be overshadowed by the more evident continuity in the efforts to promote the social and ideological functions of literary practice.

For Liang, as we have seen, the new poetry depends on the cultivation of a new imagination that is emphatically European-oriented. Colonization, naturalized as much by social Darwinist thinking as by the prevailing capitalist mode of production, provided a powerful system through which Liang could articulate the necessity of discovering a new poetic content/continent. Informed by this belief, Liang could go on and imagine Europe being colonized in turn and made to accommodate a new, expanded Chinese poetry. This incorporation is endorsed as such a heroic and self-confident deed that the indigenous identity of the anticipated new poetry is never in question. In other words, Liang did not believe that the aggressive cannibalization of European ideas and expressions would make the new poetry un-Chinese. On the contrary, his confidence in the capacity of Chinese poetry to absorb new and heterogeneous elements was unbounded.

The reasons for this confidence are complex and multifarious. One general reason is that the nationalist ideology that Liang and his generation of Chinese embraced at the turn of the twentieth century was still largely a geopolitical awareness or anxiety rather than a well-articulated historical movement or political institution. Even the ill-fated, proto-nationalist Boxer Rebellion was yet to erupt into the open and cause much consternation among the better educated, more privileged, and more cosmopolitan members of the population. As nationalist discourse began to create a collective consciousness of national destiny and difference, it also readily lent itself to legitimating the new world system, in which the modernizing colonial enterprise appeared both

---

Wenxue yichan zengkan 1961, no. 8: 73–94; Julia Lin, *Modern Chinese Poetry: An Introduction* (Seattle: University of Washington Press, 1972), pp. 18–27.

rational and natural. Thus, colonization was not so much denounced as celebrated as inseparable from civilization, a sign of industrial and universal modernity. Just as national self-determination was not at this stage pursued as a political objective both independent of and in conjunction with world civilization, so cultural nationalism was yet to be articulated as a critique of Western modernity. More specifically, the monarchy as the inherited form of centralized governance and cultural order was not yet systematically questioned or delegitimated as such. In addition, the Qing empire was so large geographically that, even though continually threatened since the mid-nineteenth century, it still served as an image of some grand and inexhaustible resilience. The consciousness of a crisis was often the negative expression of a profound disbelief that such a rich and enduring civilization as the Chinese universe would have no place in the modern world. In fact, a crucial component of modern Chinese nationalism was the rhetoric of restoring past glory, which led Liang Qichao and his contemporaries to see, for instance, striking similarities in destiny between China and Greece or Italy. This sense of a mission to restore the Chinese heritage was given full expression in Liang Qichao's "Ode to Young China" (after Mazzini's Young Italy), written to celebrate the arrival of the twentieth century and published simultaneously with his *Travels to Hawaii* in *New Citizen Journal* (February 1900). The rhetorical operation is an intricate balancing act in which both past grandeur must be unequivocally affirmed and the current bleak conditions need to be acknowledged, if only as that which temporarily eclipses the brilliance of the nation. Consequently, much of reformist discourse centered on institutional transformations that would allow the country to modernize itself quickly and strengthen the government militarily and economically. As late as 1902, for example, Liang Qichao would comment that "although China has fallen behind in almost everything, in literature alone it seems to be able to compete with the West."[24] Cultural iconoclasm of the May Fourth intensity, in other words, was not yet on the agenda. As a result there was little effort at institutionalizing a national form or "national literature," as Hu Shi would later advocate. Liang Qichao himself, too, would devote much energy, in the last decade of his life, to systematizing a national cultural heritage. Or, to put this differently, the consciousness of a crisis was not yet so comprehensive as to lead people to question the validity or usefulness of the native literary tradition in its entirety.

---

24. Liang Qichao, *Yinbingshi shihua*, p. 4.

A second and related reason for Liang's confidence is related to the status of poetry writing and its limited social value or practical impact. The ability to compose poetry was largely seen as indicative of good training in the classics and sound aesthetic cultivation, and the literati would often turn to poetry to record their personal sentiments and experiences. Poetry was predominantly a private practice, even though the flourishing of a print journalism was radically changing that situation. Prose, as Ted Huters observes,[25] was quickly becoming the preferred medium for social commentary and engagement. In what would become the standard practice in journals, in Liang Qichao's *China Discussion*, essays and treatises occupied the most prominent sections, and poetry was inevitably included as a supplement. Liang's promotion of "new fiction" in 1902 was based on his understanding of the vital relationship between the popular novel and social progress. The limited and private role given to poetry won poets a certain license, since poetry was not part of the extensive symbolism of nationalism that was rapidly developing. A good case in point is Liang Qichao's decision, only two days after he expounded his views on poetic revolution, to give up poetry as a distracting addiction.[26]

A third and also general explanation for Liang's confidence revolves around the dialectics of form and content, or the familiar tension between Western application and Chinese essence that dominated historical imagination at the time. On one level, Liang apparently believed that Chinese poetry was such a highly developed and versatile form that it could absorb fresh, even alien, elements and raw material. Classical poetry has its own metric patterns, stylistic conventions, and layered cultural associations; yet for Liang it was also an open and adaptable form that will survive through expansion. Liang did not perceive poetic form, or more specifically the formal structure of classical poetry, as a problem or hindrance. On the contrary, the embedded prestige, if not ultimate inalienability, of the form itself allows for the search for new contents. Poetic form, in other words, becomes an in-

---

25. Theodore Huters, "A New Way of Writing: The Possibilities for Literature in Late Qing China, 1895–1908," *Modern China* 14, no. 3 (1988): 243–76.

26. Liang broke his solemn resolution four days later. Toward midnight on December 31, 1899, the last day of a stormy century, while he was in the middle of the Pacific Ocean, "the most pivotal bridging area in the world," Liang wrote: "Drinking and murmuring alone, I grow bitter with boredom, / So I will sing a majestic song for my Pacific of the twentieth century" (*Xinmin congbao*, 1: 109).

nate, self-affirming practice that anchors continuity and familiarity. By assuming the "old style" to be a stable and yet open structure, Liang reaffirmed poetic form as a tradition, which would in turn offset the radicalness of his call for appropriating new poetic contents/continents. By 1902, Liang would formulate this strategic adherence to a formal continuity into the notion of "containing a new imagination within the old style," which was then defined as "the essence of the poetic revolution."[27] This approach to the question of form certainly coincided with Liang's political ideology: namely, the modernization of China was best carried out with the blessing and mooring provided by the symbolic structure of the monarchy. Interestingly enough, Hu Shi, in his critical review of literary developments from 1872 to 1912, would categorize the general tendency as "a reform movement within the boundaries of classical literature," in which he included Liang's promotion of a "poetic revolution" and poems by Huang Zunxian.[28] Yet such efforts at making classical literature useful and adaptable, in Hu Shi's account, were of a transitional nature at best and altogether misguided at worst—a value judgment enabled by a different historical vision and ideological commitment.

On another related level, the classical poetic style that Liang posited as the ultimate criterion (new concepts and expressions still had to abide by poetic conventions) helped deflect, surreptitiously, the growing concern with national essence into a question of form. In commenting on Liang's poetics, critic Xia Xiaohong suggests that Liang had a different attitude toward poetry than toward fiction.[29] Liang regarded classical poetry as superior to the novel, partly because of his elite training and emotional attachments and partly because for him these two literary genres serve different symbolic and aesthetic functions. For Liang, a novel could draw on an admixture of different genres and might even derive its strength from an equalizing heteroglossia, but poetry ought to be much more deliberate and observe the conventions. It should not lose what sets it apart as a refined and culturally specific means of artistic self-expression. If the popular novel may aspire to be fully at the service of modern society, expressive poetry is then charged with the arduous task of confronting the new and, by extension, maintaining a critical (even playful) tension with modernity. Against this background, the radicalness as much as the seriousness of the literary revolution that Chen Duxiu

---

27. Liang Qichao, *Yinbingshi shihua*, p. 51.
28. Hu Shi, *Wushinian lai Zhongguo zhi wenxue*, pp. 94–95.
29. Xia Xiaohong, *Jueshi yu chuanshi*, p. 163.

advocated at the outset of the May Fourth period becomes much more pronounced. What Chen Duxiu denounced is precisely the "old style," the deliberate, elaborate, and often restrictive form that served as an indicator of social and cultural distinctions and boundaries. Hence his well-known, sweeping characterization of the native literary tradition in terms of its formal inadequacy: "the ornate, sycophantic literature of aristocracy," "the stale, pompous classical literature," and "the obscure, abstruse eremitic literature."[30]

As I suggested in my 1996 study of Liang Qichao, there is an undeniable intellectual, spiritual, even lexicological continuity between revolutionary discourse developed in Tokyo at the turn of the twentieth century and that in the Beijing of the May Fourth period. The opening paragraph of Chen Duxiu's essay on the "literary revolution," for example, repeats verbatim several sentences from Liang Qichao's 1902 essay "Shi ge" 釋革 (Defining ge).[31] In "On Literary Revolution," Chen Duxiu articulated the same fascination with modern European civilization ("From whence arose the awesome and brilliant Europe of today? I say from the legacy of revolution"). Yet his strategy is no longer to "contain a new imagination within old style," but to revolutionize the literary form itself. The new literary form that will lead to the creation of a new society is "the plain, expressive literature of the people," "a fresh, sincere realist literature," and "a comprehensible, popularized social literature." Just as a new social content, the transformation of literary forms became as much a part of the May Fourth revolutionary agenda as the transformation of the political form that Chinese modernity sought to assume. Since its founding, the new republic had been mired in continual legitimacy crises. Similarly, if we pursue this line of inquiry and read conceptions of literary form as emblematic of larger social structure or ideology, Liang Qichao's insistence that new ideas must be creatively welded onto old style is also extremely revealing. The reformist thinking during and after the 1898 reform period consisted of preserving (in fact restoring) the monarchy as a porous structure into which new social values, cultural practices, and legal systems could be grafted and instituted. The monarchy itself was to become a largely symbolic form that functioned to signify the stabilizing per-

---

30. Chen Duxiu 陳獨秀, "Wenxue geming lun" 文學革命論 (On literary revolution) (1917); trans. from Denton, *Modern Chinese Literary Thought*, p. 141.

31. Xiaobing Tang, *Global Space and the Nationalist Discourse of Modernity*, pp. 163–64, 170–72.

sistence of the native tradition at a time when European modernity was being creatively engaged and indeed actively cannibalized.

Whereas Liang Qichao sought a European-oriented imagination as the new content for Chinese poetry, what Chen Duxiu and Hu Shi called for, in the end, was the Europeanization of the Chinese language as well as literary forms and practices. Herein lies the iconoclastic force of May Fourth thinking. "Beneath the May Fourth reification of a malignant tradition," as Kirk Denton suggests, "lay a profound unspoken anxiety about molding a culture without attachments to the past."[32] The modernist pursuit of the new and its accompanying valorization of shock value, in comparison, undergird Chen Duxiu's and his comrades' agenda for a radically new literature. In contrast, Liang Qichao's strategy for the poetic revolution was precisely to absorb the initial shock, to forestall the disorienting effect, as he would put it, of bizarre creatures plucked from remote planets. The newness of modernity is far from an absolute value or mandate; rather, Liang regards it as a replenishing resource that needs skilled and careful administering. The modern vernacular (*baihua* 白話) literature endorsed by the May Fourth movement, from free-verse poetry to the short story to the modern novel, was a heavily Europeanized literary form because both form and content were now compelled to be new, to be the negation of tradition. Such pervasive European influence would be critically rethought and even rejected, for example, by Qu Qiubai 瞿秋白 (1899–1935) in the early 1930s[33] and more poignantly during the 1940s when an extensive debate on the question of native forms erupted in drastically altered political and intellectual circumstances. A selective return to the native, even folksy, form in the disguise of revolutionary literature after the Yan'an Forum in 1942 signaled yet another turn in the enduring dialectics of form and content in the history of twentieth-century Chinese literature.

If the turn to prose is one ineluctable consequence of global modernity, Liang Qichao's concern with preserving "the classical style of poetry" was indeed a doomed effort. His effort belongs to a series of increasingly desperate attempts (one may think of Wang Guowei 王國維 [1877–1927], for instance, as such a tragic cultural hero) to resist the steady replacement of figurative language by referential language in a process of universal disenchant-

---

32. Denton, *Modern Chinese Literary Thought*, p. 11.
33. See, e.g., ibid., pp. 418–27.

ment. Although the modern ideology of unifying language and speech (its apparent triumph in the Japanese context greatly inspired Huang Zunxian and Liang Qichao) was the basis for Hu Shi's famous "Modest Proposals for the Reform of Literature" and his subsequent theorizations, it also entailed an irrevocable departure from the classical poetic world. As far as modern Chinese literary discourse is concerned, the poetic revolution that Liang proposed defined a basic issue for the first time: What role is to be given the native form when new contents demand to be expressed? Or, if this seems to be a false problem, we may understand the real question to be: How does one claim agency in making sense of and representing a new, changed world? How does one reconcile aesthetic habits with the lived experience of modernity? By addressing the need for a poetic revolution, Liang implicitly argued that form is a claim to identity and destiny. His reflections on the task of poetry in a turbulent age of cultural and historical reorientations underline a widespread desire to find a secure medium through which to process the new and the shocking. Modern ideas, concepts, images, and realities should be expressed through existing and familiar forms, because form is more than a mere external, disposable connection to the past. For Liang, it is our access to this particular form of poetry that allows us to reflect on and articulate our situated, inescapable relationship to the modern world. In this sense, the poetic form that Liang wished to preserve held out the possibility of erecting a porous and flexible structure of subjectivity that added depth to modernity even as it kept at bay the leveling experience of the modern.

For this reason, I would suggest that the concept of a poetic revolution, fleeting as it may have been in modern Chinese literary thinking, points to Liang's critical recognition of poetic form as a symbolic enactment of selfhood that we can hardly dispense with. Embedded in it is the possibility of regarding modernity as an open-ended and productive process, of proactively coping with the rift between the powerful and the disenfranchised, the rich and the impoverished, the more advanced and the less developed. It is far from a fundamentalist adherence to some immutable truth because the strategy of "welding new ideas onto an old style" suggests a playfulness in taming the exotic and in the end drives home the historical processes and subjectivities transmitted through the literary form itself. Hence Liang's prioritization of an effective, sustainable poetic revolution in 1902: "In an age of transition, there is bound to be revolution. What constitutes revolution, however, is transformation in the spirit, rather than of the form."[34] The fact that this poetic revolution is often alleged to have failed, especially when compared with May Fourth aspirations, only indicates the extent to which we have succeeded in disavowing or repressing residual forms of identity or experience that conflict with our sense of belonging in an age of globalization in which differences are increasingly the same.

---

34. Liang Qichao, *Yinbingshi shihua*, p. 51.

Index

Index

1898 reforms, 1, 2, 3, 4, 7–9, 15, 216, 220, 233

Bao Chuan hui 保川會 (Protect Sichuan society), 145
Bao Dian hui 保滇會 (Protect Yunnan society), 145
Baoguo hui 保國會 (Protect the country society), 144–46
Bao Zhe hui 保浙會 (Protect Zhejiang society), 145
Beijing 北京, 13, 124–57
Beijing nübao 北京女報 (Beijing women's news), 223, 227
Boxer Rebellion, 258

Cai Yuanpei 蔡元培, 122–23
cainü 才女 (women of talent), 14, 164–68, 169, 185–88, 210
Chen Baozhen 陳寶箴, 88, 96
Chen Duxiu 陳獨秀, 217–18, 236, 248, 257–58, 261–63
Chen Xiefen 陳擷芬, 163, 227–29
Chen Yan'an 陳嚴安, 172, 174
Chen Yiyi 陳以益, 177, 241n63
Chinese learning (zhongxue 中學), 102–4, 108, 111–22
Chunqiu 春秋 (Spring and autumn annals), 43–44

citizenship, 20, 32
Civil-service examinations, 102, 118
colonization, 15, 217–18, 249–50, 258–59
Confucius, 34, 43–44
Confucianism: and reformers, 21, 45–46; in Kang Youwei, 24–31 passim, 62–69 passim; in Liang Qichao, 34, 43–44
Constitutional monarchism, see Monarchy
Curriculum, 104, 112, 114–17, 119–21

Dao 道 (the Way), 91
democracy, 20, 22, 25, 32, 36–37, 39, 42; in thought of Liang Qichao, 33–34, 35, 45, 61. See also minquan
Ding Chuwo 丁初我, 240, 241
Dong Zhongshu 董仲舒, 28

education, modern, 188–89, 207–8
Empress Dowager Cixi, 78, 99, 102, 114, 116–17
Epistemology, 101, 110, 121–22
Europe, 248–54 passim, 258, 262–63

Fa 法 (institutions), 91
family, 213, 220–25 passim, 232–42 passim

female literacy, 158–79 *passim*
female overseas students, 159, 162–64,
　　167–69, 172–79
Feng Guifen 馮桂芬, 105–6
footbinding, 171–73

gender, 13, 212, 220; and nationalism,
　　212, 220, 242–44
gentry-activists (*zhishi* 志士), 38–39
global universal, 190–91
gong 公 (public), 35, 38, 40
gongche shangshu 公車上書 (Petition-
　　ing of the emperor by the examina-
　　tion candidates), 136–41, 146
Gongai hui 共愛會 (Humanitarian
　　association), 167–68, 169
Gu Hongming 辜鴻銘, 83
Guangxu 光緒 emperor, 19, 23, 30, 33,
　　46, 99, 102, 116, 245
Guanzi 管子, 26. *See also* Legalism
guomin 國民 (citizen / national peo-
　　ple), 218–20

He Qi 何啓, 85
He Xiangning 何香凝, 167
He Zhen 何震, 163, 175–76, 234–5
Howe, Gertrude, 188, 192–95, 198
Hu Liyuan 胡禮垣, 85
Hu Shi 胡適, 256–64 *passim*
Huang Zunxian 黃遵憲, 64, 74, 252–
　　53, 254, 261, 264
Hubei Translation Bureau (Hubei
　　yishu ju 湖北譯書局), 52, 56, 63,
　　68
Hubei xuesheng jie 湖北學生界 (Hubei
　　students), 163

Imperial University (Jingshi daxue-
　　tang 京師大學堂), 12, 13, 99–123

Japan, 99, 102, 105–6, 108–9, 117, 159,
　　160–61, 162–63, 167, 172, 177, 178,
　　245–46, 247
Jiangsu 江蘇, 163, 167, 168
Jing Yuanshan 經元善, 161, 164, 169,
　　171, 175
journalism, 48–76

Kang Aide, aka Ida Kahn 康愛德, 14,
　　180–211
Kang Guangren 康光仁, 146
Kang Tongwei 康同薇, 161, 164–72
　　passim
Kang Youwei 康有爲, 21–36 *passim*,
　　42, 44–45, 56, 64–66, 67, 72, 73, 78,
　　80–83, 91n, 97, 100, 129, 134–35, 137,
　　140–41, 143, 148, 151, 161, 246, 255
Kashiwabara Buntarō 柏原文太朗,
　　246
kingship, *see* monarchy

"Late Qing personality ideal," 82–83
Legalism, 27, 29, 31, 46
Levenson, Joseph, 103–5, 113, 121–22
Liang Qichao 梁啓超, 15, 21–23, 33–45
　　passim, 56, 57, 61, 62, 64, 69, 70, 72,
　　78, 80–83, 88, 96–97, 99, 102, 104,
　　106, 109–23 *passim*, 135, 137, 154, 161,
　　165, 169, 170–71, 172, 180–82, 218–20,
　　222, 233, 236, 245–65
Lienü zhuan 列女傳 (Biographies of
　　women), 186–87
Lin Xu 林旭, 135, 143, 146
literary revolution, 248, 257–58, 261
literati clubs, 18
Liu Guangdi 劉光第, 143
lyrical tradition, 185

Mai Menghua 麥孟華, 22, 36–38

May Fourth movement/period, 1, 7, 8, 100–101, 122–23, 183, 208–15 *passim*, 244, 248, 257, 259, 262–63, 265

Minxuehui 閩學會 (Fujian study society), 143

minquan 民權 (popular power), 11, 19, 22, 39n, 42, 47, 48, 83–86. *See also* democracy

minzhi 民智 (popular enlightenment), 54

missionaries, American, 191–94

modernity, 2, 5–7, 9, 10, 20, 31, 100–101, 103, 106, 108–9, 112–13, 119–23, 243–44, 259, 263–64

modernization, 4, 10

monarchy, 23, 45–47, 245, 259, 261–62; reformers' concepts of, 19–24; Kang Youwei on, 24–33, 44–45; Liang Qichao on, 33–36, 38–45; Mai Menghua on, 36–38; Ou Qu-jia on, 42–43

National Beijing University (*Beida* 北大), 100–101, 123

national identity, 19, 24

nationalism, 13, 158, 160, 162, 164, 167, 173–74, 175, 178, 187, 198, 208, 212, 213, 221, 222, 233, 258–60

Nationalist Party (Guomindang 國民黨), establishment of, 153–54

native-place lodges (*huiguan* 會館), 124–57

new fiction, 248, 260

"new" woman, 14

Nübao 女報 (National women's journal), 240–41

Nüxue bao 女學報 (Journal of women's studies), 163

Nüzi shijie 女子世界 (Women's world), 229, 230, 239, 240

Ou Qujia 歐榘甲, 42–43

poetic revolution, 15, 247–48, 250, 253, 265

Poland, 226–27

politics, 10, 12; and the state, 10–11, 12; and women, 213

Qiangxue hui 強學會 (Society for the study of self-strengthening), 142–43

Qingshi gao 清史稿 (Draft of Qing history), 83

Qingyi bao 清義報 (China discussion), 250, 260

Qiu Fengjia 丘逢甲, 248

Qiu Jin 秋瑾, 202, 234–35

Qu Qiubai 瞿秋白, 263

Quanxue pian 勸學篇 (Exhortation on learning), 74, 77–98

radicalism, 4n, 12

reformers, 24, 33; and the monarchy, 19–24, 45–47; and Confucianism, 21

ren 仁 (benevolence), 24, 28, 35

republicanism, 245

Rongqing, 117

Richard, Timothy, 85

sagehood, 43–46

Self-strengthening movement, 105–7

Shuxuehui 蜀學會 (Sichuan study society), 143

Shang Yang 商鞅, 26

Shimoda Utako 下田歌子, 174

Shiwu bao 時務報 (China progress), 11, 48–76, 82, 85, 181

"slavery," 14, 212–44 *passim*

society / the social, 10, 12, 13; and state relations, 18

Song Shu 宋恕, 160–61

Songyun an 松筠庵, 137–41

Songyun caotang 嵩雲草堂, 139–40, 142, 145

statecraft (jingshi 經世), 49, 62–69 passim

Sun Jia'nai 孫家鼐, 72–74, 102, 107–9, 114, 142, 149–50

Sun Yat-sen, 67, 153, 245

Tan Sitong 譚嗣同, 80, 129, 131, 135, 146, 248, 254, 256

Three Ages, 33–35, 43–44

Tianyi 天義 (Natural justice), 163, 175

Tokutomi Sohō 德富蘇峰, 254

ti/yong 體/用 (essence/function), 12, 79–83, 102–6, 111–22 passim

Tongwen guan 同文館 (Interpreters' college), 105, 107

United States of America, 245–46, 250

Wang Anshi 王安石, 91

Wang Guowei 王國維, 263

Wang Kangnian 汪康年, 22, 42, 54–62 passim, 66, 67, 68, 74, 75

Wang Lian 王蓮, 168, 172–73

Wang Xianqian 王先謙, 88

wangguo 亡國 (lost country), 217–19, 227–28, 231, 243

wangguo nu 亡國奴 (slave of a lost country), 217, 223, 227–28, 230–31, 235

Weixin pai 維新派 (Constitutional reformers), 83

Wen Tingshi 文廷式, 137–38, 147

Western Learning (xixue 西學), 102–8 passim, 111–22 passim

women, 14; and education, 158–79 passim, 188–89, 202, 232, 237–38, 239;

and nationalism, 158, 160, 162, 164, 167, 173–74, 175, 178, 212, 213–15, 221, 222, 233; and journals, 162–63; and citizenship, 170, 171, 175, 188, 198, 213, 221–22, 233, 237–41; and physical education, 171; and economics, 170, 173; and status, 182; and subjectivity, 212, 213; "as slaves" (nüzi wei nuli 女子爲奴隸), 213–16, 223, 228, 230, 235; and "the people," 221, 222, 231, 238

Women's Foreign Missionary Society, 193, 195, 198, 205

world system, 249

Xia Zengyou 夏曾祐, 248, 254, 256

Xiang xue bao 湘學報, 85

Xiao Hong 蕭紅, 210

Xie Zhen 謝震, 240–41

Xinmin congbao 新民叢報 (The new citizen journal), 251, 257

Xu Renzhu 徐仁鑄, 88

Xuannan 宣南 area (Beijing), 130, 134, 136–38, 141–47 passim, 152–53, 156

Yan Fu 嚴復, 53, 58, 59–60, 61, 80n9, 86, 107, 161, 165–66, 169–71, 173, 175, 255

Yang Rui 楊銳, 135, 143, 150

Yang Shenxiu 楊深秀, 135, 146

Yangwu pai 洋務派 (Foreign affairs group), 83

Ye Dehui 葉德輝, 88

Yijiao congbian 翼教叢編 (A general collection to protect the faith), 88, 95

yinjie 印結 (chopped bonds), 133, 140–41

Yuan Mei 袁枚, 162

Yuexue hui 粵學會 (Guangdong study society), 143

Zhang Baixi 張百熙, 111, 114–21, 123
Zhang Binglin 章炳麟, 66, 94
Zhang Xuecheng 章學誠, 162
Zhang Zhidong 張之洞, 11, 12, 49, 50–76 *passim*, 77–98, 102–3, 105, 111, 117–23, 233

Zhang Zhujun 張竹君, 202
Zhejiang chao 浙江潮 (Tides of Zhejiang), 163
Zhexue hui 浙學會 (Zhejiang study society), 143
Zheng Guanying 鄭觀應, 160
Zhou Zuoren 周作人, 257
Zhu Yixin 朱一新, 88

Harvard East Asian Monographs
(* out-of-print)

*1.   Liang Fang-chung, *The Single-Whip Method of Taxation in China*

*2.   Harold C. Hinton, *The Grain Tribute System of China, 1845–1911*

3.   Ellsworth C. Carlson, *The Kaiping Mines, 1877–1912*

*4.   Chao Kuo-chün, *Agrarian Policies of Mainland China: A Documentary Study, 1949–1956*

*5.   Edgar Snow, *Random Notes on Red China, 1936–1945*

*6.   Edwin George Beal, Jr., *The Origin of Likin, 1835–1864*

7.   Chao Kuo-chün, *Economic Planning and Organization in Mainland China: A Documentary Study, 1949–1957*

*8.   John K. Fairbank, *Ching Documents: An Introductory Syllabus*

*9.   Helen Yin and Yi-chang Yin, *Economic Statistics of Mainland China, 1949–1957*

*10. Wolfgang Franke, *The Reform and Abolition of the Traditional Chinese Examination System*

11. Albert Feuerwerker and S. Cheng, *Chinese Communist Studies of Modern Chinese History*

12. C. John Stanley, *Late Ching Finance: Hu Kuang-yung as an Innovator*

13. S. M. Meng, *The Tsungli Yamen: Its Organization and Functions*

*14. Ssu-yü Teng, *Historiography of the Taiping Rebellion*

15. Chun-Jo Liu, *Controversies in Modern Chinese Intellectual History: An Analytic Bibliography of Periodical Articles, Mainly of the May Fourth and Post–May Fourth Era*

*16. Edward J. M. Rhoads, *The Chinese Red Army, 1927–1963: An Annotated Bibliography*

17. Andrew J. Nathan, *A History of the China International Famine Relief Commission*

*18. Frank H. H. King (ed.) and Prescott Clarke, *A Research Guide to China-Coast Newspapers, 1822–1911*

19. Ellis Joffe, *Party and Army: Professionalism and Political Control in the Chinese Officer Corps, 1949–1964*

*20. Toshio G. Tsukahira, *Feudal Control in Tokugawa Japan: The Sankin Kōtai System*

21. Kwang-Ching Liu, ed., *American Missionaries in China: Papers from Harvard Seminars*

22. George Moseley, *A Sino-Soviet Cultural Frontier: The Ili Kazakh Autonomous Chou*

23. Carl F. Nathan, *Plague Prevention and Politics in Manchuria, 1910–1931*

*24. Adrian Arthur Bennett, *John Fryer: The Introduction of Western Science and Technology into Nineteenth-Century China*

25. Donald J. Friedman, *The Road from Isolation: The Campaign of the American Committee for Non-Participation in Japanese Aggression, 1938–1941*

26. Edward LeFevour, *Western Enterprise in Late Ching China: A Selective Survey of Jardine, Matheson and Company's Operations, 1842–1895*

27. Charles Neuhauser, *Third World Politics: China and the Afro-Asian People's Solidarity Organization, 1957–1967*

28. Kungtu C. Sun, assisted by Ralph W. Huenemann, *The Economic Development of Manchuria in the First Half of the Twentieth Century*

*29. Shahid Javed Burki, *A Study of Chinese Communes, 1965*

30. John Carter Vincent, *The Extraterritorial System in China: Final Phase*

31. Madeleine Chi, *China Diplomacy, 1914–1918*

*32. Clifton Jackson Phillips, *Protestant America and the Pagan World: The First Half Century of the American Board of Commissioners for Foreign Missions, 1810–1860*

33. James Pusey, *Wu Han: Attacking the Present through the Past*

34. Ying-wan Cheng, *Postal Communication in China and Its Modernization, 1860–1896*

35. Tuvia Blumenthal, *Saving in Postwar Japan*

36. Peter Frost, *The Bakumatsu Currency Crisis*

37. Stephen C. Lockwood, *Augustine Heard and Company, 1858–1862*

38. Robert R. Campbell, *James Duncan Campbell: A Memoir by His Son*

39. Jerome Alan Cohen, ed., *The Dynamics of China's Foreign Relations*

40. V. V. Vishnyakova-Akimova, *Two Years in Revolutionary China, 1925–1927*, tr. Steven L. Levine

*41. Meron Medzini, *French Policy in Japan during the Closing Years of the Tokugawa Regime*

42. Ezra Vogel, Margie Sargent, Vivienne B. Shue, Thomas Jay Mathews, and Deborah S. Davis, *The Cultural Revolution in the Provinces*

*43. Sidney A. Forsythe, *An American Missionary Community in China, 1895–1905*

*44. Benjamin I. Schwartz, ed., *Reflections on the May Fourth Movement.: A Symposium*

*45. Ching Young Choe, *The Rule of the Taewŏngun, 1864–1873: Restoration in Yi Korea*

46. W. P. J. Hall, *A Bibliographical Guide to Japanese Research on the Chinese Economy, 1958–1970*

47. Jack J. Gerson, *Horatio Nelson Lay and Sino-British Relations, 1854–1864*

48. Paul Richard Bohr, *Famine and the Missionary: Timothy Richard as Relief Administrator and Advocate of National Reform*

49. Endymion Wilkinson, *The History of Imperial China: A Research Guide*

50. Britten Dean, *China and Great Britain: The Diplomacy of Commercial Relations, 1860–1864*

51. Ellsworth C. Carlson, *The Foochow Missionaries, 1847–1880*

Harvard East Asian Monographs

52. Yeh-chien Wang, *An Estimate of the Land-Tax Collection in China, 1753 and 1908*

53. Richard M. Pfeffer, *Understanding Business Contracts in China, 1949–1963*

54. Han-sheng Chuan and Richard Kraus, *Mid-Ching Rice Markets and Trade: An Essay in Price History*

55. Ranbir Vohra, *Lao She and the Chinese Revolution*

56. Liang-lin Hsiao, *China's Foreign Trade Statistics, 1864–1949*

*57. Lee-hsia Hsu Ting, *Government Control of the Press in Modern China, 1900–1949*

58. Edward W. Wagner, *The Literati Purges: Political Conflict in Early Yi Korea*

*59. Joungwon A. Kim, *Divided Korea: The Politics of Development, 1945–1972*

*60. Noriko Kamachi, John K. Fairbank, and Chūzō Ichiko, *Japanese Studies of Modern China Since 1953: A Bibliographical Guide to Historical and Social-Science Research on the Nineteenth and Twentieth Centuries, Supplementary Volume for 1953–1969*

61. Donald A. Gibbs and Yun-chen Li, *A Bibliography of Studies and Translations of Modern Chinese Literature, 1918–1942*

62. Robert H. Silin, *Leadership and Values: The Organization of Large-Scale Taiwanese Enterprises*

63. David Pong, *A Critical Guide to the Kwangtung Provincial Archives Deposited at the Public Record Office of London*

*64. Fred W. Drake, *China Charts the World: Hsu Chi-yü and His Geography of 1848*

*65. William A. Brown and Urgrunge Onon, translators and annotators, *History of the Mongolian People's Republic*

66. Edward L. Farmer, *Early Ming Government: The Evolution of Dual Capitals*

*67. Ralph C. Croizier, *Koxinga and Chinese Nationalism: History, Myth, and the Hero*

*68. William J. Tyler, tr., *The Psychological World of Natsume Sōseki*, by Doi Takeo

69. Eric Widmer, *The Russian Ecclesiastical Mission in Peking during the Eighteenth Century*

*70. Charlton M. Lewis, *Prologue to the Chinese Revolution: The Transformation of Ideas and Institutions in Hunan Province, 1891–1907*

71. Preston Torbert, *The Ching Imperial Household Department: A Study of Its Organization and Principal Functions, 1662–1796*

72. Paul A. Cohen and John E. Schrecker, eds., *Reform in Nineteenth-Century China*

73. Jon Sigurdson, *Rural Industrialism in China*

74. Kang Chao, *The Development of Cotton Textile Production in China*

75. Valentin Rabe, *The Home Base of American China Missions, 1880–1920*

*76. Sarasin Viraphol, *Tribute and Profit: Sino-Siamese Trade, 1652–1853*

77. Ch'i-ch'ing Hsiao, *The Military Establishment of the Yuan Dynasty*

78. Meishi Tsai, *Contemporary Chinese Novels and Short Stories, 1949–1974: An Annotated Bibliography*

*79. Wellington K. K. Chan, *Merchants, Mandarins and Modern Enterprise in Late Ching China*

80. Endymion Wilkinson, *Landlord and Labor in Late Imperial China: Case Studies from Shandong by Jing Su and Luo Lun*

*81. Barry Keenan, *The Dewey Experiment in China: Educational Reform and Political Power in the Early Republic*

*82. George A. Hayden, *Crime and Punishment in Medieval Chinese Drama: Three Judge Pao Plays*

*83. Sang-Chul Suh, *Growth and Structural Changes in the Korean Economy, 1910–1940*

84. J. W. Dower, *Empire and Aftermath: Yoshida Shigeru and the Japanese Experience, 1878–1954*

85. Martin Collcutt, *Five Mountains: The Rinzai Zen Monastic Institution in Medieval Japan*

86. Kwang Suk Kim and Michael Roemer, *Growth and Structural Transformation*

87. Anne O. Krueger, *The Developmental Role of the Foreign Sector and Aid*

*88. Edwin S. Mills and Byung-Nak Song, *Urbanization and Urban Problems*

89. Sung Hwan Ban, Pal Yong Moon, and Dwight H. Perkins, *Rural Development*

*90. Noel F. McGinn, Donald R. Snodgrass, Yung Bong Kim, Shin-Bok Kim, and Quee-Young Kim, *Education and Development in Korea*

91. Leroy P. Jones and Il SaKong, *Government, Business, and Entrepreneurship in Economic Development: The Korean Case*

92. Edward S. Mason, Dwight H. Perkins, Kwang Suk Kim, David C. Cole, Mahn Je Kim et al., *The Economic and Social Modernization of the Republic of Korea*

93. Robert Repetto, Tai Hwan Kwon, Son-Ung Kim, Dae Young Kim, John E. Sloboda, and Peter J. Donaldson, *Economic Development, Population Policy, and Demographic Transition in the Republic of Korea*

94. Parks M. Coble, Jr., *The Shanghai Capitalists and the Nationalist Government, 1927–1937*

95. Noriko Kamachi, *Reform in China: Huang Tsun-hsien and the Japanese Model*

96. Richard Wich, *Sino-Soviet Crisis Politics: A Study of Political Change and Communication*

97. Lillian M. Li, *China's Silk Trade: Traditional Industry in the Modern World, 1842–1937*

98. R. David Arkush, *Fei Xiaotong and Sociology in Revolutionary China*

*99. Kenneth Alan Grossberg, *Japan's Renaissance: The Politics of the Muromachi Bakufu*

100. James Reeve Pusey, *China and Charles Darwin*

101. Hoyt Cleveland Tillman, *Utilitarian Confucianism: Chen Liang's Challenge to Chu Hsi*

102. Thomas A. Stanley, *Ōsugi Sakae, Anarchist in Taishō Japan: The Creativity of the Ego*

103. Jonathan K. Ocko, *Bureaucratic Reform in Provincial China: Ting Jih-ch'ang in Restoration Kiangsu, 1867–1870*

104. James Reed, *The Missionary Mind and American East Asia Policy, 1911–1915*

105. Neil L. Waters, *Japan's Local Pragmatists: The Transition from Bakumatsu to Meiji in the Kawasaki Region*

106. David C. Cole and Yung Chul Park, *Financial Development in Korea, 1945–1978*

107. Roy Bahl, Chuk Kyo Kim, and Chong Kee Park, *Public Finances during the Korean Modernization Process*

108. William D. Wray, *Mitsubishi and the N.Y.K, 1870–1914: Business Strategy in the Japanese Shipping Industry*

109. Ralph William Huenemann, *The Dragon and the Iron Horse: The Economics of Railroads in China, 1876–1937*

110. Benjamin A. Elman, *From Philosophy to Philology: Intellectual and Social Aspects of Change in Late Imperial China*

111. Jane Kate Leonard, *Wei Yüan and China's Rediscovery of the Maritime World*

112. Luke S. K. Kwong, *A Mosaic of the Hundred Days:. Personalities, Politics, and Ideas of 1898*

113. John E. Wills, Jr., *Embassies and Illusions: Dutch and Portuguese Envoys to K'ang-hsi, 1666–1687*

114. Joshua A. Fogel, *Politics and Sinology: The Case of Naitō Konan (1866–1934)*

*115. Jeffrey C. Kinkley, ed., *After Mao: Chinese Literature and Society, 1978–1981*

116. C. Andrew Gerstle, *Circles of Fantasy: Convention in the Plays of Chikamatsu*

117. Andrew Gordon, *The Evolution of Labor Relations in Japan: Heavy Industry, 1853–1955*

*118. Daniel K. Gardner, *Chu Hsi and the "Ta Hsueh": Neo-Confucian Reflection on the Confucian Canon*

119. Christine Guth Kanda, *Shinzō: Hachiman Imagery and Its Development*

*120. Robert Borgen, *Sugawara no Michizane and the Early Heian Court*

121. Chang-tai Hung, *Going to the People: Chinese Intellectual and Folk Literature, 1918–1937*

*122. Michael A. Cusumano, *The Japanese Automobile Industry: Technology and Management at Nissan and Toyota*

123. Richard von Glahn, *The Country of Streams and Grottoes: Expansion, Settlement, and the Civilizing of the Sichuan Frontier in Song Times*

124. Steven D. Carter, *The Road to Komatsubara: A Classical Reading of the Renga Hyakuin*

125. Katherine F. Bruner, John K. Fairbank, and Richard T. Smith, *Entering China's Service: Robert Hart's Journals, 1854–1863*

126. Bob Tadashi Wakabayashi, *Anti-Foreignism and Western Learning in Early-Modern Japan: The "New Theses" of 1825*

127. Atsuko Hirai, *Individualism and Socialism: The Life and Thought of Kawai Eijirō (1891–1944)*

128. Ellen Widmer, *The Margins of Utopia: "Shui-hu hou-chuan" and the Literature of Ming Loyalism*

129. R. Kent Guy, *The Emperor's Four Treasuries: Scholars and the State in the Late Chien-lung Era*

130. Peter C. Perdue, *Exhausting the Earth: State and Peasant in Hunan, 1500–1850*

131. Susan Chan Egan, *A Latterday Confucian: Reminiscences of William Hung (1893–1980)*

132. James T. C. Liu, *China Turning Inward: Intellectual-Political Changes in the Early Twelfth Century*

133. Paul A. Cohen, *Between Tradition and Modernity: Wang T'ao and Reform in Late Ching China*

134. Kate Wildman Nakai, *Shogunal Politics: Arai Hakuseki and the Premises of Tokugawa Rule*

135. Parks M. Coble, *Facing Japan: Chinese Politics and Japanese Imperialism, 1931–1937*

136. Jon L. Saari, *Legacies of Childhood: Growing Up Chinese in a Time of Crisis, 1890–1920*

137. Susan Downing Videen, *Tales of Heichū*

138. Heinz Morioka and Miyoko Sasaki, *Rakugo: The Popular Narrative Art of Japan*

139. Joshua A. Fogel, *Nakae Ushikichi in China: The Mourning of Spirit*

140. Alexander Barton Woodside, *Vietnam and the Chinese Model.: A Comparative Study of Vietnamese and Chinese Government in the First Half of the Nineteenth Century*

141. George Elision, *Deus Destroyed: The Image of Christianity in Early Modern Japan*

142. William D. Wray, ed., *Managing Industrial Enterprise: Cases from Japan's Prewar Experience*

143. T'ung-tsu Ch'ü, *Local Government in China under the Ching*

144. Marie Anchordoguy, *Computers, Inc.: Japan's Challenge to IBM*

145. Barbara Molony, *Technology and Investment: The Prewar Japanese Chemical Industry*

146. Mary Elizabeth Berry, *Hideyoshi*

147. Laura E. Hein, *Fueling Growth: The Energy Revolution and Economic Policy in Postwar Japan*

148. Wen-hsin Yeh, *The Alienated Academy: Culture and Politics in Republican China, 1919–1937*

149. Dru C. Gladney, *Muslim Chinese: Ethnic Nationalism in the People's Republic*

150. Merle Goldman and Paul A. Cohen, eds., *Ideas Across Cultures: Essays on Chinese Thought in Honor of Benjamin L Schwartz*

151. James Polachek, *The Inner Opium War*

152. Gail Lee Bernstein, *Japanese Marxist: A Portrait of Kawakami Hajime, 1879–1946*

153. Lloyd E. Eastman, *The Abortive Revolution: China under Nationalist Rule, 1927–1937*

154. Mark Mason, *American Multinationals and Japan: The Political Economy of Japanese Capital Controls, 1899–1980*

155. Richard J. Smith, John K. Fairbank, and Katherine F. Bruner, *Robert Hart and China's Early Modernization: His Journals, 1863–1866*

156. George J. Tanabe, Jr., *Myōe the Dreamkeeper: Fantasy and Knowledge in Kamakura Buddhism*

157. William Wayne Farris, *Heavenly Warriors: The Evolution of Japan's Military, 500–1300*

158. Yu-ming Shaw, *An American Missionary in China: John Leighton Stuart and Chinese-American Relations*

159. James B. Palais, *Politics and Policy in Traditional Korea*

160. Douglas Reynolds, *China, 1898–1912: The Xinzheng Revolution and Japan*

161. Roger Thompson, *China's Local Councils in the Age of Constitutional Reform*

162. William Johnston, *The Modern Epidemic: History of Tuberculosis in Japan*

Harvard East Asian Monographs

163. Constantine Nomikos Vaporis, *Breaking Barriers: Travel and the State in Early Modern Japan*

164. Irmela Hijiya-Kirschnereit, *Rituals of Self-Revelation: Shishōsetsu as Literary Genre and Socio-Cultural Phenomenon*

165. James C. Baxter, *The Meiji Unification through the Lens of Ishikawa Prefecture*

166. Thomas R. H. Havens, *Architects of Affluence: The Tsutsumi Family and the Seibu-Saison Enterprises in Twentieth-Century Japan*

167. Anthony Hood Chambers, *The Secret Window: Ideal Worlds in Tanizaki's Fiction*

168. Steven J. Ericson, *The Sound of the Whistle: Railroads and the State in Meiji Japan*

169. Andrew Edmund Goble, *Kenmu: Go-Daigo's Revolution*

170. Denise Potrzeba Lett, *In Pursuit of Status: The Making of South Korea's "New" Urban Middle Class*

171. Mimi Hall Yiengpruksawan, *Hiraizumi: Buddhist Art and Regional Politics in Twelfth-Century Japan*

172. Charles Shirō Inouye, *The Similitude of Blossoms: A Critical Biography of Izumi Kyōka (1873–1939), Japanese Novelist and Playwright*

173. Aviad E. Raz, *Riding the Black Ship: Japan and Tokyo Disneyland*

174. Deborah J. Milly, *Poverty, Equality, and Growth: The Politics of Economic Need in Postwar Japan*

175. See Heng Teow, *Japan's Cultural Policy Toward China, 1918–1931: A Comparative Perspective*

176. Michael A. Fuller, *An Introduction to Literary Chinese*

177. Frederick R. Dickinson, *War and National Reinvention: Japan in the Great War, 1914–1919*

178. John Solt, *Shredding the Tapestry of Meaning: The Poetry and Poetics of Kitasono Katue (1902–1978)*

179. Edward Pratt, *Japan's Protoindustrial Elite: The Economic Foundations of the Gōnō*

180. Atsuko Sakaki, *Recontextualizing Texts: Narrative Performance in Modern Japanese Fiction*

181. Soon-Won Park, *Colonial Industrialization and Labor in Korea: The Onoda Cement Factory*

182. JaHyun Kim Haboush and Martina Deuchler, *Culture and the State in Late Chosŏn Korea*

183. John W. Chaffee, *Branches of Heaven: A History of the Imperial Clan of Sung China*

184. Gi-Wook Shin and Michael Robinson, eds., *Colonial Modernity in Korea*

185. Nam-lin Hur, *Prayer and Play in Late Tokugawa Japan: Asakusa Sensōji and Edo Society*

186. Kristin Stapleton, *Civilizing Chengdu: Chinese Urban Reform, 1895–1937*

187. Hyung Il Pai, *Constructing "Korean" Origins: A Critical Review of Archaeology, Historiography, and Racial Myth in Korean State-Formation Theories*

188. Brian D. Ruppert, *Jewel in the Ashes: Buddha Relics and Power in Early Medieval Japan*

189. Susan Daruvala, *Zhou Zuoren and an Alternative Chinese Response to Modernity*

Harvard East Asian Monographs

190. James Z. Lee, *The Political Economy of a Frontier: Southwest China, 1250–1850*

191. Kerry Smith, *A Time of Crisis: Japan, the Great Depression, and Rural Revitalization*

192. Michael Lewis, *Becoming Apart: National Power and Local Politics in Toyama, 1868–1945*

193. William C. Kirby, Man-houng Lin, James Chin Shih, and David A. Pietz, eds., *State and Economy in Republican China: A Handbook for Scholars*

194. Timothy S. George, *Minamata: Pollution and the Struggle for Democracy in Postwar Japan*

195. Billy K. L. So, *Prosperity, Region, and Institutions in Maritime China: The South Fukien Pattern, 946–1368*

196. Yoshihisa Tak Matsusaka, *The Making of Japanese Manchuria, 1904–1932*

197. Maram Epstein, *Competing Discourses: Orthodoxy, Authenticity, and Engendered Meanings in Late Imperial Chinese Fiction*

198. Curtis J. Milhaupt, J. Mark Ramseyer, and Michael K. Young, eds. and comps., *Japanese Law in Context: Readings in Society, the Economy, and Politics*

199. Haruo Iguchi, *Unfinished Business: Ayukawa Yoshisuke and U.S.-Japan Relations, 1937–1952*

200. Scott Pearce, Audrey Spiro, and Patricia Ebrey, *Culture and Power in the Reconstitution of the Chinese Realm, 200–600*

201. Terry Kawashima, *Writing Margins: The Textual Construction of Gender in Heian and Kamakura Japan*

202. Martin W. Huang, *Desire and Fictional Narrative in Late Imperial China*

203. Robert S. Ross and Jiang Changbin, eds., *Re-examining the Cold War: U.S.-China Deiplomacy, 1954–1973*

204. Gwanhua Wang, *In Search of Justice: The 1905–1906 Chinese Anti-American Boycott*

205. David Schaberg, *A Patterned Past: Form and Thought in Early Chinese Historiography*

206. Christine Yano, *Tears of Longing: Nostalgia and the Nation in Japanese Popular Song*

207. Milena Doleželová-Velingerová and Oldřich Král, with Graham Sanders, eds., *The Appropriation of Cultural Capital: China's May Fourth Movement*

208. Robert N. Huey, *The Making of 'Shinkokinshū'*

209. Lee Butler, *Emperor and Aristocracy in Japan, 1467–1680: Resilience and Renewal*

210. Suzanne Ogden, *Inklings of Democracy in China*

211. Kenneth J. Ruoff, *The People's Emperor: Democracy and the Japanese Monarchy, 1945–1995*

212. Haun Saussy, *Great Walls of Discourse and Other Adventures in Cultural China*

213. Aviad E. Raz, *Emotions at Work: Normative Control, Organizations, and Culture in Japan and America*

214. Rebecca E. Karl and Peter Zarrow, eds., *Rethinking the 1898 Reform Period: Political and Cultural Change in Late Qing China*